D0855075

DISMANTLING THE MEXICAN STATE?

LATIN AMERICAN STUDIES SERIES
General Editors: Philip O'Brien and Peter Flynn

This series is an initiative designed to give a comprehensive analysis of some of the many complex problems facing contemporary Latin America and individual Latin American countries.

Selected titles

David E. Hojman (*editor*)
NEO-LIBERAL AGRICULTURE IN RURAL CHILE

Dermot Keogh (*editor*)
CHURCH AND STATE IN LATIN AMERICA

David Slater
TERRITORY AND STATE POWER IN LATIN AMERICA: The Peruvian Case

Dismantling the Mexican State?

Edited by

Rob Aitken
Lecturer in Anthropology
University College, London

Nikki Craske
Lecturer, Department of Government
University of Manchester

Gareth A. Jones
Lecturer, Department of Geography
University of Wales, Swansea

and

David E. Stansfield
Lecturer in Politics
Institute of Latin American Studies
University of Glasgow

First published in Great Britain 1996 by
MACMILLAN PRESS LTD
Houndmills, Basingstoke, Hampshire RG21 6XS
and London
Companies and representatives
throughout the world

A catalogue record for this book is available
from the British Library.

ISBN 0–333–64248–1

First published in the United States of America 1996 by
ST. MARTIN'S PRESS, INC.,
Scholarly and Reference Division,
175 Fifth Avenue,
New York, N.Y. 10010

ISBN 0–312–16003–8

Library of Congress Cataloging-in-Publication Data
Dismantling the Mexican state / edited by Rob Aitken . . . [et al.].
p. cm. — (Latin American studies series)
Includes bibliographical references and index.
ISBN 0–312–16003–8 (cloth)
1. Mexico—Politics and government—1988– 2. Political parties–
–Mexico. I. Aitken, Rob. II. Series: Latin American studies
series (Houndmills, Basingstoke, England)
JL1281.D57 1996
320.972'09'049—dc20 95–53128
CIP

---

10 9 8 7 6 5 4 3 2 1
05 04 03 02 01 00 99 98 97 96

Printed and bound in Great Britain by
Antony Rowe Ltd, Chippenham, Wiltshire

Table of Contents

List of Tables

List of Figures

Acknowledgements

The initial motivation for the conference held at the University of Manchester arose from a discussion between the editors and the Committee of the Society of Latin American Studies (SLAS). The Society provided initial pump-priming for the conference, which attracted additional sources of funding from The British Academy, The British Council (Mexico City), the Foreign and Commonwealth Office and The Department of Government, University of Manchester. When the idea of an edited collection took shape, SLAS was once more on hand with moral and financial support. The editors hope that the confidence placed in them by the Society and others is at least partly repaid with this book.

The involvement and generous comments from those who participated at Manchester helped to make the conference enjoyable and proved to be useful in pulling this volume together. Those in attendance were: Judith Clifton; Fransisco Flores Rosas; Natividad Gutierrez; Gerardo Mixcoatl Tinoco; Leticia Fierra Garcia; Susana Rostas; Leticia Ruano; VJ. Vaitheeswaran and Steve Wiggins. The editors would like to acknowledge the help of those who assisted with the production of the final text. Jasmine Gideon helped with the translation of one chapter and provided assistance with the proof-reading, as did Vicky Knight, while Russell Gibbon speedily compiled the index. Rob Aitken is thanked by the "other three" for efficiently producing a desk-top manuscript as the deadline loomed.

1 North Baja California
2 South Baja California
3 Sonora
4 Chihuahua
5 Coahuila
6 Nuevo León
7 Tamualipas
8 Sinaloa
9 Durango
10 Zacatecas
11 San Luis Potosí
12 Nayarit
13 Aguascalientes
14 Jalisco
15 Guanajuato
16 Querétaro
17 Hidalgo
18 Veracruz
19 Colima
20 Michoacán
21 State of Mexico
22 Federal District
23 Morelos
24 Tlaxcala
25 Puebla
26 Guerrero
27 Oaxaca
28 Chiapas
29 Tabasco
30 Campeche
31 Yucatán
32 Quintana Roo
Pacific Ocean
Gulf of Mexico
International Boundaries
State Boundaries
0
400
800 km
N

Introduction

The central concern of this book is the political impact of the socio-economic reforms introduced since the mid-1980s, which gained strength during the administration of President Carlos Salinas de Gortari (1988-94). Few commentators have questioned the radical nature of these reforms and many have suggested that they are inexorably bound to change the nature of political discourse, structure and action. Since the Mexican political system has long been regarded as authoritarian and/or corporatist, the prospect of change has been seized upon by many as likely to lead to a more open and democratic polity; that political liberalisation is the inevitable consequence of economic reform. Even Pedro Aspe, Salinas' *Secretario de Hacienda* (Treasury) declared that 'You cannot have an open economy and a closed political system'. Thus, by implication, the Salinas administration was setting the stage for the dismantling of the Mexican State. In this volume we assess this idea, asking whether the State has been, or is in the process of being, dismantled and, if so, what are the political consequences?

What emerges is, perhaps, to be expected. The extent and significance of change has been inconsistent. Although, as John Weiss indicates, there was an overall coherence in the neoliberal economic project pursued by Salinas, political change was far from coherent and more piecemeal in character. In fact we were struck by the persistence of entrenched patterns and practices. 'New' procedures are frequently no more than novel forms of authoritarianism or disguises for the old ones. That is not to say that political change is a *chimera*. Old institutions and habits have been abandoned or sidelined and fresh ones introduced. However, it has become clear that political change has had ideological and regionally differentiated dimensions, being more likely to have occurred (or be permitted) when the beneficiaries share the basic economic tenets of the regime or are operating at subnational and, as yet, financially dependent levels of government. Other reforms were difficult to classify as products of systemic change linked to the new economic model. Thus, Salinas' removal of such notorious *caciques* as Joaquin (La Quina) Hernández Galicia of the petroleum workers union and Carlos Jonguitud Barrios of the teachers union had echoes of 'housekeeping' purges carried out by previous presidents at the beginnings of their *sexenios*. Similarly, intra-PRI tensions over party organisation and strategy have a history which goes back further than 1988. The difference may be that these changes and divisions occurred in a new atmosphere, in which political reform or renewal was the watchword of the President and his coterie of advisers.

The challenge posed to established orthodoxies has been dramatically evident in ideological debates. The neoliberal schema runs counter to modes of economic, social and political thinking long held dear and propagated by the postrevolutionary elite. As a consequence, reactions to and elaborations of the new 'philosophy' have been intense. In this volume Alan Knight reviews critically the newly coined *salinista* version of social liberalism against its historical antecedents. Based on their anthropological fieldwork in Michoacán, Rob Aitken and Kathy Powell examine the ways in which the regime has sought to reformulate the concepts of the State and national identity into its legitimating discourse.

Any political reform must perforce address the overwhelming power of the governing party, the *Partido Revolucionario Institucional* (PRI), which has dominated the political system for over six decades. Salinas declared in 1988 that 'the era of the virtual one-party system [in Mexico] has ended', and much attention has been given to assessments of the demise of authoritarianism and the consolidation of democracy. Victoria Rodríguez and Peter Ward analyse the tensions between the new-style PRI and electoral politics in Nuevo León and conclude that whilst there are significant changes, the new PRI is having difficulties in establishing itself. Nikki Craske, similarly, argues that internal 'democratising' reforms within the PRI have done little to alter the corporatist nature of the party.

Another issue in this process of assessment concerns the conduct and interpretation of elections. Electoral reform predates the Salinas term, but election results had been consistently questioned by the opposition, culminating in the allegations of massive fraud in the 1988 diet which brought Salinas himself to power. A commitment to clean elections became a major plank in the new governments platform and, for the first time since the PRI's formation, governors representing an opposition party, the *Partido de Acción Nacional* (PAN) took office: in Baja California in 1989, as an interim in Guanajuato in 1991, in Chihuahua in 1992 and in Jalisco in 1995. Opposition election victories, however, are not guaranteed recognition, as witnessed in 1993 with the denial of the PAN's almost certain victory in the Yucatán. Elections in states where the leftist *Partido Revolucionario Democrático* (PRD) was strong were less "transparent" and continued to generate complaints of fraud and intimidation. The high turnout of around 75 per cent of the electorate in the 1994 federal elections, however, suggests that a degree of faith in the electoral process had been restored by the regime. On the whole the contest was perceived by most observers as less tainted by fraud than before – helped by the new system of photocards for electors to reduce the incidence of impersonation, the establishment of the semi-independent *Instituto Federal Electoral* (IFE) and the presence of civic and foreign observers to monitor the polling. As David Stansfield points out the result was a highly regionalised pattern of political competition with the PRI facing different oppositions in different parts of the country and with the PAN continuing to gain support. Jorge Regalado, on the other hand, suggests that the poor showing of the PRD was the product of its failure to capitalise on the energy of the 1980s protest movements and its obsession with elections.

At the sub-national level political reform appears to have been less influential with traditional authoritarian practices persisting in the face of official reformist statements. Colin Clarke in his study of Oaxaca demonstrates that the PRI continues to exploit its historic links with the local economic, social and political elites to dominate elections and to vet its representatives. In states where the PRI faced strong opponents, old habits and structures are seen to persist. In San Luis Potosí Wil Pansters shows that the *navista* opposition has tended to reproduce many of the undemocratic features associated with the PRI – particularly a tendency towards *caudillismo*. In Baja California, Gustavo Vicencio finds that the *panista* governor, Ernesto Ruffo, has encountered strong local *priísta* obstructionism and a federal financing system which severely limits the scope for regional autonomy.

Ideological exegesis and electoral probity, however, are only part of the story. The *salinista* project has also meant the reformulation of existing structures and institutions, and the creation of new ones. These changes give the appearance of being the deliberate result of the neoliberal emphasis on privatisation, attempts to maintain Mexico's comparative advantage in international labour markets and political legitimation strategies. Appearances, however, can deceive especially, as John Gledhill examines, in the ways these audacious reforms work through in practice. What emerges is a series of reforms that contain a high degree of improvisation. Thus, while official discourses have stressed an end to paternalism and the free market, practice has aimed to maintain political consent and opportunities for patronage. Such ambiguity over intention and outcome is explored by Gareth Jones who argues that the dismantling of *ejido* land reform has allowed the State opportunities for more efficient intervention. The enhanced efficiency of the State to deliver the goods is investigated by Ann Varley for Salinas' flagship welfare programme, PRONASOL. Varley sets out to unpack the degree of continuity with the past behind a public relations component which has been capable of giving the appearance of a President with something new to offer. Jane Hindley also portrays the apparently new elements of Salinas's reforms as a legitimation strategy. Taking the emergence of a new indigenism,

Hindley concentrates upon how the promises to extend justice, rights and institutional support to indigenous peoples, for which the regime received favourable international attention, have been subverted in scope and meaning.

This volume shows that the 'dismantling' of the Mexican State has been limited, uneven and reversible. These observations pose a number of challenges for President Zedillo who seems committed to the economic project of his predecessor, but who is faced with the collapse of many of its apparent economic successes. Balance of payments problems, the drastic devaluation of the peso and the country's burgeoning international debts have produced a crisis of investor confidence and a new spate of tight austerity measures. These difficulties are likely to sharpen the contradictions between social needs and the economic project at a time when the regime is faced by scandals and divisions within the ruling party and the simmering embarrassment of the *zapatistas* in Chiapas. Violence, which many commentators believed to be more a feature of the rural and urban margins of the political system, has reappeared in elite circles with the assassination of the PRI's first choice presidential candidate, Luis Donaldo Colosio, in Tijuana, Cardinal Posada Ocampo in Guadalajara and the PRI's General Secretary, José Ruiz Massieu in downtown Mexico City. The recent allegations of the Salinas family's complicity in the latter assassination and the spectre of narcotics dealers involvement with the political class have raised the frightening prospect of the 'Colombianisation' of Mexico. It is too early to assess Zedillo's chances of dealing successfully with these problems, but it seems unlikely that he will deviate greatly from the lines of economic policy inherited from Salinas and may, therefore, be forced to return to old authoritarian procedures in order to contain the consequences of discontent. To borrow from Mark Twain, reports of the death of the Mexican State might well be exaggerated.

Rob Aitken
Nikki Craske
Gareth Jones
David Stansfield
April 1995

Abbreviations

ADN:	Alianza Democrática Nacional
ANAGSA:	Aseguradora Nacional Agrícola y Ganadera SA
AGROSAMEX:	Agricultural Branch of Aseguradora Mexicana
ARDF:	Asamblea de Representantes del Distrito Federal
BANRURAL:	Banco Nacional de Crédito Rural
CADER:	Centro de Apoyo al Desarrollo Rural
CANACINTRA:	Cámara Nacional de la Industria de la Transformacíon
CANACO:	Cámara Nacional de Comercio
CCE:	Consejo Coordinador Empresarial
CD:	Coalición Democrática (Coaltion of PSUM, PRT, PMT and COCEI in 1986 in Oaxaca)
CD:	Corriente Democrática
CDE:	Comité Distrital Electoral
CEE:	Comité Estatal Electoral
CEMEX:	Cementos Mexicanos
CEN:	Comité Executivo Nacional
CFE:	Comisión Federal Electoral
CIDH:	Comisión Interamericana de Derechos Humanos
CME:	Comité Municipal Electoral
CNC:	Confederación Nacional de Campesinos
CNOP:	Confederación Nacional de Organizaciones Populares
CNJPI:	Comisión Nacional de Justicia para los Pueblos Indígenas
CNPP:	Confederación Nacional de Pequeños Productores
COCEI:	Coalición Obrero Campesino Estudiantil del Istmo
COCEO:	Coalición Obrero Campesino Estudiantil de Oaxaca
COFIPE:	Código Federal de Instituciones y Procedimientos Electorales
CONASUPO:	Companía Nacional de Subsistencias Populares
COPLAMAR:	Coordinación General del Plan Nacional de Zonas Deprimidas y Grupos Marginados
CORETT:	Comisión para la Regularización de la Tenencia de la Tierra
CP:	Centro Patronal
CPEI:	Comité de Profesionistas e Intelectuales
CPI:	Consumer Price Index
CRESEM:	Comisión para la Regularización en el Estado de México
CROC:	Confederación Revolucionaria Obrera y Campesina
CROM:	Confederación Revolucionaria de Obreros de México
CTM:	Confederación de Trabajadores de México
DGRT:	Dirección General de Regularización Territorial del Distrito Federal
EZLN:	Ejército Zapatista de Liberación Nacional
FAN:	Frente Antireelecionista Nacional

FCP:	Frente Cívico Potosino
FDN:	Frente Nacional Democrático
FEO	Federación Estudiantil Oaxaqueña
FIVIDESU	Fideicomiso de Vivienda y Desarrollo Urbano
FNOC	Federación Nacional de Organizaciones y Ciudadanos
FONHAPO	Fondo Nacional de Habitaciones Populares
FRCP	Frente Reinvicador de la Ciudadanía Potosina
FUCOPO	Fusión Cívica de Organizaciones Productivas de Oaxaca
GATT	General Agreement on Tarrifs and Trade
GDP	Gross Domestic Product
IFE	Instituto Federal Electoral
ILO	International Labour Organisation
IMF	International Monetary Fund
INFONAVIT	Instituto del Fondo Nacional de la Vivienda para los Trabajadores
INI	Instituto Nacional Indigenista
IRCA	Immigration Reform and Control Act
ISAI	Impuesto Sobre Adquisición de Inmeubles
ISIM	Tax of Mercantile Incomes
IVA	Impuesto de Valor Agregado
LCF	Fiscal Coordination Law
LICASCEO	Liga de Comunidades Agrarias y Sindicatos Campesinos del Estado de Oaxaca
MIT	Massachesettes Institute of Technology
MT	Movimiento Urbano Popular Territorial
NAFINSA	Nacional Financiera SA
NAFTA	North American Free Trade Agreement
NGO	Non-Governmental Organisation
NPP	Nava Partido Político
OECD	Organisation for Economic Cooperation and Development
OTV	Organismo Técnico de Vigilancia
PAN	Partido Acción Nacional
PARM	Partido Auténtico de la Revolución Mexicana
PDM	Partido Democrático Mexicana
PED	State Development Plan
PFCRN	Partido Frente Cardenista de Reconstrucción Nacional
PIDER	Programa Integral para el Desarrollo Rural
PMS	Partido Mexicano Socialista
PMT	Partido Mexicano de los Trabajadores
PNR	Partido Nacional Revolucionario
PPJ	Partido Popular Jaliciense
PPS	Partido Popular Socialista
PRD	Partido de la Revolución Democrática
PRI	Partido Revolucionario Institucional
PRM	Partido Revolucionario Mexicano
PROCAMPO	Programa de Apoyos Directos al Campo

PROCEDE	Programa de Certificación de Derechos Ejidales y Solares Urbanos
PRONASOL	Programa Nacional de Solidaridad
PROVIMET XXI	Programa Vial Metropolitano (Nuevo León)
PRS	Partido de la Revolución Socialista
PRT	Partido Revolucionario de los Trabajadores
PSBR	Public Sector Borrowing Requirement
PSE	Pacto de Solidaridad Económica
PST	Partido Socialista de los Trabajadores
PSUM	Partido Socialista Unificado de México
PT	Partido de Trabajo
REE	Registro Estatal de Electores
RER	Real Exchange Rate
RFE	Registro Federal de Electores
SARH	Secretaría de Agricultura y Recursos Hidráulicos
SAM	Sistema Alimentaria Mexicano
SAW	Special Agricultural Worker
SEDESOL	Secretaría de Desarrollo Social
SEDUE	Secretaría de Desarrollo Urbano y Ecología
SHCP	Secretaría de Hacienda y Contaduría Pública
SNTE	Sindicato Nacional de Trabajadores de la Educación
SRA	Secretaría de la Reforma Agraria
UABJO	Universidad Autónoma 'Benito Juárez' de Oaxaca
UNAM	Universidad Nacional Autónoma de México
UN	United Nations
UNE	Une - Ciudadanos en Movimiento
UNO	Unión Nacional Opositor

Notes on the Contributors

Rob Aitken is Lecturer in Anthropology at University College London. He held a CONACYT scholarship at the Colegio de Michoacán, Zamora, from 1987-9, and has subsequently taught there. His contribution to this volume arises out of his doctoral thesis, *Cardenistas de Hueso Colorado?: the State, Political Culture and the Dynamics of Popular Mobilisations in Ciudad Lázaro Cárdenas, Michoacán.* He has published various articles on political culture and the local responses to economic and political change in Michoacán.

Colin Clarke is Lecturer in Geography at Oxford University and an Official Fellow of Jesus College. He has taught at the Universities of Toronto and Liverpool, where he was, until 1981, Reader in Geography and Latin American Studies. He has carried out numerous field investigations in Mexico and the Caribbean, and has published more than ten books. He is the author of *Kingston, Jamaica: urban development and social change, 1692-1962*, *East Indians in a West Indian Town: San Fernando, Trinidad, 1930-1970*, and editor of *Society and Politics in the Caribbean.*

Nikki Craske is Lecturer in Politics at Queen's University, Belfast. She is author of *Corporatism Revisited: Salinas and the Reform of the Popular Sector* and co-editor (with Victor Bulmer-Thomas and Mónica Serrano) of *Mexico and the North American Free Trade Agreement: who will benefit?*. She has published articles on women's political participation in grassroots urban politics, both government and opposition, in Mexico.

John Gledhill is Reader in Anthropology at University College London and an Associate Fellow of the Institute of Latin American Studies of the University of London. A specialist in political and economic anthropology, he has been researching on rural society in western Mexico for the past fifteen years, and has also taught in Mexican universities. His publications include *Casi Nada: A Study of Agrarian Reform in the Homeland of Cardenismo* (also revised and published in Spanish), and *Power and Its Disguises: Anthropological Perspectives on Politics*. He is managing editor of the journal *Critique of Anthropology* and editor of the series *Explorations in Anthropology* for Berg Publishers.

Jane Hindley is a postgraduate student in the Government Department at the University of Essex. Her doctorate thesis *Indigenous Mobilization and Political Reform in Mexico, 1988-94* examines grassroots indigenous mobilisation in the state of Guerrero. She spent 1994-5 as Researcher in Residence at the Center for US-Mexican Studies, University of California-San Diego.

Gareth A. Jones is Lecturer in the Department of Geography, University of Wales, Swansea. He held a CONACYT scholarship at the Universidad Autónoma Metropolitana-Azcapotzalco in 1988 and obtained his doctorate from the University of Cambridge in 1991. He is joint editor (with Peter M. Ward) of *Methodology for Land and Housing Market Analysis* and is author of numerous articles, notably on urban land markets and the conservation of historic centres in Mexico and Ecuador.

Alan Knight is Professor of the History of Latin America, Director of the Latin American Centre, Oxford University, and Fellow of St. Antony's College. He was formerly Professor of History at the University of Texas at Austin and Visiting Fellow at the Center for US-Mexican Studies, University of California-San Diego. He is author of the two volume, *The Mexican Revolution.*

Wil Pansters is Associate Researcher at the Department of Cultural Anthropology at the University of Utrecht. He has conducted research and published widely on regional political history, *caciquismo*, social movements and urban problems in Mexico. His books include *Politics and Power in Puebla: the Political History of a Mexican State, 1937-1987*, and co-editor (with A. Ouweneel) of *Region, State and Capitalism in Mexico: Nineteenth and Twentieth Centuries* (both CEDLA, Amsterdam). He is currently engaged in a research project on politics and *caciquismo* in the Mexican state of San Luis Potosí (1938-1958) and is editing a volume on Mexican political culture.

Kathy Powell is a postgraduate student of the University of London. Her doctoral thesis examines political culture and socio-economic change in the sugar growing regions of Los Reyes, Michoacán. She has forthcoming articles on political culture and the impacts of the privatisation of the sugar industry.

Jorge Regalado is Head of the Departamento de Estudios sobre los Movimientos Sociales (DESMOS) in the Universidad de Guadalajara. He is also a doctoral student on the University's programme of social sciences and the Centro de Investigaciones y Estudios Superiores en Antropología Social (CIESAS), Mexico. He has published numerous articles on social movements and opposition politics in Mexico and has been a long-time activist in grassroots urban politics in Guadalajara.

Victoria E. Rodríguez is Assistant Professor at the LBJ School of Public Affairs, The University of Texas at Austin. She is author of *Decentralization in Mexico: The Facade of Power* and of several articles and book chapters dealing with Mexican politics and public administration, particularly intergovernmental relations and municipal politics. In 1993-4 she served as a consultant to the World Bank on a project on decentralisation and regional development in Mexico. With Peter M. Ward she has co-directed a major research project on opposition governments in Mexico. They are co-authors of *Political Change in Baja California: Democracy in the Making* and *Policymaking, Politics and Urban Governance in Chihuahua: The Experience of Recent Panista Governments*, and editors of *Opposition Governments in Mexico*. Her recent work includes a pathbreaking research project on women in Mexican politics.

David E. Stansfield was educated at the University of Wales and the LSE and is currently Lecturer in Politics in the Institute of Latin American Studies at the University of Glasgow. He has held posts in the Universities of Lancaster, New Mexico, LaTrobe and CEDLA, Amsterdam. He was President of the Society of Latin American Studies from 1992-4. He is editor of *Dependency and Latin America*, and has written articles on Cuban foreign policy and Mexican politics.

Ann Varley is Lecturer in the Department of Geography, University College London. She has been working on urban Mexico since 1980. Her contribution to this book arose out of her long-standing interest in the regularisation of illegal settlements and the political implications of this process. She has also worked on rental housing and alternatives to ownership. She is co-author (with A. Gilbert) of *Landlord and Tenant: Housing the Poor in Urban Mexico* and editor of *Disasters, Development and Environment*. Her current research concerns gender issues in housing and urban development.

Gustavo Vicencio is Director of the Research Secretariat of National Executive Committee of the Partido Acción Nacional (PAN). A former student of sociology at the Universidad Autónoma Nacional de México (UNAM), he was a doctoral student of The Institute of Latin American Studies at the University of Glasgow, from which he also has a Masters' degree. He is author of *Memorias del PAN IV* and co-editor of *Así Nació Acción Nacional*.

Peter M. Ward was Lecturer at the Universities of London and Cambridge before moving to the University of Texas at Austin in 1991 where he is a Professor in the Department of Sociology and the LBJ School of Public Affairs. Since 1992 he has been Director of the Mexican Center of the Institute of Latin American Studies at UT. In addition to numerous articles and book chapters on public policy in Mexico and Latin America, his most recent books include *Housing, the State and the Poor: Policy and Practice in Three Latin American Cities* (co-author with Alan Gilbert), *Welfare Politics in Mexico: Papering over the Cracks* and *Mexico City: The Production and Reproduction of an Urban Environment* (all translated into Spanish), *Corruption, Development and Inequality* (editor), and co-editor and multiple contributor (with Gareth A. Jones) of *Methodology for Land and Housing Market Analysis*. He is currently completing two research projects: that of opposition governments in Mexico (with Victoria Rodríguez), and a study on residential land values and development policy in Mexico. His principal research interests are housing, planning, urban development, and the politics of public administration in Mexico. He has served as advisor to the Mexican government and to several international development agencies.

John Weiss is Reader in Development Economics at the Development and Project Planning Centre, University of Bradford. He worked in Mexico 1980-2 as an economic advisor to the then Ministry of Industry and National Resources and continues to visit the country regularly. He is the author of *Industry in Developing Countries* and co-author (with Steve Curry) of *Project Analysis in Developing Countries*. He is author of a forthcoming book, *Economic Policy in Developing Countries: the reform agenda*. He has worked as a consultant to several international agencies including the World Bank, the United Nations Industrial Development Organisation and the European Investment Bank.

1 Salinas and Social Liberalism in Historical Context

Alan Knight

There are two basic attractions to history – as opposed to politics – which might be called the misanthropic and the methodological. First, history involves a cloistered existence in libraries or, better still, archives, in which the historian communes with dusty tomes rather than real live people. Second, and more important, history does not get regularly upstaged by recent events. Of course, historical interpretation changes – sometimes quite dramatically – and change is often related to contemporary changes in the 'real' world. E. H. Carr explained the renewed emphasis on chance evident in the work of early twentieth-century British historians in terms of the 'mood of uncertainty and apprehension which set in with the present century and became marked after 1914' (Carr, 1964: 100). Cuba and Vietnam helped stimulate a fresh interest in revolutions and peasant studies in the 1960s. However, these are shifts of glacial lentitude compared to the sudden upheavals experienced by students of contemporary politics – especially students of Mexican politics who, since 1982 (if not 1968), have ridden a rollercoaster of crisis, speculation, re-evaluation and recantation. Basáñez enumerates four crises – one political, three economic – between 1968 and 1987, to which we may add three more: 1988 (political), 1994 (political) and 1994-5 (economic) (Basáñez, 1990: 9).[1]

As this chronological clustering emphasises, the final year of the Salinas de Gortari *sexenio*, like previous sexennial endings in 1976, 1982 and 1988, was one of crisis, which began with Chiapas, was punctuated by political assassinations and their fall-out, and ended with the economic crisis of

1 Obviously, the distinction between 'economic' and 'political' crises is a somewhat arbitrary one, and usually hinges on the crisis's *origins*; 'economic' crises (like that of 1994-5) clearly have political consequences, just as political crises have – to varying degrees – economic consequences. It is, nevertheless, ironic that the Salinas presidency, applauded for its economic achievements (and often cricitised for its political failings), should end with a successful election, followed by a crisis of economic confidence.

December 1994. If 1993 was *annus horribilis* for the House of Windsor, 1994 was no better for the PRI (and this, I shall suggest, is not a wholly fanciful comparison). What is particularly striking is that 1993 ended on a triumphal note, with the conclusion of NAFTA and the *destape* of Salinas' *delfín*, Luis Donaldo Colosio. The crisis/es of 1994 did not, therefore, roll in like a gathering storm, but struck like bolts from the blue, disconcerting *políticos* and pundits alike. Salinas' prestige, consistently high through 1993, sank in early 1994, picked up in the summer, then plummeted along with the peso at the end of the year. Some 54 per cent of Mexicans now say they think the ex-president should face judicial proceedings, and only 20 per cent say that he shouldn't (MORI/*Este País* poll, 18 January 1995). As for that great tribe of voodoo economists (I use the noun loosely) who make a comfortable living reading the entrails of the market, they could not have got it more wrong: Salinas had emerged 'a clear winner', *The Economist* told us in August 1994; Zedillo would be a strong president and the election 'will bring increased economic growth', the shamans of Salomon Brothers told us in the same month (*The Economist*, 27 August-2 September 1994: 44; *Emerging Markets Research*, 12 August 1994).

Given the proven fallibility of pundits and the volatility of events, it is clearly risky to attempt a review of Salinas and social liberalism 'in historical perspective'. My original paper was written at the end of 1993, when *priísta* triumphalism prevailed. It was delivered, at the Manchester conference, as the Chiapas revolt sent reverberations around the world. It is being rewritten a year later, following a decisive PRI victory in the August 1994 elections and a no less decisive repudiation by the markets of Mexico's much-trumpeted neoliberal achievements. This raises awkward problems of analysis. There is the temptation, at one extreme, to write an entirely new paper; or, at the other, to append a quick update to the original. A third, suitably postmodern, alternative might be to follow the example of Orlando Fals Borda and produce a dual text on facing pages, juxtaposing – without integrating – the January 1994 and January 1995 versions. In the end, I have opted for a fourth approach. I have retained the bulk of the original paper, believing that its argument has not lost all validity in light of later events. However, I have interpolated references to those events, trying, wherever possible, to alert the reader to these interpolations; and I leave it to the reader to decide whether they constitute sneaky efforts to be wise after the event, or *ex post* confirmations of the original argument.

Mexicanists are familiar with the notion that parties, *políticos* and presidents place great emphasis on establishing their historical, symbolic and intellectual legitimacy. Historical precedents are religiously cited; presidents choose emblematic historical mentors; history itself becomes a significant political battleground (Riding, 1986: 19-25). The classic recent example was the controversy provoked by the new school textbooks introduced by – as he then was – Education Secretary Zedillo. Thus we encounter the paradox of a revolutionary regime that, more than most regimes, has relentlessly harked back to the past. The onset of neoliberalism presented certain problems, since the neoliberal project involved substantial departures from the past, particularly in the realms of economic practice and international relations (as regards the realm of domestic politics, more anon). These departures from tradition could easily be justified in the Jesuitical manner which some Mexican *políticos* – and intellectuals – have developed into a fine art.[2] The Revolution means change, President Salinas proclaimed in his first *informe*, therefore the flurry of reforms he had begun to introduce were eminently revolutionary. However, this was not entirely convincing. Not entirely convincing to whom? To the country at large, many of whom retained some sort of attachment to the revolutionary heritage; and, perhaps more important in official eyes, to the political elite who had to implement the neoliberal project in circumstances of considerable instability.[3] The PRI itself had split in 1987; Cárdenas had mounted a surprisingly strong challenge in 1988; Muñoz Ledo and other critics within a resurgent Congress would not swallow the strictures of neoliberalism – free trade, NAFTA, privatisation, the elimination of the *ejido* – without a fight. The regime was therefore keen – perhaps desperate – to find some sort of attractive ideological wrapping for its chosen project.

As we know, the answer was social liberalism: a term and concept which acquired enormous currency during the second half of the Salinas *sexenio*. Future historians will no doubt dredge the archives in order to deconstruct the origins of social liberalism. Any contemporary analysis is bound to be premature and partial. A couple of aspects stand out. First, the effort and energy which have been invested in the concept are remarkable. Keynes' dictum – 'nothing possesses the power of an idea whose time has come' – always struck me as idealistic waffle until social liberalism reared its Hydra

---

2 With apologies to any Jesuits who may read this.

3 This broaches the knotty question of legitimacy, about which two points may be made. First, I would distinguish between a broad popular legitimacy, and a legitimacy generated by, for, and among the ruling elite (Abercrombie *et al.*, 1984: 3ff.). Second, I would question the strength of the former, which is too often gratuitously assumed. While accepting that the ideology of the Mexican Revolution has – to a degree which is subject to debate – underpinned the hegemony of the PRI, I would see the latter's 'legitimacy' as residing less in positive endorsement than a sort of fatalistic acceptance; in other words, I would stress the PRI's 'thin' rather than 'thick' legitimacy ('the thick theory claims consent; the thin theory settles for resignation': Scott, 1990: 72).

head. In fact, as I shall suggest, the ideological content of social liberalism is hardly intellectually compelling, and it was less the case of a momentous idea generating practical action, than of political expediency elevating a somewhat mundane idea – or, if you prefer, legitimating discourse. However, the political leverage – and, hence, the historical significance – of ideas and discourses often has little to do with their intellectual cogency or novelty. What is remarkable about 'social liberalism' is the sheer discursive output: the recurrent references, the media coverage, the learned disquisitions, the rote repetition of catch-phrases, the publication of glossy symposia; all of which, taken together, convey a faintly Orwellian flavour. We now have an Institute of Social Liberalism, spreading the word; and one of the communities analysed by President Salinas in his doctoral dissertation – a seminal work in the social liberal canon – has now renamed itself Tetla de Solidaridad (*La Jornada*, 8 September 1993).

Second, social liberalism is the ideological offspring of PRONASOL (the *Programa Nacional de Solidaridad*, or 'Solidarity'). Even allowing for Salinas' seminal doctorate, in which aspects of social liberalism were adumbrated, it appears that practice preceded ideology: the success of Solidarity encouraged the administration to develop a full-blown ideology claiming – as, in a sense, it had to do – a combination of reformist novelty and historical prescription. Social liberalism was designed to marry neoliberal economics, which afforded the very basis of the *salinista* project, to a characteristically Mexican brand of social paternalism. As the Mexican economy adjusted to the rigours of the market, PRONASOL would address the casualties of the market, targeting needy groups, encouraging self-help (*autogestión*). In Denise Dresser's neat encapsulation, it offered 'neopopulist solutions to neoliberal problems' (Dresser, 1991).

In developing an ideology that would (retrospectively) justify PRONASOL, the administration displayed an inspired eclecticism. The discourse of PRONASOL displays no clear parentage. There are recurrent references to traditions of collective work (such as the *tequío*) dating back to the Colony or beyond. Some commentators discern a covert Catholic influence – for example, in the concern for 'subsidiarity', the valorisation of intermediate groups in society. The very name 'Solidarity' itself conjures up images of an insurgent people confronting a ricketty State. The Revolution, inevitably, is invoked, but in somewhat half-hearted and qualified fashion: the references are to 1910 rather than to 1938 (C. Rojas, 1991: 22). For, negatively, apologists of PRONASOL are at pains to deny any debt to traditional 'revolutionary' populism – populism, in fact, is now a dirty word – even though the debt is quite apparent and future historians, I suspect, will see PRONASOL as fitting (*mutatis mutandis*) within that established tradition

(Knight, 1994a). Indeed, some perspicacious political scientists have already begun to explore that link and to argue for the compatibility of neo-liberalism and neo-populism (Weyland, 1994). Meanwhile, some 'social liberal' enthusiasts have adapted neoliberal economic jargon to the political lexicon: PRONASOL is an example of 'supply-side politics' (Aguilar Villanueva, 1991: 128).

However, as the movement acquired ideological coherence – at least in the minds of its makers – so the chief point of reference became nineteenth-century 'social liberalism'. The trouble with – or perhaps the advantage of – this invocation is that 'social liberalism' is both historically remote and conceptually ambiguous. The fullest and best-known formulation is that of Jesús Reyes Heroles, whose paean to nineteenth-century liberalism introduced the notion of a liberal left-wing, typified by Ponciano Arriaga, who, recognising those acute social inequalities which narrow political programmes could not address, advocated 'social' policies, including the redistribution of property (Reyes Heroles, 1957-61, v. III: 539-674). This, therefore, we may designate a 'redistributionist' social liberalism, quite radical in content, and embodying a threat to the sacred right of property. However, the term 'social liberalism' has also been used to describe a quite different facet of liberalism, namely, the liberals' concern for those rampant social vices – drink, disease, gambling, bloodsports, sloth, absenteeism – which they saw as impeding the development of a modern productive capitalist Mexico and which required an active social engineering to eradicate (Knight, 1985a: 61-2, 68-9). We have here, then, a species of 'developmentalist' (*desarrollista*) social liberalism. Though quite distinct, both these views stress the *social* dimension of liberalism, arguing – rightly – that late-nineteenth and early twentieth-century liberalism went far beyond a narrow political platform, as sometimes – wrongly – asserted. But the social dimensions stressed are plainly different: the first 'redistributionist' (Reyes Heroles) brand of 'social liberalism' anticipates the social reforms of the Revolution, such as *agrarismo*; the second 'developmentalist' version relates liberalism (be it *Juarista*, *Porfirista* or *Callista*) to an evolving – essentially capitalist – view of society and the social impediments to capitalist progress which need to be removed. Both views agree in crediting liberalism with a social message, even a social conscience, and they represent useful contributions to Mexican historiography, in which respect they contribute to that powerful reassessment of Mexican liberalism which is evident in the works of Anderson (1974), Thompson (1990) and Mallon (1994).

Thus, in opting for a 'social liberal' discourse, the theorists of *salinismo* have – wittingly or not – struck a rich historiographical vein. However, it is not at all clear what the historians' 'social liberalism', just described, has to do with the *salinista* version. The contemporary project of PRONASOL forms part of a long tradition of State paternalism, which, if we wished, we certainly *could* dignify as 'social liberalism', implying by that a liberal concern for social problems and a recognition that the market – whatever the economic benefits it may bring – cannot solve all society's problems. However, there is no good (intellectual) reason for picking particularly on Ponciano Arriaga and the 'social liberalism' of the 1850s, for there have been plenty of closer precedents – such as the State-sponsored educational, agrarian and anti-poverty programmes of the period c. 1920-1980 (Knight, 1994a). Furthermore, Arriaga, like many of his twentieth-century revolutionary successors, advocated policies which would not sit happily within the current neoliberal project: for example, an agrarian reform which challenged the property rights of large commercial farms. In this respect, *salinismo*, in sounding the official death-knell of the *ejido*, sets its face against the 'social liberal' tradition, as defined by Reyes Heroles and exemplified by Arriaga. In respect of the second historical brand of 'social liberalism', the connection is again somewhat tenuous. Today's 'social liberals' do not inveigh against popular vices, at least not in public. The day when bullfights, alcoholism, prostitution and venereal diseases were seen as the *lacras sociales* retarding Mexico's development are long gone, at least among the technocratic elite who run the country. That's not what they learned at Harvard and MIT.[4]

In short, the historian's 'social liberalism' – or 'liberalisms' – is/are only tenuously related to the contemporary version, now being actively peddled in Mexico. The lowest common denominator of all three species (and it is pretty low) is a marriage between liberal – now 'neoliberal' – economics and a modicum of social conscience, or social awareness. How that awareness should be translated into political practice is quite open; 'social liberalism' – as a historical phenomenon – offers no consistent answers. Ponciano Arriaga wanted to expropriate property; revolutionary social liberals wanted to extirpate alcholism; Salinas and Carlos Rojas want to alleviate poverty by blending government resources with communal self-help. All that social liberalism *per se* can be said to imply is a belief that the market alone cannot solve social problems: a perfectly reasonable belief, which would be unremarkable were it not for the excesses of doctrinaire *laissez-faire* liberalism which have been visited upon Latin America and Eastern Europe in recent years. In this sense, social liberalism – however unoriginal or manipulative – probably qualifies,

4 Among provincial elites, *políticos* and priests, however, this traditional discourse almost certainly endures.

in Sellar and Yeatman's terms, as A Good Thing.[5] Indeed, we should credit the architects of PRONASOL not only with political ingenuity, but also with political prescience, since they anticipated the later drift of official thinking worldwide, as considerations of 'sustainable' growth and 'governability' began to make inroads into the doctrinaire economistic 'Washington consensus' of the late 1980s. Ironically, this prescience did not avert the Chiapas revolt at the beginning of 1994, or the economic crisis at the end. Social liberalism was insufficiently 'social' in the first case, and insufficiently 'liberal' in the second.[6]

However, as I mentioned before, the appeal of particular slogans cannot be attributed to their intellectual novelty or coherence; quite the reverse. Politicians – even Mexico's politicians, who are a sophisticated lot, by global standards – need convenient alibis, excuses and rationalisations. History – and political philosophy – are ransacked accordingly (Adam Smith being a particular victim of recent casuistical citation). But there is usually some logic in this process of appropriation: ideas are not infinitely fungible. In this case, the choice of a mid nineteenth-century concept had clear advantages. It involved a vast leap over both Revolution and *Porfiriato*, which enabled the regime to play down – but never repudiate – its revolutionary legacy, without falling into the trap of neo-*Porfirismo*. (Enough critics – including the proverbial man or woman on the Insurgentes omnibus – were already labelling the regime xenophile, *vendepatria*, neo-*Porfirista*, *científico*, even *gachupín* [Gilly, 1989: 85-6, 105, 203-4, 233, 236]; it would hardly do to emphasise that ancestry by invoking outright Porfirian concepts. School textbooks might – at a price – rehabilitate Díaz and Don Porfirio might star in up-market *telenovelas*, but it was clearly premature to parade a Porfirian political lineage. 'Social positivism' would hardly do the trick). On the other hand, invoking the nineteenth-century liberal tradition offered a means to marry liberalism to social responsibility – and, it should be added, to patriotism.[7] If Ponciano Arriaga had never existed, he would have had to be invented.

---

5 Sellar and Yeatman (1930) the historian's canon, contains 103 Good Things, but none later than 1918 when America became top nation and history came to a .

6 That is to say, despite ample PRONASOL resources, Chiapas remained a powderkeg; and, despite his enormously high standing in international financial circles, Salinas could not avert the crisis of late 1994. This occurred, of course, shortly after he left office (and another highly-regarded economist and technocrat replaced him). We may consider the timing a perverse tribute to Salinas' personal prestige, but the outcome remains a stinging indictment of his economic project.

7 Recent research on ninteenth-century liberalism stresses the powerful fusion of liberalism and patriotism which occurred under Juárez and profoundly affected subsequent Mexican

But why this ingenious invention of tradition? What contemporary political imperatives were at work? Here we can depart from discourse and enter the real world of contemporary political economy. This is, of course, a complicated, messy world, which several chapters in the volume address. I will confine myself to a simplistic overview, which is all the more tentative in light of recent (1994-5) events. The proclaimed goals of *salinismo* were economic restructuring and political reform (and Zedillo, by training and temperament, and in terms of both previous career and initial presidential rhetoric, does not appear to promise a radical change). Salinas held out the prospect of a dynamic modern economy and transparent modern politics. The first involved liberalisation of both the domestic economy and foreign trade and investment. The second promised an end to the old, authoritarian monopoly of the PRI and a shift towards a genuinely free competitive pluralist politics. This is, of course, a classic liberal project, with ample (rhetorical) precedents in Mexican history: Madero, 1910; Vasconcelos, 1929; Almazán, 1940; both Alemán and Padilla, 1946; even de la Madrid in the early 1980s. In practice, of course, *salinismo* delivered the economic goods but stalled on the political reform. Following precedents set by de la Madrid – or, we should say, by Salinas and de la Madrid – the economy was significantly liberalised. State enterprises were sold off, Article 27 was reformed to allow the privatisation of the *ejido*, Mexico entered GATT and NAFTA. On the political front, there were genuine changes: electoral and human rights reforms, a more diverse and lively congress, a handful of oppositionist state governors, a greater opposition presence in municipal government.[8] But the national monopoly of the PRI remained and remains firm (and all the firmer following the August 1994 elections); the party itself was not substantially reformed; and, under Salinas, the figure of the president/*tlatoani* was, if anything, reinforced. Even when the opposition 'won' and the PRI 'lost', this often came about thanks to presidential fiat. Meanwhile, critics allege, the PAN sold its political birthright for a mess of electoral pottage; and the PRD felt the force of *priísta* repression, which was in turn justified by oblique

---

history, down to and beyond the Revolution. It is obviously attractive to today's neoliberals that, as they dismantle an old *economic* nationalism, they can lay claim to a yet older *political* patriotism; how much they are believed is another matter which, to my knowledge, has been little researched.

8 We should, however, beware of applauding fictitious novelties. While the scale of opposition victories in municipal elections is unprecedented, municipal pluralism in itself is not entirely new; in several states there is a long tradition of genuine political competititon, either between the PRI and its opponents, left and right, or within the PRI itself, (see Bailón, 1992).

references to the PRD's primitive, populist, and personalistic tendencies (Gómez Tagle, 1994).

Thus, even if we recognise that Mexican politics have been in flux (as they have been for much of the twentieth-century), it is not clear that we have been witnessing a clear progression towards a consolidated democracy. Limited local concessions to the opposition may, in fact, serve to bolster the PRI and presidentialism at the national level.[9] In a situation of rapid economic change and ambiguous political reform, the utility of PRONASOL and its discursive reification, social liberalism, is obvious. Even critics grudgingly admit that PRONASOL – following well-worn Mexican traditions – has directly bolstered the president, indirectly benefited the PRI, undermined the opposition, especially the PRD, and thus given the political system a new lease of life (Knight, 1994a: 33; Molinar Horcasitas and Weldon, 1994:136-40; Arroyo Alejandre and Morris, 1993). The political turnaround since 1988 has been striking, and the PRI's revival was confirmed by the August 1994 election results, despite the death of the PRI's chosen candidate and the lacklustre campaign of his substitute. True, Zedillo's vote (in percentage terms) was about the same as Salinas' in 1988. But the turnout was exceptionally high (77 per cent compared to some 50 per cent in 1988); the scale of fraud was appreciably less; and the PRI displayed an ability to recover lost ground in states like Chihuahua, as well as the key battleground of the Federal District (DF). No doubt the ruling party was also more relieved by the drop in the *cardenista* (FDN/PRD) vote than it was alarmed by the growth of the PAN's (see Stansfield this volume).

A multiplicity of factors, of course, contributed to this electoral success: media bias, party resources, the conquest of inflation, the celebrated *voto miedo* – the fear vote, which PRI propaganda actively sought. But it cannot be doubted that PRONASOL – and its more recent neopopulist cousin, PROCAMPO – decisively paved the way for the PRI's victory. Had Colosio survived and won, it would have been reasonable to have anticipated a further extension of the shelf-life of PRONASOL. Perhaps SEDESOL – like *Pro-*

9 I am eliding 'PRI' and 'presidentialism'. Clearly, the two constitute key pillars of the Mexican political system, and are to a degree mutually reinforcing. During the last *sexenio* both president and party rebounded from the trauma of 1988; however, the party's rebound has been less vigorous and – to an unquantifiable degree – a reflex of presidential recuperation; hence the recurrent gossip of a split between Salinas and the PRI, which was supposed to lead to [another] schism and the birth of a new *Partido de Solidaridad*, or something of the sort. That did not happen, of course. However, Manuel Camacho's indignant departure, brief exile, and recent political return offer a variant on this theme, which further adds to the current political uncertainty. Can Camacho, *quemado* in the spring of 1994, rise, Phoenix-like, from the ashes?

gramación y Presupuesto (Ministry of Budget and Planning) in the 1976-88 period or *Gobernación* (Ministry of the Interior) during 1946-70 – was destined to be the incubator of presidents, the training ground of *tapados*; maybe Carlos Rojas fancied his chances for 2000. Perhaps he still does. But the turbulent events of 1994 make any prediction concerning the future of PRONASOL difficult, not least because pro's and con's appear to be finely balanced. Budgetary austerity may doom the programme; on the other hand, further 'belt-tightening' may make it more necessary than ever, whether as an anti-poverty programme or as an electoral machine. Zedillo is cast more in the mould of neoliberal than neopopulist, but his initial presidential statements – including his inaugural – included repeated references to social justice. The backlash against the Salinas administration is currently powerful, but the principal victims are the architects of *economic* rather than *social* policy. It seems probable, therefore, that PRONASOL will survive (it still retains an undoubted political utility), but it may live a more humdrum, less brash, existence. And if the programme undergoes, let us say, a routinisation of neopopulist charisma, we may in future hear a lot less about its ideological rationale, social liberalism – which, given its intimate association with Carlos Salinas, cannot but have suffered a certain guilt by association.[10]

Historians, however, do not lose interest in phenomena simply because they fade from contemporary attention or future predictions. On the contrary, the passage of time affords access to archives (there are, presumably, massive PRONASOL and related 'social liberal' archives) and confers the added benefit of hindsight. As of early 1995, any evaluation of PRONASOL, social liberalism, and the Salinas *sexenio* is plainly premature. But it is worth making a tentative try. By developing a neopopulist programme of this kind – while sedulously denying its neopopulist credentials – the Salinas administration displayed an adherence to traditional Mexican politics which was striking, if not, perhaps, surprising. Salinas, after all, comes from an established political family; like Alemán (whom he resembles in several respects), he is a *cachorro de la revolución* who, we may surmise, acquired a certain political nous with his mother's milk. He is no doubt aware that one of the strengths of the Mexican system – whose longevity is all the more impressive now that that the 'revolutionary' regimes of Eastern Europe have fallen like ninepins – has been its capacity for mediation, patronage, and manipulation. Dissent may be repressed, as in 1968; but, often, dissent is recognised and

10 This begs some obvious but unanswerable questions: how deep and long-lasting will Salinas' discredit prove and will Zedillo both strive – and manage – to deflect criticism away from himself and against the preceding administration?

dialogue is established (perhaps after some salutary repression). Erstwhile dissenters are then readmitted to the fold.[11] Such tactics require a good deal of discretionality. Politics (including elections) are conducted according to well-known unwritten customs as well as formal prescriptions. Journalists are warned off – and bought off – before they are, occasionally, bumped off. Mexico is also familiar with both policy and budgetary discretionality. Major decisions – such as the 1982 bank nationalisation – can emerge from small kitchen cabinets. The *dedazo*, of course, involves only the presidential finger. Lázaro Cárdenas, we are told, went around with a man carrying a sackful of pesos to distribute – and certainly his budgets show a good deal of slippage (Gledhill, 1991: 68; Cothran, 1986). But even today, in an age of computerisation and fiscal rigour, the Salinas administration is regularly accused of deploying public funds for political purposes: PRONASOL – which, as a programme, emerged from the *Presidencia* – is a classic example of executive autonomy and discretionality.

In other respects, too, the Salinas presidency displayed several 'traditional' political features, which contrasted with its rhetorical claims to gleaming modernity.[12] Mexican politics are habituated to a degree of corruption and violence. Neither were eliminated by the Salinas administration; arguably, they increased. Corruption is difficult to measure, and may follow cyclical swings: de la Madrid was a less egregious offender than his predecessor. But a given quantum of corruption is endemic, even in ostentatious new programmes such as PRONASOL (*Proceso*, 23 August 1993: 33). In addition, the increasingly close relationship between government and big business encouraged collusion and corruption.[13] So, too, with political violence (and I am concerned chiefly with the violence perpetrated by the State against opponents rather than vice versa). Again, there is a recognisable Mexican tradition (Knight, 1994b). Compared to the bureaucratic authoritar-

---

11 A key – if not novel – feature of the Salinas administration was its ability to recruit erstwhile critics and independent intellectuals, including veterans of 1968: Rolando Cordera, Hector Aguilar Camín, Gustavo Gordillo and Arturo Warman (the latter now holding a cabinet post under Zedillo and enacting agrarian policies distinct from those advocated in his earlier writings).

12 The argument presented here encapsulates some points made at rather greater length in Knight (1993b).

13 This is a big question which, for want of time, expertise and even temerity, I shall pass over. The famous businessmen's breakfast at Los Pinos has already passed into *salinista* folklore: future historians may see it as symptomatic of the administration's increasingly intimate relationship with the private sector, especially the blatant new rich of the early 1990s. A related theme, also ducked in this paper, is the Moussavi case: the scandal that – some said – was going to break Salinas, NAFTA, and the PRI, but didn't.

ian regimes of the southern cone, not to mention Central America, the regime of the PRI has been restrained; it has blended coercion with conciliation; it has contrived to displace political violence away from the centre to the murky provincial periphery; and, far from trumpeting its bloody achievements, as some national security doctrinaires have done in South America, it has sought to avoid root-and-branch repression. Thus, while political intimidation, disappearances, and outright assassinations occur, the federal government – and, above all, the President – has usually managed to avoid responsibility. The smoking gun – if found at all – has been found in the calloused hands of local *caciques* and *guardias blancas*. Indeed, the federal government has, in some instances, interposed itself in local political conflicts, offering mediation, ousting egregious *caciques*, sometimes sponsoring genuine social reform. PRONASOL – as a federal government initiative not necessarily welcome to local elites – thus has a long pedigree: compare the agrarian reform or the federal education programme of the 1920s and 1930s, which similarly depended on the reformist efforts of the 'centre', and often elicited the strenuous opposition of local vested interests.

For a variety of reasons, the federal government has both the will and the capacity thus to hold itself above the fray of local politics, red in tooth and claw; and to intervene selectively, judiciously, and often paternalistically, demonstrating, if you like, its relatively autonomy of local interests. Its *capacity* derives from its superior fiscal resources (far greater than the states' or the municipalities'), its control of the federal army, and its recruitment of reformist cadres, whether the *maestros rurales* of the 1930s or the *pronasolistas* of the 1990s. Thus, historically, the 'centre' is often seen as a source of resources, reform, and useful political contacts (Craig, 1983, is a good historical example). Certainly, it can repress popular movements; but it can also empower them, and it can serve as a counterweight to local forces which are more directly and often more draconianly hostile. The centre's assumption of this role – its *will* to conciliate and patronise – is also capable of several explanations. To a degree, it may reflect a genuinely enlightened politics. Salinas no doubt delighted in parading down main street, jacketless and folksy, backslapping the *campesinos* (I doubt we will see much more of this, even in Tetla de Solidaridad). Conversely, no president wants to go down in history as the architect of another Tlatelolco (compare, say, Guatemala or El Salvador, where massacres of this scale have been commonplace and their architects not only escape effective censure but may even win plaudits). Mexican political culture admits of a good deal of violence, but it does not condone and reward deliberate, culpable, official repression: hence the massive outcry against military repression in Chiapas in early 1994. In addition, the president and his entourage operate under the watchful eye of the print media, foreign and Mexican;[14] a consideration all the more compelling as Mexico groomed itself to enter NAFTA and the OECD; or, today, as Mexico faces the alarming prospect of a conservative Republican Congress setting conditions for the country's financial lifeline. Particularly along the border, violence and electoral chicanery are to be avoided: hence, in part, the concessions made to the PAN in Chihuahua and Baja California, which contrast with the treatment meted out to dissidents in, say, Michoacán.

If these considerations restrain executive violence, and encourage a more decorous political deportment, it must also be recognised that localised fraud, violence, and corruption continue. Indeed, some have discerned an increase in local violence during recent years: the result of *narcotraficante* activity (a vast and ramified theme which I shall not attempt to unravel); of local class and ethnic conflict (most obviously in Chiapas); and of enhanced political competition and polarisation, particularly in states like Michoacán, Guerrero, and Tabasco (Gómez Tagle, 1994). It may be that, even as the political system gradually and painfully 'opens up' – and as opposition parties of left and right campaign more openly and strenuously – so infringements of civil rights increase rather than decrease. Consolidated democracies may, as Huntington (1991) argues, have a good record on human rights; but the *process* of democratisation – which is often contentious and sometimes protracted – may involve greater conflict, violence, and arbitrary use of power.[15]

What is more, on two dramatic occasions during 1994, deadly violence affected the very *cúpulas* of the PRI. We still do not know – and probably we will never know – the true causes of the assassinations of Colosio and Ruiz Massieu. Hence it is as risky to incorporate them into this general discussion of the Salinas *sexenio* as it would be ingenuous to leave them out. But it seems quite probable that they reflected – at national level, at the summit of the political volcano – some of the same pressures which, for years, had been simmering at the base, amid the hot lava of provincial politics: *narcotraficante* influence; the stresses produced by incipient democratisation and party competition; the growing political polarisation between and also

14 I stress *print* media, since Mexican television is not noted for its investigative zeal. Another interesting aspect of the last *sexenio*, especially during the final year of Chiapas and the presidential elections, was the mounting criticism of Televisa and its skewed news coverage – criticism which ranged from informed journalistic comment to street graffitti and protest banners. It is, however, difficult to see the present administration responding to this criticism and biting the hand that fed it.

15 This hypothesis appears to receive some statistical support from the interesting comparative research on citizenship, participation and protest in Mexico, Spain, Brazil and Chile currently being done by Joe Foweraker and Tod Landman at the University of Essex.

within parties (a polarisation sometimes presented in terms of dinosaurs versus reformers, *políticos* versus *técnicos*, and – as a glance at Zedillo's ephebocratic cabinet suggests – generations versus generations). What is surely significant is that these conflicts, hitherto confined largely to the base and to the provinces, have now erupted at the top, among the PRI's national elite, even on the streets of the capital. We do not know if the violent events of 1994 were freak aberrations or incipient trends. In the unlikely eventuality that they marked a new trend, the implications for Mexican political stability would be grave, suggesting a return to the internecine elite feuding of the 1920s and 1930s; in which case, the Salinas *sexenio* will be judged to be one, not of political advance, or even stagnation, but of outright regression. Again, the welter of events, the tug-of-war of pro's and con's, makes any evaluation of this factor almost impossible. The shock of twin assassinations, coupled with Chiapas, a triumphant election, and a swift economic debacle, may reinforce the PRI elite's customary party discipline: 'better to hang together or, assuredly, we shall all hang separately', as Ben Franklin put it.[16] But the rifts of 1994 will be hard to heal: Camacho is still sulking in his tent; and Zedillo's cabinet purge has added to the list of disaffected *camarillas*, while further reducing his own – never that extensive – political base. Although, we may conclude, Salinas enabled Zedillo to enter Los Pinos with a modicum of legitimacy (as the witticism went: Salinas lost his own election in 1988 but won Zedillo's in 1994), it is now clear that he bequeathed his successor a *damnosa haereditas*, both economic and political.

We may finally ask why, given the consistent democratising 'first-world' rhetoric of the Salinas administration, progress in this direction was relatively slow, certainly if comparison is made with the rapidity of economic reform, and why old political traits – executive discretionality, 'neopopulism', alchemical or 'negotiated' elections, the incidence of violence and corruption – remained notoriously hard to eradicate.[17] First, the federal government may *want* to clean the Augean stables of local politics, but lack the power. Sporadic initiatives – the ouster of flagrant offenders: labour bosses like La Quina or the *priísta caciques* of Chiapas – do not add up to a systematic house-cleaning. One *cacique* tends to give way to another; the worst offenders are shown the door; scandals are soon forgotten. But the system remains and the people at the top survive these recurrent embarrassments: PRI politics

16 On the PRI's party discipline, especially at the top, which – despite schisms in 1952 and 1987-8 – has generally been a key element in its maintenance of power, (see Purcell and Purcell, 1980).

17 These points are also discussed in Knight (1993b).

therefore invite comparison with the Papacy or, as already suggested, the British royal family. Historically, even reformist administrations have protected their own and relied on some dubious backers: the centre needs its supporters, nationally and locally; it dare not offend too many of its own people, for it depends on them to make the system work (Gledhill, 1991: 66, 107; Pansters, 1990: 50-2; Knight, 1994c). Note, in this context, the role of Carlos Hank González and the Atlacomulco group in Zedillo's electoral victory.

There is also a long history of Federal initiatives running into the sands of provincial – especially *priísta* – inertia or outright opposition: the socialist education programme of the 1930s; Madrazo's attempted party reforms in the 1960s; de la Madrid's promise of free elections in 1985. Colosio's attempts to reform the PRI encountered a good deal of subterranean resistance – and, in part for that reason, were limited in success (Garrido, 1994; see also Craske this volume). Some have even speculated that Colosio's death derived from PRI resentment at the PAN's gubernatorial victory in Baja California in 1989. Thus, as Dale Story has convincingly argued in respect of Mexico's industrialists (Story, 1986), powerful sectional – and regional – interests have the capacity to stymie initiatives they dislike. Conversely, the central government (whose powers are regularly exaggerated by statolatrous historians and social scientists) cannot ride roughshod over such interests; the supposed decline of the presidency in the 1970s and 1980s had a lot to do with ill-advised policies which offended powerful interests well capable of confronting, resisting and influencing the State (Elizondo, 1993). Perhaps the central government could have staked all on victory and won, *cueste lo que cueste*, as Victoriano Huerta liked to say. But the success – in terms of stability and 'systems-maintenance' – of the Mexican State has depended precisely on avoiding such unequivocal confrontations, such prodigal squandering of political capital. To a greater extent than some – statolatrous – analyses recognise, the Mexican system has involved a delicate balance of political interests (one which, since it reflects a highly unequal society, has necessarily tended to favour the rich and powerful: Knight, 1993a). No president will want to jeopardise this – for him – providential dispensation unless the ultimate prize fully justifies the risk. In short, reform and democratisation are fine if they are roughly compatible with the socio-political *status quo*; but they in no way justify subverting the status quo and squandering the carefully hoarded capital of three 'revolutionary' generations.

To a substantial degree, therefore, the central government is a prisoner of the system and the political culture which brought it into being. However much the imperatives of modernisation and North American opinion may – and I stress 'may' – require democratisation, it is hard to envisage the

Mexican Leviathan voluntarily beaching itself and expiring. At best, it may slim down, the better to survive and forage. Thus, talk of 'dismantling' the State seems to me misguided; perhaps Leviathan is simply turning into a leaner, meaner shark.

Furthermore, there are reasons for thinking that systematic reform – a concerted clean-up of the dark corners of Mexican political culture – are not only risky for the central government, but also basically undesirable. That is to say, the urge to democratise is offset by the practical, quotidian, functional needs of the State, as it strives to govern a large, complex, heterogeneous, unequal society, which has known a turbulent history and which also happens to share a 2000 mile border with the United States. Thus, the notion of *la patrie en danger* can be used to justify repression (for example, in 1968); a similar rationale underlies the practice of so-called 'patriotic fraud'. Domestic social control is enhanced by selective deviations from strict constitutional practice. We do not know whether presidents encourage, sanction, or reluctantly tolerate local abuses (electoral alchemy, illicit pressure on the media and opposition, and worse). But the notion of discretionality, raised earlier, suggests that it can be in the interests of the central government to maintain a degree of uncertainty and illegality. As Frans Schryer points out, in his excellent study of peasant politics in the Huasteca, local violence and *caciquismo* create an atmosphere of uncertainty which the federal government can exploit to its own advantage – monitoring, mediating, standing back, intervening, dividing and ruling (Schryer, 1990: 221). Local actors are kept on the hop, the rules of the game remain flexible, the centre has the final say. The discretionary intervention of the federal executive in gubernatorial elections – another echo of the turbulent 1920s – could be said to obey a similar rationale: by avoiding strict adherence to constitutional nicety, the executive retains the initiative, keeps local actors (both PRI and opposition) in a state of uncertainty, and pragmatically determines the final outcome.

Such a strategy, anathema to strict legalists and doctrinaire (representative) democrats, both Mexican and foreign, carries risks: the central government's manipulation of Chiapas politics – conditioned, no doubt, by the demands of NAFTA – ended in disaster. But the centre's strategy can work, so long as it is run by competent *políticos*, tolerably resistant to the temptations of office, including that *delirio de la grandeza* that has affected some presidents/*tlatoque*. It has helped preserve a degree of social stability: the *sesenta años de paz social* which the PRI placards proclaimed in 1989. It has also facilitated a concerted economic policy, making possible Mexico's conquest of inflation, thorough programme of privatisation, and successful attraction of foreign investment. However, even this achievement – the pride of *salinismo*, the envy of Latin America, and the object of repeated World

Bank and 'expert' encomia – now looks decidedly hollow, a tactical rather than a strategic victory.

I have argued that the Mexican political system, while far from static, has retained certain enduring characteristics, which have proved quite compatible with structural economic change. The hegemonic party, forged by Calles and Cárdenas in a society that was still heavily rural and illiterate, reinforced its dominance during the post war years of industrialisation and urbanisation, and, under Salinas, spearheaded Mexico's neoliberal economic transformation. Its demise has frequently been predicted (never more vociferously than in 1988), but each demise has proved premature. In grand and schematic terms, we might say, the PNR/PRM/PRI has served as the institutional carapace of Mexico's bourgeois revolution, promoting the conditions within which national integration and capital accumulation can proceed apace (Knight, 1985b).

Some might shy away from this formulation: as too abstract, too unfashionably *marxisant*, or – alternatively – too lacking in Marxist rigour, all of which would be true. The third objection – lack of rigour – leads me to my final point, which involves matching the politics and economics of *salinismo*: the former, as I have said, quite 'traditional' and cautious; the latter bolder and more innovative. Classical Marxism – that is, Marx's own analysis of British capitalism – assumed some sort of affinity between industrial capitalism and 'bourgeois democracy'. Like several of Marx's assumptions, this was arguably eurocentric. We have seen plenty of cases of fast-developing capitalist societies which have avoided bourgeois democracy. But the presumption of an affinity remains. Furthermore, the presumption is often shared by those who would not give Marx the time of day. What Fukuyama argues on a global scale, experts on Mexico, such as Sidney Weintraub, argue for the present conjuncture in Mexico: for them, the shift to a more open, free, *laissez-faire* capitalism carries with it, as a necesary corollary, a transition to a more free, open, and transparent democracy (Weintraub, 1990: 202). As the State dismantles its barrage of economic controls – subsidies, regulations, tariffs, quotas – so it will divest itself of its concomitant political hegemony. It will relinquish the means to control civil society, and the latter – lusty, revivified, and independent – will take charge of its own political destiny. The *estado papá* will shuffle off to the nursing home, leaving a mature people to run their own adult lives, both politically and economically.

The argument – whether of Marxist or non-Marxist provenance – displays a certain economic determinism and, in my opinion, fails to do justice to the autonomy of politics and to the durability and flexibility of the Mexican political system. The latter, as I have said, has proved compatible with shifting socioeconomic conditions over decades. Neoliberalism has happily accommodated a large dose of neopopulism. Does it follow that neoliberal economics will sound the death-knell of the PRI, presidentialism, and the familiar structures of Mexican politics? And – a crucial follow-up question, in light of recent events – if it does, if economic debacle finally breaks the power of the PRI, does it follow that the outcome will be a 'transparent', orderly, liberal democracy (rather than, for example, a descent into authoritarianism, factionalism, and violence – what is sometimes glibly referred to as the 'Colombianisation' of Mexico)?

The systemic argument posits that economic development – of a capitalist, market-oriented kind – is hostile to archaic political practices (violence, *caciquismo*, rigged elections, arbitrary executive power). This argument can be of two kinds. First, it can stress the logic of capitalist political economy, contending – in Schumpeterian style – that capitalism cannot abide archaic practices which undermine confidence and inhibit market rationality. Even if there is some truth to this argument, it is offset by a countervailing argument, already touched upon: while a model representative bourgeois regime may be optimal (a big 'if'), this may not in fact be the practical alternative to the *status quo* which is on offer. In the real world of Mexican political economy – as elsewhere in Latin America, perhaps even Europe – capitalists, while they may not love the State, are not blind to its utility, nor to the (worse) possible alternatives they may confront. In fact, the relationship between the Mexican State and private capital has been a complex, shifting, but fundamentally collaborative one, at least since the 1940s. Although business, especially big business, has not enjoyed formal representation in the PRI, it has exercised real influence, through both formal and informal channels. By most standards – rate of profit, tariff protection, taxation, subsidies, control of organised labour – it has had a good deal. For that reason, no doubt, it has had little reason to flirt with praetorian solutions. Only with Echeverría and, briefly, with López Portillo, did business fear for its future; and, as a result of those scares, it mobilised, lobbied, threatened and cajoled with conspicuous success (Story, 1986; Maxfield and Anzaldúa, 1987; Luna, 1992; Elizondo, 1993) Its weapons were varied and effective: support for the PAN, use of the mass media, an investment strike, capital flight. In response, State and party have since 1982 placed a high priority on reassuring the private sector, tailoring both policies and candidacies to this end. While the neoliberal project should not be seen as a State concession to business (no such simple agency can be assumed; and not all items in the neoliberal project are necessarily favoured by business), equally, it would be wrong to conceive of that project as a pure technocratic conceit, or a knee-jerk reaction to changing global fashion. Future historians who evaluate the economic restructuring of the1980s and 1990s will, I suspect, place considerable emphasis on the capacity of the private sector to influence public policy; and they will also point to the rise of a new generation of entrepreneurs and interests who have emerged as the beneficiaries of liberalisation. Salinas' millionaires, to use the popular phrase, may come to be seen as the 1990s counterparts of Sanford Mosk's 'New Group' who rode to prominence on Alemán's coattails during the 1940s boom (Mosk, 1950).

But the relationship between this important economic shift and the – at best – incipient democratisation of the day is far from clear. Business spokesmen made a good deal of play with democratisation in the mid-1980s, as they reacted to the bank nationalisation and, in some cases, aligned themselves with the PAN. Today, however, the PRI appears to have recovered the entrepreneurial higher ground (helped, of course, by its cosier relationship with the PAN). Mexican entrepreneurs, like their counterparts elsewhere, are likely to keep their options open – thus, for example, they are ready to listen to Cuauhtémoc Cárdenas, if not to bankroll him (*La Jornada*, 4 Sept. 1993). However, to the extent that a *neocardenista* coalition offers the chief national threat to the PRI, business is likely to retain its historically congenial relationship with the PRI; a relationship which, I would hypothesise, has been the more effective because of the formal separation of the two entities. In short, a PRI that does not obviously *represent* business, but which can maintain the broad framework within which business can invest, accumulate and prosper, may be optimal; business and the Catholic Church, one might say, are better off if they keep the State at arms' length, and do not succumb to a close embrace. If true, this suggests a caution: Mexico's capitalists – whether the import-substituting 'New Group' of the 1940s or the neoliberal 'Newer Group' of the 1980/90s – did not and do not need a PRI that was/is in thrall to their interests, responsive to their every need. A PRI of this kind – an 'agent' State, subservient to capital – would forfeit legitimacy, lose its capacity to mediate social conflict, and, perhaps, prove unable to maintain the broad framework within which business could thrive. It is for this reason (among others) that programmes like PRONASOL, however distasteful to hardnosed neoliberals, are politically functional.

My argument, then, is that the reformulation of capitalism currently taking place in Mexico does not necessitate – and may not even favour – a breakthrough to genuine democracy. A strong version of this argument – and the mirror image of Weintraub's – would be that a vigorous and dynamic capitalism will actually bolster the PRI and deter democratisation. A weak version would incline to agnosticism, and avoid any presumed connection between economic restructuring and democracy: as Peter Smith has argued concerning NAFTA, the political consequences of economic liberalisation may pull in different directions, and defy any neat correlation. Both of these arguments

– the pessimistic and the agnostic, we might call them – seem to me to be more historically sound than the optimistic conclusion which posits a necessary and positive relationship between economic liberalisation and democratisation.

If this systemic argument focuses on business and its relationship to the State, a second treats society in its entirety. Roughly, it is assumed that as society 'modernises' – that is, becomes more literate, technological, urban, mobile, secular, achievement-oriented – so archaic political forms give way to more rational, *ergo* democratic, ones (Huntington, 1991). This second systemic argument seems to me to carry more weight than the first. History suggests that representative democracies are more likely to take root and flourish in 'modern' societies – although we should take note of major exceptions (Costa Rica, India) and regressions (fascist Europe, the Southern Cone in the 1970s). Among the supposed causal explanations for this apparent correlation are the fact that literate urban populations are more difficult to dragoon than illiterate rural populations; thus, as the cities swell, so traditional *cacical* authority is likely to give way to modern mass parties (although, Germani warned, there may be an unfortunate hiatus as the rural migrants, lugging their 'traditional' cultural baggage with them into the city, reproduce a political *rus in urbe*, to the detriment, rather than to the advantage, of representative democracy; if this process continues for the long term, of course, it could contribute to a long term democratic deficit (Germani, 1978).

In the Mexican case, there are limited grounds for endorsing this thesis. Cities have tended to produce sizeable votes for the opposition, while the more backward rural regions remained – at least during the heyday of the PRI – solid for the ruling party (González Casanova, 1970). However, even the historical argument has its drawbacks. If the thesis is watertight, one might have expected the regularly rising literacy rates of the 1940s, 1950s, and 1960s to yield growing political dissent and opposition; yet the Mexican countryside – though never as docile and quiescent as sometimes imagined – was more thoroughly controlled by the State in the 1950s and 1960s than it had been in the 1920s and 1930s. Furthermore, evidence of a 'backward' political culture, replete with abuses and inimical to democracy, appears to defy both temporal and spatial logic. Tamaulipas – a relatively 'modern' northern state – was a nest of *caciquismo* in the 1930s and still yields plenty of examples of murky – as opposed to transparent – politics (*La Jornada,* 29 August, 5 September 1993). Mexico's burgeoning cities, too, have produced plenty of *caciques* and *cacical* abuses (Ugalde, 1970; Cornelius, 1973; Vélez-Ibáñez, 1983: Eckstein, 1988).

Of course, over time the modes of *caciquismo* change: in San Luis, as the ('traditional') Cedillo *cacicazgo* was consumed, the ('modern') Santos *caci-*

cazgo rose from its ashes (Márquez, 1988; see also Pansters this volume). The Figueroa family of northern Guerrero produced a first generation of old-style (parochial, military) *caudillos* in the 1910s and 1920s and second generation of new-style (centralising, bureaucratic) *caudillos* in the 1930s; the third generation of the dynasty remains powerful in Guerrero politics today (Jacobs, 1980; *Proceso*, 9 November 1992). In Puebla the powerful and durable *cacicazgo* founded by the Avila Camacho family depended on – and did not react against – the centralising drive of the central government; rather, this regional power bloc drew sustenance from the centre, which in turn allowed *avilacamachismo* to dominate the state politically and economically (Pansters, 1990). A roughly comparable case might be the Atlacomulco group of the state of Mexico, whose enduring influence has been mentioned (Arreola Ayala, 1985). Local – as well as regional – studies also reveal persistent nodules of *cacical* power which, while they necesarily differ from, say, the praetorian fiefdoms of the Revolution, similarly inhibit the implementation of transparent democratic politics – and do so, often enough, with the support of the centre, sometimes with genuine support from sections of the local population, and in apparent defiance of the rapid 'modernisation' which their communities have undergone. The contemporary Huasteca, for example, is a far more literate, market-oriented, accessible, and integrated region than it was in the days of the early revolutionary *caciques* (for example Lárraga, Santos); yet, as Schryer graphically shows, *caciquismo* and violence remain endemic. Indeed, ('modern') *caciquismo* may even nurture itself on those modernising influences – roads, radio, federal agencies, foreign investment – which are supposedly agents of its dissolution.

Of course, I have selected cases to support my argument – or, more strictly, to question the argument implied by Lipset, Huntington and others (Huntington, 1991: 59-72). It may well be that, over the long term, 'modern' urban industrial societies offer more propitious circumstances for the development of democracy. On the other hand, there can be no doubt that historical and cultural factors exercise great influence – whether positive or negative – and that, as a result, structural preconditions are only a part, perhaps a small part, of the story. Within Latin America itself the range of stable, unstable, and absent democracies has been wide and fluctuating. Even if it could be shown that the progressive 'modernisation' of Mexico is, over the long term, conducive to democratisation, it is clearly a very long term, since Mexico has been 'modernising' at least since the *Porfiriato*, if not the *Reforma*, and no stable, functioning democracy has, as yet, emerged. And in the Mexico of today, amid the white heat of Salinas' technological revolution, the vestiges of 'traditional' political culture remain strong, extensive, and recalcitrant; while the regime, bent on its project of economic restructuring, may regard root-and-branch democratisation as a secondary priority, certainly a risk, perhaps, even, an ill-advised surrender of the State's historic resources.

Thus, while Salinas' administration developed and deepened Mexico's 'bourgeois revolution', insofar as the economy is concerned, it appeared to drag its feet in respect of the representative democracy which, according to some, both Marxists and non-Marxists, is the natural political expression of 'modern' developed capitalism. Perhaps, in the long term, the presumed elective affinity will materialise. Perhaps, paradoxically, the failings of the neoliberal project – evident as I write – will prompt a democratising of the regime, as Zedillo casts about for political allies and makes genuine political concessions in return for yet another bout of 'belt-tightening'.[18] But those are hypothetical future developments. My tentative and premature post-mortem of the '*Salinato*' suggests that economic neoliberalism did not significantly promote political democratisation (indeed, it may even have inhibited it); that, the events of 1994-5 notwithstanding, major structural changes were wrought in the Mexican economy, particularly to the advantage of big business, yet no corresponding structural reform of the Mexican political system took place; and that even the political innovations of the period – PRONASOL, 'social liberalism', *panista* governorships – were less genuinely innovative than often imagined. Like that other *cachorro de la revolución*, Miguel Alemán (who also left office under a cloud, and whose successor promptly devalued the peso), Salinas is therefore best seen as an aggressive and creative president, dedicated to the modernisation of Mexico along capitalist lines, prepared to deploy the coercive and patronage powers of the State to further these goals, solicitous for but not subservient to private capital, and committed to the maintenance of a State which, while it might eschew old-style economic dirigisme and public ownership, contradictorily combined promises of 'modern' democratic reform with ample use of 'traditional' discretionary powers. Alemán, building on the work of his more cautious predecessor, Avila Camacho, constructed a durable political and economic system, overcoming the debacle of the 1940 election, collaborating with the US (and, to a degree, the Church), inaugurating a generation of pax

18 If such a crisis-induced democratisation does occur, which is possible but not, I think, probable, then it would be wrong – though no doubt tempting to some – to see such an outcome as proof of the democratising influence of neoliberal economics. After all, such a scenario can be envisaged precisely because neoliberal policies have – by neoliberal as well as other criteria – proved a failure, by virtue of bringing renewed devaluation, inflation, market instability, and falling living standards. An accelerated democratisation at this juncture – thrust on a reluctant regime by adverse circumstances – would seem, if anything, to support the notion that succesful neoliberal economics obstructed rather than promoted democratisation.

priísta and so-called economic miracle. I imagine that Salinas, having overcome the trauma of 1988 and undertaken a second reformulation of Mexican capitalism, would like to be remembered in similar terms. In January 1994 I concluded: 'it is not impossible that he will be'. If Zedillo and the PRI can survive to see the benefits of a devalued peso; if the *bolsa* recovers, the US plays ball and Chiapas does not flare up again; if the political opposition fails (or is not allowed) to benefit from the PRI's discomfiture; and if the PRI stop killing each other – then, perhaps, my original conclusion, which now seems excessively sanguine, may not be far wrong. But these are big 'ifs' and more dramatic outcomes are clearly within the bounds of possibility. It is these 'ifs' and outcomes, however, which will finally determine history's verdict on Salinas, social liberalism, and the '*Salinato*'.

2 Neoliberalism and Identity: Redefining State and Society in Mexico

Rob Aitken[1]

Knight (this volume) argues, parties, *políticos* and presidents in Mexico have placed great emphasis on historical precedents and symbols in legitimating themselves; this also holds true for much of the Mexican population who have constructed their identities and ideas of their places in Mexican society, at least in part, in terms of the discourses and symbols of Mexican history. In this sense history is a political battleground, but one that is not simply contested by politicians but also by a diversity of social groups, and thus forms an important arena for the cultural negotiation of rule in Mexico (see Lomnitz-Adler, 1992; Joseph and Nugent, 1994). The Salinas administration has seen important changes in the way in which the ruling political group has tried to legitimate itself and its policies, even if as Knight argues, 'social liberalism' is more a practical result of these policies than a coherent ideology. Nevertheless, these changes in the legitimating discourse of the Salinas administration, as well as the changes in political and economic policies, have had important implications for the way that Mexican people perceive their place within the society. The neoliberal policies and ideology espoused by the Salinas government challenged the types of identities formed around the ideology of the Revolution and the categories of workers, peasants or *ejidatarios*. These popular identities have been shaped in relation not only to people's experiences of political and economic power, but also in relation to popular and elite discourses. In particular elements of dominant discourses have been taken up, reinterpreted and embedded in local discourses and identities. Much of the Mexican population now faces an abrupt change in official discourse which challenges their own imaginings of the national

---

1 I would like to thank the *Consejo Nacional de Ciencia y Tecnologia* and the Central Research Fund of the University of London for funding fieldwork in Michoacán between 1987 and 1993. I am indebted also to John Gledhill, David Stansfield, Gareth A. Jones and Nikki Craske for their invaluable comments on earlier drafts of this paper.

community and their place within it.[2] Neither do their responses to these changes occur in an anomic vacuum but in relation to the intersection of different discourses and their experiences of power. So there is not likely to be any single response, though I hope to point out some potential ones.

The neoliberal policies of the 1980s and 1990s with their emphasis on the opening of the country and the end of large-scale direct State investment have implied a restructuring of the economy, although it could be argued that the neoliberal ideology of the Salinas administration was above all an attempt to rationalise and legitimise changes that were already occurring. It is also important to emphasise that neoliberalism in practice has not implied a withdrawal of the State from the economy but rather a redefinition of its role, such that it is no longer to be the motor of development through direct investment, but rather to construct the conditions for (mostly certain types of large-scale) private investment. This redefinition has not implied a decentralisation of power, but rather a recentralisation justified ideologically in terms of discourses about the necessity to free society from bureaucracy. Thus the increase in attacks on trade unions and workers' rights has been justified in terms of the corruption of unions, and by arguments that workers' struggles are not only against the national interest but also against their own interests as they will be putting themselves out of work. They have been accompanied by a massive ideological intervention by the State to attempt to impose these new norms.[3]

The changes in the 1980s, then, have not been simply economic, the removal of subsidies on basic goods, privatisation and so on, but have involved an ideological transformation. The resurrection of modernisation as the principal goal of State policy, at least in the government rhetoric, forms part of a global tendency in the ideological terrain, which has denigrated any form of 'statism' – to the extent that the statism of Latin America in the 1970s, like communism, has been depicted as a failed ideology. The discourse of President Salinas formed part of a global transformations even as it reinterpreted and embedded these discourses into others such as nationalism within Mexico. The neoliberal policies are presented in Mexico in a manner remi-

---

2 I should stress that my interest in this paper is not to analyse the changes in the Salinas administration's official discourse *per se*. Rather I am interested in the responses of local social groups to their perceptions of shifts in the official discourse. These will obviously be multiple and varied, however, in illustrating some of them with reference to social groups in Michoacán, I aim to show some of the problems involved in the redefinition of the State in Mexico.

3 Although as O'Connor (1984) notes for the case of Reagan's United States the different ideological elements of the redefinition of the State and society may actually be in conflict with each other.

niscent of Mrs. Thatcher's repeated cry of 'there is no alternative' to the extent that anyone who doubts the policies is accused of being anti-patriotic. As Kathy Powell (this volume) argues, recent changes in official discourses in Mexico have included attempts to redefine Mexican nationalism through an abandoning of economic nationalism, and at the same time linking the Salinas modernisation project directly with the nation rather than the State, to legitimise it and maintain it above the arena of politics.

Obviously, the rhetoric and practices of the Salinas government go beyond simple neoliberalism, and particularly through its 'anti-poverty' programme, the *Programa Nacional de Solidaridad* (PRONASOL), involve an appropriation of popular discourses on autonomy and *autogestión* (self-help). Clearly this is not unrelated to neoliberal discourses. Although the government is keen to stress PRONASOL as a particular Mexican solution to Mexican problems, it seems to fit in very well with the tendency of World Bank and IMF programmes to emphasise the targetting of resources and community participation. PRONASOL is presented as an attempt to transform State-society relations in Mexico and create groups within civil society which are capable of presenting demands to the State. While this interpretation does have some academic support (see Cornelius *et al*., 1994), I am more inclined, from my experiences of the political use of Solidarity funds to see the programme, like Denise Dresser, as a 'neopopulist solution to neoliberal problems' and as representing much more continuity than change in the clientelistic nature of political culture (see Varley this volume).

Despite the continuing clientelistic practices of the political system, the Salinas administration has placed a greater emphasis in its discourses on concepts of autonomy. These discourses on autonomy, as well as international discourses on ecology and the rights of indigeneous peoples, have nevertheless presented strategic opportunities for some popular movements and for the construction or reconstruction of certain types of identities. Haber (1993) demonstrates the use of PRONASOL by both the *Comites de Defensa Popular* (CDP) in Durango to build their movement and also by the national government to disassociate the CDP from the *Partido de la Revolución Democrática* (PRD). In the case of rural movements, Harvey (1990) has argued that movements with an emphasis on production issues seem to have fared better than those which have stressed land issues. Similarly, a number of indigeneous groups which emphasise cultural rights and ethnic identities have had some success at allying with urban and even international ecological groups and bringing pressure to bear on the political system.

While these new discourses do provide the potential for new forms of mobilisation and the construction of identities, they do so in the context of popular political cultures that have been formed historically in relation to the official discourses of the State and the political practices of the local dominant class (see Lomnitz-Adler, 1992).[4] The effect of these processes of reinterpretation and embedding of elite discourses in everyday life and in popular discourses is that the same ideological elements become part of processes of both domination and resistance. This is not a new process in Mexico; the history of the nineteenth century involved processes of the popular reinterpretation of liberal ideas, of European or North American origin, appropriated by Mexican elites. Within the one country, elements of the liberal discourse were appropriated and reinterpreted in different forms by different social groups. This occurred to the extent that in 1910 the supporters of Porfirio Díaz as well as his opponents, from both elites and the broader population, used elements of liberal ideology in their discourses (Knight, 1990a). Since the Revolution, revolutionary nationalism, the official ideology of the Revolution, has achieved a similar status in contemporary Mexican political culture through a long and conflictual process. The neoliberal discourses of the government attempt to reinterpret or abandon much of the discourse of the Revolution, threatening the identities previously constructed on the basis of these discourses.

While the current modernisation project requires not only the passive acceptance of workers and peasants, but also considerable economic sacrifices from them, and at the same time it denies them a role as significant actors in the development of the nation. While the representation of peasants and workers in the official unions of the PRI may have been corrupt and controlling, nevertheless, the ideology of the Revolution did give them a place in society where they were portrayed as important for national development. The modernisation project of the Salinas administration viewed what much of the working population perceived to be hard won rights as obstacles to modernisation and development. For the majority of those who saw themselves as peasants and workers this implied not only an economic exclusion from the development and modernisation of the Salinas period, but also the denial of their importance and rights. As the *sexenio* progressed there was also an increasing political exclusion. Not only was the importance of the channels of official representation (limited though they were) greatly weakened, but the early policy of *concertación social* (social pacts) with independent popular movements, seemed to diminish in importance.

4 The *zapatista* rebellion in Chiapas provides an example of a movement that has used discourses about indigenous peoples rights, democratisation and citizenship, but combined them with an appropriation of the ideology of the Revolution, particluarly through discourses of the Revolution betrayed, of which Zapata himself is a key icon (see Powell this volume).

Democratisation was increasingly identified with electoral liberalisation and negotiation with political parties to frame new electoral laws. Clearly clean and democratic elections have been a popular demand and many peasants and workers have struggled to have their political rights recognised. However, the concentration on elections has diminished the importance given to other forms of social rights and representation. The modernisation project of the Salinas administration therefore posed considerable threats to the forms of self-identification and collective organisation of a large part of the Mexican population. Their reactions to these economic and ideological threats are not anomic, but involve a reinterpretation and transformation of the significance of these identities, and a re-evaluation of the importance of different identities; I will return to these points later. However, before doing so I will discuss the importance that the ideology of the Revolution attained through its interrelation with the construction of local identities.

THE IDEOLOGY OF THE REVOLUTION AND LOCAL IDENTITIES

Processes of State formation in postrevolutionary Mexico have involved not simply an expansion of the central power of the State and the creation of bureaucratic institutions, but also projects of cultural revolution, which are both totalising and categorising (see Joseph and Nugent, 1994: 19-20). They can be described as totalising in the sense of the existence of projects for the construction of an imagined national community, that is the nation. The particular vision of this imagined community in postrevolutionary Mexico was one in which the State sat above society and acted, at least in the official discourse, as an arbitrator between different social groups. The totalising vision of the modern nation-state has the effect of politicising social and cultural issues, which now must be resolved in the public domain with reference to the State (Asad, 1991; Gledhill, 1994). Struggles over land become struggles for State recognition of land claims, working class struggles become struggles over labour law, or, as is often the case in Mexico, struggles to make the State implement its own laws or recognise a strike.[5] At the same time, official discourses and new bureaucratic structures of representation,

5 It should be noted that this was by no means new in Mexico. Land issues in the colonial and independence period had often involved appeals to the State. However, it would be mistaken to take a revisionist position and argue that the Mexican Revolution changed nothing. The postrevolutionary State achieved a far greater penetration of civil society than earlier regimes even if this was never total and was often contested.

such as trade unions, peasant unions, *ejidos* (land reform communities) and so on, have the effect of categorising people as workers, peasants or *ejidatarios*.

Clearly there was considerable resistance from a 'recalcitrant people' to the cultural projects of the postrevolutionary political elites. Many of the more extreme attempts to redefine the identities and popular cultures of the Mexican population can best be described as 'failed cultural revolutions' as Bantjes (1994) argues for the case of the defanatisation campaign in Sonora in the 1930s. In western Mexico the implementation of the postrevolutionary project in the 1920s and 1930s often met strong local resistance. While land reform was clearly a popular demand, the implementation of land redistribution was often a violent process in which certain agrarian leaders created political careers for themselves as intermediaries between the population and the State on the basis of pressing for land reform. Resistance to land reform was often a resistance to the perception of the increased penetration of rural life by the State as well as opposition to the violent behaviour of the new local intermediaries between the State and people. This resistance to the increased penetration of local society by the State was expressed in the popular mobilisations supporting the *cristiada* (see Meyer, 1976).

The ideology of the Revolution and the categories of *ejidatario*, peasant, and worker that it created were not initially popular. However, over the following decades much of the revolutionary ideology, as well as the laws and institutions that supported it, has been appropriated by the population and even used to mobilise resistance to the failure of the actions of the State's local representatives to match the claims of the ideology. The postrevolutionary State may well have been a 'swiss cheese' (Knight, 1990b), in that its institutional structures had limited penetration of many regions and may often have been rejected or reinterpreted at the local level in terms of local projects. Yet, it created an image of a national community and the place of social groups within it.

Local Identities in Michoacán

In the case of Ciudad Lázaro Cárdenas, Michoacán, the devaluation of the role of workers in the development of the country and the virtual elimination of the nationalised industries during the Salinas administration has had serious implications for the economic position of the majority who perceived themselves as working class, which in turn has had an impacted on their identity. Ciudad Lázaro Cárdenas was constructed as a new town at the behest of the State and its economy has been dominated by nationalised industries, principally the *Siderúrgica Lázaro Cárdenas - Las Truchas SA* (SICARTSA) steelworks and the *Fertilizantes Mexicanas* (FERTIMEX) chemical factory.

Although the massive immigration to the region had also created a large 'informal' and service economy employing the majority of workers, the steelworks remained central to the region's economy and the reason for the city's construction. Furthermore, the steelworks gave the region its economic and especially its political importance. Given the massive investments in the region it seemed unlikely that the State would abandon it, even if subsequent development plans were frequently postponed. The militancy of the local steelworkers union also gave the local population the feeling of being in the vanguard of trade unionism. Section 271 of the Miners' Union, the union of SICARTSA workers, had not been formed due to the initiative of the workers but had been imposed by the State in order to prevent the workers forming an independent local union. Nevertheless, Section 271 won a reputation for defending the economic and social interests of the workers. During the 1970s fought over questions of housing, schools and transport as well as wages, and maintained a reputation for defending the local autonomy of the union section against the national union. Section 271's first major strike in 1979 was against a fraudulently elected leadership who were perceived to have been imposed by the national union, and later strikes in 1985 and 1989 were not recognised by the national leadership.

Furthermore, the internal organisation of the local union, which included delegates in each area of the factory as well as general assemblies of the workers and an elected local executive committee, created activists with the experience of having negotiated in the plant to resolve the problems of fellow workers and of having spoken in assemblies and meetings. Some of these workers later became leaders of neighbourhood movements pressing for titles to their land and services. In as much as a regional identity existed in this new town it was focused on the memory of the struggles of the Section 271 and a pride in its achievements and the importance of the steelworks. One of the main sources of this pride in the Section 271 was the autonomy it had achieved from the official national union it was part of.

Discourses on autonomy and particularly local autonomy have a long history in Mexican political culture. In the case of Ciudad Lázaro Cárdenas, in both the trade union and neighbourhood movements the major confrontations of the people were with representatives of the State or the PRI. During the 1980s many of these movements developed a tactical autonomy – an autonomy that balanced the necessity of maintaining the possibility of relations and negotiations with at least some representatives of the State, but with the importance of remaining independent from it and being able to pressurise the authorites through marches, sit-ins, strikes and occupations. In their mobilisations they felt themselves to be fighting for their rights, not only their rights under the law but also their rights under the ideology of the

Revolution, against a political system that sought to deny them. It was a common perception that the State, or rather the elite in control of the State, had betrayed the rights expressed in the ideals of the Revolution and hijacked it for their own purposes.

The daily experiences of the political system by the local working class population shaped their discourses about power and the State. People would say, often as they were apologising for the food or drink they were generously offering me, '*soy pobre pero honesto*' ('I'm poor but honest'); a saying whose corrollary is that the rich are by definition corrupt. The bureaucrats, factory managers, national leaders of the trade union and local authorities that the people confronted in their mobilisations were by definition politicians, who were seen as rich and corrupt as well as acting in their own interests despite the rhetoric of claiming to do otherwise. The workers, neighbours and families I lived with expressed these attitudes in their interpretations of the actions of bureaucrats and politicians. During the steelworker's strike in 1989 many people interpreted the changes in the collective contract that SICARTSA was seeking to impose were motivated by a desire to increase their potential earnings from bribes, rather than by a desire to increase the efficiency of the plant.This was particularly true of the proposal to allow the company to use outside contractors for maintenance work previously carried out by unionised workers. Nevertheless, to be corrupt or to be a *cacique* (political boss) was not necessarily seen in solely negatively terms. A corrupt *cacique* who fulfilled his role as a patron and responded to his people in moments of crisis may be preferable to a bureaucrat who applied the rules in a form that did not respond to the people's needs, even if the bureaucrat were honest.

The popular cultures of a diversity of social groups in Ciudad Lázaro Cárdenas valued the ideology of the Revolution. They emphasised the sacrifices that previous generations had made for the nation and to win rights for the people and their betrayal (almost all Mexican heroes end up betrayed and assassinated). At the same time their experiences in relations with representatives of the State and the PRI created a distrust of politicians, the political system and their own power to achieve real change. Many supported the ideology of the State but were critical of its practice. It would seem reasonable to suppose that this type of situation was common in many parts of Mexican society and not just in Ciudad Lázaro Cárdenas. After more than 70 years of an imposed official ideology it should not be suprising that popular cultures have appropriated at least some aspects of official ideology and at times used it to mobilise against the actions of representatives of the State, even in areas which had resisted the imposition of the State's ideology. The legitimacy of popular mobilisations lies in their attempts to enforce rights given to them in law and the ideology of the Revolution. The power of the symbols of the ideology of the Revolution lies in their very ambiguity, and in the fact that their meanings are contested (see Powell this volume).

To this extent then the local ideology in Ciudad Lázaro Cárdenas seems to be similar to that of *ejido* communities in western Michoacán based upon *ejidos*. These communities had often been bitterly divided in the 1920s and 1930s between *agraristas* and *cristeros* with both groups inflicting random violence on each other and the rest of the population. Despite these deep divisions and the economic differentiation within villages, over time a certain sense of identity has been created around their self-identification as *campesinos* and *ejidatarios*. Their conflicts at least until the early 1980s were as often with the bureaucrats of BANRURAL and other agencies, as with the *neolatifundistas* and commercial farmers from inside as well as outside the community. Attacks by the Salinas modernisers upon the corruption of the State bureaucrats clearly have an appeal, yet the era of BANRURAL now seems like a lost golden age, since at least some credit did reach peasants. Much of this region which was once heavily involved with commercial production by both *ejidatarios* and commercial farmers is now being sown with maize or not sown at all (Gledhill, 1991 and this volume).

The importance of the ideology of the Revolution then is not that it and the institutions of the post-revolutionary State succeeded in penetrating and controlling all of Mexican society. They never did. Rather, their importance is in the extent that they have become foci of contestation and the construction of local identities. Clearly, the ideology of the Revolution was never the only element in local political cultures and local identities. Instead these are constructed in the intersection of a diversity of ideological elements from the discourses of the colonial caste system, nineteenth century liberalism, the ideology of the Revolution, gender, violence and religion among others. However, in challenging the identities constructed around the ideology of the Revolution, or at least in taking actions which many would perceive to be challenging these, the Salinas administration has not only challenged the local identities of many people, but also the political culture that allowed for some articulation of their demands. In replacing this with a discourse of social liberalism the Salinas administration has tried to legitimate itself in terms of the symbols of Mexican history, even if the symbols of Mexican liberalism are not without their problems.[6] There were many forms of liberalism in nineteenth century Mexico and popular interpretations of the meaning of

6 The conflict caused by the rewriting of Mexican history in the school textbooks is one example of the problems involved.

liberalism may be quite different from those of the administration (see Knight this volume) .

VISIONS OF SOCIETY

The ideology of the Revolution is clearly not the first to present a vision of Mexican society, of the imagined national community. In its day and since, colonial Mexican society was compared to the *ancien régime*, in its domination by a landholding elite whose status allowed them to buy into at least some political offices which held possibilities for further enrichment. Lomnitz-Adler (1992: 261-74) goes beyond the notion of the colonial system as a corporate one and stresses the importance of hierarchy (in a Dumontian sense) and caste in the Spanish ideological system.[7] The relationship between the Church and State in Spain, he argues, had a hierarchical and complementary nature, in which the political order was subordinated to the religious. The placing of religion at the apex of the social order permitted the emergence of a social hierarchy in which pure blood Spaniards were elevated above the New Christians, who were tainted with Jewish, Moslem or heretical antecedants and were therefore untrustworthy. However, the social hierarchy in colonial Mexico was not a simple colour bar system of stratification with the whites at the top, above *mestizos*, Indians and blacks, but rather a triangle with a variety of different castes existing between the three poles of pure blood. The emergence of this system therefore linked race and culture. Spanish domination was legitimated by its greater purity, expressed not only in religion but also in purity of blood. *Gente de razón* (civilised people - whites) were contrasted with *naturales* (natural people - Indians). Social status was then based not only on caste position but also on culture, and the colonial system had the effect of linking race and culture in a way that continues to exist in contemporary Mexico. Urban social groups in Mexico continue to define their identities in part as *gente de razón*, and contrast themselves with Indians and poor *mestizos* in terms of education and culture (see Lomnitz and Lizaur-Pérez, 1987). An example is the discourses that blame Mexico's incomplete democracy on the backwardness and lack of a

7 Dumont (1986: 279-80) makes a distinction between hierarchical ideological systems that see the element or individual as existing in a set of relationships which constitute the whole and individualistic ideologies that valorise the individual as an autonomous moral being. Both Lomnitz-Adler (1992) and Damatta (1991) stress that Latin American societies are based on a complex mixture of hierarchical and individualistic ideologies.

proper democratic culture among the poor. These appear to be very 'modern', but are, I would argue, based on the way in which urban social groups construct their identities and legitimate their power in terms of culture and education. These discourses have their roots in the continuing colonial distinctions based on the caste system and the linking of race and culture.

During the colonial period the dominant vision of Mexican society was of a number of nations encompassed by the religious-political figure of the King. In contrast, liberal rhetoric was egalitarian and based on the models provided by the French and American revolutions. The concept of the liberal State implied not the encompassment of many nations by the sovereignty of one king, but a single people all equal before the law. Independence, therefore, brought substantial changes to the dynamics of race and class in Mexico. Slavery was abolished, the *castas* (mixed race castes) and slaves were mostly reclassified as 'the masses' and absorbed into the general category of *mestizo*. Many liberal thinkers wished to go beyond this simplification of the racial hierarchy into the categories of white, *mestizo* and Indian, and impose a class model of distinction in place of the old racial categories. The old distinctions of Indian and non-Indian were to be replaced with those of poor and rich. In the liberal model the Indians were to become, not a separate nation or race, but simply a part of the poor masses who could in theory recieve all the benefits of society. During the nineteenth century liberal policies attempted to replace Indian communal property with private property and eliminated all the legal distinctions between Indians and other citizens. These policies were also seen to have positive benefits for the development of the country by removing the block of Indian communal property and practices from the more dynamic practices of the creole population. However, as Lomnitz-Adler (1992) emphasises, despite the egalitarian rhetoric of liberalism, the ideal of whiteness did not disappear in ninteenth century society. Class became conflated with race so that the term Indian became synonymous with a combination of material poverty and cultural 'backwardness', while the rich could be 'whitened' (Knight, 1990c). Thus, the complex racial dynamics of the colonial period were simplified in the nineteenth century into a bipolar model (Indians/whites) with an intermediary class of '*mestizos*' (Lomnitz-Adler, 1992, 275-6). The old type of social status distinctions were maintained by the association of culture with race.

While liberalism in Mexico achieved a position of dominance by the late nineteenth century, it did not entirely eliminate Catholic conservatism. Rather, through the struggles between them, both achieved a deep penetration into the political culture and influenced local feuds and mobilisations (Knight, 1992). Liberalism's success was in large part due to the emergence of a popular patriotic liberalism. The stress of liberalism on federalism, local militias and opposition to foreign interventions generated a popular support which reinterpreted liberalism to mean a respect for local autonomy (Thomson, 1991).

The stress placed on local autonomy in popular reinterpretations of liberalism continued to be important in the Revolution. Popular participation in the Revolution of 1910-20 came from movements attempting to regain the material basis for a reconstruction of local autonomy such as the *zapatistas* of Morelos, as well as multi-class *serrano* movements of whole communities opposed to increased State interference in their internal affairs and the encroachment of politically connected landowners, such as the *villistas* of Chihuahua (Knight, 1990a). For both types of movements autonomy was an important concept even if its implications were quite different. In one case the recreation of the autonomous corporate community, in the other the protection of the individualistic autonomy, honour and dignity of the *ranchero* communities in often mountainous regions where great value was placed on men's skills with horse and arms. While in the postrevolutionary period these discourses on autonomy have been related to the ideology of the Revolution and the economic and political circumstances of the communities in which they existed have been transformed, they have by no means disappeared. Rather, they live on in struggles for autonomy from or within the postrevolutionary political system and in discourses about male identities and honour (see Aitken, forthcoming a).

Thus, it is important to stress that while the ideology of the Revolution has been central in the construction of local identities for many social groups in Mexico it is not the only source of these forms of self-identification and political culture. Indeed it may not be the dominant one. Nugent (1988; 1993) argues that in the case of the *serrano* community of Namiquipa, Chihuahua, there exist opposing ideological points of view between the State and the population. This and the view of progress as disorder and immorality that Alonso (1988) finds in the same community could be common of *ranchero* communities with their emphasis on individual autonomy and private property. Lomnitz-Adler in his study of the political culture of the Huasteca Potosina describes *ranchero* self-identification in terms of:

> ... a particular understanding of a ninteenth century liberal tradition, wedded to an ethos of courage, manliness, and knowledge of weapons, of the countryside and of horses. In a word, ranchero self-image and self-legitimacy is contructed upon liberalism wedded to a mode of production that required a *don de mando* (the gift of commanding) (1992: 204).

The ideology of *ranchero* communities in Michoacán would appear broadly similar with an emphasis on individual skills, on being white and a denegration of Indians and *mestizo ejidatarios* as clients of the State (Barragán López, 1990). It is probable that the location of these communities within an historic 'ideological field' will lead to different responses to the current neoliberal ideology. Some elements of the project of President Salinas, such as its emphasis on private property and the privatisation of the *ejido* correspond with the popular ideology of these communities, while other elements such as the emphasis in the modernisation programme on large scale or international capital do not have the same attraction.

The importance of earlier colonial and liberal ideologies and visions of society, however, extends beyond the fact that some social groups in Mexico continue to construct their identities in relation to these ideologies. They serve rather to illustrate the continuing tensions in the construction of Mexican society and political culture, particularly around questions of race and ethnicity and the contradictions between the coexistence of individualistic and hierarchical ideologies.

Race and racial hierarchy remain essential elements of political culture. The ideology of the Revolution once more transformed discourses on race and ethnicity in Mexico, but did not eliminate them. The revolutionary nationalism produced a new hero, the *mestizo*, as the new official protagonist of Mexican history. Where the colonial society had seen Indians as a nation encompassed by the Spanish nation, and in the nineteenth century the Indians had come to be seen as a backward class retarding the development of the European-oriented nation, revolutionary nationalism saw Mexico as the product of the clash of these two cultures. 'The new hero of the Mexican nationalism became the *mestizo,* who was physically both Indian and Spanish, and whose spiritual qualities avoided both the atavisms of the Indian and the exploitative nature of the Europeans' (Lomnitz-Adler, 1992: 277). This transformation involved a revalorisation of Indian culture and the Indian past in the movement which became known as *indigenismo*. However, this was a revaluation in which the *mestizo* Mexican nation and the postrevolutionary State became the successors to the glories of the Indian past, so that contemporary Indians would have to be incorporated into the *mestizo* nation in order to share in the symbols of the glorious past or in the fruits of development (see Powell and Hindley this volume). Moreover, this new discourse on the *mestizo* nation also had implications for poor *mestizos* who felt themselves to be excluded from the benefits of the Revolution.

Many *mestizos* in Michoacán perceive their rulers to be foreigners, who have usurped the Revolution, the State and revolutionary nationalism from its true protaganist, the *mestizo*. They argue that surnames such as López Portillo, de la Madrid and Salinas are not Mexican, but Spanish names. They respond to their feelings of exclusion by attempting to reclaim the national community and the history of the Revolution by labelling the ruling political class as 'foreigners and whites'. Yet, they also value whiteness and generally associate lighter skin with beauty and, while they identify with the Indian past, they denigrate the Indian present and look down on *inditos* or *naturales*. The incorporation of organisations of mass representation into the State party and particularly the practices of the local representatives of these organisations is often resented and is the focus of oppositional mobilisations. Nevertheless, the corporatist vision of society implied the protection of a national community in which people had some place. The rush into integration with the USA in the 1980s and 1990s seems to threaten this national community.

The threat to the revolutionary vision of society and the national community posed by the shift in official discourse could be assuaged by a revaluation of liberalism. The neoliberal turn in official discourses appears to promise that Mexico will finally arrive at a promised land of liberal democracy and individual citizenship. However, the promise of individual citizenship, desirable as it is, is tempered by doubts about the reality of that citizenship. Liberalism had achieved dominance in Latin America at the level of consititutions and laws by the late nineteenth century. However, it was grafted onto societies which had been organised on principles of a person's position within a hierarchy of social relations. These did not disappear but continued to coexist with the individualism of liberalism. Damatta (1991) from his work in Brazil, shows how the anonymity of the street and the law can be avoided by making claims to social position – to who you are and whom you know. This allows the more priveleged sections of the population to avoid the inconveniences and perils of the law by invoking social rank. Lomnitz-Adler (1992) points out for the case of Mexico that while corruption may be opposed by everyone it is intrinsically linked to highly valued social relations, to friendship and family ties. The coexistence of principles of individualism with those of social hierarchy, challenges the credibility of any claims to move to individual citizenship and equality before the law. Such a move would require the denial of highly valued social relations.

At the same time, the elements of liberalism that are most valued, principally those related to personal and local autonomy, are not those that many people would associate with the modernising project of the Salinas administration. As Knight (this volume) argues, the social liberalism of the Salinas adminstration appears to be largely economic liberalism with an element of social paternalism. The centralisation of power during the *sexenio* also limits the possibilities of a popular appropriation of this social liberalism as meaning local autonomy.

CONCLUSIONS

This is the centre of the problem. The aspects of liberalism that might have the greatest popular appeal, those related to discourses of autonomy, are in large part negated by people's experiences of economic and political reality. At the same time, neoliberalism implies a negation of the national community as understood in the ideology of the Revolution in which the corporatist State encompassed the community but gave the corporate sectors a place within the development of Mexico. The promise that Salinas and now Zedillo hold out, of a liberal democratic order and a reconstituted civil society, seems very distant from the majority of the population's experiences of the State. PRONASOL, which is claimed to be an attempt to restructure State-society relations, is widely perceived to be administered in a partisan way and its resources used to buy votes for PRI candidates in crucial elections and disarticulate the opposition. The form of the future 'imagination' of the national community of Mexico is unclear, but the realisation of the promise that it will be Mexico's final arrival at modernity, democracy and advanced capitalism seems distant, supposing it is desirable. The economic policies pursued by the government make it hard for many people to interpret their own future as being anything other than simply a mass of individuals serving the interests of Amercian capital and a small transnationalised elite, whom many of them would contend have never been part of the national community.

3 Neoliberalism and Nationalism

Kathy Powell[1]

The principles of nationalism identified with Mexico's emergence as a modern nation state are intimately bound up with the experience of the Revolution, the postrevolutionary state-building project and the politico-symbolic meanings attached – sometimes retrospectively – to these processes. Of central importance have been the principles of national sovereignty and of social contract, establishing the rights of Mexican peasants and workers, inscribed in the 1917 Constitution.

The extent to which these principles have been adhered to or pursued has long been a matter of fierce debate and ongoing struggle, which for the past 65 years has taken place within the context of continuous government by the PRI at national level. However, since the espousal of a neoliberal ideology and economic agenda prompted by the crisis of 1982, many of the tenets of the postrevolutionary state have been abandoned or displaced, and a problem for the party of government has been to present these departures as the evolution or continuation of revolutionary nationalist principles, rather than as a betrayal.

This paper does not attempt to offer an overview of the meanings of nationalism or national consciousness within Mexico.[2] Instead it focuses

---

1 These observations are drawn from field research carried out principally from July 1990 to August 1991, kindly funded by the Wenner-Gren Foundation and by the Centro de Estudios Mexicanos y Centroamericanos. A subsequent short field trip in early 1993 was funded by the Central Research Fund of the University of London. This paper is based on an earlier version presented at the Institute of Latin American Studies in November 1992.

2 I refer to Anderson's (1991) definition of the nation as an imagined community; imagined because its members will never know or experience the whole community, yet share a sense of its continuity and identity through time and history, which imparts to those members living in the community at the same historical time a kind of 'horizontal comradeship', even where other inequalities divide them. Nationalist sentiment and national consciousness indicate this *sense* of nationality, which attaches to the perceived fundamental qualities and historical characteristics of the nation, and which, as Kapferer (1988) demonstrates, respond to symbolic elements such as founding myths, legends of death and sacrifice in the national cause, which constitute the integrity of the nation.

upon those aspects of national consciousness which articulate a regional and rural political culture, and upon ways in which the regime has latterly sought to appeal to nationalist sentiment in order to reassert its claims to legitimacy *as* a regime, which in turn promotes its radical conversion from a statist and corporatist to a neoliberal ideological framework.

These efforts have not been concerted, but have involved ad hoc rhetorical attempts to redefine national consciousness in a manner more consistent with the neoliberal worldview, which so far appear to have met with little success. As Lomnitz-Adler (1992) points out, in the government's retreat from a statist economy towards an open market one, it has not yet formulated a coherent new nationalism. I suggest that this lack of success is due to both the regional and the global implications of neoliberal policies, to the ahistoric nature of neoliberal ideology and to the difficulties in dislodging those features of postrevolutionary national consciousness which have historically informed certain forms of political culture. One of these difficulties lies in the extent to which the nature of the State party's own role has constituted some of the more ambivalent of these features.

The political culture from which these observations are drawn belongs to an area of Michoacán dominated by the cane sugar agro-industry, where the 'presence' of state/corporatist principles of socio-economic organisation has been relatively high (in comparison to other regions within the state) and has taken the form of: *ejidal* production; state takeover of the sugar mills between 1968-1991; the presence of large unions affiliated to the *Confederación de Trabajadores Mexicanos* (CTM), the *Confederación Nacional Campesina* (CNC) and the *Confederación Nacional de Pequeños Productores* (CNPP), and the status of sugar production as a process falling within the domain of the 'public interest'. Because of this, both the nature and the impact of 'destatisation' and its concomitant subversion of corporatism has undoubtedly been more apparent in the region.

The neoliberal 'renewal' constitutes an attempt to carry through the first major hegemonic shift since the Revolution, and as such can be, and widely is, perceived as an attempt to dismantle the Revolution, and to displace its political symbolism as a focal point of national consciousness. Of particular importance in this regard are those principles of the social contract such as Article 27 of the Constitution which laid out agrarian reform and Article 123 defining workers' rights in relation to capital, which intended to guarantee representation of popular and class interests within the political economy and which subsequently underlay long processes of struggle to convert these guarantees into political reality.

The difficulty which the neoliberal regime is encountering in establishing a meaningful relationship to national consciousness, however, is not because of the conservative embeddedness of postrevolutionary ideology *per se*, nor because it is to some extent being espoused by opposing political forces. More fundamentally it is because the Revolution and the struggles it engendered remain central processes in the construction of the modern national imagination. Both the Revolution and its political and social imperatives continue to carry a great deal of symbolic weight and enjoy substantial ideological currency, not because the 'social contract' is regarded as something that has been won and must be cherished, but precisely because it is still being struggled for and still perceived as something worth struggling for. I would argue that in fact the historical experience of these dynamic processes produced the modern nation, and thus provide the source of those founding myths and symbolic heroes which, as Kapferer (1988) argues for nationalisms more generally, impart to the nation a sense of higher purpose, of the sacred, and which gain their significance within historical and ontological realities.[3]

These are points I hope to clarify presently, but I will begin by looking at areas in which attempts have been made to 'reorient' nationalist horizons and will make some suggestions as to why these have been unsuccessful.

First, the *necessity* for the regime to make efforts to reclaim the ideological initiative was made more urgent by the manner in which the neoliberal programme was imposed and by the nature of the political opposition which it provoked. While in a global context this comprehensive politico-economic reorientation can be seen as part of an ideological thrust following upon the demise of communism and late capitalism's 'conquest of history', what was surprising in the domestic context was that:

> ....the initial imposition of the project was made possible by transmutations within the state party, rather than being the product of struggle between political forces. That is, a 'coup d'état' took place within the state party. This description seems fully justified, as almost absolute presidential power was used to impose a project and then a regime to guarantee it, thereby violating the premises, agreements and practices of the state party itself and without any form of negotiation having taken place' (Laurell, 1992: 50)

This exacerbated divisions within the PRI during the 1980s at national and local level. The mass sectoral organisations in particular were increasingly

---

3 I am following Kapferer's use of *ontology*: 'in reference to those constitutive principles of being that locate and orient human beings within their existential realities. Meaning in ontology does not precede the reality of experience but is inseparable from it and is simultaneous with it' (1988: 220).

distanced from the executive and, as Gómez Tagle points out, their weaknesses 'revealed by their inability to oppose the executive's austerity policies and particularly those aspects which undermine the party's negotiating capacity *vis-à-vis* the members' (1993: 75).[4] The absence of democratic consultation within the party had also prompted the disaffection of Cuauhtémoc Cárdenas and his departure from the PRI, enabling him to head a coalition of growing left-wing, popular and middle class opposition movements, equally disaffected by the way the crisis of the early 1980s was being managed.

Although the 'neoliberal renewal' has its roots in the de la Madrid *sexenio*, it was largely Salinas who inherited the task of trying to claw back consensual support and legitimacy for the regime, as well as of stemming widespread social unrest. The urgency of these efforts was due to the doubts surrounding the 1988 elections and a continued challenging of the electoral process since, which resulted in the ongoing phenomena of almost inevitable post-electoral conflict. This task was made both more difficult and imperative because of the need to consolidate and justify the coup internally and because of the character and extent of the opposition movement. Confronting *neocardenismo* has been a complex task because to an important extent the PRD was challenging the PRI precisely *with* the ideological legacy of the Revolution, presenting itself – or, at least, widely perceived to be presenting itself – as its authentic representative. This is not to suggest that the *perredista* programme is identical to that of postrevolutionary statism, but that it claims strong kinship in spirit, placing great emphasis on social justice and sovereignty. The PRD has reappropriated these elements of revolutionary ideology on the uncomfortable grounds that the PRI ultimately betrayed it by consistently failing to fulfil it. In doing so it is seen by some to have robbed the PRI of access to its own historical roots.

Salinas' response to this was to present his vision relentlessly as a modernising project, a vision of the future by which Mexico will emerge from the Third and into the First World. Aided by northern triumphalism following the demise of the eastern bloc, platitudes relegating statist ideologies to an inward-looking past have been readily available. Statism was now being held responsible for the failure of many Third World countries to develop,

4 The CNC leadership felt particularly isolated by these developments. Early in the Salinas *sexenio*, formal representations were made to the President protesting the implications of policy changes upon the rural sector, which received extremely short shrift; though it was not clear whether the CNC leadership feared more for the wellbeing of the *campesinado* or for the possibility of the ultimate demise of their constituency, and hence their powerbase.

particularly in Africa, and was becoming associated in the north with the almost wilful reproduction of Third World status. Illustrative of these received wisdoms – as well as of the success of Salinas' projected image abroad – were the comments of the US Ambassador to Mexico to the US State Department, outlining his enthusiasm for the prospect of a successfully negotiated NAFTA, in regard to the economic dimension:

> Concurrent with the *replacement of Third World demagoguery by responsible internationalism,* was the decision to reform the internal economy to make it more open to foreign investment and competition (Negroponente, cited in Puig, 1991; author's translation and emphasis).

Consequently efforts have been made to consign the PRI's identification with the politics of postrevolutionary statism to history and to emphasise instead its identification with an ideologically renewed *nation.* This renewal is based ostensibly on the principles of a strengthened democracy, characterised by electoral reform and political pluralism; of a nation which values its social and cultural pluralism; and of modernisation, defined by state withdrawal from the economic sphere in favour of market forces, and international competitiveness. While this is an astute move – nationalism, as Kapferer (1988) points out, makes the political religious and places the nation above politics, so that the more a party can claim identity with the nation, the more it can assert its 'natural right' to rule – it is also a problematic one when these declared principles vary so sharply from reality.

DEMOCRATISATION

As far as the declared intention to create a nation that is democratically stronger is concerned, the almost exclusive control of State media to disseminate *priísta* propaganda[5] and the handling of criticisms of the PRI in such a way that they are presented as offences against the integrity of the nation, indicate that the party continues to display a conspicuous disdain for dissenting political opinion, in spite of the proclaimed commitment to pluralism within the party political field.

---

5 Anderson (1991) makes a persuasive argument for the centrality of print capitalism in the development of modern nationhood; of equal importance subsequently has been the ability of many States to monopolise mass communication for purposes of ideological control. In countries with high levels of poverty and illiteracy, the role of television has taken on particular importance in this regard.

Despite repeated promises to eradicate fraudulent practices within the electoral process, in many cases experience is that fraud often accompanied by repressive violence on the part of the authorities has continued unabated. Although claiming to have been the most transparent in history, the 1994 presidential elections were nonetheless beset by accusations of irregularities,[6] while the results of the 1994 gubernatorial elections in Chiapas are still being vigorously contested.

This situation has been compounded by similar practises within the PRI itself as fragmentation sets one faction against another and the favourites of state politicians are imposed over local candidates. In the 1992 municipal elections in Los Reyes, Michoacán, there were as many as 18 PRI *pre-candidatos* each competing for a following. In the selection of a candidate for deputy in 1991, although local *priístas* had objected to the imposition of a candidate *por dedazo* and insisted upon elections, the ballot boxes were spirited away to the state capital to be counted and the popular local contender displaced by a widely disliked *cacique* and friend of the governor.

The compilation of a new electoral register in 1991 did little to improve the situation since even according to official figures it left some nine million people off the register, some 20 per cent of the voting population. Together with increases in the incidence of political violence against academics, journalists, union militants and local opposition activists, the democratic credentials of the regime remain extremely shaky.

Furthermore, the perceived willingness to subordinate Mexican economic interests to those of the United States in NAFTA also served to highlight the issue of political rights in relation to national sovereignty. It has not escaped attention in Mexico that the government's attitudes with regard to political rights and national sovereignty tend conveniently to divide. As Jorge Chabat pointed out in 1991, the notion of economic nationalism had been ditched in favour of the notion of comparative advantage within a world economy, a virtual recipe for the reproduction of a low wage economy. At the same time the notion of political sovereignty was quickly wheeled in to resist any suggestion that the electoral process should be open to international scrutiny and to reject any criticism from international bodies about Mexico's record on the investigation of human rights abuses; even though the Mexican government has never questioned the competence of bodies like the Organ-

---

6 Complaints included manipulation of the electoral register, insufficient ballot papers in the special booths for voters who were outside their district, missing or 'stuffed' ballot boxes, people voting without credentials, as well as the suspicion of 'technological' fraud within the computing system (Ramírez, 1994).

isation of American States' *Comisión Interamericana de Derechos Humanos* (CIDH), to proclaim on the issue of political or human rights in other Central and South American countries.

This stance provides an excellent example of the desirability for the ruling party of placing the nation above politics and identifying itself with the nation. Similarly, when Cárdenas on a visit to Spain in 1991 was reported to have expressed criticisms of government practices and support for the idea of international vigilators during elections, Salinas was able to accuse him of little less than treason and to make a virtue out of his own reluctance to guarantee the integrity of the electoral process in any convincing way.[7]

CULTURAL PLURALISM

Appeals to pluralism beyond the party political field have carried little more conviction. Attention to cultural plurality within the national community has also undergone a shift away from postrevolutionary perspectives. As Lomnitz-Adler (1992) remarks, after the Revolution it was the *mestizo* who emerged as the official image of the national protagonist (see also Aitken this volume). In regard to indigenous peoples, while, during the course of the century, Mexico became 'an epicentre of the theoretical-political elaboration of the ethnic question' (Díaz-Polanco 1992a: 297, author's translation), the perspective of the postrevolutionary State, consistent with the promotion of the *mestizo*, emphasised national cultural *homogeneity*. This emphasis was based, Díaz-Polanco argues, on the erroneous conception that the modern, 'occidentalist' state somehow required ethnic/cultural homogeneity (*ibid*: 303).

While the notion of national homogeneity did not represent any form of coherent State policy, nevertheless under the rubric of the modernisation theory in vogue at the time, the existence of different ethnic and cultural groups was readily reduced to a dichotomous modern/traditional problematic, or suffered the attentions of an *indigenismo integracionista,* although:

---

7 Subsequently, international vigilators were allowed to observe the Presidential elections in 1994. However, some of the vigilators complained (to British TV news crews) that their observations had been very selectively reported in the Mexican media. This supports those who, during the debate on the question of international observers in 1991, opposed the idea, not for reasons of sovereignty, but because it would not serve any useful purpose since much fraudulent practice occurred before polling. Much of the argument at the time, however, revolved around perceived willingness to make the electoral process more transparent.

> Strictly speaking, the integrationist impatience was due to the requirements of capitalist expansion in the ethnic regions and of implementing the new political order there rather than to a goal of cultural homogenisation (Díaz-Polanco, 1992a: 302, author's translation).

This emphasis on homogeneity provoked an *etnicista* reaction from indigenous political groups and from within critical anthropology, some representatives of which took up the polar position of emphasising cultural and ethnic diversity to the point of asserting that a *national* culture did not exist.

While this was clearly not the position of the Salinas regime, official discourse certainly moved towards a new form of *indigenismo*, celebrating cultural pluralism and seeking to promote specifically indigenous projects. While making a gesture in recognition of indigenous identities, this position at the same time continues to serve as a technique of power.

Characteristic of many contemporary States, this current valorisation of cultural plurality acts, in aestheticising both popular and indigenous cultures, to dehistoricise, as Morris demonstrates in the case of Australia.

> The particularity of Aborigines' social and historical experience – their conquest, domination and loss of sovereignty – is reduced to a recognition of a reified and restricted notion of cultural particularity, an exaggerated essence. Thus decontextualised, Aboriginality is removed from ... contemporary experience... which includes an interpretation of the past (1989: 219).

Once aestheticised in this way, indigenous cultures may then be exhibited (often literally) as testimony to the deep antiquity of 'national' culture.[8] The promotion of cultural plurality in this form becomes a technique for avoiding confrontation of profound socio-economic, cultural and ethnic divisions and inequalities. This technique is compounded by a view of history which is reoriented to focus upon an appropriated ancient past. Such a focus has the unfortunate effect of reducing *processes* like the conquest, the independence wars and the Revolution itself, to *episodes* of historical conflict which have long been resolved – as if history could be conceived as being over in some way. This is particularly unfortunate in regard to the question of indigenous identities and national consciousness, which remains highly ambivalent in a number of ways.

Indigenous peoples, (as well as the *mestizo campesinos*), remain for the urban middle classes and for bourgeois and political elites a distant socio-

---

8 The elaborate and much publicised *Thirty Centuries of Splendour* exhibition, which also toured the United States as what seemed to be a cultural supplement to the NAFTA talks exemplifies this tendency, as does the promotion of ethnic 'culture' by the tourist industry.

cultural – and racial – Other, yet who exist within the limits of the nation and who, again with Australian Aborigines, share the discomforting status of not merely representing a plurality of cultural forms, but of being the nation's original inhabitants. Their history and marginality constitute a fierce critique of the 'glorious ancient past' view of history as well as of current politico-economic realities.

Attitudes to sharing a national identity with indigenous communities are perhaps even more ambivalent among *mestizo campesinos*, where, to borrow G. Lewis' (cited in James 1992) phrase, a 'multilayered pigmentocracy' persists, reproduced on the one hand by the perceived 'Europeanness' of the elites and on the other by varying degrees of uncertainty over how to feel about 'having Indian blood'. Social distance from indigenous communities is characterised by attitudes ranging from deep respect, though even some of these are qualified by a persistence in classifying indigenous people as *gente natural* (natural people) as opposed to *gente de razón* (civilised people), to total disdain, and in the case of some *ranchero* communities, which define themselves as white and continue to emphasise their Spanish origins, a refusal of any social intercourse with indigenous communities, even when they are close neighbours.

While on the one hand, the promotion of an aestheticised cultural pluralism may do little more than appeal to the middle classes, on the other hand, as Díaz-Polanco argues, the concentration on the part of *etnicistas* on specifically indigenist projects, separated from the struggles of other oppressed sectors, precludes orientation towards alternative national projects.This separateness and independence could militate against the development of any counter-hegemonic initiative. The action of the EZLN in Chiapas, which began in January 1994, represents a powerful critique of both these trends. The mobilisation of indigenous and *mestizo* peasants has been characterised by a clarity of focus upon national and global socio-economic and political rights issues which both transcends specifically indigenous concerns and exposes the irrelevance of the discourse on cultural pluralism.

Furthermore, the valorisation of socio-economic pluralism over the anonymity of the class-based sectoral bloc has not had better success in deflecting attention from the strategy of undermining organised labour, abolishing collective contracts and reducing real wages in both the industrial and agricultural sectors.[9] This offensive against the Mexican working class takes

---

9 'It is not insignificant that the unions under greatest attack have included those which belong to the biggest companies in the country, such as Pemex, Ford, Telmex, Aeroméxico, Mexicana de Aviación, AHMSA, Cervecería Modelo, TAMSA, Sicartsa and Minera de Cananea. Nor is

place under the auspices of the lofty principle of entrepreneurs' 'freedom to manage'. The neoliberal vision of a renewed nation is one in which labour rights are presented as restrictive obstacles, antithetical to this freedom – obstacles specifically to the free operation of transnational capital.

MODERNISATION

This kind of rhetoric closely accompanies that relating to 'modernisation'. A discourse at once imperative and vague, its inherent critique of the failures of statism (which, perplexingly, was also a modernising project until recently) lacks the integrity to confront the logic of that failure and seeks instead to implicate the unprogressive nature of members of the declining corporate constituencies.

Deficiencies in the agricultural sector, it was implied, were the responsibility of a *campesinado* which had for so long passively benefited from the subsidies of a paternalistic state.[10] Ejidal land tenure stood in the way of the inevitability of the free market,[11] as did restrictions on commercial capital operating within the ejidal sector; deregulation would liberate individual enterprise and capitalisation would quickly follow.

Implications of this nature, not surprisingly, give deep offence. At a time when local *cañeros* were struggling with reduced credits, compound interest rates, low sugar price, escalating costs of production, and had not received payment for their crop due to the financial straits of the now privately owned mills,[12] an official of the *Reforma Agraria*, charged with justifying the

---

it a coincidence that the most concerted attacks have been on the para-state companies where the workers' gains had achieved the most systematic consolidation' (Laurell, 1992: 49).

10 The rhetorical line which scorned as paternalism what, in most other countries was referred to as agricultural policy, corresponds to the period before PROCAMPO, when much was suddenly made of comparisons of levels of agricultural subsidies between Mexico and other parts of the world, as if this were news to Mexican producers. This abrupt about-face in regard to subsidies, which had the appearance of an ad hoc response to deepening crisis, reveals rather than negates the specious nature of earlier rhetorical excursions, as well as a lack of coherence.

11 Opponents of the changes to Article 27 discerned a not-very hidden agenda here; as Calderón Salazar stated during the debate on the reforms in the Cámara Pública on 4 December 1991, 'We [PRD] have sustained on various occasions that although they have not wanted to recognise it explicitly this process of privatisation is part of a dynamic to create conditions favourable for the signing of NAFTA' (1992: 155-6, author's translation).

12 Privatisation of the state-owned sugar mills was part of the deregulation programme. The lifting of import barriers was another, which left the new private sector owners in the position

changes to Article 27 of the Constitution, arrived at a meeting to exhort, 'You must all learn how to work, how to commercialise!' One of the *cañeros* interrupted angrily: 'Listen: do you mean to tell me that up to now, we have not known how to work? I remind you that we worked all these years according to a *system.*[13] Now that system doesn't suit you any more you come here to tell me I'm a *pendejo* who doesn't know how to cultivate cane?'[14]

Any attempt to bring about an ideological shift which entails negating the experience and disdaining the expertise of a sizeable sector is unlikely to persuade; but furthermore, a fundamental problem of conviction in regard to the neoliberal vision of national renewal lies in the consequences of its policies. The socio-economically disadvantaged feel less that they are taking their place within new national horizons, than that they are becoming or at risk of becoming part of an expanding transnational underclass. Mexican small producers, agricultural day labourers and industrial workers alike are well aware that in an international economy they are competing not only with their rich neighbours to the north, but globally and that the tendency of the market is to level product price and incomes downwards everywhere. The vulnerability felt after constitutional changes to Article 27 effectively privatised *ejido* land has consolidated these fears. This vulnerability is felt not only in regard to increasing exposure in the financing of production,[15] but also in regard to the implications for the *ejido* plot as a familial unit of production, since the amendments to Article 27 left the question of the rights of spouses and heirs extremely vague. And as far as the landless *campesinos* are concerned, the premise that there is no more land to be distributed seems to have removed them from the agenda altogether.

Such fears are not unfounded; the neoliberal doctrines of the open market and the minimalist state, promoted in debtor countries of the south by IMF

---

of being unable to sell their product since the country was inundated with cheap foreign sugar imported by speculators.

13 The conditions governing the cultivation and contracting of cane, together with its industrialisation, are laid down in the annually revised *Decretos Azucareros*.

14 The exhortation of the *Reforma Agraria* official that the *cañeros* should 'learn how to commercialise' was all the more galling since soon afterwards the new private owners of the mills were appealing to the *cañeros*' goodwill to accept a delay in payment for their cane, since the mills were in such dire financial straits largely due to a failure to commercialise.

15 The possibility which now exists of using land to secure loans is widely viewed as a potential *loss* of power over land tenure, rather than an increase – a reasonable view given recent ratios of input to income for many crops. Likewise the ability of commercial capital to enter into *ejido* production is perceived as a potential route to a new kind of *latifundismo*.

loan conditionality, act to determine the distribution of wealth.[16] IMF policy has been much criticised, particularly by the dependency school, on the grounds that it does not meet its proclaimed objectives, and on the grounds that it actually inhibits growth. Pastor (1987), however, argues that actual effects on growth have been variable and not necessarily negative but that instead the consistent effect of IMF policy has been the redistribution of wealth away from labour, whether growth occurs or not. IMF conditionality can therefore best be understood not only by the embedded class interests of IMF officials as they increasingly become managers of the international finance system and representatives of the interests of strong core capital over weak peripheral capital, but also, and equally importantly, by the class interests of the capitalist elite of debtor countries. 'There is a general danger that the typical Fund mission will avoid suggesting cuts that impinge on the politically powerful... and not specifying spending cuts leaves discretion in the hands of local governments, who are hardly likely to place the burden of adjustment on powerful elites.' (Pastor, 1987: 57)

Not that readjustment brings unqualified benefits for all types of domestic capital. On the contrary, it has been responsible for a fair degree of differentiation within the entrepreneurial classes. As Ghai and Hewitt de Alcántara (1991) demonstrate, the segment of the elite which has benefitted most from the crisis originating in the early 1980s is that where the parameters of activity are no longer national, but international; a transnational elite whose class interests are not confined within national boundaries.[17]

It is in this respect that neoliberal political economy can be regarded as antinationalistic; that it promotes the transfer of wealth and, concomitantly, the undermining of labour rights, away from those major sectors of the

---

16 IMF policy is often described as being *imposed* upon debtor countries. It is, however, perhaps best to qualify the notion of imposition of IMF policy. The degree of deregulation which has taken place since the early 80s, appears to exceed, for example, the requirements of Extended Fund Facility loans (1983), to which lower conditionality is attached (Pastor, 1987), in the same way that the freeing of trade restrictions far exceeded the requirements of the GATT (Acosta, 1991). This demonstrates a positive commitment to IMF policy on the part of domestic policy-makers and suggests that they share ideological common ground with their IMF counterparts – illustrated by Salinas' eagerness to head the World Trade Organisation which replaces GATT. At the same time such policies are introduced in the domestic context as government initiatives. The notion of imposition is best understood in class terms.

17 The behaviour of transnational capitalists in exacerbating the external debt problem through capital flight is relevant here. See Petras and Morley (1990), who argue that a significant proportion of external debt has been used to finance capital flight; guaranteed by the State, the increased burden of debt repayment falls upon the working classes in the form of decreased State expenditure, the holding down of wages, and so on.

working population which have, since the emergence of Mexico as a modern nation-state, been consistently defined as *constituting* the foundations of the national community. As the logic of 'market economy' exacerbates an already critical degree of socio-economic polarisation, there exists the evident possibility that Anderson's (1991) 'horizontal comradeship' between unequal sectors of the national community could break down entirely.

The critique of statism in neoliberal modernisation discourse – particularly in regard to labour and land rights – is perceived as a critique of working class and *campesino* political culture. Its agenda, which proceeds from an ideology supporting class interests located in the transnational sphere, seeks to make the historical struggles for these rights redundant and irrelevant to the 'natural' logic of late capitalism. The negation of history constitutes the negation of identity and is likely to be resisted. But it is, moreover, the specific nature of the political culture formed from these historical processes which makes this negation equally a problem for the regime since its own consolidation of power is rooted in the same historical processes.

THE DYNAMICS OF POLITICAL CULTURE

I remarked earlier that those features of postrevolutionary national consciousness which inform political culture were difficult to dislodge. I do not mean by this to suggest that *campesinos* and workers are naively committed to the elevated principles attributed to the Revolution and enshrined in the 1917 Constitution. On the contrary, the nature of the revolutionary experience and the processes of State-building which it generated gave rise to a political culture located precisely *between* the divergent paths of political ideology and political reality, a divergence increasingly mediated by relationships with the State party.

Nationalist sentiments generated from these processes are characterised by an ambivalence towards the State of a specific nature; an ambivalence which is the product of the particular political organisation of the modern Mexican State and which has its roots in the Revolution and in the centralisation of the State which followed.

While Mexico became a nation long before the Revolution, the nationalism of independence was qualitatively different from the nationalism produced by revolutionary struggles. As Anderson has pointed out, the independence movement was characterised by creole nationalism; a movement on the part of creole communities who were in the unusual position of 'simultaneously constituting a colonial community and an upper class' (1991: 58), who, as Spanish speaking Americans, were asserting their rights to themselves control a two centuries old administrative unit. Far from being a movement to incorporate the lower classes of indigenous peoples and the rural *mestizo* into political life, it was a movement inspired in part by fear of these classes and a conflict for the right to control and administer these classes. While indigenous and *mestizo* communities were nominally nationals, they were not incorporated politically and only incorporated economically in the sense of representing sources of labour and of land.

Even up to the eve of the Revolution, as Knight (1990a) has demonstrated, for many parts of Mexico regional identities remained of far greater importance than national identity and in many regions there existed little, if any, perception of living 'in Mexico'.

The 1910 Revolution, on the other hand, was characterised by unstable coalitions between popular and bourgeois factions; the latter needed popular armed support but was at the same time dismayed by its size and strength, and age-old fears about the consequences of mass uprisings were heavily reinforced. This was the point at which a nationalism based upon the political incorporation of the masses seemed to be the prudent way forward; to incorporate and then to gain firm control of the 'natural majority' through the apparatus of government and the political system. The tensions of the revolutionary coalitions persisted; the difference in the postrevolutionary period was not only that an unusually progressive constitution now existed, but also that a natural political majority now existed with a substantial stake in the Constitution's guarantees.

It was however an irony that the emergent structures of State centralisation which contained the possibility of making the social contract a reality also offered the means to make control over the popular classes by incorporation into the political system complete and to guarantee the system's reproduction; the sectoral division of society and its representation through a state party apparatus.

Though this was intended to be the structural basis for a system based on participatory, representative democracy, the operation of the system became increasingly unilateral. The principles of the popular Revolution were thus seen to have been appropriated from their popular base and converted into instruments of control of an increasingly distant political elite. This seems especially to have been seen to be the case after the presidency of Avila Camacho, whose successors have been, as some elderly *campesinos* disdainfully noted, '*puros licenciados*'. This is not to minimise in any way the achievements of popular struggles, but rather to outline the extent to which these were subjected to systematic attempts to assimilate them within the corporatist structure, or they were qualified by, and subordinated to, the requirements of political control and the reproduction of political power.

While at the same time claiming to be the ideological heirs of the Revolution, the ruling elite persistently violated its principles in pursuit of these goals.

The meanings invested in the symbolism of the Revolution reflect the logic of the processes underlying *all* of this experience. It is not that symbols of the noble principles of the Revolution persist in spite of the corruption of those principles and *create* a contradiction; that symbolic meanings are *composed* precisely of the contradictory nature of those processes.

An important and exemplary element in the symbolism of revolutionary struggles and of political culture is that of the logic of deceit, or betrayal. The Revolution itself is often described as having been betrayed by an emergent political elite, as indeed is the social contract – betrayed because subverted. The significance of the myths of two of the Revolution's best known popular heroes, Villa and especially Zapata, does not lie exclusively in the fact that they fought and led popular armies to important victories, but also in the fact that they were subsequently assassinated – deceived and betrayed – by the upcoming *caudillos*. It is also significant that both these characters *and* their assassins have been hailed as heroes of the Revolution; in juxtaposition they almost seem to represent the duplicity of postrevolutionary political processes.

On a different level, the same type of symbolism attaches to an heroic figure in the history of the unionisation of the canegrowers. Roque Spinoza, to whom several of the most important achievements within the movement are attributed, was assassinated ostensibly in circumstances related to drug-trafficking. Whatever the actual circumstances of his death, however, what is significant is that his assassination is widely perceived to have been the work of those who were to become his successors within the union hierarchy. In the same way, it seems almost inevitable that at least some of the interpretations of the assassination of Colosio and Ruiz Massieu will follow similar lines.

The concept of betrayal within political culture seems complex, central and is much discussed. A possible reason for its centrality may be that the logic of betrayal, symbolic or otherwise, is in a sense reflected on an ontological level, connected with the consummation of political transactions even on a local, daily, routine level.

Understandings of local level politics seem to be burdened by two unhelpful concepts. Firstly, regional political practices are often theoretically characterised as demonstrating the contradiction between modern, centralising tendencies and the embeddedness of 'traditional' *caciquismos*. However, Pansters (1990), in the context of the political history of Puebla, has demonstrated how the logic of regional *caciquismos fused* with that of a centralising State institutionalisation, bureaucratisation and corporativisation to form a specific type of political organisation characterised by authoritarian leadership and mass patronage. I suggest that this insight has more general relevance, in that

> This conceptualisation does away with the modern-traditional dualism... Instead of pointing to the uneasy coexistence of two conflicting forms of political organisation it *emphasises the fusion of these forms and the way this produces a political organisation in its own right.* (Pansters, 1990: 75. Emphasis added).

Secondly, the organisation or system of party patronage is regularly described as corrupt. While the notion of corruption may serve descriptive purposes, it has little explanatory value, since it does not account for the dynamics or the 'reach' of the system; the fact that so many find themselves engaging in this dynamic in spite of the fact that it is widely perceived as corrupt. There must surely be some meaning achieved in the reality of practice, however ambivalent, in order for the system to be reproduced. While party patronage became the means and provided the resources to secure the reproduction of its power structure, principles, again, were regularly betrayed in favour of political expediency (often in the form of redirecting resources). It was not so much the blatant hypocrisy of a party on the one hand publicly upholding the issue of rights and the equitable distribution of resources, while on the other running a political system which prevented people receiving them; rather it was that receipt of rights or resources was made systematically *conditional*.

To the extent to which these practises, on a banal, day-to-day, local level, become an extension of significant community practices of reciprocity, *compadrazgo*, extended kin relations, then mass patronage entails mass *implication* in this logic of inexorable conditionality.

The feeling of implication carries appreciable constraints. For example, on the evening before elections for union representatives, one of the candidates, a *cañero* and a *priísta*, commented, 'to tell you the truth, I'm more afraid of winning than of losing. If I win tomorrow they [mill management] will be round here the day after saying, come and have supper, come and have a drink, but just come on your own, don't bring any of the boys.' In his interpretation of the situation, whether he accepted or refused these hospitalities would compromise either his ability to do the job or his credibility as a political leader.

Not everyone has such scruples: a mill worker expressed concern that he now felt a burdensome obligation towards his local union leader (a *cacique* who owed his position to party contacts rather than to the electoral support of the membership), since he had helped him out with a problem concerning the mill management. Even though the leader had in fact simply been carrying out the duties for which he was paid as a union representative, this duty was both performed and received as a favour.

On the other hand, efforts to avoid feeling implicated are not uncommon; cane cutters in the region refused hand-outs in exchange for votes during electoral campaigns, and some poorer *campesinos* refused the offer of *creditos a la palabra* (credit given with a promise of repayment 'on one's word') because these were explicitly perceived as being handouts from the PRI. It may not be insignificant that these people have no union representation and exist to a greater extent beyond the realm of institutional activity.

Lomnitz-Adler remarks that:

> 'Corruption' is almost universally disliked in Mexico, but it is a practice that at times involves maintaining highly valued relationships such as friendship, family solidarity and trust. For corruption to be strongly resisted in Mexico, it must be redefined in such a way as to be a more unambiguously negative experience for Mexicans. (1992: 253)

This is an important point since it is precisely the ambiguity engendered by the implication of valued social and political relationships in the clientelist methods of guaranteeing the reproduction of political power which is functional.

'Implication' has the dual effect of making people feel either protected, and/or compromised, and ultimately powerless.[18] It is this, more than – often in spite of – the policies or performance of government which is instrumental in consistently delivering a substantial PRI vote, whilst, at the same time, the government is consistently criticised. To the extent that participation in the dynamics of mass patronage reflects the symbolism of betrayal, with all its historical weight, it provokes both censure and self-blame.[19]

---

18 One of the results of the rise of the PRD has been to throw this system into higher relief, in that the refusal of patronage and resources to its militants has exposed the extent to which it can be used as a threat and is ultimately oppressive.

19 Both self-blame and censure on the part of people involved on the one hand, as well as the ultimately derogatory use of the notion of corruption as an explanation on the part of analysts on the other, seem to evade the fundamental issue, which concerns the distribution of power. As Blok puts it: 'Attitudes towards the government and involvement in tasks in society on the part of the people who form it will only change with changes in the society at large. Only by studying these interrelations and seeing them as aspects of the distribution of power and the division of labor in society will we get beyond the mere description of corruption and help account for its genesis, development and decline. Furthermore, to see corruption as something which is morally bad needlessly burdens the task of analysis... We must expect... that people who act in particularistic and corrupt ways in not making a clear distinction between public and private affairs have few other options. They are part of societies in which the distribution of power is

CONCLUSIONS

Some of the equivocal meanings which constitute national consciousness therefore are routinely represented and accomplished in context. I suggest that a neoliberal nationalism cannot readily displace this for two related sets of reasons.

Firstly, neoliberalism has anti-nationalistic characteristics, expressed not in its rhetoric but in the logic of its economic policies – a logic which, moreover, militates against the socio-cultural and political integrity of *campesinos* and working classes globally. Representing elite class interests located in a rootless transnational sphere, the argument of neoliberalism implies a homogenisation of the global political economy which threatens to produce a form of totalitarianism which would prove far more difficult to confront than that associated with the most exclusionary forms of nationalism. This is suggested by its persistence in promoting its policies despite abundant evidence that they are unable to deal with socio-economic and political problems either in the south or in the north.[20]

Secondly, despite its espousal of neoliberal policies and ideology, the Mexican regime continues to reproduce the logic of betrayal referred to above. In attacking corporate structures its threatens to cut adrift many of its own activists; long-standing union bureaucrats are now painfully aware of the extent to which the corporate structures in which they are lodged are being mobilised by the regime in order to promote their own demise. In removing from the agenda altogether those postrevolutionary principles such as land reform which remain meaningful but unfulfilled and yet continue to be pursued, the regime has committed a serious betrayal. And it may be obliged to consider committing another; the financial crisis besetting Zedillo has led to recommendations of further privatisations, which is likely to focus attention once again on the petroleum industry, the most valuable and politically significant of Mexico's natural resources.

Certainly as long as the regime needs to have recourse to the embedded system of power reproduction and oppression in order to survive, then it is

far more uneven than in certain nation-State societies societies where people can, quite apart from personal merits, afford to be "honest".' (1974: 229).

20 The 1994-5 financial crisis in Mexico provides an example. The response to the failure of economic policy barely a year after the signing of the NAFTA has been to recommend more of the same; 'In spite of vast poverty and escalating social problems, Mexico is now pledged to a fresh round of spending cuts, deregulation and privatisation which, whatever their "efficiency", imply further dramatic cuts in social provision for the bottom 50 per cent of Mexicans.' (Will Hutton in *The Guardian*, 31 December 1994).

still caught up in the logic of these processes and no meaningful renewal is possible until it relinquishes them. There is no inevitability that this renewal should either continue to take the form of an anti-nationalism (or Negroponte's 'responsible internationalism') which exposes large sectors of the national community to the caprices of transnational capital, or, at the other extreme, of the kind of exclusionary nationalism currently afflicting Europe. A more creative nationalism might be based not merely upon a devalued form of democracy, but upon principles of self-determination exercised by the diverse components of a national community both in respect to each other and in respect to the communities of other nation-states.

4 Economic Policy Reform in Mexico: The Liberalism Experiment

John Weiss

The 1980s were a turbulent decade in economic terms in many countries, however in few were there more profound reforms introduced than in the case of Mexico. The reforms of the 1980s, whilst at times appearing to lose momentum and direction, none the less can be seen as a consistent strategy of 'economic liberalism', defined broadly as one of reducing the size of the State sector and allowing markets greater scope for determining resource allocation. A recent Banco de México survey sets out clearly the redefinition of the appropriate role of the State in the liberalism model. The reform of the public sector has sought to exclude it from commercial activities and to concentrate its action on basic functions of the State and the development of an economic framework that stimulates the efficient use of resources by the private sector. The public sector now concentrates on the provision of health and education services, the fight against poverty, the provision of infrastructure and the administration of justice and other traditional public services (Banco de México, 1993:164).

The reform programmes date from the emergence of the Debt crisis in 1982 and the consequent peso devaluations of that year. It is important to stress that in the pre-reform days of the early 1980s, Mexico was far from a State-driven closed economy. However it did have a very serious internal macro-economic imbalance, caused primarily by the public sector budget deficit, which in nominal terms reached 17 per cent of Gross Domestic Product (GDP) in 1982.[1] Further it was hit by two serious external shocks in the form of rising international interest rates on foreign debt and declining oil prices. In response to the foreign exchange crisis, in 1982 import licences, which had been removed for some goods in previous years and had become easier to obtain, were reimposed for all commodities. Also, in response to the

1 Unless otherwise indicated data on Mexico come from Banco de México (1993)

massive capital flight out of the peso, foreign exchange restrictions on capital flows were tightened and the banking system nationalised to enforce these.

To respond more fully to the crisis, there is no doubt that macro economic adjustment – what is now termed stabilisation – was required. There can be some dispute over the exact degree of adjustment that was necessary, but the need to reduce internal imbalance (as reflected in the public sector deficit) and external imbalance (as reflected in the balance of payments current account deficit) was clear. What is more controversial is the subsequent supply-side or micro elements of the liberalism programme: these include wide-ranging trade reforms and privatisation, combined with a reassessment of the roles of the public and private (particularly the foreign private) sectors.

An overall assessment of such an ambitious adjustment programme is not possible in the confines of a single chapter, and the aim here is relatively modest, in giving a broad overview. The discussion is in three sections; the first describes the main dimensions of the reform programmes, distinguishing somewhat arbitrarily between macro economic, micro economic and social dimensions. The second section considers some selective evidence on the impact of these various reforms, drawing in particular on results from the author's own work. Since the reforms are relatively recent it is not surprising that it is difficult to come to definitive conclusions on their impact. Nonetheless there is a need to counsel against placing too much reliance on highly optimistic assessments from official publications and much of the international financial press, which has reintroduced the term 'Mexican Miracle' in a very misleading manner.[2] Finally the third section considers briefly future developments in the light of entry into the North American Free Trade Area (NAFTA). The key uncertainty here is the extent to which foreign capital will continue to flow to Mexico to allow the financing of the large current account deficit that has emerged as a result of trade liberalisation and economic recovery – an uncertainty all the more prophetic given events since writing this chapter for the Manchester conference (see editors' introduction).

MAJOR ASPECTS OF THE REFORM PROGRAMME

Macro Policy

In conventional discussions of stabilisation it is argued that to meet two objectives (that is removal of internal and external imbalances) requires at

2 See, for example, the *Financial Times* country survey of 10 November 1993 which has the headline 'The Miracle seems to have faded'.

least two policy instruments (see Dornbusch, 1980). The instruments normally used are the level of the government budget deficit and the exchange rate. Hence it is not surprising to find these central to policy in Mexico.

Taking the budget deficit first, it is important to note that economic theory is ambivalent on its optimal size. Strictly, there is no case for a zero deficit, since if a government can borrow to finance expenditure with returns above the appropriate discount rate, this will be socially desirable. For any particular economy the desired level of the deficit will depend upon a range of factors including, the extent of underemployed resources, the returns on marginal government investment and the costs associated with the deficit's financing. The implication is that governments should aim to keep deficits within manageable limits. They should not be so high as to stimulate inflation, depress private investment or create unsustainable external debts. All of these effects occurred in Mexico in the early 1980s. On the other hand, deficits should not be so low as to hold back growth through their depressing effect on domestic demand.

In Mexico in the early 1980s there was general agreement on the need to reduce the budget deficit as a proportion of GDP. Lustig (1992: 26) is likely to be correct in arguing that had the government followed a less expansionary fiscal policy (i.e. a lower deficit) in 1980 and particularly in 1981, the crisis of 1982, triggered by the unfavourable external shocks, would have been milder. In 1983, the deficit was reduced rapidly primarily by a combination of expenditure cuts and higher non-tax revenue. However, in an environment of high inflation it is necessary to distinguish between different measures of the budget deficit. This is because some items of expenditure (principally interest payments on domestic government debt) will be outside government control and will rise automatically with inflation, thus worsening the deficit. Thus the deficit can be both a cause and a consequence of inflation. Three measures of the deficit have been used in discussions of policy in Mexico. The nominal deficit or Public Sector Borrowing Requirement (PSBR) is the difference between the monetary value of government expenditure and income. The operational deficit is government expenditure minus income, where only the real not the monetary value of government domestic interest payments are included as expenditure. Finally the primary deficit is expenditure minus income, where no interest payments on either foreign or domestic debt are included.

Table 4.1 gives these three measures of the deficit over the period 1982-92. It shows that the nominal deficit (PSBR), whilst falling in 1983, remained high for much of the 1980s; however the primary deficit, which is the best indicator of whether policy is depressing or stimulating demand in the economy, went into surplus immediately after the crisis year of 1982. For all

Table 4.1: Alternative Measures of the Government Deficit (1982-92) (percentage of GDP)

	PSBR	*Primary Deficit*	*Operational Deficit*
1982	-16.9	-7.3	-5.5
1983	-8.6	4.2	0.4
1984	-8.5	4.8	-0.3
1985	-9.6	3.4	-0.8
1986	-16.0	1.6	-2.4
1987	-16.0	4.7	1.8
1988	-13.0	8.0	-3.6
1989	-5.6	7.9	-1.7
1990	-3.9	7.8	2.2
1991	-1.5	5.3	3.3
1992	0.5	5.6	3.6

Source: Banco de México (1993: Table 34).
Note: negative sign indicates a deficit.

of the period since then, excluding interest payments, government expenditure has been below income. Initially budget targets were set solely in nominal terms, which ran the risk of creating excessively large primary surpluses. By 1986, however, the nominal deficit was no longer the key focus, being replaced by the operational deficit in the agreement between the government and the International Monetary Fund (IMF). The social consequences of the reductions in government expenditure that were part of this process are taken up below.

Exchange rate policy was the second key area of the macro strategy. The important target was the real exchange rate, which in its simplest form is the nominal rate adjusted for differential inflation between a country and its trading partners.[3] In principle, there will be a unique real exchange rate that will bring external balance for a particular level of domestic activity.

During the 1980s, policy in this area changed significantly with different theoretical views being influential at different times. At the outset of the crisis in 1982 the exchange rate had become significantly overvalued; in other words the real rate had appreciated relative to the level necessary for external balance. Policy sought to address this through a series of devaluations initially single (or stepwise) adjustments and then on a gradual or crawling peg basis. In addition, between 1982 and 1991, a dual exchange rate system was employed. This involved a controlled or official rate, for approved commodity transactions and foreign debt servicing, and a market-determined rate for

3 Edwards (1988) surveys the real exchange rate concept and gives more rigorous definitions.

capital and other commodity transactions.[4] Initially the latter rate was considerably more depreciated than the former, but this premium was reduced considerably to less than five per cent by 1986, and remained low apart from the exceptional period linked with the stock market crash in 1987 until the dual system was abandoned in 1991.

About 1985 a decision was taken to accelerate the real depreciation of the exchange rate through a single adjustment and a faster rate of crawl. The objective was to deliberately undervalue the real rate to replace protection by import tariffs and controls by 'exchange rate protection' and to encourage greater exports (see Corden, 1985).

Combined with continued fiscal restraint, this policy succeeded in holding down demand for imports and contributed to growth of non-oil exports. However this was at a serious cost in terms of acceleration in inflation. Import prices normally rise almost automatically with a devaluation and the more open an economy, in terms of the share of internationally traded goods in total activity, the more serious this problem will be.

Inflation, as measured by the Consumer Price Index (CPI), was just over 60 per cent annually in 1985, rising to over 100 per cent in 1986 and nearly 160 per cent in 1987 (see Table 4.2). At the end of 1987 price stability became the key objective and policy towards the exchange rate changed with it becoming an 'anchor' against inflation. This involved holding the nominal exchange rate (both official and market) virtually constant during 1988 and resuming the crawling peg system in 1989, but only at a pace that did not fully offset the inflation differential with the US. The exchange rate anchor was combined with a prices and income policy – the *Pacto de Solidaridad Económica* (PSE) – and this unusual or heterodox policy package is credited by most observers as being a major factor in reducing inflation, by operating on inflationary expectations, without significant losses in output (Kiguel and Liviatan, 1992). By 1993 it is estimated that inflation was below ten per cent.

Real exchange movements are also shown in Table 4.2. The real exchange rate index depreciated in 1982 and 1983, as a result of the nominal devaluations in those years, but appreciated again in 1984 and 1985 as the rate of crawl did not keep pace with inflation differentials with trading partners. This was reversed dramatically in 1986 and 1987 with the conscious policy of undervaluation and exchange rate protection. However since 1988 and the

---

4 The theoretical rationale for a dual system of this type is that with a separate market-determined rate for capital transactions, the exchange rate for key commodity trade can be protected from the effects of short-run capital flows; Dornbusch and Tellez Kuenzler (1993) discuss the dual rate concept drawing on Mexican experience.

Table 4.2: Inflation and Real Exchange Rate Index (RER) (1982-92)

	Annual Change in CPI	*RER*[1]
1982	98.8	86.80
1983	80.8	79.73
1984	59.2	97.20
1985	63.7	100.94
1986	105.7	69.15
1987	159.2	63.64
1988	51.7	77.44
1989	19.7	84.09
1990	29.9	84.22
1991	18.8	92.61
1992	11.9	98.90

Source: Banco de México (1993: Tables 26 and 23).

Note: [1] Based on a comparison of consumer price movements in 133 countries. A rise in RER indicates an appreciation of the peso.

pursuit of price stability as the key objective of exchange rate policy, there has been a steady real appreciation.[5] In terms of institutional arrangements, with the abolition of exchange controls on capital flows, in November 1991 the dual exchange rate system was abandoned with all transactions to be carried out at a unified market rate. A band system was introduced with the bottom rate fixed and the ceiling deprecating a crawl. It is hoped that widening the band in this way will increase foreign exchange risk and thus discourage short-term investment in peso denominated assets and encourage relatively longer-term capital inflows.

During most of the 1980s the issue of resource transfers abroad was a critical one for macro policy. Capital outflows exceeded inflows for all of the period 1982-90 (see Table 4.3). These outflows comprised payments on foreign debt and capital flight;[6] in some years net resource transfers (the difference between capital outflows and inflows) were as high as seven per cent of GDP, implying a major real reduction in resources available for internal use. The reversal of this position required action on three fronts: a reduction in the foreign debt service burden; encouragement of capital repatriation (that is the return of flight capital) and attraction of new foreign investment. Each of these objectives became a priority.

---

5 Whether this should be a cause for concern is not clear, since the long-run or equilibrium real exchange rate will depend in part on the level of foreign capital inflows. Since these have risen significantly since the late 1980s the observed real appreciation of the exchange rate may not reflect a misalignment: more work is needed to assess this question.

6 This is the shift by domestic savers into foreign currency denominated assets.

Table 4.3: External Resource Transfers (1982-90)

	Foreign Debt Service Ratio[1] (%)	*Net Resource transfer* (% of GDP)	Capital flight[2] (billions of US$)
1982	62.2	6.3	6.5
1983	50.4	7.6	2.7
1984	42.8	6.8	1.6
1985	43.8	6.9	0.7
1986	48.6	4.2	-2.2
1987	42.8	2.9	0.3
1988	43.4	6.8	1.1
1989	35.9	1.2	-2.9
1990	29.4	0.4	n.a.

Source: Lustig (1992: Tables 2.2 and 2.4).

Notes: [1] Interest plus amortisation as a percentage of total exports.

[2] Excludes interest earned on foreign capital. Negative figures show net inflow.

n.a. is not available.

Efforts at debt rescheduling were made in 1983, 1986 (the Baker Plan) and again in 1989 (the Brady Plan). Of these the rescheduling in 1986 was probably more significant in terms of savings in payments, but the indirect effect on private sector confidence of the 1989 rescheduling is seen as critical by many observers (Lustig, 1992: 56). Encouragement of capital repatriation was pursued by a combination of debt rescheduling, attempts to restore the credibility of government policy and high domestic real interest rates. In addition to these measures new foreign investment was targeted through legislative changes and entry into NAFTA, both of which we discuss below.

Micro Reforms

The distinction between macro and micro measures is arbitrary in some areas. Here we class trade and privatisation reforms as essentially micro-oriented on the grounds that their primary aim was to improve producer efficiency at the enterprise level (although both have had significant macro economic effects).

Trade reform is seen by some as the most radical element of the liberalism package. This is slightly misleading in that Mexico had never been a very protected economy by developing country standards, although at times of balance of payments crisis import licensing was used to restrict demand for imports.[7] As we have noted these controls were tightened in 1982 and were not loosened significantly until 1985, the year which saw the beginning of

7 See the estimates of effective protection for Mexico and other countries reported in Weiss (1990: Table 5.4).

the trade reform programme. The immediate objective, it appears, was to boost non-oil exports and greater access to imported inputs, through trade liberalisation, was seen as essential for this. Other justifications included the incentive effect of greater import competition and a contribution to reducing inflation, with world prices providing a ceiling that domestic prices of traded goods could not exceed.

The dismantling of the import licensing system proceeded relatively quickly. The proportion of imports not subject to licences rose from less than 20 per cent in 1985 to more than 70 per cent by 1987 (see Weiss, 1992a, 1992b). By the end of the decade licensing had been removed from all but the most sensitive sectors (such as automobiles, computers, pharmaceuticals and certain agricultural products), where the aim was a gradual phase-out to prevent serious disruption to domestic import-competing producers.

Import tariffs were also lowered with a view to both reducing the range of rates as well as the overall average tariff. In 1987, the number of tariff rates were lowered to five, with a maximum of 20 per cent. At present most imported inputs and raw materials face rates of no more than ten per cent, with most consumer goods subject to the 20 per cent tariff. The weighted average tariff is around ten per cent.

Recent changes have taken the trade reform process a stage further. In 1990 the government announced its intention to seek a free trade agreement with the USA. NAFTA, which finally came into force in January 1994, is seen by many as the final step in the trade liberalism programme and one which renders the process irreversible. Its central feature is the general removal of trade barriers and tariffs between the US, Canada and Mexico. This dismantling of barriers is not instant, since restrictions on intra-NAFTA trade remain, primarily the trade in agriculture, automobiles, textiles and clothing; these are to be phased out over periods of up to 15 years (see Hufbauer and Schott, 1993).

Historically foreign investment has played a major role in Mexico, however in recent years as part of the liberalism package encouragement of further inward investment has become a central part of policy.[8] The aim is both to use the finance, technology and management skills of foreign investors to modernise the productive assets of the economy and also use foreign capital inflows to cover the growing trade imbalance that has emerged, in part as a consequence of trade liberalisation. NAFTA is seen as critical in creating favourable expectations amongst foreign investors, who, it is hoped, will

8 Evidence on the role of foreign investment up to 1980 is given in Casar *et al.* (1990), and Fajnzylber and Martinez (1975).

invest in Mexico to take advantage of by far the lowest labour costs within the NAFTA region.[9]

This welcoming attitude towards foreign investment has prompted significant legislative changes. Until recently foreign investment in Mexico was subject to potentially restrictive legislation dating from 1973 that set limits on foreign equity holdings, allowed the imposition of performance contracts (such as the domestic content and trade balance requirements in the automobile sector). In 1989 a decree gave a more liberal interpretation to the 1973 law and allowed automatic approval of foreign investment, up to certain limits and provided a number of conditions were met.

NAFTA superseded the earlier legislation for firms from member countries, since it guarantees US and Canadian firms 'national treatment'; this means that they must be treated as favourably as nationally owned firms. Under NAFTA, performance requirements can no longer be imposed and existing requirements (principally in the automobile sector) are to be phased out. Guarantees are also given since profit remittances cannot be restricted except for short-term balance of payments reasons, and any expropriation of assets must be after due process and with fair compensation.

This liberal treatment of investors from NAFTA countries has been extended to those from other countries in the new foreign investment law that came into force in December 1993; in effect this extends national treatment to foreign firms for most activities. The few remaining areas of restriction relate to investment in financial services (where under NAFTA domestic institutions are protected up to 2007), and in certain sectors that are either reserved for the State (such as petroleum and related activities, the ports, the railways and postal services) or for national investors (such as auto transportation services and printing and publishing newspapers).[10]

Another major and controversial legislative change involves the opening up of the agricultural sector to foreign investors through an amendment to the federal Constitution (see Powell, Gledhill and Jones this volume). This allows foreign investors to acquire agricultural land and establish joint ventures (up to 49 per cent of capital stock) with Mexican farmers.

Encouragement of the foreign private sector is linked with another important strand of the liberalism experiment – privatisation. Privatisation in Mexico has had at least three key objectives:

---

9 In 1992, for example, average wages in maquiladora plants were only 15 per cent of those in US manufacturing (Hufbauer and Schott, 1993: 172).

10 Additional complementary measures designed to encourage foreign investors include the removal of controls on technology transfer and the introduction of greater patent protection.

- to improve the operating efficiency of enterprises by a transfer to the private sector;
- to contribute to a reduction in the government budget deficit either from the sale proceeds, or from the disposal of loss-making enterprises whose losses no longer have to be covered by the government;
- to foster confidence in the private sector and thus encourage new investment.

Privatisation proceeded in phases. In the early years between 1983 and 1985 non-viable and non-priority State enterprises, mostly small in size, were either liquidated or merged within the public sector. From 1986 to 1988 experience was built up through the sale of medium and small companies, generally in non-sensitive areas. It was only after 1988 during the Salinas administration that the larger, more strategic, public enterprises were sold; these include the telecommunications company (Telmex), whose sale attracted considerable foreign investment, the two airlines, the large steel, fertiliser and sugar companies and more recently the commercial banks, nationalised in 1982. This latter move is generally interpreted as having a critical role in confidence building, since it completed the series of policy reversals since the crisis years of the early 1980s.

By 1993, little more than 200 public enterprises remained as compared with 1155 in 1982. In the early 1980s the public enterprise sector was a net drain on government resources, with an operating deficit of more than two per cent of GDP in 1982 (SHCP, 1991). On the other hand, the revenue proceeds from the privatisation sales of the period since 1988 have been a major source of revenue for the government. Since 1990 they have been placed in a 'contingency fund' and used to pay off government debt. The resulting decline in annual interest payments has in turn contributed to the government budget surplus.

In the liberalism experiment privatisation has also had a wider interpretation than simply the sale of public sector assets. In this wider context it refers to an opening up of new investment opportunities for the private sector in areas previously reserved for the State. Recent examples of this include private sector road building under schemes in which private firms operate toll roads for a period of time and then sell the ownership to the State; other new initiatives include private investment in electricity generation, although the State through the *Comisión Federal de Electricidad* continues as the sole owner and operator of the distribution network. The consequence of this policy shift towards the private sector has been a marked decline in the share of the public sector in total investment, from a peak of 46 per cent in 1981 to 23 per cent in 1991 (Pfefferman and Madarassay, 1992).[11]

Social Measures

As we have noted the liberalism experiment has entailed a clear shift in perceptions of appropriate government responsibility, with a withdrawal from most forms of production and much less direct control over the private sector. However official policy has stressed the State's continued responsibility for social and distributional issues.

The crisis of the 1980s, arising from a situation of internal imbalance in which aggregate expenditure exceeded aggregate income, meant that real incomes in the country had to decline to restore balance. However, the manner in which these falls in income were distributed was strongly influenced by the policies pursued. Two aspects of policy are of particular concern here, first the cuts in government social expenditure (primarily on health and education), and second the removal of universal food subsidies which were replaced by financially smaller targeted subsidy programmes. Both of these were part of the austerity measures required to reduce the budget deficit.

Between 1983 and 1988 central government expenditure fell in real terms by nearly 30 per cent for education and around 23 per cent for health (Lustig, 1992: 79).[12] Since 1988 there has been a reorientation of government expenditure priorities and a real rise in these categories. The government argues this has been possible due to their success in reducing interest payments on government debt, which has allowed resources to be freed for social measures. In terms of food subsidies, the key move away from a universal system was in 1984 with the end of the tortilla subsidy. This was replaced by a targeted scheme in which CONASUPO stores either sold cheaply, or gave away, tortillas in limited amounts to those who were eligible to receive them. In addition over the decade other general subsidies on beans, cooking oil, bread and eggs were eliminated gradually.

A central tenet of the social policy of the liberalism experiment is that assistance to the poor and vulnerable must be as closely targeted as possible. Since 1988 the main focus of policy has been the Solidarity programme (PRONASOL), which aims to provide both short-term and long-term support to the very poor. The programme covers four broad areas: provision of food;

11 However it must be pointed out that private investment remains far from buoyant, being only a slightly higher proportion of GDP in the early 1990s, than in the early 1980s.

12 There is uncertainty about these figures which are derived by deflation by the general GDP deflator that may not reflect the actual price rises for these sectors.

finance of small-scale high risk projects; health and education provision; and infrastructure development for poor communities. The active participation of the beneficiaries, particularly in building and preparing their own projects, is stressed. Since 1988 activities under the programme have grown substantially, so that it has become the primary social welfare scheme in the country. In 1992, for example, PRONASOL accounted for nearly 60 per cent of government physical investment.

SOME EVIDENCE ON EFFECTS OF POLICY REFORMS

Macro-Economic conditions

The macro strategy with its conventional combination of expenditure reducing and expenditure switching measures has undoubtedly been successful in both restoring growth and reducing inflation. As Table 4.4 shows, after the low point in 1986, the economy has recovered steadily, although GDP growth has been modest and has not approached the historical average for the 1970s, of over six per cent annually. As we have seen also inflation has been reduced very significantly to an official figure of around ten per cent in 1993.

None the less there can be legitimate criticism of several aspects of the overall strategy. In the 1983-5 period, for example, a focus on a target government budget deficit in nominal rather than real terms (the PSBR rather than the operational or primary deficits) may have contributed to an excessive deflation of the economy, with output reduced excessively below productive potential (Brailovsky *et al.*, 1990). Also from 1985-7 exchange rate policy seems to have been misconceived with the deliberate undervaluation of the peso and its excessive real depreciation, contributing to both inflationary and deflationary tendencies at the same time. Inflation was stimulated by the impact of nominal deprecations of the peso on traded good prices, whilst deflation arose through the reduced purchasing power of those with dollar-denominated debts and the fall in the real wage relative to traded good prices. In addition, the trade liberalisation programme commencing in 1985 had little effect in reducing inflation. Most observers now agree that the exchange rate policy of 1985-7 was an error and that the heterodox package, which combined exchange rate stability, price and wage controls and fiscal restraint, was a major step forward.[13]

---

13 See, for example, Ten Kate (1992) and Lustig (1992). The relative failure of attempts at stabilisation 1983-85 has also been put down to the difficulty of stabilising effectively in the absence of supply-side reforms, particularly in terms of foreign trade (Nash, 1991: 511).

Table 4.4: GDP and Balance of Payments Current Account (1982-90)

	GDP Growth (%)	*Current Account* (as % of GDP)[1]
1980	9.1	-5.5
1981	8.8	-6.4
1982	-0.6	-3.6
1983	-4.2	4.5
1984	3.6	2.7
1985	2.6	0.8
1986	-3.8	-1.3
1987	1.9	2.9
1988	1.2	-1.4
1989	3.3	-2.7
1990	4.4	-2.9
1991	3.6	4.8
1992	2.6	-6.9

Source: Banco de México (various issues); INEGI (various issues) and data supplied by *Economia Applicada*.
Note: [1] negative sign indicates deficit.

One measure of the ultimate success of macro policy is the restoration of Mexico's international credit worthiness. Since 1989 Mexico has again been able to borrow on the international capital market, having been excluded from 1982; this return is due in part to debt rescheduling, but no doubt also reflects international confidence in economic policy. Foreign investment inflows, particularly portfolio rather than direct investment, have also increased substantially.[14] Portfolio investment in Mexico was non-existent before 1989, yet with the internationalisation of stock exchanges and changes in foreign investment regulations in Mexico, it represented over two-thirds of total foreign investment in 1992 (see Table 4.5).

This very substantial rise in capital inflows, and the subsequent capital account surplus on the balance of payments, has as its other side a rise in the current account deficit; as shown in Table 4.4 this latter deficit has risen to nearly seven per cent of GDP in 1992. Exports have grown rapidly during the second half of the 1980s (for example rising annually at 13 per cent in current dollars between 1986 and 1992). There has also been a significant

However it is by no means obvious that the economy could have coped with far-reaching trade reforms as early as 1983 and 1984, when international reserves were low. Also, as we have seen, it is not clear what trade reforms can contribute to stabilisation.

14 Whilst direct investment covers ownership of productive assets, portfolio investment includes purchase of bonds, equity-related instruments, and the direct purchase of shares in the domestic stock exchange.

Table 4.5: Foreign Investment Inflows (1983-92)

(billions US dollars)

	1983	1984	1985	1986	1987	1988	1989	1990	1991	1992
Direct Investment	2 192	1 541	1 984	2 401	2 635	2 880	3 176	2 633	4 761	5 366
Portfolio Investment							493	1 995	9 870	13 553
- Stock Market							493	1 995	6 332	4 780
- Money Market									3 538	8 773
Total	2 192	1 541	1 984	2 401	2 635	2 880	3 669	4 628	14 632	18 919

Source: Banco de México (1993: table 55).

diversification away from oil, so that manufactured exports have risen from under 40 per cent of total exports in 1985 to nearly 80 per cent in 1992. Further, there is evidence that this growth of manufactured exports is due to growing price competitiveness within Mexican manufacturing.[15] However imports have increased even more dramatically (for example rising by 52 per cent annually in current dollars between 1986 and 1992). A high income elasticity of demand for imports has been a long-term problem, with previous periods of growth terminating in balance of payments crisis. The present surge in imports is no doubt due to a combination of restocking, after the abnormally low import levels of the crisis years in the early and mid-1980s, normal growth associated with rising incomes and the easier access to imports and lower import tariffs that have resulted from trade liberalisation. So far, the growing trade deficit has been more than covered by higher capital inflows, and particularly since 1990 foreign exchange reserves have risen rather than fallen.

The Salinas government dismissed arguments that a future balance of payments crisis loomed by reference to a further strand in the liberalism case. This is that unlike previous current account deficits, the present one is due to private rather than public sector behaviour. As of 1992 the government fiscal account was in surplus (see Table 4.1), so that the aggregate excess of investment over savings implied by the current account deficit must be due to private sector investment in excess of private savings (that is private dissaving).[16]

A current account deficit due to private decisions is not an economic problem, it was argued, since rationally-made investment will generate future income to cover debt, profit repatriation and import bills, and rational consumption expenditure will result in resource use for purposes, which are as valuable as investment. Apart from the assumptions of foresight and perfect markets that are implicit in this argument, it assumes critically that the capital inflows that cover the deficit are long-term. By definition short-term capital can be withdrawn at short notice, placing pressure on foreign reserves and the exchange rate, and not adding to the productive potential of the economy as recent events have proven.

15 Evidence on this for export growth during the period up to 1987 is in Weiss (1992b).

16 A fundamental identity of macro economics is (I-S) = (M-X) where I is total investment, S is total savings, M is total imports and X is total exports. Thus an excess of investment over savings is reflected in a trade deficit. Since I and S can be decomposed into private and public components, if public savings exceeds public investment (so there is a budget surplus) it follows that with a trade deficit the private sector must be dissaving.

As we show in Table 4.5, most recent foreign investment inflows have been portfolio rather than direct investment, and although not all portfolio investment need be short term, a significant proportion seems to be of this type.[17] Thus, although the current account deficit may not be the issue it was in the early 1980s, it is premature to dismiss it as a macro problem. As we discuss below, entry into NAFTA was designed to address this by encouraging further long-run capital inflows.

Micro Economic conditions

Whilst in general macro policy has been consistent with conventional economic theory, there is more controversy over micro level changes. For example, despite the authority with which trade reform has been recommended to developing countries there is still legitimate dispute concerning its impact (see Pack, 1988; Havrylshyn, 1990). Theoretically there is a strong case that the removal of trade barriers should improve the allocation of resources, however whether once-for-all gains can be translated into higher longer run growth is more open to question. Long-run growth will be determined by factors like investment levels, technical change and economies of scale, and whilst correction of macro imbalances is clearly essential for this process, it is less obvious that an open trading environment will inevitably put an economy on a higher growth path (Rodrik, 1992).

For Mexico several studies have looked at the short-run allocative effect of trade reform, finding a tendency for a modest rise in productivity growth in the second half of the 1980s (Ros, 1992: 64-5; Lustig, 1992:121-2). However demonstrating a causal link with trade reform is more difficult. The present author examined this question in detail in Weiss (1992b) and (1992c), finding evidence of a significant but relatively weak relationship between trade reform and improvements in efficiency (as measured by labour and total factor productivity growth) at the branch level in manufacturing. Whilst there is evidence that, other things being equal, more liberalised activities (as measured by the change in the nominal rate of protection) tended to have faster productivity growth, there were clearly other causal factors at work and the quantitative impact of liberalisation has been relatively small, at least up to 1988, the last year included in the study. Another aspect of the case for trade liberalisation – that import competition 'disciplines' domestic producers to keep down their prices – receives only weak support. There is a

17 In the balance of payments statistics there is a distinction between short and long term capital flows, although the accuracy of this distinction is not clear. In 1992 the net short-term balance was around 30 per cent of the long-term balance.

tendency for more liberalised activities to have lower increases in price-cost margins (that is, price mark ups over operating cost), but the relationship is only very weakly significant. The implication of these results is that whilst trade reform has had none of the harmful effects, in terms of collapses in many domestic import-competing activities, that critics predicted, neither have its initial positive effects been very dramatic.

The other key area of micro reform – privatisation – has been recommended enthusiastically to developing countries. Here also economic theory is more guarded, providing no clear guidelines on the optimum size for the public sector. Cross-country comparisons of the public sector fail to provide unambiguous evidence that a rapid growth of State activity is inevitably associated with poor performanc (Lindauer and Valenchik, 1992). Further, at an enterprise level many suggest that what matters for performance is not ownership, but the market environment in which enterprises operate (Commander and Killick, 1988).

In Mexico, privatisation can be described legitimately as a major success, in the technical sense of a rapid dismantling of the public enterprise sector, at reasonably realistic prices. Its efficiency effects are not yet well understood, however, and there is some conflicting evidence. Three cases of privatisation in Mexico – those of Telmex, Aeroméxico and Mexicana – have been examined in detail by the World Bank as part of an international research project on privatisation (Tandon, 1992). The study attempts to assess the national costs and benefits of privatisation. The findings are that for Telmex and AeroMexico the outcome was clearly positive, with benefits above costs, but that the reverse was true for Mexicana.

There are considerable uncertainties involved in this exercise, particularly the projection of expected post-privatisation performance into the future, but the distributional results are of particular interest. For Telmex, for example, consumers were found to lose due to the major rise in charges (although it is argued that society as a whole gained from this rise since previous rates were well below the scarcity value of the service) and purchasers of the enterprise (particularly foreign investors) gained substantially. The effect on workers of the enterprises was found to be positive in the two successful privatisations and in that of Mexicana their net position was judged to be unaffected. The unsuccessful experience of Mexicana after privatisation is put down to mismanagement, resulting in an over-ambitious investment programme.

There is clearly a limit to the generalisations that can be made from these (albeit high profile) case-studies. An alternative approach by the present author (Weiss, 1994) looks at the performance of a sample of the largest enterprises in the country for 1985-90, whose operating results are reported in the magazine *Expansión*. A cross-firm regression analysis is conducted attempting to explain various measures of performance by firm characteristics, such as size, factor-intensity, level of trade protection and ownership. If the economic model underlying the liberalism experiment is correct, a dummy variable for public ownership should be significantly and negatively related to performance. In other words, other things being equal, for a given set of characteristics, performance should be poorer if a firm is in the public rather that the private sector. The analysis found no support for this interpretation, however, with the variables reflecting public ownership not being statistically significant.

Whilst casting some doubt on the efficiency case for privatisation this result does not necessarily undermine the whole of the strategy. It may be, for example, that the effect of privatisation, in reducing the public sector debt and improving the investment climate for the private sector, may still have been important. None the less it cautions against uncritical acceptance of all of the claims made for privatisation.[18]

Social Conditions

Economic theory provide little guidance on how the distribution of income will be affected during a process of stabilisation and longer-term adjustment. Outcomes will depend on exact circumstances and the package of policies adopted (see Demery and Addison, 1987). However, the expectation must be that in liberalism experiments with cuts in government expenditure, many of the poor may suffer, particularly in the short-term.

For Mexico there is evidence that the 1980s were a decade of growing poverty and widening income disparities. Indicators of real wages show a major fall during the 1980s, with the minimum wage falling consistently during the decade and the average wage per worker falling until 1989, after which point it starts to recover. Average household consumption fell by much less, reflecting dissaving and extra reliance on non-wage income, however with the removal of general food subsidies it seems that the food intake of the very poor has declined.[19]

These trends are reflected in the broad indicators of poverty and distributional shifts that are available. The World Bank (1993: Table 4.2) estimates

---

18 Another issue to be resolved is the establishment of an appropriate regulatory framework for newly privatised monopolies, such as Telmex. It is not clear how far moves to curb monopoly abuses have gone.

19 Evidence for these statements comes from Lustig (1992: 68-9), who shows that average real wages fell by 40 per cent per worker 1983-8, whilst average consumption fell by 11 per cent. Real minimum wages fell by nearly 50 per cent over the same period.

that those below the poverty line were 17 per cent of the total population in 1980 and 23 per cent in 1989; those in extreme poverty are estimated to have risen from 2.5 per cent to over seven per cent.[20] The same source also finds a worsening of income distribution, with a rise in the Gini coefficient from 0.51 in 1984 to 0.55 in 1989. Given this increasing inequality, it is not surprising to find the share of the bottom 20 per cent of the population in total income falling from 4.1 per cent to 3.2 per cent between 1984 and 1989. It is worth noting that of 18 Latin American and Caribbean countries covered by World Bank (1993) only four (Brazil, Guatemala, Honduras and Panama) have a lower share of income going to the bottom 20 per cent (also Lustig, 1992: Table 3.12). The conclusion must be that the social side of the liberalism experiment clearly needs further consideration, if development in the wider sense is to result, and indeed if the experiment is to be sustainable socially.

FUTURE ECONOMIC TRENDS

The future development of the economy is seen by many as bound up closely with the NAFTA treaty, and here we comment briefly on its likely impact. The important general observation is that most academic studies, whilst agreeing that NAFTA should have a positive effect on the economy, tend to downplay its quantitative significance (Ros, 1992). The common-sense of this is that since most trade barriers and tariffs on US-Mexico trade had already been lowered significantly prior to the treaty, the additional trade and resource reallocation that will follow after its implementation will be relatively modest. However more significant effects on growth are expected from the higher capital inflows – both direct and portfolio investment – that are expected to result, as US investors in particular, look to Mexico as a location for either production sites, or money market and stock exchange investments. There is considerable uncertainty, however, regarding the scale of additional capital inflows. A survey of current estimates suggests a wide range of possible total inflows to Mexico in the period up to the end of the century, of between US$25 billion to 60 billion (Hufbauer and Schort, 1993: 174).

The most optimistic of the available economic models predicts an increase of no more than eight per cent of current GDP due to NAFTA. This is

---

20 The poverty line is set at US$ 60 per month and the extreme poverty line at US$30 per month. There are some technical problems with the data which lead the authors to caution against placing too much weight on the results.

approximately equivalent to a half of one percentage point increase in annual GDP growth, spread over a 15 year period. If significant new capital inflows do not result from NAFTA, however, gains could be no more than a quarter of this figure, or an increase of only 0.125 percentage points on GDP growth annually over 15 years (see Sobarzo, 1992; Grennes and Krissof, 1993).

Thus NAFTA is unlikely to transform economic prospects. These will depend upon the viability of the liberalism model itself. So far progress has been positive, but initially slow in the period before 1988 and certainly not of 'miracle' proportions. The key issues at the end of the Salinas *sexenio* are the financing of the current account deficit of the balance of payments and the extent to which, general recovery, if it can be sustained, will address the poverty and distributional problems that worsened in the reform decade of the 1980s. Final judgements on the liberalism experiment as an economic package must await the resolution of these issues.

5 Dismantling or Retrenchment? Salinas and Corporatism

Nikki Craske[1]

When Carlos Salinas de Gortari took office in 1988, it was clear that the *sexenio* (six-year presidential term) was going to be one of change, both economic and political. There was not much doubt about Salinas' economic policies since he had been the architect of many reforms during the de la Madrid administration (1982-8), however his political vision was less clear. Salinas' party history did not give a clear indication of his political views but his role in the *Secretaría de Programación y Presupuesto* put him on the side of the new breed of technocratic administrators. However, unlike previous generations, these technocrats were also politically capable; *tecnócratas* rather than *técnicos* (Centeno, 1994). Salinas' inauspicious ascent to the presidency in the wake of the 1988 elections damaged his and the *Partido Revolucionario Institucional*'s (PRI) legitimacy, however through audacious economic projects such as NAFTA and the much publicised social welfare project *Programa Nacional de Solidaridad (*PRONASOL) (see Varley this volume) Salinas managed to cast aside doubts and soon his popularity ratings soared. Certainly the economic project was radical but political change was less clear and its trajectory not unilinear. Despite the rhetoric of 'modernisation and democratisation', Salinas increased the authoritarian character of the regime in key areas and did little to attack the anti-democratic practices of clientelism, the highly centralised nature of the political system, arbitrariness in the decision-making process, unclear regulatory principles and presidentialism. There are also indications that human rights abuses have increased (Foweraker, 1994). In one area which Salinas identified as being in need of change, party reform to make the PRI a party of individuals rather than organisations, – that is the dismantling of corporatism – success was patchy

1 Many of the arguments put forward here are discussed in greater detail in Craske (1994). I thank the Institute of Latin American Studies, University of London, for allowing me to reproduce the work and for contributing to the funding for the fieldwork.

and regionalised and little structural change was achieved despite many projects.

One of the problems for Salinas, or anyone else who may want to carry out extensive reform, is the PRI itself. Here I argue that the six years of party reform has left the PRI relatively unchanged organisationally and continuing to practice authoritarian corporatism but with increasing divisions between the reformists and the traditionalists. Indeed, one attempt to develop a new political structure within the PRI came in the guise of a project called *Movimiento Urbano Popular Territorial* (MT). The fate of this project is illustrative of the obstacles to reforming the political system as shall be seen below. Regardless of its rhetoric of modernisation and democratisation, PRONASOL also reflected corporatist tendencies in its organisation (cf. Lomelí Meillón, 1993). Despite the need for, and talk about, political reform it was never prioritised and there was little in the way of a coherent strategy on the part of the elite. This lack of direction, in contrast with the commitment to economic change, allowed the regrouping of the traditionalists within the party. Consequently, throughout the administration the reform of the party was characterised by project launch followed by U-turn.

Salinas's failure to reform the party may pave the way to another approach to strengthening the pluri-party system in Mexico; the slow withering away of the party as PRONASOL takes over the clientelistic resource distribution and the economic programme is safe in the hands of the opposition – as long as it's *Partido Acción Nacional* (PAN). Figures for the 1994 elections indicate a political geography of bi-party contest in most regions, thus the PRI's position is clearly not as strong as it was (see Stansfield this volume) and few of the technocratic elite have a firm commitment to the PRI. However, attentio to social and political reform, which appeared to be key areas for Zedillo at the outset of his administration, may now have to be shelved. It was assumed that Salinas' radical economic programme had dealt with the most important economic problems, however the economic chaos into which the country was plunged as a result of currency devaluation in December 1994 has shifted attention away from social and political issues. Whatever the policies Zedillo chooses to follow, it will be a challenging time for him since he has yet to prove himself to be politically capable.[2]

2 Although we have to remember that Salinas was considered politically inexperienced he managed to reinvent himself through PRONASOL and regain the political initiative to become a highly popular president during his administration despite his failure to challenge the PRI's outmoded practices (see also Varley this volume). However, as a result of the economic chaos his reputation has been tarnished resulting in his being accused of economic mismanagement and being behind the assassination of presidential candidate Luis Donaldo Colosio by some.

The chapter will be divided into three sections; in the first I will discuss the attempts by the reformers at dismantling corporatism focusing primarily on the PRI, then I will go on to examine two forms of retrenchment of corporatism, one as the old guard re-assert themselves within the party and secondly, the modernisers' corporatist project PRONASOL. Finally the outcome of these reforms are assessed with the Salinas *sexenio* at an end. Salinas always prioritised the economic over the political and tried to minimise the contradictions between the economic model and social demands by limiting the political arena to elections and excluding other socio-economic issues. Through judicious use of the system the PRI has improved on its 1988 position but the reactive nature of reform has resulted in limited change alongside rapid change in electoral law. The underlying political instability is still evident from the number of electoral reform projects, the need to centralise the system further and continued problems in the exercise of rights. We also see a fragmentation of the party on regional grounds as the tensions between the two factions are played out. On balance it appears that Meyer's observation that reforming the PRI is a 'mission impossible' is still salutary (1989).

DISMANTLING CORPORATISM?

The principle characteristic of corporatism is the vertical, hierarchical and 'functionally differentiated organisations' which separates potential allies (see Schmitter 1979 for a discussion of corporatism). These organisations are sanctioned by the state which gives them privileged access to resources in return for loyalty. Although Mexico does not correspond to an ideal type of corporatism in that not all organised groups in society are affiliated to the PRI as the terrain of corporatism, there are clearly corporatist elements at work.[3]

Although Mexico enjoyed greater political stability than most of its neighbours, there was increasing disenchantment with the authoritarian political system which relied very heavily on cooptation and coercion. Throughout the 1970s and 1980s, popular discontent focussed on issues of independence (from both political parties generally and the PRI in particular)

3 The party has three main 'pillars': the labour sector, the *Confederación de Trabajadores Mexicanos* (the CTM); the peasant sector, the *Confederación Nacional Campesina* (the CNC); and the catch-all Popular Sector originally called the *Confederación Nacional de Organizaciones Populares* (CNOP).

and autonomy. The increasing sophistication of the political actors involved in these popular organisations indicated that the PRI was no longer efficient at orchestrating support for the executive in return for favours. The very position of the party was uncertain as the new political elite owed less and less allegiance to the party whilst the party faithful were increasingly excluded from top government positions. Independent organisations were also more successful at forcing the authorities to negotiate with them but without guaranteeing votes in return. The 1988 elections illustrated well the precarious position of the party, and by association, the government with the majority of people doubting the legitimacy of the new president. The development of popular protest organisations had forced a new conception of citizenship onto the Mexican political arena which was incompatible with traditional political practices of clientelism, arbitrariness and coercion. Consequently the methods of the PRI were unable to cope with the new political reality and its reform became inevitable.

The PRI has two facets; it is there to generate support for the elite and it is also a political machine with its own agenda increasingly at odds with that of the elite. Each faction has its own supporters; the modernisers from those who are pressuring for transparent procedural practices, and the traditionalists from those who fear change and who are more deeply incorporated into the clientelistic system.[4] However, whatever the perspective, the old sectors were failing, particularly the Popular Sector whose remit included low-income neighbourhoods where much of the popular protest activities originated. However all the sectors would be under pressure during the Salinas administration. A quiescent labour force was key in the economic restructuring particularly important in Mexico's search for foreign investment; Mexico's comparative advantage with the US and Canada in the NAFTA is cheap labour. The CTM leader, Fidel Velázquez, was given a clear warning against opposing the economic project at the outset of the Salinas administration when two key union bosses were removed from their posts and in one case imprisoned. Since then Velázquez has done little to impede economic reform but he has tried to slow the pace of party reform. Similarly the peasant sector was also under pressure with the 1992 changes to Article 27 of the Constitution and the massive displacement of farmers as a result of this and the impact

4 The dichotomy between moderniser and traditionalist is a complex one, which is often too simply equated with the centre and older regional bosses. Here I wish to draw the distinction between planners who are largely in Mexico City and those who work 'on the ground'. However, the practices employed by any one person may vary between the two; many so-called modernisers employ traditional practices when politically active in the regions, particularly when confronted with active opposition movements.

of the NAFTA and reduced access to credit for small farmers (Appendini, 1994; Gledhill this volume). However, it was the Popular Sector where the attempted restructuring took place during the Salinas administration. This Sector was chosen for three reasons; first, the PRI was worried by the degree of middle class discontent – the CNOP had been founded to absorb the middle classes into the party in the 1940s; second, the Sector had failed to co-opt the alienated groups emerging in the low-income neighbourhoods also under its remit; and finally, the Sector was considered more docile and therefore easier to reform.

At first the reform appeared to be the precursor for the dismantling of corporatism but the lack of consistency on the part of the elite allowed the old guard to mount their defence. Consequently, the structure of the PRI barely changed during the six years, but the emergence of PRONASOL as an important new actor had an impact on the party (see below). Despite the need of each president to distinguish himself from the previous one by distancing himself from that administration's policies, the last two *sexenios* (and quite possibly the current one) have shown more consistency. This consistency is most marked in the modernising of the economic arena. There is enough evidence to illustrate that the Salinas administration in particular made radical changes through privatisation of parastatal companies, the opening up of the economy to foreign investors and free trade and the removal of most subsidies. Bizberg maintains that this modernisation is incompatible with corporatism mainly because of the contradiction in the sphere of labour relations (1993: 309). However this supposes that corporatism necessarily includes an agreement whereby labour has a principle role as one of the 'functionally differentiated categories' which is not the case, although it has generally been a norm particularly in Europe.

Bizberg's assertion that the modernisation process demands the dismantling of corporatism ignores the tendencies towards a reorientation of corporatism away from the party, whose reform is a project riddled with problems as Salinas discovered. Bizberg does suggest an alternative scenario of 'neo-corporatism' which is not to be confused with the neo-corporatism in the general literature which is synonymous with European corporatism of the 1960s and 1970s where the corporatist groups have influence in policy design and implementation, which clearly would not fit the Mexican case. His version would be to remove some of the prerogatives of the strongest unions but keep the basic structures of corporatism, but, he argues, this would still be difficult to achieve since so many groups are already active in the independent arena where they 'have found in the electoral arena new spaces for political expression.' (ibid.: 312). This again over-emphasises the place of labour within a corporatist structure. With the increased casualisation of labour the future of labour organisations has been fluid and Salinas was keen to promote Mexico as a country without major labour disputes and flexible in the global market place. Consequently, a rigid labour organisation such as the CTM is not necessarily an important element to such a political system.

With the changes in the economic sphere, Salinas's goal was to keep people tied to the political system and maintain political stability whilst carrying out the economic restructuring. Consequently, if the PRI is to lose its dominant position, which in the long-run appears likely, there needs to be something to take its place to generate support for the government and particularly its economic policies; hence the shift of corporatism to PRONASOL which organises people into vertical, hierarchical groups focusing on issues of 'community' which have emerged over the past twenty years. It is increasingly obvious that the PRI will continue to be a problem area for the government, but a continuation of the economic modernisation project can be guaranteed with certain changes locked in under NAFTA, and Zedillo supports these, and a social welfare project which contains discontent, which Zedillo again seems set to continue.

There is no doubt that there needs to be some policy which will mitigate the contradiction between the economic model and social needs. The popular protests of the 1980s politicised socio-economic issues, however the neoliberal economic project puts these questions outside politics and the arenas opened up by grassroots political organisations were gradually closed off by Salinas and the political arena increasingly focussed on elections.[5] Consequently, by 1994, the degree of political liberalisation was measured by the 'transparency' of the August elections, despite the choice in the elections being constrained by continued human rights abuses, negotiations and fraud in regional and local elections during the *sexenio* and continued clientelism through PRONASOL.

Salinas's attempted reform of the PRI followed the usual practice of ad hoc developments and grafting on of new ideas which had successfully challenged its power. Hence the new emphasis on natural leaders, social

---

5 At the outset of his administration, Salinas promoted *convenios* which were agreements with independent organisations aimed to bring them into the fold and scupper any alliances with the opposition, particularly the PRD. Perhaps the best known was one signed with the locally powerful *Comité de Defensa Popular* in Durango. In 1988 it had supported the FDN, but after signing the *convenio* it gained its own local registration, gained a local councillor and access to state resources (Haber, 1993); there were similar agreements with other organisations including the victims of the 1985 earthquake (see Eckstein, 1990). In the second half of the *sexenio* such agreements virtually disappeared and independent organisations found it increasingly difficult to negotiate with the authorities.

organisation and grassroots participation and decentralisation. The modernisers' ideal was to streamline the PRI into an electoral operation and to separate the party from government with the consequent removal of service provision from the party's influence.

The Popular Sector was to be one of the first areas to be reformed. There were four stages of this reform which first moved towards the modernisers' view before the retrenchment phase. The Sector was founded in 1943 and by 1988 it consisted of eleven 'participatory' and nineteen bureaucratic branches. The first stage of reforms tried to develop an organisation for Urban Popular Movements, however it was soon clear that a more wide ranging reform was necessary; that is, not just the grafting on of another structure but an overhaul of the Sector itself. This lead to a second reform to separate the Sector's branches which dealt with the 'community' from those related to 'citizens'' issues such as the environment, women's groups and youth groups since it was the coming together of such groups which contributed to the pressures on the PRI in 1988. This second stage lead to a sharp decrease in bureaucracy reducing it to four 'support branches' and a more structured participatory organisation with five branches: citizens; urban; professionals; trades' unions (*sindicatos*) and white collar unions (*gremios*). At this stage there was also a name change to *Une - Ciudadanos en Movimiento* (a slogan rather than an acronym: Unite - Citizens on the Move). The five participatory groups were acknowledged to be at different stages of political development with the citizens and urban groups the least developed. There was then an attempt to take the reform one step further with the removal of community issues into a new organisation which would embrace all who were interested in *gestión social* including members of the opposition and PRONASOL committees *but* which would still be affiliated to the PRI; this organisation would be called *Movimiento Popular Urbano Territorial* (MT).

This project merits greater analysis here. It was developed with the idea of copying the urban popular movements particularly regarding horizontal linkages, networking, community-based organisations and mobilisation around consumption issues. However, unlike many of the elite, the architect of the project, José Parcero López, did not believe that you could separate the social from the political and that political will was necessary to solve social questions. The stated goal of the project was to develop autonomy within the communities and to be as inclusive as possible going 'house to house' to encourage everyone to participate. Parcero López also believed that representational democracy was going to be the organisational feature of the project to avoid the *dedazo* (the presidential, or occasionally governors', naming of a candidate).

Although the project rhetoric corresponded with notions of political liberalisation, there were many anomalies. First, the *priísta* organisations which had dealt with service distribution did not form the basis of the MT but remained within the Popular Sector. Second, the MT was supposed to incorporate all who were interested in *gestión social* but it would become a new sector of the PRI thus incorporating PRONASOL Committees and independent groups into the party. Consequently, it was repeating clientelistic patterns and cooptation. Third, it also failed in its attempt to break with the *dedazo* when Carlos Sobrino was designated its leader which, some believed was designed to him give a launching pad for his bid to become governor of Yucatán. Finally, the MT did not become a major force within the neighbourhoods and its failure to establish itself gives an indication of the obstacles to developing a more open democratic forum within the party for service provision. Here there were two more problems; first the project itself stopped short of embracing genuine democratic forms, and second the project was scuppered by the traditionalists who wished to keep service provision within their control and who continued to participate within the Popular Sector.

In many areas the changes to the Popular Sector, the emergence of PRONASOL and the MT did lead to the ousting of local leaders who were antipathetic to change and who had vested interests in the old clientelistic system. Consequently, there was as much opposition to the new organisations from within the PRI as from the opposition and increasingly members of the PRI, rather than the PRD and PAN, engaged in anti-regime behaviour (Morris, 1992). In other instances however, as shall be seen below, the old guard appropriated these new channels of resource distribution which were then merged with the traditional idiosyncratic system. In terms of rhetoric, the changes which were being promoted for the party were largely about making it more responsive to the grassroots, however in reality the target audience was not the grassroots of the party but those who were (potential) opposition sympathisers; the party grassroots were often confused by the change or were against it. For many, the series of changes within the Popular Sector between 1989-93 were ill-conceived and were actually losing the party support. The reform projects caused increased tensions between the modernisers and the traditionalists which were reflected in the uneven nature of reform within the party which is itself regionalised with the north and centre generally being more receptive to change whilst in the south and west party members have rejected many of the centre's ideas.

Part of the problem has been elections themselves. To control the reform project, both regarding the party and as well as broader political and economic questions, the elite need to stay in power and the PRI, whilst not as effective as it has been, still provides a substantial contribution to the maintenance of power. Consequently, a complete dismantling of the system was not carried out giving the old guard important political leverage allowing them to counter attack. This limited room for manoeuvre along with the prioritisation of economic project has lead to U-turn and retrenchment of corporatism. The final stage of the Popular Sector reform returned it to the same basic structure as 1988 albeit with a streamlined bureaucracy and with the five participatory groups. However, the membership was left virtually intact since it generally failed to attract members from the independent organisations and, more importantly, the political practices remained largely the same. There was another (the third) name which incorporates the notion of citizenship without extending it in a meaningful way: *Federación Nacional de Organizaciones y Ciudadanos* (FNOC).

The experience of the Popular Sector was not repeated in either of the other two Sectors, other than their half-hearted 'pact' (*Pacto Obrero Campesino*). In a time of limited resources and an economic project which was attempting to promote decision-making based on rational/technical criteria, rather than political considerations. Any attempt to incorporate dissident groups into the political system necessarily meant less access for those already participating within. This lead partially to the opposition from the old guard who were also worried that many of the current cohort of decision-makers in Mexico City have little identity with the party since they have not risen through the ranks. There is no doubt that there have been some changes which has lead to the downfall of local party bosses who have abused the system, there are more elections within communities to decide on grassroots leaders and new people have become active which has contributed to changing some of the excesses of the traditional system. In some cases PRONASOL has not only contributed to ousting local entrenched *priístas* but has allowed the opposition access to government resources which may have been impossible only a few years ago. The worrying issue in terms of a genuine political liberalisation, not to mention democratisation, is the arbitrary nature of these changes.[6] They are not uniform nor irreversible and remain largely controlled from the top which has contributed to increased centralism in contradiction with the rhetoric on decentralisation. These indicate that corporatism is not only *not* being dismantled but that it is increased in key areas.

6 Here I wish to draw the distinction between political liberalisation which focuses on electoral practices, obviously a key issue in Mexico, and democratisation which also includes broader questions of equality including income distribution, access to adequate education, healthcare, housing and other basic services.

THE RETRENCHMENT OF CORPORATISM

The retrenchment of corporatism takes two forms; first the way in which the old guard of the PRI has been mobilised to defend its position and gained support from those who at least know the system despite its arbitrariness. Second, the emergence of a programme such as PRONASOL using the familiar vertical, hierarchical structures this time organised around production, services, the regional fund and other projects such as *Mujeres en Solidaridad*. These are designed to bind people to the government rather than to the party *per se*.

The fragmentation of the PRI which we have been witnessing over the past years, along with the partial liberalisation of the political system, has highlighted the deep problems in trying to reform the party. The failure of the Popular Sector reform project launched by Salinas has stalled a more complete party reform. It seems that the party will not so much be reformed from the centre as allowed to become more regionalised where the old authoritarian PRI is visible in some states, taking advantage of the coercive apparatus available to it and in others a modern party which is competing in a more open political system.[7] However, the continued repression of the PRD indicates that the elite are not prepared for total openness. It will only relinquish the use of non-democratic practices when it is assured that the overall 'modernising' project will not be undone. In terms of the economy this is now more secure since the signing of the NAFTA and the failure of an alternative economic project to emerge. The challenge to Zedillo will be to extend the modernisation project to the political arena, but without losing control of the economic project.

The project to restructure the PRI to make it a party of individuals was aimed to reduce the party's dependence on the three pillars of labour, peasants and 'popular' sector for support. However, the reform project took time in being developed and implemented, evident from the four stages outlined above, at which point much of the pressure coming from popular protest activities had eased off with the subsequent downgrading of the reform process. This in turn allowed the old guard to regroup itself and make a counter attack. The efforts of the traditionalists resulted in halting of the separation of the Popular Sector from service provision in low-income neighbourhoods. Whilst this may be a key victory for this camp, it means that there are too many organisations targetting the same constituency: the FNOC,

7 These regional dimensions are discussed in many of the chapters in this volume: see particularly Rodríguez and Ward; Vicencio; Stansfield; Pansters, and Clarke.

the *Movimiento Territorial* and PRONASOL. Consequently, service provision in some communities is more complicated than before resulting in tensions between the different *priísta* organisations. A further consequence was that the reform of the Popular Sector stalled and the expected reform of the CTM and CNC never materialised; although both are finding it increasingly difficult to represent their members (if they ever did) in the current economic climate. The retreat of the reformists and the return to old party structures and cadres ratified in the party's XIV National Assembly boosted the confidence of local leaders even if their power *per se* has not increased. Many of the party supporters and activists in the neighbourhoods are keen to keep the system the way it is since they at least understand the rules of the game and have often spent a long time cultivating the clientelistic relationships necessary to gain access to State resources.

PRONASOL is also an element of the corporatist retrenchment. It has provided both opportunities and constraints for the PRI. In terms of opportunities PRONASOL was to provide massive funds for projects which have previously been distributed largely through the party, however despite the parallel organisation the party was still used to develop programme projects and organise the contributions through co-responsibility of participants, frequently strengthening the old *caciques*. Indeed the links between the party and PRONASOL were such that many PRONASOL commitments were made by PRI candidates on the campaign trail. The constraints came from the way in which the programme was also used to circumvent the obstructionist strategies of local *priístas* opposed to modernising tactics. In these cases the resources were channelled through 'natural leaders' (those organising groups independently of parties) whom the elite wanted to co-opt into the system. PRONASOL was also a constraint in that funds were often distributed through opposition local governments as a demonstration of the President's commitment to political liberalisation. Which of these permutations is evident in a given context depends upon the complex local-regional-federal relations, timing of elections in the locality, the strength of local opposition and the local party; in my own experience in Guadalajara, PRONASOL has largely been hijacked by PRI traditionalists, however there are other examples (see Cornelius *et al.*, 1994).

PRONASOL did not represent a great break away from previous administrations' social policies, there have been a number of similar policies, but PRONASOL did introduce new elements. It dealt with opposition local governments and it also developed the notion of co-responsibility where beneficiaries were to contribute to the resources available aping the self-help tactics of independent organisations. There is not sufficient room here to discuss PRONASOL in depth (see Varley this volume), but what interests us here is how it complimented party reform and reflects a modernisation, rather than a dismantling, of corporatism.

There are two key elements about the functioning of PRONASOL and the impact it has on the overall political system. First, it reinforces centralism since it was originally directed from the Presidency itself and then formed the central part of a new 'superministry' SEDESOL (which the assassinated presidential candidate Luis Donaldo Colosio first directed). The decisions over which projects would be followed through were authorised by the centre. Furthermore, there is little evidence that PRONASOL eliminates arbitrariness in the decision-making process since few people seem to understand which criteria are used for judging the worthiness of petitions. Second, it is also organised in stratified, hierarchical and non-competing organisations where demand-making is channelled in a top-down structure and horizontal linkages are contained. It mirrors the organisation of the PRI albeit with structures which focus on different issues; instead of labour, peasant and popular sectors, we now have services, production, the regional fund, women and schools. In regions where the Popular Sector's traditionalists have been able to maintain their dominant position, it has often served to strengthen their hand by becoming another resource for them to distribute. In many of the neighbourhoods I studied, little if any distinction was made between PRONASOL and the Popular Sector or the PRI. Thus rather than replacing clientelism with clear rules which may represent 'pork-barrel politics' but nothing more, it is actually reinforcing many of the trends which the modernisers want to change.[8] In these cases, the input of local people who are not PRI participants is as negligible as ever. Most grassroots party activists see privileged access to government resources as a right and resent anything which changes this. In other areas where there has been opposition to the PRI and local opposition government has emerged, it is also possible that the realities of regulated political decision-making may not be the panacea to demands; the PAN's vote dropped dramatically in Chihuahua in August 1994 despite their example of 'good governance' at state level. With a new opposition PAN governor in Jalisco and *panista* municipal governments in metropolitan Guadalajara, we may soon be able to assess the impact on PRONASOL in the region rather than a social welfare project filtered through the PRI.

---

8 Molinar and Weldon (1994) conclude that in many cases PRONASOL represents pork barrel politics and not a new clientelistic network.

CONCLUSIONS

The Salinas administration was one of great change and in some ways very successful. By the end of the *sexenio*, it appeared that the economy was more able to deal with the rigours of the international market, albeit at a cost, but political liberalisation had been patchy. However, perhaps one success of Salinas was to focus people's attention on the electoral arena and, despite a number of fraudulent elections during the course of the *sexenio*, produce presidential elections which have largely been accepted as fair and a genuine representation of the votes cast at the ballot box. In doing so, there has been a narrowing of the meaning of citizenship to equate it with electoral competition to the exclusion of equally important issues such as access to the nation's wealth, the freedom of association, open discussion of government policies (the negotiations over NAFTA are a good example of 'backroom' deals), an independent judiciary, which Salinas himself admitted was one area which he failed to reform (*Financial Times*, 7 November 1994), and clientelism to name but a few of the current concerns.[9] The popular protest organisations of the 1970s and 1980s politicised previously social issues. Now, in the 1990s, with the notion of democracy confined to the ambit of elections, the moral health of the nation is measured purely in terms of whether the latest round of elections have been fair and 'transparent'. Increasingly we see a more genuine form of party competition and the 1994 elections indicated a greater degree of bi-party competition emerging in many areas of the country (Rodríguez and Ward this volume; Stansfield this volume), however, during the Salinas administration there were many counts of fraud, some which were overturned by the centre (Guanajuato and San Luis Potosí) but others were sanctioned. It was clear that despite its co-governing status, the PAN was not immune to being denied its vote as happened in Yucatán in 1993 (Cornelius, 1994). But in order for political liberalisation to reach its fullest conclusion, there needs to be a separation of the PRI from service distribution as the party fulfils its role *as* a party rather than as a political machine. The role of PRONASOL is to take over where the PRI needs to leave off and oversee service distribution and contribute to the development of social and political stability; however the evidence to date shows that this

9 In many ways this reflects the experience of other Latin American countries which have returned to civilian rule where the political arena has been subordinated to the needs of a neoliberal economic project despite popular mobilisations which have campaigned on questions of socio-economic justice. However, in many of these countries the electoral system and the judiciary are more open which aid political liberalisation and the clientelistic networks are not so deeply entrenched.

is going to be a difficult aim to achieve. The events which have taken place since the elections, the assassination of José Ruíz Massieu and the subsequent accusations by his family of PRI involvement, and the arrest of the ex-president's brother, Raúl Salinas, for the intellectual murder of Luis Donaldo Colosio, as well as the renewed activity by both the *Ejercito Zapatista de Liberación Nacional* (EZLN) and the Mexican army in Chiapas, are indications that the next six years are not going to be easy. It appears that some of the six scenarios that Cornelius, Gentleman and Smith painted in 1989 could still hold true; not the least of which is an authoritarian crackdown. Certainly the political liberalisation project is not so far advanced that it could not be reversed and the 'mission impossible' of reforming the PRI remains a moot point.

6 The New PRI: Recasting its Identity

Victoria E. Rodríguez and Peter M. Ward

INTRODUCTION: IS REFORMING THE PRI 'MISSION IMPOSSIBLE'?

During the Salinas presidency, Mexico experienced the most dramatic changes in its economic and political structures since the administration of Lázaro Cárdenas (1934-40). Our purpose in this essay is to examine one arena where political change can be clearly observed – namely, in the performance of the *Partido Revolucionario Institucional* (PRI) in state and local government. Although still in its early stages, we will describe the emergence of the so-called 'New PRI' insofar as it is composed of a different breed of politicians and administrators, a changing rationality underpinning decision-making procedures, new relations with citizens, greater accountability and openness in governing, a distancing from old traditions of party patronage, and a different type of relationship among the different levels of government. As yet, this new *modus operandi* of the PRI in government is not pervasive across the nation, but has emerged forcefully in the more progressive states of the northern part of the country, particularly in those where the opposition has its principal strongholds. We shall argue that the primary stimulus for these new patterns of government is, precisely, the opening of the political space and a cleaner, more closely contested electoral environment in which the PRI can no longer automatically assume victory.

While the focus of analysis in this chapter is the performance of the PRI in government, it is necessary to discuss briefly how the PRI is changing, both internally as a party and within Mexico's political system as a whole. How far-reaching are these changes? How genuine? Can the PRI truly change, or as Lorenzo Meyer (1989) put it, is reform of the PRI 'mission impossible'? We believe there are several areas in which changes of both the PRI and the Mexican political landscape are observable.

First, the political arena has become more competitive than ever before. In certain regions where the PRI formerly enjoyed an undisputed monopoly, it now at best retains hegemony and, more often than not, finds itself engaged in competitive pluralism (Molinar Horcasitas, 1989; 1991). Although nationally three political parties compete regularly in elections, regionally the pattern is one of *bi-partidismo*, that is PAN versus PRI in the north, PRI vs PRD in the south, and so on. In Congress, the expansion in the number of seats tied to a system of stratified proportional representation has meant that two fifths of seats are held by non-PRI deputies. This has bolstered reforms in the electoral framework, specifically the passage of the COFIPE (*Código Federal de Instituciones y Procedimientos Electorales*) in 1990, and reforms of the same in 1993 and 1994 which imposed major constraints upon both the party itself and its control and influence over the conduct of elections.

Furthermore, electoral victories of opposition parties at the local level since the early 1980s, and at the state level since the late 1980s, have further challenged the PRI's former monopoly on government. During the Salinas administration approximately ten per cent of municipalities were governed by the opposition and, although it can be argued that this percentage is rather low, what is significant is that some of these are major cities or urban centres, not small rural municipalities. Moreover, in many cases they were being retained by these opposition parties in subsequent elections (for example, Tijuana and Ensenada in Baja California, and León in Guanajuato). As a result of electoral competitiveness, political awareness and participation have increased among the Mexican people. Therefore, more space has been opened within the political landscape for the expression of democratic demands.

Second, the PRI has been obliged to undertake reforms on its internal structure, support base and recruiting patterns (Camp, 1993a). Historically, the PRI has been organised as a 'party of the masses' with three main sectors: labour (CTM), peasants (CNC) and popular (previously the CNOP, now FNOC). This corporate structure enabled it to channel demands, mobilise broad electoral support and, more importantly, to co-opt large sections of the population. This arrangement was effective (although with occasional use of repression) from the 1940s to the early 1980s, a time during which Mexico enjoyed steady economic growth. However, the economic crisis of 1982 and the subsequent decline in Mexico's economic performance generated an environment of dissatisfaction within many social groups, some of which began to realise that the sectoral leadership was no longer capable of delivering the benefits that would satisfy their demands. This strengthened the emergence of some independent labour unions and social movements which frequently allied themselves with opposition parties. As a result, the viability of the labour sector as a basis of support for the ruling party eroded badly. This situation occurred in the other sectors as well, as became evident in the 1988 elections – generally considered a disaster for the PRI. Together, these events provoked a re-evaluation and a move toward restructuring the party.

Instead of relying on the sectors, and after much internal deliberation, the PRI launched a new strategy to organise its support on a territorial basis and transformed the former CNOP into the *Federación Nacional de Organizaciones y Ciuadanos* (FNOC) and founded a new organisation, the *Movimiento Urbano Popular Territorial* (MT). Also, for the first time in history, it allowed and promoted individual citizen membership without any sectoral affiliation (Colosio, 1993). These reforms appear to have had considerable immediate effect, since the PRI won back in 1991 much of the ground it had lost in 1988. However, some analysts argue that this PRI victory owed more to President Salinas' programmes, especially PRONASOL, than to the party's reforms (Dresser, 1991; Molinar and Weldon, 1994).

An additional internal reform effort within the party has been in the candidate selection procedures. Traditionally, candidates have been selected by high ranking PRI and government officials in Mexico City, often with little or no input from local party members (either through primary-type elections or as actual candidates). With the implementation of the new territorial strategy, local party officials have tended to play a more relevant role in the selection of lower and mid-level candidates and functionaries. However, when it comes to selection of candidates for federal deputies, senators, and the presidency, *dedazo* from Mexico City remains the order of the day. It appears this is likely to change significantly in the near future, beginning with Jalisco and Guanajuato in their 1995 elections, and continuing in 1997, in which President Zedillo has vowed to not intervene.

A third dimension of internal reform has been in the area of PRI recruiting patterns. Whereas in the past much could be made of the difference between the *técnicos* who dominated the federal bureaucracy and the *políticos* who dominated the party structure, that difference has increasingly narrowed in the recent past (Centeno and Maxfield, 1992; Cornelius and Craig, 1991). We believe the difference has narrowed for two principal reasons (Rodríguez and Ward, 1994a). One, the importance of the old style so-called 'dinosaurs' has been progressively eclipsed, although they remain a significant force of resistance. Two, the new political leadership within the party has tended to come from highly qualified, well educated *técnicos* who were formerly considered to have little or no political savvy. For these two reasons, party recruits and leadership tend to be more and more a blend of technically competent politicians. The same pattern applies when assessing the state and local levels. Whereas in the past it was possible to clearly discern significant differences in the professional and educational background of high-level federal government officials compared with their national and local counterparts, that difference has also narrowed. Nonetheless, the trend among federal officials toward high educational achievement and graduate studies at premier institutions in Mexico and abroad continues to be less frequent at the state and local levels, which reduces the pool of suitable candidates for local office. But at the local level, too, the exigencies of governing in a more demanding political arena and in a more complex social, economic and political context also demand more educational background; increasingly, the personal qualifications and expertise of the individual are what matter.

In addition to these major changes, there are several other items on the current agenda: separation of party and government; modernisation of the party structure through internal (local) candidate selection procedures; the formulation of a clear ideology that distinguishes the PRI in government from other parties; making local candidates and party offices responsible for campaign fundraising and party activities; adjusting to a decline in centralism and to the demands of a 'new federalism', and moving the party away from rubber-stamping executive initiatives in Congress.

In our view, the pressures for all the changes described above derive from a growing recognition that in order to survive as a viable political party, the PRI has to meet the demands of an increasingly competitive and open electoral arena. Specifically, the PRI must present candidates that are credible and acceptable at the local level. The PRI must also prove itself capable of performing effectively in government. Unlike in previous decades, when PRI candidate selection depended upon connections and patronage, and performance was measured in term of party loyalty, now the rationale has changed to emphasise government ability through technical competence. Moreover, in order to win an election, the PRI must now demonstrate that its outgoing administration did a good job and that its new candidates for office will keep up the good work. Given the no re-election clause and term limitations in office, it is not possible for proven government officials to be re-elected successively to the same office or to fulfil all of their government programme. The idea, therefore, is to convince the electorate that there will be continuity if another *priísta* is elected. While this may not seem unusual in other settings, it is something of a novelty for the PRI. Interestingly, as we shall demonstrate below, our work suggests that the PRI's response to these challenges has often been informed by patterns of government practice that have been developed by opposition parties, especially the PAN.

LEARNING FROM THE OPPOSITION: PATTERNS AND PRACTICES OF *PANISTA* GOVERNMENT

With some arguable veracity, the PAN sustains that part of its traditional policy agenda and ideological platform was 'stolen' by the Salinas administration (Alvarez, 1993: 144). This would especially appear to be the case for economic liberalisation, privatisation, deregulation of the *ejido* and so on. However, it is not our intention in this essay to evaluate the extent to which the PRI has moved into the right of the political spectrum and converged with the *panista* platform. Rather, our aim is to provide an overview of the principal features of state and local government under the PAN, drawn from our research (Rodríguez and Ward, 1992; 1994b; 1995). In summary form, these features are the following.

Recruitment and Background

While there are observable differences among our own sample of *panista* officials in local and state government, there are several characteristics that appear consistently (cf. Camp 1995). Invariably they have little militancy within the PAN prior to holding office (either elected or appointed), and overwhelmingly are drawn from the private sector, where they have distinguished themselves as successful businessmen (Guadarrama, 1987). Their educational backgrounds are more likely to be in accounting and management, rather than law and economics, and they have no experience in the public sector. A large number of *panista* officials have graduated from private universities, most notably the *Tecnológico de Monterrey*. Given this general background, these officials tend to use in government the same management principles they did in their private practices, as will be described below. Finally, because the pool of available *panista*s to serve in public office is so small, it is commonplace for them to retain for service in their administrations those *priísta*s who have proven competency and commitment to public service, even in some key positions (treasury, public works).

Transparency, Accountability and Efficiency

Under the slogan of *honestidad y eficiencia*, *panistas* have sought to reform local government practices. In particular, they have opened up public finances to public scrutiny by publishing regularly their operating budgets and by responding to citizen inquiries. They have cleaned up the government payroll inherited from previous *priísta* administrations and fired long lists of so-called *aviadores* (people who 'fly in' to collect their paycheque without performing any duties). Similarly, they have discontinued the practice of paying the rent for (PRI) party buildings and their operating costs out of the public purse. In a variety of ways, they have modernised and streamlined government and public administration by eliminating positions, merging departments, reducing duplications and overlap, thereby seeking to 'do more with less' (Ward, 1995).

Intergovernmental Relations

Unlike *priísta* administrations which have traditionally been obliged to follow party orthodoxy and policy direction imposed from above, opposition governments, upon taking office, do not have these constraints. Indeed, they enjoy much greater political autonomy from state and federal overlords, such that they can implement the policies and programmes of their own choosing (Rodríguez, 1995). By and large, opposition governments continue to receive the share of federal monies to which they are legally entitled, but their lack of personal and party relations with the PRI and the central government results in a lower likelihood of funding for special projects (such as highways, dams, housing). In order to overcome this likely shortfall, opposition governments have aggressively pursued alternative sources of financing, namely through local taxation opportunities afforded to them under Article 115 of the Constitution and through effective collection of fees for public services (Rodríguez, forthcoming).

As far as intra-governmental relations are concerned, at the state level we have observed a greater measure of decentralisation and separation of powers, particularly between the executive and legislative branches. This is especially so in the case of Baja California, where we observed a greater degree of autonomy of the legislature even among *panista* deputies. This led to major policy amendments and checks upon the executive. Although not strictly legislative, the *cabildo*, at the municipal level, showed a similar tendency and functioned as an increasingly effective watchdog (Rodríguez and Ward, 1994b).

Partisanship and Public Policy

Arguably, *panistas* are less overtly partisan in formulating and implementing their policy agendas. They do not enjoy long-standing and closely cultivated relationships with working class communities, and have tended to be even-handed in their treatment of such areas. Instead of cultivating the grassroots, they have preferred to adopt an open door policy for citizens to make their demands. Nevertheless, *panista* administrations do appear to privilege certain constituencies through various day-to-day policies (garbage collection, removal of street vendors, security, street lighting), all of which overwhelmingly favour the middle classes. However, it is also true that these are the areas of activity under the sole aegis of the municipality and do not require collaboration with higher levels of government.

Interestingly, many of these principles of government have not automatically been jettisoned where the PRI has won back the municipal presidency. Often, the incoming PRI government picked up the policy agenda left by the outgoing *panista* administration and enjoyed some of the newly found political space that they had created *vis-à-vis* the centre. However, in the case studies that follow, we are not describing this reversal of fortune, but rather how the PRI has sought to recast its identity and project itself in a new light. We examine two instances of the 'New PRI' in government: at the state level in Nuevo León, and at the local level in the municipality of Monterrey, both of which have experimented with modernisation along the *panista* lines described above. We consider a state or municipal government to be representative of the New PRI if it meets the following criteria: 1) campaigns on and implements an agenda which is clearly defined and appropriate to the needs of the area; 2) delivers services in a technically rational manner; 3) administers government in an efficient and accountable manner; 4) promotes economic development in the spirit of social liberalism, and 5) decentralises and democratises the governmental decision-making process.

SOCRATES RIZZO AND THE PRI IN NUEVO LEON

In the 1991 gubernatorial elections in Nuevo León, Sócrates Rizzo García, a career PRI party official and the Monterrey mayor from 1988 to 1991, was the party candidate. He ran a traditional PRI-style campaign on a platform that tended to be rather broad and all-encompassing, although when specific issues arose in the race Rizzo responded with more focused policy options. The only agenda item which Rizzo raised during the campaign on his own initiative was the modernisation of finances and public administration (*El Norte*, 23 June 1991 and 26 June 1991). However, once in office, Rizzo issued a more specific plan for his administration, labelled the *Pacto Nuevo León*. The plan listed seven theses which were to be the administration's goals: internationalisation of Nuevo León; decentralisation and regional development; growth with order; improvement of the quality of life; security and justice; modernisation of finances and public administration, and democracy and Solidarity (Rizzo, 1992a).

While the ideas and goals themselves are rather broad, their meaning is spelled out in more detail in the document. Our analysis of the Rizzo administration will focus on these goals, grouped into four categories: modernisation, technical rationality of service delivery, democratisation, and economic development. As will be discussed later in the Monterrey case study, progress made in these four areas at the state level has created an environment conducive to reform at the municipal level.

Modernisation of Public Administration and Finances

Governor Rizzo has set out to professionalise the 'industry' of public administration during his term (1991-7). One indication of this trend is the utilisation of Edward Deming's system of Total Quality Management, a management philosophy which seeks to decentralise administrative controls and encourage all employees toward quality performance. Rizzo has sought to delineate clearly the lines of authority and areas of responsibility of the various Ministries and reduce the number who report directly to the governor. Additionally, he has sought to reduce personnel and to improve and give greater transparency to the salaries of public servants.

The computerisation of offices and services is a major component of Governor Rizzo's strategy to modernise public administration. Since 1991, the number of computers in use for the *Dirección de Informática* has increased over 100 per cent. While in 1991 there were only 227 computers, by February 1993 there were 480 (Rizzo, 1993: Anexos). In addition, the extent of computer training and general employee 'quality' training provided, as well as the number of participants in these training sessions, has increased. Similar advances are observable in the area of public finances.

By 1991, Nuevo León had accumulated a sizable public debt that would require the new governor's immediate attention. In the first five months of his term, Rizzo's administration developed a two-tier plan to negotiate the terms of the debt. In the first stage, the administration renegotiated the public debt payment strategy, consolidated loans and decreased the debt interest rates. This resulted in a 26 per cent decrease in debt service. The second phase entailed consolidation of the Metro construction and debt development of a financing plan for the Monterrey-Cadereyta highway, based on revenue anticipation notes from the highway's tolls. The savings generated by these changes permitted the government to free up 105 billion pesos for the general budget (Rizzo, 1992b). In Rizzo's *Segundo Informe*, he proposed to create a *Ley de Administración y Planeación Financiera* to regulate the debt and to establish clear laws for state financing of projects (Rizzo, 1993).

The urgent need for more modern public and fiscal administration was illustrated by the ISSTELEON crisis in late 1993. The pension fund for state workers and teachers went bankrupt due to problems which began under the administration of Governor Jorge Treviño, Rizzo's predecessor. Teachers went on strike and occupied the Macro Plaza in front of the Government Palace for weeks, and schools were closed during that time. Rizzo managed to avoid the conflict, until on 1 December 1993, an agreement was finally reached to revise the law within 60 days. The new law was eventually passed without PAN support.

Technical Rationality of Service Delivery

Traditionally, decisions regarding service delivery in Mexico have often been linked to the corporatist sectors of the PRI and other political and electoral considerations. In contrast, the Rizzo administration appears to be moving towards a more technically rational decision-making process. When decisions are made according to technical rationality criteria, this means, essentially, that decisions are based on the rational and technical evaluation of the needs of the community, rather than on political motivations (Gilbert and Ward, 1985). Governor Rizzo began moving in that direction through the *Plan Estratégico 1994-2020*, a plan which summarises the state government's efforts to analyse problems and challenges in the area of urban development, as well as to design an appropriate strategy. Rizzo has received great praise for including municipal governments and other interested parties in the development of this document, which illustrates his commitment to decentralisation and regional development – an observation which also emerged strongly from our research in Baja California. Altogether, Governor Rizzo has focused on several major modernisation and enhancement projects designed to improve services and the quality of life for the citizens of Nuevo León (Rizzo, 1993).

Included in the administration's efforts are issues of water and sanitation, traffic and transportation, and housing. For example, to address the region's chronic water problems, the Rizzo administration created the *Sistema Estatal de Agua Potable y Saneamiento*, which is charged with creating a strategy to effectively treat, ration and deliver water. The largest project is *El Cuchillo-Solidaridad* on the San Juan river, which includes a dam, a treatment plant and an electrical power plant (Rizzo, 1993). To deal with increased traffic congestion, the *Programa de Vialidad Alterna* was created in cooperation with the municipality of Monterrey. The mission of the programme was to build 16 vehicular and eight pedestrian bridges that would increase 'transversal circulation' during the period of construction (Rizzo, 1993). Governor Rizzo also created the *Programa Vial Metropolitano* (PROVIMET XXI), which will supervise the construction of a beltway around the metropolitan area that will directly benefit the people of the municipalities of San Pedro, Guadalupe, Monterrey and San Nicolás as well as facilitate easy access between the rest of the area's municipalities (Rizzo, 1993).

The Rizzo administration has taken several steps to increase public security in Nuevo León, including both criminal justice and preventive approaches. Police salaries, benefits and training have grown (Rizzo, 1993: Anexos). The administration has also increased the number of surveillance vehicles by 38 per cent, as well as police equipment (including high-tech radio communications and video equipment). It has also created 24-hour 'security corridors' within Monterrey to protect commercial and tourist districts. In recognition of an increase in the number of juvenile delinquents, laws have been changed to require more severe punishment for juveniles (Rizzo, 1993).

Democratisation

A critical element of the New PRI is the advances made toward democratisation. In general, the trend in Nuevo León has been towards increased democracy, not only within the party itself, but also in the electoral process and in governance. While the primary focus of our analysis is on the PRI in government, changes in the other two areas deserve mention.

First, the PRI in Nuevo León has made several internal reforms, including the liberalisation of the candidate selection process. The state party has experimented with a number of techniques, such as internal elections and consultation with the base membership of the party (interview with local priísta deputy César Lucio Coronado Hinojosa). Second, the electoral environment in Nuevo León has become more open. The 1991 race for governor was described as competitive and transparent, with few irregularities reported. The PAN did not protest its defeat, but rather accepted it as fact. This is a striking contrast with the allegations of fraud committed by the PRI and the massive protests that took place after Jorge Treviño's 1985 gubernatorial victory (Guadarrama, 1987). In 1991, Rizzo won 60 per cent of the vote, followed by the PAN's Rogelio Sada with 31.5 per cent. The conduct of this election, to a large extent, helped to restore credibility in the electoral system of Nuevo León (GEA Político, 1991).

It is in this more open political environment that the party in government appears to be moving towards more democratic procedures. Both PRI and PAN officials interviewed said that Governor Rizzo is more open than his predecessors and that relations between the governor and the mayors of *panista* municipalities are cordial.[1] For example, when Rizzo presented his second *Informe de Gobierno*, it was the first time that the opposition was allowed to make an official response to the governor's annual statement; also, the Rizzo administration provided them with a copy of the *Informe* in advance, allowing them ample time to prepare a formal response.

But perhaps the most important sign of democratisation by the party in government was the passage of a new State Electoral Law in October 1993.

---

1 Interviews with José Armando Jasso and Antonio Elosúa Muguerza (local PAN deputies), César Lucio Coronado Hinojosa (local PRI deputy) and Alfonso Garza Junco (Subsecretary for Housing, Léon state).

Rizzo stated that reforming the law was a necessary part of establishing a new political culture in the state and, as Antonio Elosúa Muguerza, the PAN leader in the state legislature, said, the law shows a 'new willingness' on the part of the government to make reforms (*Estrategias del Pacto Nuevo León*, 1992). Major provisions of the law include the establishment of independent Citizens Commissions to monitor the elections and require financial disclosure by political parties. Each of these provisions was expected to make the electoral environment more hospitable to competition and the party in government more accountable (*El Norte* 30 October 1993:1). We will discuss below how this new law was put into practice in the 1994 election.

The relationship of the PRI government with various groups in society has also changed in recent years. The Rizzo administration wanted to establish a new political culture by 'modernising relations between the government and social groups'. It proposed to do this by increasing the dialogue with formal and informal groups such as neighbourhood associations, service clubs, business associations, and labour unions, which seems to indicate that the three-sector corporatist model is being replaced by more direct relationships with important groups in Nuevo León. Altogether, it appears that Governor Rizzo has sought to establish a climate of respect for pluralism and dialogue (Rizzo, 1992a).

Economic Development and Social Liberalism

President Salinas attempted to validate social liberalism as the new doctrine that would guide the actions of his government and of PRI governments at all levels as the party philosophy during his *sexenio* (Bailey, 1995: 175). This doctrine acknowledges the excesses of government intervention in the economy by modifying its traditional role, rejecting the dilemma of state versus market and accepting that each one of those has a distinct and uniquely important function. Consequently, the government must relinquish much of its direct participation in the economy and instead foster job creation within an economic development strategy that emphasises internationalisation and infrastructure improvement. social liberalism also attempts to provide for the basic needs of those who are not successful in the free market through PRONASOL. Although this approach was generally accepted at the highest levels of the administration, it did not hold strong appeal at lower levels of the party apparatus and failed to generate a new broad consensus. Differences in regional needs, political culture, costs associated with the macroeconomic restructuring, increased electoral competition, and the inability of the party structure to accommodate pressing social demands, have made social liberalism a hard sell as the universal ideology of the New PRI.

In Nuevo León, the Rizzo administration has promoted economic development in the spirit of social liberalism by emphasising internationalisation and infrastructure development. As an industrial base for Mexico and as a border state, Nuevo León is an important link in an increasingly global economy, and NAFTA presents Nuevo León with a unique opportunity to advance itself internationally. Moreover, internationalising the state enhances its revenue generating ability and decreases its dependence on federal allocations. In addition to hosting international business and political leaders, the Rizzo administration has been successful at recruiting new businesses into Nuevo León (Rizzo, 1993). Measures to improve the transportation infrastructure in order to increase the accessibility of Nuevo León and the metropolitan area of Monterrey have also figured in Rizzo's plan. For example, major highways linking Monterrey to the border cities of Laredo and Reynosa are nearing completion, and are expected to substantially increase the trade flow between the United States and Mexico (Rizzo, 1993).

THE PRI 'EMPANIZADO' IN MONTERREY, 1991-94

The PAN appears to have established a stronghold within the metropolitan area of Monterrey, both in the rich suburbs of the municipality of San Pedro Garza García, which it won in consecutive elections since 1988, as well as in other nearby municipalities. Although the PRI managed to retain control over the central municipality of Monterrey itself, even here the PAN was edging closer to victory. This threat to the PRI in the very heart of the state capital helps to contextualise why, unlike at the state level, local elections in Monterrey have tended to be hotly contested and controversial. When (now governor) Sócrates Rizzo won the municipal presidency in 1988 with 65.3 per cent of the vote, his *panista* opponent, María Teresa García de Madero, strongly alleged fraud (*El Norte*, 13 November 1991: B1). She later became a city councillor (1991-4), but commented retrospectively of her defeat to Rizzo: 'I won. He got the job'. In the 1991 elections a local businessman, Benjamín Clariond, won the election with 58.4 per cent of the vote, but these elections were also marred with controversy (*El Norte*, 13 November 1991: B1). His adversary, former PAN gubernatorial candidate Gerardo Garza Sada, was not as magnanimous in his defeat this time and sought nullification of the result. *Inter alia*, the PAN complained of orchestration of the vote on election day and of campaigning within 72 hours of the election itself. Nonetheless, the State Electoral Commission declared Clariond the official winner three days after the election (*El Norte* 12 November 1991: B2).

At the time, the selection of Benjamín Clariond appears to have been an astute move to counteract the strong candidacy of Garza Sada. Clariond did not fit the traditional PRI mould. A successful businessman from a well known family empire, he had little militancy in PRI politics before being invited by his former schoolboy acquaintance and later president, Carlos Salinas, to run for federal deputy for the 1st District of Nuevo León (Monterrey). He was imposed over the heads of the local PRI party leaders and, as such, owed them no allegiance. Nor did he owe allegiance to the recently inaugurated governor, Sócrates Rizzo, who ordinarily might have hoped to have someone in city hall who was loyal to him personally or, at the very least, someone chosen with his blessing.

Thus, he was able to break with precedent and exercise considerable autonomy in his election campaign, which was innovative insofar as it actually presented a concrete municipal policy agenda. Clariond appeared in early October editions of *El Norte* saying he would improve water, lighting and garbage collection, and restrict the number of street vendors (*vendedores ambulantes)*, from the city streets. These pronouncements were incorporated into his *Plan Monterrey 1992-94* campaign speech to CANACINTRA executives; *El Norte* quoted him the following day: 'The goals and objectives are to achieve social justice within our community, in the form of equality of security and opportunity, that is, everyone united and progressing in society, and to develop greater efficiency in municipal public administration through the *Plan Monterrey*, Solidarity, and the budget, in order to achieve an integrated development of Monterrey' (25 October 1991: B1, authors' translation).

In response, Garza Sada stated in the same edition that he would eliminate the 2000 *aviadores* that existed on the city payroll. Although Clariond could not follow suit and make a similar denouncement for fear of embarrassing his predecessor and recently elected governor, Sócrates Rizzo, the elimination of such positions would come to be one of Clariond's key accomplishments in modernising the Monterrey government, as we shall observe below. Moreover, he was not shy about adopting a number of his *panista* competitor's proposals, both during his campaign and in his list of priorities once in office. When we interviewed him in January 1994, he jokingly admitted that 'we stole their agenda'. Although a member of the PRI, he was far from being a 'PRI man' or a militant of the party. Indeed, some have suggested that he was in reality a *panista* in *priísta* clothing – *un PRIísta emPANizado.*[2]

2 In cooking, to *empanizar* is to coat with a light breaded batter before cooking. Bread, in Spanish, is *pan*; hence *empanizar* is used here in a double meaning to give *emPANizado*.

Once in office, Clariond put his promises into practice by systematically implementing the agenda on which he had campaigned. The following section briefly explores that agenda in four areas: modernisation of public administration; the restructuring of public finances; technical rationality of municipal service delivery, and the democratisation of city governance. As will be observed, these patterns of government bear a close resemblance to those we identified earlier in our assessment of the state level. In both cases these are increasingly being adopted by the New PRI in an attempt to raise its level of credibility in local elections. Although we do not discuss them here, Clariond's government priorities and manner of governance were virtually indistinguishable from those of the *panista* municipal president in neighbouring San Pedro Garza García.

Modernisation of Public Administration

Upon taking office, Benjamín Clariond immediately began the process of streamlining and modernising the municipal government, a process he described as 'housecleaning'. In the first days of January 1992, this included informing the labour unions that he was about to implement a new contract with the municipal workers' union which eliminated many unnecessary positions, increased the work week from 35 to 40 hours, and provided higher salaries for city employees. He also set out to improve the records system for municipal personnel, since he had found that only 20 per cent of municipal employees had a file in the city's records; not surprisingly, this created havoc with retirement schedules and pensions, given that the city often had no record of an employee's tenure. Moreover, the government frequently could not determine the exact job function of those receiving paycheques. By December of 1993, the personnel filing system had been completely updated and compiled into a computer database, showing around 7000 people on the city's payroll and all positions properly accounted for. Clariond also created a centralised Solidarity office within the city government, equipped with high-tech presentation equipment that would help the city gain leverage to win PRONASOL support.

Similar to the state level, computerisation was adopted throughout the municipal government. This included the purchase of sophisticated technology to prevent the counterfeiting of official documents, such as drivers licenses and car registrations. The Urban Development department increased its use of computerised imaging of development site plans. Overall, by the beginning of its third year in office, the administration was using approximately 150 computer terminals, compared to a single machine during the previous municipal administration (Rizzo's).

Traditionally, *priísta* mayors have recruited personnel for important municipal positions on the basis of party affiliation. As noted earlier, one of the characteristics of the New PRI is a trend toward recruitment based on the personal and professional qualifications of the candidate. Clariond seems to have reduced the role of partisanship in the selection of personnel for top positions within the municipal administration. Two department heads we spoke with mentioned that they did not consider themselves to be affiliated with the PRI. Whatever their party affiliation, most of the appointees appear to have been hired primarily on the basis of their professional qualifications. For example, the city's Secretary of Urban Development and Ecology was a successful architect who worked for CEMEX (*Cementos Mexicanos*) and taught at the *Tecnológico de Monterrey* for many years, who claimed to care little for politics and certainly did not consider himself a PRI militant. A new city treasurer was hired in July 1992 when her predecessor moved across to a senior position in the state government, and although Mayor Clariond did not know her personally, he hired her solely on the recommendations of members of the city council for her extensive experience as a public accountant both in the private sector and with the Treasury in Mexico City.

These examples of professional hiring policy notwithstanding, it appears that certain positions within the administration remain the preserve of seasoned politicians with a strong sense of party loyalty. One example is César Lazo Hinojosa, the Secretary of Public Works who was himself a former mayor of Monterrey (1967-69) and a former state deputy. He also directed the Popular Sector of the PRI in Nuevo León and, according to one PRI council member, his placement in Public Works ensured the fulfilment of the party's social commitment to the underclass. But as *panista* councillor García de Madero stated, Lazo is both a skilled engineer as well as a skilled politician and, according to her, did an excellent job. Once again, it appears that competence was probably more important than political loyalty and connections.

Restructuring Public Finance

In another New PRI initiative, Mayor Clariond sought to make the local government more financially independent from higher levels of authority by taking greater advantage of the provisions of Article 115, specifically those which allow municipal governments to raise their own revenues in order to fund normal operating expenses. Historically, the federal government in Mexico has controlled about 85 per cent of public revenues, the state governments less than twelve per cent and the municipal governments scarcely three per cent of the total. The average municipality depends on the state and federal governments for about 80 per cent of its income (*participaciones*); only 20 per cent usually comes from local sources (Rodríguez, 1995).

In 1990, Monterrey received the equivalent of 94.8 million new pesos in federal revenue sharing (*participaciones*). This increased to 149 million in 1993 – an increase of ten per cent in real terms – which suggests that Monterrey was neither punished nor rewarded financially by state authorities during the early 1990s. On the other hand, Clariond was successful in raising the total amount derived from city-based incomes (*ingresos propios*). During the last year of the Rizzo municipal presidency, internal (city) revenues constituted 41 per cent of a total budget of 163 million pesos. This increased to 58 per cent of the total budget of 413.4 million pesos under Clariond, constituting a 151 per cent increase in real terms. The two main sources of additional tax revenues came from the *Impuesto Predial* and from the *Impuesto Sobre Adquisición de Inmuebles* (ISAI).[3] On the *impuesto predial* alone, revenues increased by 378 per cent in real terms over the second year of the Rizzo administration. Moreover, initiatives were taken to expedite collection, including a ten per cent discount for full payment by February 15 of the year (rather than in bi-monthly instalments), by doubling the number of collection booths throughout the city and by allowing the tax to be paid at local banks. The ISAI tax on the sale of real estate was further reduced from eight per cent in 1991 to two per cent in 1994 in order to free up the property market and to encourage additional revenue collection, which despite the lowering in percentage terms, showed a 70 per cent increase in real terms between 1990 and 1993.

Moreover, the year-end financial results were published in local newspapers such as *El Norte*, and were much more detailed than ever before. This greater transparency appears to be a part of the better working relations Clariond established with the PAN council members (see below) and of the administration's willingness to incorporate some of their suggestions in the *Informe Financiero*. Another first was for the city's books to be audited by the state's *Contaduría Mayor de Hacienda.*

The Technical Rationality of Service Delivery

A litmus test for the New PRI is the extent to which it is less partisan and more technically rational in its delivery of municipal services. The Clariond administration took this approach in providing services to the people of Monterrey. For example, in order to monitor complaints, a telephone 'hot line' called *Quejatel* was set up and the distribution of complaints was

3 These are roughly equivalent to rates and land purchase tax in Britain.

published in the widely respected newspaper *El Norte*. In January 1994 the administration received 529 calls to complain about telephone service problems or deficiencies (6.8 per cent), lighting (27.2 per cent), road maintenance and pavement (22.1 per cent) and water services (3.5 per cent).

In the arena of water and drainage, Clariond tapped into PRONASOL funds in order to increase provision. When he took office in January 1992, 26 000 homes in Monterrey's *colonias* were without water and sewage; by the end of 1993, 91 per cent of those homes had received water and drainage services and the remainder of the homes were scheduled for 1994 (Clariond, 1993). Nearly all of these projects, as well as *El Cuchillo* dam mentioned earlier, have been funded by PRONASOL. With two long-time PRI *colonia* leaders included on the council in order to maintain direct contact with the people of the *colonias*, PRONASOL was a key source of financing, accounting for 116 million pesos – an additional 73 per cent over municipal funding put into public works (Monterrey, 1992; *El Norte*, January 1992 and January 1994). While some of these projects appear to have been targeted at Monterrey's *colonias* by PRONASOL in order to maintain electoral support for the PRI in these neighbourhoods, even here the administration prioritised those neighbourhoods which had gone without such services longest.

Finally, and following the state government's lead, another area of concern has been to upgrade the city's infrastructure in order to develop its status as an international centre of commerce and tourism. Clariond increased municipal spending on public improvement projects from 24 per cent of total expenditure under Rizzo in 1990 to 33 per cent in 1993, a 140 per cent increase in real terms (Monterrey, 1990 and 1993; Clariond, 1993). These investments were primarily directed at street paving, measures to relieve traffic congestion, improved rain drainage, and the remodelling and improvement of public buildings.

Democratisation

The Clariond administration attempted to foster a more democratic structure of governance by improving relations with the city council (*cabildo*), and by making the functions of government generally more open and accountable to the public and to other levels of government. Specifically, the *panista regidores* (councillors) had opposed several of the initiatives that he proposed; in his *Informe de Gobierno* Clariond explained what their objections had been and why he and the PRI *regidores* had proceeded regardless, paralleling Governor Rizzo's decision to allow the opposition in the state congress to prepare an official response to his second *Informe de Gobierno* in 1993. Greater tolerance and respect for political opposition appeared to be a clear priority for state and local governments under the New PRI in Nuevo León.

Certainly there were several areas where the *panista regidores* were successful in getting their way: the payroll lists was one such area, and they applauded Clariond's cutting of the *aviadores*. One issue upon which they had him on the ropes was when in June and July 1992 he purchased garbage trucks and equipment from *Camiones y Tractocamiones S.A.*, a business which was connected to his family. The *panista regidores* claimed that this contravened the Law of Responsibilities for Public Functionaries, and after meeting in special session unanimously admonished him but resolved to let the contract stand due to the high cost that would be incurred were it to be broken and the vehicles replaced. In fact, even the opposition *regidores* interviewed by the authors admitted that Clariond had obtained the best possible price for the trucks, but it was a matter of principle that he had not declared it was a family interest. However, when he was later accused by the president of the *Colegio de Abogados* of Monterrey of purchasing printing services for the municipality through a firm in which it was claimed he held a 50 per cent share of company stock, the council gave him a unanimous vote of confidence, citing documentation that he had sold his interest in the company in March 1991. This activation of the *cabildo* is another indication of recent attempts to revitalise the process of local government and to involve greater active participation of city councillors, even though this may reduce the autonomy of the municipality's executive offices and, as in these cases, may create political and personal difficulties for the incumbent.

Unlike many of his *priísta* municipal president counterparts, Clariond did not treat the unions with kid gloves. As part of his two-pronged strategy of improved basic services, and in order to foster economic development and tourism, upon taking office he immediately instructed municipal inspectors to permanently remove the street vendors who had occupied the Macro Plaza in central Monterrey. These 217 vendors were affiliated with the *Confederación de Trabajadores de México* (CTM) and a moderately radical *Tierra y Libertad* urban social movement. Although Clariond's action touched off a heated conflict with the workers' unions, he refused to back down and managed to secure the unanimous backing of the council, as well as other support from among the general citizenry and from business organisations such as CANACO de Monterrey. Ultimately, after lengthy negotiations with CTM leaders, Clariond agreed to sell monthly permits to street vendors, the proceeds of which would be used to help finance a new market where they would eventually be relocated. Until such time, however, they would have to do business in downtown streets outside the Macro Plaza.

Although Clariond's particular style of administration sometimes caused political headaches, overall he seems to have made more friends than enemies and was quite successful in modernising, democratising and making more rational the municipal government's administrative structure and delivery of services. In January 1994, *El Norte* gave his administration a rating of 7.85 out of 10 and 72 per cent of surveyed respondents believed that Clariond had done a good job. His programme represents a good example of the sort of programme that the New PRI must contemplate if it is to be successful in confronting the challenges of managing a city the size of Monterrey. That he was able to achieve so much probably relates to his relative autonomy of the party apparatus and orthodoxy; his independence of the governor to whom he owed no loyalty and had no reason to seek to please; his high personal standing among the powerful business community and middle class, and, one should not forget, his good contacts with President Salinas, which were crucial in his gaining access to PRONASOL funding. Also important were the priorities he chose to adopt and the manner in which he implemented them which, we suggest, resembled much more closely the *panista* agenda than that traditionally associated with the PRI.

THE NEW PRI IN NUEVO LEON AND MONTERREY: A FAILED EXPERIMENT?

Thus far in this essay we have described the emergence of the New PRI in state and local government. Our argument is that this evolution is in response to a) the need to modernise an anachronistic structure, and b) the need to rise to the electoral imperatives of the day in order to win the vote fairly. However, recent evidence suggests that this revamping of the PRI is not having the expected results. As noted above, the PAN has always had an important presence in Nuevo León (particularly in the Monterrey area) and has mounted a dramatic challenge during the Salinas presidency. Among an expanded electorate which almost doubled between 1991 and 1994, the PAN quadrupled its vote statewide, while the PRI's vote barely doubled (IFE, 1994a; 1994b). In the 1991 senatorial and congressional election, the PRI's margin over the PAN was approximately 69 per cent to 26 per cent. By 1994, this had narrowed to 48:40, and in the presidential elections the result was almost identical. In 1994, the PAN won 2 out of the 11 federal deputyships outright (IFE, 1994b).

Nuevo León was one of the few states in which local elections also took place on 21 August. For the PAN, locally, the results were even more dramatic. In the state Congress the PAN now holds a majority, and in the municipal elections it won six out of 51 municipalities, adding three to the three that it already held in the Monterrey area (San Pedro, San Nicolás and Santa Catarina). Most dramatically of all, it 'won' the city of Monterrey itself, which means that 82 per cent of the state's population of just over three million is now governed by the PAN. In the Monterrey election, the results initially disclosed by the *Comisión Municipal Electoral* (CME) showed that the PRI's candidate, Jorge Manjarrez, polled 233 461 votes, compared to 227 331 for the PAN's candidate, Jesús Hinojosa – a victory of approximately 7000 votes. Despite the fact that the PAN contested some of the precinct results, the review of the CME and the electoral tribunal confirmed the PRI's victory and, on 28 August, Manjarrez received his *constancia de mayoría*. Several weeks of behind the scenes negotiations (mostly in Mexico City) followed and on the 21 September, in the no-recourse-to-appeal chamber (*Sala de Segunda Instancia*), 42 of the 103 *casillas* were annulled, giving the PAN a 1200 margin of victory over the PRI. When Jesús Hinojosa took office as the new mayor of Monterrey, the PAN's grip on the area was complete.

There seems little doubt in our minds that the PRI probably won the Monterrey election and that the reversal of the electoral results was due to intense pressure from the PAN in Mexico City. Certainly it appears that the PAN was unwilling to vote in the Congress for ratification of Zedillo's victory unless it was able to win, in exchange, some concessions from the PRI. Among these concessions was the municipal presidency of Monterrey. If the Clariond administration had been as impressive and popular as we have argued, why did the PRI not win with an overwhelming, uncontestable margin? How can one explain the apparent paradox between our assessment of the New PRI's achievements in Monterrey and the electoral results? If the New PRI governed so well, why was this not reflected in the election? These were questions we asked ourselves and put to some New PRI officials, including Manjarrez. There are several reasons which help explain this apparent anomaly.

First, and one of the reasons given to us by Manjarrez, was that many PRI municipal presidents in the state had performed poorly in office relative to their PAN counterparts. Invariably they were not among the modernisers of the New PRI. Clariond was an exception. Second, and most importantly, Clariond was never really viewed as a new *priísta*. We have demonstrated how he and his programme were really *priísmo empanizado* and, even if his political trajectory was in the PRI, he was seen to be clearly *panista* in type and style. There was little apparent difference between him and his *panista* counterpart in San Pedro. Third, the candidature of Manjarrez owed much to the personal support he received from Sócrates Rizzo, under whom he had developed his career in its entirety, serving as his *Secretario Particular*, his

Secretario de Gobierno, his campaign coordinator and his *Secretario de Desarrollo Social*, among others posts, before moving to become the Secretary General and subsequently an official at the Presidency of the PRI in Nuevo León. This close relationship created certain difficulties for him. One of these was that when it came to the election, many voters were probably uneasy about Manjarrez's clear ties to Sócrates Rizzo and his militancy in the party (albeit within the new wing). But of much greater significance is the fact that Manjarrez was not the candidate of Clariond and his team; their selection was Teresa García de Madero, a *panista*, or, alternatively, Clariond's chief of public works and former mayor of Monterrey, César Lazo Hinojosa. This seems to support the idea that, ultimately, internal divisions within the PRI are what made the PRI lose. In retrospect, a Clariond look-alike would have probably generated greater support and consensus within the party and would have weakened the *panista* hand in subsequent negotiations with Mexico City.

One important implication arising from this particular case study is the uncertainty in the electorate's mind about the sustainability of the New PRI and its representatives. Given the no re-election clause in Mexico, people are likely to vote for candidates in whom they can have confidence. Voters are now voting for individuals, rather than for parties. This means that the New PRI must project effective, competent candidates if it is to win over the electorate. Moreover, it must demonstrate that there can be continuity of good government from one *priísta* administration to the next – as the *panistas* have demonstrated in San Pedro and other cities. Currently, these goals are overridden by internal divisions within the party which do not allow the PRI to showcase that they can also govern, consistently, along the lines described in this essay.

7 The PAN's Administration in Baja California: The Struggle for a Free and Sovereign State

Gustavo A. Vicencio

In 1989, for the first time in Mexico's postrevolutionary history, the victory of an opposition party in a state gubernatorial election was recognised by the regime. In Baja California Ernesto Ruffo, from the National Action Party (PAN), became the first non-*priísta* governor since 1929, when the current political system was founded. This fact would provide the first example of how power might be renegotiated between central government and the states. It would also highlight the differences between two political projects, especially in two areas; decentralisation and democratisation.

Traditionally, Mexican politics has been described as living under two kinds of rules: the written and the unwritten ones. While the Constitution of 1917 is constantly referred to in government speeches with principles like democracy, federalism, effective suffrage, a fair party system and the division of powers are verbally venerated by all the administrations, the political system has, in fact, been built with the structures of an authoritarian presidentialism and of a corporatist official party (Reyna and Weinert, 1977; Cornelius *et al.*, 1989). This has meant that the Presidency is endowed with not only legal, but paralegal and de facto powers, which allow it to overshadow the legislative and judicial branches, and to maintain a highly centralised style of governing (Carpizo, 1972; Garrido, 1989: 417-34). This situation is reinforced by the way in which the official party and the political system as a whole are structured. This has helped the *Partido Revolucionario Institutcional* (the PRI) win every single presidential election since 1929, all the governorships up to 1989 and all the Senate seats up to 1988. The PRI has never lost its majority in the Chamber of Deputies and has won an overwhelming percentage of all municipal elections.

Within this national context, the PAN's history had been referred to as 50 years of electoral opposition disappointments, especially at state and presidential levels. Because of this, the *panista* victory in 1989 gave way to hypotheses and speculation. On the one hand, it has been said that Salinas allowed the PAN to win because he needed to increase his democratic credibility, not only nationally but also at the international level, in the light of his own dubious electoral victory the previous year. Other observers alluded to murky 'under the table' negotiations between PAN and PRI, which allowed for this *panista* victory in exchange for PAN support for the national Salinas project.[1] Both assertions imply that Ruffo owes his post to Salinas and therefore 'nothing is new under the sun'. It also infers that the structures of the political system remains substantially unchanged, and that the PAN is governing thanks to and within *priísta* procedures.

The objectives of this paper are, first, to analyse the political context surrounding the PAN's victory in Baja California; second to examine how the power is being renegotiated between the state and the central government, and finally to outline the steps followed by Ruffo in his attempts to fulfil the constitutional mandate of a free and sovereign state.

THE BEGINNING

On 3 January 1989 Xicotencatl Leyva left office as governor of Baja California, nine months before the constitutional end of his term. The official version was that President Salinas had invited Leyva to join the NAFINSA (*Nacional Financiera SA*) team, working on the debt-restructuring programme. However, in reality he was sacked by Salinas because levels of corruption, nepotism and violence in the state had divided the local '*priísta* family', and had jeopardised the chances of a PRI victory in the 1989 elections (Guillén López, 1992: 147). On presidential orders, Oscar Baylón was elected as interim governor by the local Congress. His main and urgent aim was to restore peace within the PRI and deliver public services to rescue the Bajacalifornians' trust in his party before the elections of 2 July 1989. The new governor, with considerable economical help from Mexico City, was able to deliver several public services like new roads, school buildings, electrification and land property titles. Legal charges were even initiated against members of the Leyva team. However, the political structure of previous administrations remained unchanged; corruption within the *Procuraduría de Justicia* and within the judicial police was untouched, public

1 The first hypothesis was supported by Jesús Blanco Ornelas, director of the Bajacalifornian weekly newspaper *Zeta*. The second hypothesis was supported by some PRD leaders.

resources continued to be used to support *priísta* expenses and the Congress continued to act as the rubber stamp for the Governor's bills.

By the beginning of 1989 the race to become the PRI's candidate for governor had begun. Several possible candidates had emerged. 'Kicks under the table' were a common practice among *camarilla* members seeking to weaken opponents and to chalk up merits in order to be selected, *por dedazo*, by the 'great elector'. Suddenly, on 28 May, two ex-governors – Castellanos and de Lamadrid – together with some of the most powerful entrepreneurs of Tijuana and Mexicali were brought to Mexico City where President Salinas informed them that Senator Margarita Ortega would be the PRI's candidate. After their initial surprise, since no one had considered her a serious contender, they agreed with the President's 'good choice' and promised to support her, both as a candidate and as governor. Salinas committed himself to help the would-be new administration in making Baja California a 'model state'.

Although Ortega was born and had made her political career in Baja California, winning previous elections, accumulating wide administrative experience and with no particular links to any one local *camarilla*, her candidacy was seen as dubious, particularly after the PAN chose as its candidate the well known municipal president of Ensenada, Ernesto Ruffo.[2]

From the PRI's national headquarters a team of delegates, led by Luis H. Ducoing, had been sent to Baja California several months earlier to restructure the party and to implement a national strategy to win the elections. They seemed to have had little concern for the wishes of the Bajacalifornian *priístas*; for example, at the same time that President Salinas was meeting with the Baja California entrepreneurs in Mexico City, Ducoing in Mexicali was notifying the leaders of the CNC, CNOP and CTM, who the 'unveiled' (*destapado*) was. That decision taken, the next stage was to choose candidates by *dedazo* for other posts: deputies, municipal presidents and *regidores* (appointed municipal councillors). Not unexpectedly, many politicians disagreed with the process because their interests were not taken into account. The national strategy, however, was finally imposed.

In the PAN's corner, the selection of candidates followed a quite different path. For an opposition party, in a one-party dominated system, recruitment is a difficult task. An electoral campaign means that the candidates have to

2 Ruffo, as municipal president of Ensenada (1986-9) suffered humiliations and lack of economic support from Governor Leyva. Knowing this, the Ensenadenses began to back Ruffo's actions in order to increase municipal resources, overcoming the Governor's obstructions. The battle was won by the *panista* president and thus the social phenomenon called *Ruffomanía* was born.

neglect their own jobs or businesses and spend time and money without any guarantee of success. Even Ernesto Ruffo, the PAN's strongest prospect and the most popular politician in the state, denied several times that he intended to become the party's candidate for the governorship; however under pressure from the PAN leadership he accpeted the nomination (Guillén López, 1992: 163).[3] A similar predicament, but with a different outcome existed in Tijuana, where a 'good man' with no record of previous militancy and with hardly any political experience was elected as the PAN candidate to the municipal presidency due to the lack of alternative prospects.

Help from the PAN's national headquarters meant only partisan leaflets, posters, a little cash and occasional visits by federal deputies and members of the party's national executive committee (CEN). Another form of assistance, which later became crucial in obtaining the recognition of Ruffo's triumph by the federal government, was the CEN's role as a mediator between Baja California and the *Secretaría de Gobernación* (Ministry of the Interior) in Mexico City.

By the end of May an electoral poll commissioned by the local weekly newspaper *Zeta*, predicted a 'technical draw' between Ortega and Ruffo.[4] *Panista* leaders, however, taking into account the popular response to Ruffo's campaign, had no doubt of victory. Their main concerns were how to counteract the possibility of pre-electoral fraud and how to find out on election day who had won and lost, in order to obstruct any later attempt to falsify the results. The campaign had created so much interest that thousands of volunteers came forward as PAN representatives at each of the 1166 polling stations placed around the state. Hundreds more acted as observers outside the polling booths in response to a *Zeta* invitation to be an active participant in the elections and to prevent possible irregularities. Finally, a sophisticated communication system around the state was devised, which allowed the PAN to detect and successfully counteract the traditional fraudulent manoeuvres carried out by *priístas* on election day. These tricks included the non-recognition of opposition parties representatives at polling stations,

---

3 In October 1988, on the PRI's orders, an exhaustive survey, called '*Proyecto Calafia*', was carried out in Baja California. The main objective was to understand popular attitudes towards 'the current public administration, the governors succession, and the impact of federal actions in the state'. When asked about who would be the next governor, Ruffo obtained the highest percentage, 30.1 per cent of the responses. See *Zeta*, 24-31 March 1989.

4 This survey was a joint operation between *Zeta* and the newspaper *El Norte of Monterrey*. It gave 39 per cent of votes to Ortega and 35 per cent to Ruffo, with a margin of error of five per cent. See *Zeta*, 16-23 June 1989.

the violation of the right to a secret vote, the alteration of results, the pressurising of peasants and workers to vote for the PRI and so on.

The struggle between local and national authorities within the PRI was present again when, at the end of the election day, Baja California *priísta* leaders announced that 'the electoral tendency of the state is favourable to Margarita Ortega' (Valderrábano, 1990: 141). The following day, however, Luis Donaldo Colosio, the PRI's national president, publicly recognised that the tendency was favourable to the PAN's candidate. Colosio's declaration was a political earthquake. Few people could believe it and *priístas* felt themselves betrayed. Eventually, however, not without tensions between Baja California and Mexico City, between PAN and the *Secretaría de Gobernación* and between state and national PRI leadership, the outcome was as follows: the governorship, Tijuana, Ensenada and nine deputies for the PAN; Mexicali, Tecate and six deputies to the PRI; and the PARM, PFCRN, PPS and PRD received one deputy each, by proportional representation.

Once it was clear that the next administration would be a *panista* one, the incumbent Governor, Oscar Baylón, began to send bills to the Congress modifying laws in order to create problems for the new governor. For example, he increased the number of bureaucrats as well as their benefits,[5] the presentation of municipal reports before the Congress were put forward to be approved by the still *priísta* majority, he also tried to increase the repayments to the municipalities from 20 to 35 per cent of the state's budget, and finally the period of offices of judges appointed by him, and therefore committed to him, was extended by five years. Due to later negotiations in Mexico City between Ruffo and the *Secretaría de Gobernación*, the latter two maneouvres were cancelled. This legacy was complemented by a state budget deficit of nearly 20 000 million pesos, and with the removal or burning of files, especially those in *Oficialía Mayor* and Secretary of Finance.[6]

PANISTAS IN POWER

Analysing *panista* documents and speeches we can observe that the ideological issue have been a central and critical points for the Ruffo government.

5 During the Leyva period, only 75 new jobs were allowed per year, but with Baylón ten times more bureaucratic posts were created in his nine-month administration.

6 René Corella, *Oficial Mayor* (Chief of Staff), and Eugenio Elorduy, Secretary of Finance. Interviews with the author.

The first chapter, for instance, of the State Development Plan (PED) 1990-95, is dedicated entirely to describing in general terms the '*Postulados de Humanismo Político*'. Based on this ideology six main objectives were proposed in the Plan; the democratisation of the political system, the encouragements of civil society, economic promotion including redistribution of income and free competition, decentralisation for regional development, the enforcement of state sovereignty and the redevelopment and enforcement of social welfare.

As the Ruffo administration draws to a close, it is possible to conclude that important changes have been achieved in Baja California in the struggle to fulfil the PED objectives. Among those related to power structures we can identify a clear separation between government and the party in power, the revitalisation of the local Congress and the independent working of the judicial power, the reinforcement of municipal autonomy with both political and economical resources, negotiations among parties due to the lack of a hegemonic party, effective implementation of anti-corruption measures and finally a media with no illegal links to the government (Rodríguez and Ward, 1993; Guillén López, 1993).

The second aim of this paper is to analyse the problems involved in the renegotiation of relations between the centre and the state, particularly in the attempts of the Ruffo administration to achieve fiscal autonomy and a democratisation of the local political system.

THE STRUGGLE FOR FISCAL FEDERALISM

Without doubt, the most critical issue upon which to evaluate the autonomy of any state with respect to the central government is finance. In 1989 President Salinas stated:

> Modernisation means healthy public finances in order to give constant attention to welfare expenses. For that reason, it is essential to strengthen the administrative structures of collection in municipalities and states... Modernisation means states with stronger finances, more competent, more responsive to the necessities of their people and to their aspirations...(cited in Elorduy, 1991: 2; author's translation).

This declaration of presidential sympathy for strengthening local government looked promising, but three years later Governor Ruffo claimed that little, if anything, had changed:

> We have always complained about centralism in Mexico. I believe that the clearest evidence of centralism is the budget, and it is centralised (Konrad Adenauer Foundation, Interview with Ernesto Ruffo 1992).

The story of the fiscal issue goes back to 1973 when the *Ley de Coordinación Fiscal* (LCF) was created to legislate an agreement between the federal government and each state to simplify the existing great diversity of taxes charged by local governments.[7] People throughout the country had been paying several local and federal taxes. The LCF, through its establishment of the *Impuesto Sobre los Ingresos Mercantiles* (ISIM; equivalent to a trade tax), allowed the states to make one charge only, 51 per cent of the total to be remitted to the federation and 49 per cent to remain in each state. In 1980 the ISIM was eliminated when the new fiscal law created the Value Added Tax (IVA). Henceforth duties would be collected by the federation, but with a claim that there should be no detriment to the various states levels of funding. It was decided moreover to establish a General Fund of Repayments, which would be distributed among the states, and which represented 13 per cent of the total federal collection. In a second period, from 1984 to 1987, the law was modified, creating a mathematical formula to reward those states which exceeded the projected collecting goals; a bonus for their work and effort. During a third period, from 1988 to 1989, the law was changed again, the federal government established a fixed base of 17.36 per cent of the total payments for distribution to the states, thereby eliminating rewards for collection efficiency. From 1990 that percentage was increased to 18.26 but with a new distributing formula: 91.58 per cent to be delivered according to the amount collected and 8.42 per cent in an inverse proportion of per capita income, so the lower the per capita income the greater the federal grant.

In short, since the IVA was born, state governments have seen the erosion of their fiscal powers in favour of the central administration. As a result, at present, 81 centavos of each peso collected remain in federal hands, 16 centavos go to the states and only three centavos are distributed among the municipalities.[8] Another consequence of the Fiscal Coordination Law is that local treasurers or secretaries of finance do not know how much money is collected via taxes in their own territories, because the federal government which receives those funds has no legal obligation to notify them. Since they do not know how much was collected initially, they are also unable to judge

7 Cesar Coll in *La Nación,* 18 November 1991; Eugenio Elorduy in *La Nación*, 4 May 1992.

8 *Boletín Estatal*, Government of Baja California, 30 June 1993.

whether the amount repaid to the states is correct or not. In fact they have to accept it – trusting in the good faith of the central government.

In the case of Baja California, the Ruffo administration has pointed out to the federal government the need to replace the centralised fiscal structure with a new one, in which each state has greater responsibility and knowledge of the taxes collected within their boundaries. Such a reform is designed, on the one hand, to fulfil the constitutional mandate of 'free and sovereign states' and, on the other hand, to make Salinas' open commitment to modernisation and fiscal decentralisation come true. For example, the Baja California Secretary of Finance has proposed a decrease in the IVA rate proportional to the amount currently remitted back to the states. Each state could then charge its own local taxes without harming people's disposable income. He has also suggested that the integral administration of IVA and other duties should be in Baja California's hands, that businesses or enterprises operating in the state but with headquarters outside should inform the Secretary of Finance of their activities which would then be subject to IVA and that there should be a return to the system of rewards for the fulfilment of tax-collecting goals.

In other words, the *panista* government has demanded, with no success thus far, that the distributive pyramid has to be inverted, there should be more money to municipalities and states, collected by themselves, and less to the centre. The Ruffo administration's main success was the signing of an agreement with the *Secretaría de Hacienda y Crédito Público* (SHCP) which required that the Baja California government should be informed about the amount of IVA collected in that state, thus becoming the only local administration to gain access to this powerful information (Guillén López, 1993: 93).

Latterly, the Baja California-Federation relationship has been troubled by two concrete issues.[9] First, since the IVA Law was created in 1980 the state has been receiving less money in repayments from the federation than it received under the former system (ISIM). Second, what Baja California receives from the central government through repayments and federal expenses is an unfair fraction of what the federation collects.

Ruffo's collaborators reached these conclusions taking into account tax data from 1987, a year chosen because the information is available. SHCP authorities, however, have insisted – with the same data – that in both cases Baja California has been privileged above other states; up to 21.4 per cent better off with the new IVA and it receives up to 13.5 per cent more from

9 The following paragraphs are based upon *Secretaría de Finanzas de Baja California*, 1993; *Diario*, 29 June 1993 and *Boletín Estatal*, 30 June 1993.

central government. Although since 1991 several meetings had been held to unify criteria, no agreement has been reached. When negotiations became stuck, Ruffo proposed the intervention of an independent third party to arbitrate. On 22 April 1993 in the presence of Fernando Gutiérrez (the Secretary of *Gobernación*), Governor Ruffo and Pedro Aspe (the Secretary of *Hacienda*) agreed to resolve their differences through an 'Arbitration Group' selected by the governor. During the following weeks both sides handed over their respective files and computer tapes, and held regular meetings with the Group. On 2 June their preliminary conclusions were published. The Bajacalifornian governor was surprised when the Group concluded that the SHCP was right. Given that this assertion was supported by the evidence of the federal computer tapes, Ruffo asked for a copy in order to check them against the state's records. After some obstacles were overcome the federal computer files were delivered, but minus the password, 'by superior orders'. Personnel of the computing department had to wait twenty four hours until they got access to the information, where substantial differences between the SHCP's and Baja California's figures were found. With respect to the first issue (ISIM versus IVA), the central government had registered 26 435 taxpayers, while Baja California had registered 28 603. However 4851 of the official list were reported as zeros – meaning that they paid no IVA – while the Baja California files reported IVA payments.

On 6 June a meeting with the Arbitration Group was held in Mexicali in order to report its findings. To be sure about the veracity of the information, state authorities suggested checking both computer tapes against the 28 603 taxpayers physical statements kept in the Secretary of Finance. Nevertheless, the following day SHCP delivered a revised and final computer tape with only 21 584 reported statements; data which was imposed as 'the only one' for use by the Group. The final verdict repeated the earlier conclusion in favour of SHCP.

With regards the issue of central government funding, local authorities discovered that various taxes collected by the federation in Baja California

Table 7.1: Comparison of figures on Taxpayers and Tax Paid in BC

	No. of Taxpayers	Amount Paid
SHCP	21 584	5 833.2
Government of BC	28 603	7 725.3
Difference	7 019	1 892.1

Source: *Boletín Estatal Baja California* No. 31

Note: Figures in thousands of millions of pesos

(in agricultural activities, education, enterprise branches, imports, petrol, and others) had not been taken into account when determining whether the proportion of Baja California's taxes devoted to repayment. Governor Ruffo pointed out these irregularities to President Salinas and insisted that: a) if the physical verification had been carried out it would have proved that 7019 taxpayers were omitted, and b) if the tax data eliminated by SHCP were included, Baja California's generated income would reach 201 000 million pesos. Consequently, the repayment to Baja California (160 000 million pesos) would be short by 20 per cent. On 26 June, the last meeting was held, where SHCP ratified its position, and Baja Californian authorities considered it useless to present more arguments.

With no agreement reached between local and federal executives, Ruffo's next move was to report to the state Congress. On 22 July he and his collaborators spent nearly five hours answering the deputies' queries. The Congress proposed a change of strategy including a possible appeal before the Supreme Court of Justice in order to get Baja California the fair repayment for its tax contribution to the federation. In any case it was the Congress's turn to decide the next stage.

THE ELECTORAL ISSUE

Constitutionally a free and sovereign state on the political arena means strong institutions, led by authorities democratically elected and then given legitimacy from the bottom. However, the unwritten rules of the Mexican political system have determined an inverse way to choose rulers, from top to bottom, designed and, in many cases, removed by the 'superior elector'.[10] This practice has been reinforced by the PRI-government duo that has controlled the electoral processes at both federal and local levels since 1929. The PRI, as the official party, not only employs illegal resources from public treasuries but maintains control of the electoral organisms such as the Federal and Local Electoral Commissions (CFE and CEE), the Federal and Local Electoral Registers (RFE and REE), and the Municipal and District Electoral Committees (CME and CDE). Another weapon is its invariable majority in local and federal Electoral Colleges. Within that context critical local decisions are not generally taken by local authorities, but by central ones, who seek not the best solution for states or municipalities but the well-being of the political system.

10 During the Salinas *sexenio*, 17 governors were removed on presidential orders.

Thus, when an opposition party wins an election at any level and its achievement is recognised by electoral authorities, it is because: a) the party and its candidates achieved enough popularity to overwhelm the PRI's real votes and its possible tricks; b) the party was able to find out the real results and to get proofs of its triumph, and finally c) in the prevailing local, national and in some cases international conditions, the recognition of an electoral defeat by the PRI meant less political cost than a fraudulent victory. Taking into account those elements it is possible to evaluate the PAN's triumph in 1989.

A somewhat different scenario was set up during 1992 in Baja California when elections to renew municipal authorities and the local Congress were held. For the first time in Mexico's postrevolutionary history the process was organised and controlled by a non-*priísta* bureaucracy. The outcome of this new experience would have a national impact, showing the ability or inability of an opposition force to fulfil the constitutional mandate of 'effective suffrage'. Given that the 1989 elections were carried out with a law dating from 1976, that according to the *panistas* did not guarantee fair elections, Governor Ruffo convened an open assembly in order to achieve popular consensus for a bill modifying the local Constitution and thus creating a new electoral law. In October 1991, the bill was presented at the Chamber of Deputies containing the following changes: more guarantees to the political parties throughout the whole electoral process; the right to use the media by all the parties; creation of an autonomous electoral court and, consequently, the abolition of the Electoral College; an increase in the number of deputies and municipal *regidores* (appointed municipal councillors); and the recognition that the electoral process is a state function in which the executive, the legislative, the political parties and the citizens are jointly responsible (Ruffo, 1992). The proposal, however, was unsuccessful because the main opposition party, the PRI, voted against it, and the PAN could not obtain the support of four more deputies from the other parties to reach the two thirds of the votes needed to modify the Constitution.

Despite the defeat, Governor Ruffo still had the option of proposing changes in the electoral law – which only needed a simple majority to pass – rather than attempt constitutional amendments again. In February 1992, new guarantees were voted through by the deputies, among them regulations for public debates – on radio and television – by candidates from all the parties; clearer procedures for the use of public finance; the introduction of random methods to designate the officials at polling stations; the inclusion of electoral crimes in the Baja California Penal Law; and the creation of a local electoral card with the voters photograph and other security measures to prevent its fraudulent use.

After its own experience in opposition, the PAN's priority was to produce a trustworthy electoral roll with non-falsifiable voting cards. Local authorities asked the federation for both the lists and the cards. On 5 April, 1991 an agreement was signed stating that the basic electoral roll data would be given by the federation, but cards with the voter's photograph would be Baja California's responsibility.

Another crucial event at the beginning of the 1992 was the foundation of the Local Electoral Commission, which would be totally in charge of the election. By law the Commission had to be made up by representatives of the state and municipal executives, the legislative and each political party. Thus, the 15 seats were occupied as follows: the PAN six (the CEE president and secretary, one deputy, Tijuana and Ensenada representatives and the party representative); the PRI four (one deputy, Mexicali and Tecate representatives and the party representative); the PRD two (one deputy and the party representative); the PPS, the PFCRN and the PARM one seat each. This meant that a unified opposition could be in control of the CEE, something unthinkable at federal level.

The first task for the Local Electoral Commission (CEE) and the Local Electoral Register (REE) was to organise the *photocredentialización* process.[11] The estimated total number of citizens in Baja California was 1 042 000, but the electoral rolls contained only 993 405. The electoral authorities had a six month period (from January to June 1992) to fulfil two goals; to issue and supply photocards to the electors and to draw up local electoral rolls based on the federal data with the photo of every voter. Four steps were followed; from 2 January to 6 February, a preliminary implementation of the process in Tecate was undertaken, to test and adjust procedures. Then from 7 February to 20 April, the 'One hundred days, five minutes' programme, when 80 fixed and 10 mobile modules were installed around the state with the objective of handing over photocards in no more than five minutes per person. This was followed by the 'Programme of Approaching the Citizen' of the 'Mahoma Plan' from 21 April, which tried to intensify the delivery of cards in those zones where people had not collected them. Finally on 17 June, 'a day for Baja California', when around five thousand volunteers were gathered to contact 150 thousand citizens who had not yet obtained their photocard.

The electoral authorities also organised – for each of the parties – direct access to any related information about the credentialisation process, not only through their representatives in the CEE, REE, CME and CDE, but within a

11 *Boletín Estatal*, 24, 31 August 1992.

new entity, the *Organismo Técnico de Vigilancia* (OTV), created by the *panista* administration to check every step taken by the electoral authorities in order to achieve clean elections. Finally, each party had its own computer terminal with direct access to the data base of the electoral roll and of the photocard delivery progress.

Throughout the procedure the opposition was pressuring the electoral authorities, denouncing what they considered irregularities, such as the intensive card deliveries in the PAN's voter areas, slower execution in PRI areas, the late handing-over of electoral rolls to the parties, the lack of control in the cards elaboration and so on. These claims contributed to the detection of mistakes, clarification of procedures and the improvement of methods. Even the PPS, supported by the PRI, demanded that if a high percentage of photocards had not been delivered, the federal card should be used to vote on 2 August. Nevertheless, by the end, *priísta* militants worked hard promoting the 'credentialisation' among their followers to avoid a possible *panista* '*carro completo*' (PRI, 1992).

The task was finished on 30 June, with a total of 822 151 photocards issued and delivered, at a cost of 6 500 million pesos. That meant 82.76 per cent of the citizens registered on the federal voter lists, at a cost of 7906 pesos each card. In comparative figures, 10.81 per cent more cards were distributed than the federal elections of 1991 and the total cost of each photocard was six times cheaper than the federal one, first printed in 1993 (Anaya in *Zeta*, 992, April 1993).

Another important aspect of the 1992 electoral process was the way that decision-making was carried out within the Local Electoral Commission. Though no one party had a majority of votes, several important decisions were taken unanimously including the integration of the 15 district committees and of the four municipal ones, the procedure to designate all officials at the 1855 polling stations, the standards of the material to be used during the electoral day (ballots, ballot box, documentation, and so on) and the decision to place the results outside the electoral booths when the election was over. On controversial points the PRI, PPS, PARM and PFCRN (seven votes) acted as a block, while the PRD supported the PAN (eight votes). However, three months before the elections, the PRD deputy, Catalino Zavala, resigned from the CEE to be a candidate for an elected post. In the Chamber of Deputies the PAN could not designate a *panista* as his substitute because Zavala was the 'point of balance' in Congress and he did not want to choose a *panista* candidate. Then an ex-PRD deputy was appointed, who had been expelled from his party because of corruption charges. Although some decisions continued to be unanimous, there were others which the CEE president at that time believed were carried out by the opposition block with the objective of boycotting the elections.[12] Three weeks before polling day, when the Congress had risen, its Permanent Commission – in which the PAN on its own has a majority – decided to change the ex-PRD deputy as its representative in the CEE for a *panista* one. Although that procedure was legally supported, the opposition representatives within the CEE denounced it as 'illegal and arbitrary', trying unsuccessfully to reverse it. Thus the eight to seven pro-PAN proportion returned. Within this context the elections of 2 August took place.

The 1992 local elections in Baja California provides an opportunity for comparison with those organised in the traditional style of the Mexican political system. The 15 district committees and the four municipal committees worked autonomously, coordinated by the CEE but taking their own decisions according to legal procedures. In all the 1855 polling stations not the electoral roll contained not only the name and address of the electors but also their photographs to prevent multiple voting. Not one of the 19 702 party representatives at the polling stations was expelled or obstructed in their function to watch over the proper administration of the elections. No illegal procedures were detected such as the '*carruseles*' (a group of people voting several times in different booths), or the '*operación tamal*' (a breakfast organised by a *priísta* leader for committed voters, going on together to vote), or the '*urnas embarazadas*' (stuffed ballot boxes – multiple voting by electoral officials). Nor was there evidence of '*robo de urnas*' (stolen ballot boxes), or '*tacos de votos*' (a person introducing several ballot slips into the box). It is also important to emphasise that 78.49 per cent of the registered voters participated in the elections, meaning only 21.51 per cent abstained, figures unprecedented in the state (Ruffo, 1992).

On polling day some mistakes were made by personnel of the electoral bodies as well as by officials of the polling stations which were used later by the opposition parties – especially the PRI and PPS – as proof of 'the least clear and least trustworthy elections in recent years' (Castro and Cantú, 1992). However, independent observers from the *Procuraduría de Derechos Humanos y Protección Civil de Baja California* and the *Academia Mexicana de Derechos Humanos* drew quite different conclusions. On 4 August, their conclusions were published.

> ... in general terms, the electoral process in Baja California differs from the disputes caused by elections held in other parts of Mexico. This was possible due to various factors. First and above all, the maturity of the citizens, a great number of whom voted, with the certainty that their vote would be respected. In second

12 Rodolfo Valdes, president of the Comisión Estatal Electoral. Interview with the author.

> place, there was greater competition among the political parties. The merit of these elections, exemplary in many senses although with some incidents and anomalies, has been imputed by different sectors of the community to a) the political parties, who carried out good campaigns, and b) the presence of the first opposition local government in Mexico's modern history, which committed itself to implement substantial reforms in the electoral law and procedures; this contributed, no doubt, towards creating an environment of confidence for the electors...' (*Procuraduría de Derechos Humanos,* 1992: 10; author's translation).

The final outcome of polling day was as follows: the PAN won three municipalities (Tijuana, Ensenada and Tecate) and eight deputies (six from Tijuana, one from Mexicali and one from Ensenada); the PRI won one municipality (Mexicali) and seven deputies (five from Mexicali, one from Tecate and one from Ensenada); the PRD got four deputies by proportional representation, while the PPS, PFCRN and PARM did not get any deputies since none of them achieved 1.5 per cent of the votes.

Post-election, the PRI used a double tactic to be acredited with more seats; while it complained about the 'electoral fraud' carried out in Tijuana, it recognised the 'peacefulness and clarity' of the elections in Mexicali (Perez Tejada, in *El Mexicano*, 4 August 1992). Within the six Tijuana district committees, the PRI fought vote by vote, trying to prove its assertion. Without precedent in other Mexican elections, the votes of 169 polling stations were counted again and in 477 the null votes were checked. In some instances mistakes made not only by officials but also by party representatives were detected and rectified. Once it was confirmed that none of these were 'serious irregularities', the original results remained unchanged. In some districts of Tecate for example, the PRI's tactics were complicated by split-ticket voting by its own supporters. While they voted PRI for the deputy, they voted PAN for the municipal president. Faced with this dilemma, *priístas* complained only about the municipal results, considering acceptable the district election. Given that it was not possible for the PRI to reverse defeats, its last recourse was to organise 'The March of Dignity' trying to influence deputies in the Electoral College, where *panistas* had a majority.

Finally, after the whole process was over, the *panista* authorities suggested the implementation of two measures. First the CEE proposed the auditing of the REE by an independent firm in order to decide whether the credentialisation process had been correctly executed. Second Governor Ruffo asked the Congress to exhibit publicly the electoral documents so that they could be checked by any person with queries about the development and outcome of the 1992 local elections. While the audit disproved claims of malpractice, the Governor's proposal was rejected by the *priísta* deputies.

CONCLUSIONS

The arrival of an opposition force to the governorship in Baja California demonstrates the differences between the written and unwritten rules in Mexican politics. The *panista* bureaucracy, lacking interests within the traditional structures of the political system, has been able to develop an administration more in-keeping with the norms established in the Constitution and in local laws. Thus, in order to counteract *priísta* practices, one of the main aims has been to reinforce Bajacalifornian political institutions, such as the Congress, the judicial tribunal, the municipalities and the electoral system, while limiting the executive's power. The most important obstacle to this scheme has been the financial issue, especially since its solution lies not in Bajacalifornian hands but in the federal government's. Salinas' modernisation has meant the reinforcement of centralism, rather than the strengthening of states; only 20 centavos of each peso collected via taxes goes to the states and municipalities, while a billionaire budget is administered by PRONASOL from Mexico City (Dresser, 1991). The Baja California authorities have complained that the *Secretaría de Hacienda* uses the same tactics as the *Secretaría de Gobernación* uses to limit the growth of opposition votes; *'rasuramiento del padrón'* (selected elimination from the electoral roll of opposition party supporters). In this case the lists shaved are those of the taxpayers, with the outcome of not less votes but less money as repayments to the state. The centralised budget has not only negative implications for Baja California, but for all states. For that reason, while some governors support Ruffo's negotiation with SHCP 'in private', others from Nuevo León and Jalisco, for example, have begun to raise their voice against the unfair fiscal structure.

The experience of Baja California gives cause for both hope and frustration. On a positive note, an opposition administration at state level is demonstrating that it is possible to govern outside and even against the traditional rules of the political system. What it is achieving in Baja California is having repercussions at the national level. The *Instituto Federal Electoral* (IFE), for example, was forced to implement a photocard in the 1994 elections. Also, the austere and moderate style of the governor's annual report before Congress has been adopted by other states. Furthermore, in the absence of a hegemonic political party, open debate among all the political parties, where negotiation and dialogue have replaced the traditional overwhelming vote of the PRI, has assumed a much more active role acting as a real balance and counterweight to the executive.

However, it is clear that the pace of change is not wholly controlled by either the local authorities or opposition forces, but involves the federal government. It seems that Salinas allowed limited opposition victories in governorship and municipalities to increase his credibility at national and international level, but only so far. Beyond that, the traditional rules are imposed as usual. In any case this tactic is double edged since the structures of the unwritten rules are being undermined in Baja California as an example of what is possible to achieve in other regions of the country, beginning with Chihuahua and Guanajuato. While some political writers agree that the struggle in Baja California for a free and sovereign state should be consolidated by *panistas* in power for another six year period (Guillén López, 1993; Espinoza and Hernández, 1993), the final decision will be in Bajacalifornian hands, according to how they perceive and support that assertion, independently of the federal government's will.

8 The PAN: The Search for Ideological and Electoral Space

David E. Stansfield[1]

Most academic studies of the political effects of the change in economic priorities in Mexico since the 1982 debt crisis have been concerned with the implications for the governing party and/or the extent to which the left was able to profit from the social strains which followed this change. The surge of electoral support in 1988 for Cuauhtémoc Cárdenas, as the presidential candidate for a coalition of defecting *priístas* and an assortment of small leftist parties, seemed to presage a dramatic shift in power. The compelling issues seemed to be why and how the PRI was decomposing/reforming and how the left was responding. Much of the discussion was concerned with the implications of the regime's abandonment of 'revolutionary' values, particularly its commitment to reduce the role of the State in the economy and its apparently reduced ability to provide funds for social development. These shifts in policy triggered deep nationalist fears and raised the possibility of a large-scale realignment of lower income groups away from the PRI and towards a State-led and socially more caring alternative represented by Cárdenas and the *Frente Democrático Nacional* (FDN).

The other major party in the political system, the *Partido de Acción Nacional* (PAN), has attracted far less attention. This is not too surprising or, indeed, novel. Despite surviving over 55 years in a frequently hostile political environment and with a share of the presidential poll that has increased steadily, the PAN has been the subject of only three substantial scholarly monographs and a small collection of academic articles (Mabray, 1973; Nuncio, 1986; von Sauer, 1974). In recent years the work of Soledad Loaeza, Enrique Krauze, Roger Bartra and Leopoldo Zea has helped to fill some of the gaps but the overwhelming body of research on Mexican politics has concentrated on the governing party and the left.

1 The author would like to thank the Carnegie Foundation for the Universities of Scotland and the University of Glasgow for their financial support of the research for this article.

Immediately after the 1988 elections the PAN and its prospects continued to be a low priority for political analysts. In the elections it had failed to capitalise on the PRI's unpopularity, increasing its vote by only one per cent and suffering a drop of 400 000 votes from its 1982 levels.[2] Ideologically the PAN was also struggling to cope with the PRI's conversion to two long-standing *panista* campaign demands, free enterprise economic policies and a reduced state apparatus. This left the PAN with a major identification problem. In the face of this stagnant electoral performance and a shortage of 'ideological space' it is not surprising, therefore, that observers looked elsewhere for clues about the future development of the political system.

In this chapter it is my intention to redress this imbalance and to examine the PAN's responses to the changes in economic and political priorities of the governing party. By doing so it is hoped not only to fill in some the empirical gaps, but also throw light on the problems faced by opposition parties operating within an evolving authoritarian regime.

THE DEBT CRISIS

The 'electoral transparency' promised by de la Madrid on taking office in 1982 was severely tested by the political reaction to the debt crisis and the austerity measures subsequently adopted. Opposition to the regime grew alarmingly for the PRI managers with murmurs of internal dissent and the PAN winning a spate of mayoral elections in the northern and central cities of Monclova, San Luis Potosí, Hermosillo, Durango, Chihuahua and Ciudad Juárez. López Portillo's nationalisation of the banking system had also alienated important sectors of the financial and business communities and figures from this grouping had begun to establish semi-formal links with the PAN. There was a very real prospect of the PRI losing the governorships of Nuevo León, Sonora and Chihuahua and the mayoralties of several important cities along the US border. In the face of this scenario the regime tightened its control of the electoral process and was able to produce a series of controversial *priísta* victories.[3]

2 These figures are disputed by the PAN, which claimed a much greater share of the vote than officially awarded. The party, however, did not claim a victory and admitted that Cárdenas had been able to profit more from the PRI's drop in support.

3 The PAN's monthly journal *La Nación* published details of the various ways in which the regime falsified the results of these elections. The frauds were also covered extensively in the international press.

However, the PAN's electoral strength, frustrated by corrupt practices or not, was only part of the story. The PRI's adoption of neoliberal, IMF-sanctioned economic strategies in the wake of the debt crisis reawakened long-standing ideological debates within the PAN. Over the years several strands of economic thinking had surfaced within its leadership. The founding fathers of the party who had opposed Lázaro Cárdenas' communalism with a call for a less politicised State within a market-led economy had, by the 1960s, been joined by Christian Democrats who looked for a state with a paternalistic, reformist role firmly committed to the protection of the *bien común* and in favour of redistributive policies. The party's policy of active recruitment of local members in the northern states in the late 1960s and 1970s had produced another equally disturbing strand of thought. In a sense this was a 'generational change of gear'. Many of the older cohort of *pensador* leaders had died and those who remained saw their dominance challenged by a new batch of younger, 'realist' *norteño* politicians who had cut their teeth in municipal and state politics. These *neopanistas*, as they became known, were self-made men, running small- and medium-sized businesses, who had made their fortunes despite an interfering and corrupt State which had placed a brake on economic growth. They did not dress up their ideas in the patrician philosophies of the capital city intellectuals and argued forcefully for the introduction of a fully fledged free enterprise system in which the State had a limited economic function. They claimed to know what was wanted in the streets of Tijuana or Hermosillo and had little time for discussions of the *bien común* or state corporatism. There was more of Thomas Hobbes than St Thomas Aquinas in their philosophical apparatus.

Tension between these ideological strands in the party simmered during the early 1980s but the choice of the Sinaloan businessman, Manuel Clouthier, as its presidential candidate for the 1988 elections seemed to suggest that this more robust tendency had prevailed. This ideological shift was given more piquancy by the *priísta* government's programmatic realignment after the debt crisis. The abandonment of the State-driven development model, which had held sway since 1945, in favour of a neoliberal, monetarist and export-led model meant that the PRI had appropriated large areas of economic policy associated with the PAN, particularly the *neopanistas*. The PRI's later assassinated presidential candidate for the 1994 elections, Luis Donaldo Colosio, for example, declared that:

> The PRI proposes a state which complements the work and effort of the citizens and social organizations in Mexico and does not supplant their initiatives. A new society requires a new state. If having the state own enterprises helped to

> ameliorate the unequal distribution in the past, that is no longer the case (cited in Centeno, 1991:27)

The PAN now had the task of differentiating itself ideologically from the regime. For years the party had complained that the regime had consistently used the State's resources to build up its political support and had thereby handicapped the development of private initiative. Now the government was close to admitting this and proposing to loosen its control on the economy – by privatisation, by reducing subsidies, by simplifying taxation and by encouraging foreign investment.

For the older intellectualist group within the PAN this provoked a re-examination of the party's attitude towards the State and its legitimate functions. Although still supporting the need for a more open, less politicised economy along the lines suggested by the IMF and accepted by the modernising elements within the government, they insisted that the PAN had never favoured a State which evaded its responsibility to manage the economy for the benefit of its citizens. The State had a duty to protect the *bien común* and to prevent individuals or groups from taking unfair advantage of the poor, the weak and the needy. Individual opportunity should be allowed, even encouraged, but should be subject to the concept of what is good for the society as a whole. The State should act to advance the well-being of all of its population. The PRI was criticised for having perverted the State's supervisory functions for its own political purposes. For the PAN, the State was not seen as an evil in itself.

The other reaction, more popular among the younger, more populist *neopanistas,* was less retrospective. In a desire to differentiate themselves from the new PRI commitment to free enterprise and a 'small State', they tended to stress their experience as businessmen and argue for an acceleration of the process of economic liberalisation. On questions of social policy they favoured individual responsibility and a State with defined and limited functions as the defender of national territory and as an 'enabler' of economic growth. People like Clouthier, for example, dismissed a PAN claim for a revolutionary pedigree. He suggested that the country's revolutionary history had been wrong, mistaken and corrupt and that Mexico should make a complete break with the past. He looked to encourage individual merit and argued that poverty was not a matter of collective shame, but of individual responsibility. The contrast with the traditional *panista* line was clear and his campaign for the presidency in 1988, although appreciated for its verve, worried some of the older, more contemplative leaders with its harsh libertarianism.

These ideological differences ran parallel to a series of tensions between the party's national headquarters and the various state organizations. In the early days the National Executive Committee (CEN) in Mexico City was able to dominate the party machines through a combination of financial strength and intellectual prowess. As the northern party machines began to amass victories in mayoral and state elections and to attract local sources of finance, the primacy of the national leadership became less secure. In the struggle for votes state machines adopted local issues and interpreted national doctrine to suit local conditions. National discipline became much harder to impose on these '*bárbaros del norte*'.

THE 1988 ELECTIONS

Although an embarrassment to the national leadership these differences within the PAN were not the main reason for the party's modest showing in the 1988 elections. This modest showing was a slightly increased share of a much reduced turnout, particularly in the context of a governing party smarting from high level defections and widespread unpopularity. Carlos Salinas de Gortari, the PRI's presidential candidate, despite a widely-criticised and overly sympathetic count, was able to claim only 50.7 per cent of the poll – a drop of 24.2 per cent and an haemorrhage of nearly eight million votes from the 1982 totals. The main beneficiary of the government's problems was Cuauhtémoc Cárdenas, who had defected from the PRI in October the previous year and had attracted to his candidature a collection of small leftist parties which fought the election together as the FDN. He increased the left's share of the vote by about 20 per cent and more than tripled the votes it had received in 1982 in the 'official' count and claimed that massive fraud by the PRI had robbed him of victory. He was recognised as having won majorities in five and coming second in seventeen states. Clouthier and the PAN, on the other hand, was unable to win a majority in any of the states and came second in ten.

The PAN fared slightly better in the congressional elections, where party affiliation was rather more important than the candidate's personality or reputation and where the FDN affiliates fought as separate parties. PAN candidates out-polled the *Partido Frente Cardenista de Reconstrucción Nacional* (PFCRN) and the *Partido Popular Socialista* (PPS) by 200 per cent, the *Partido Auténtico de la Revolución Mexicana* (PARM) by 300 per cent and the *Partido Mexicano Socialista* (PMS) by 400 per cent. This produced 101 PAN congressional seats with the FDN/PMS amalgam claiming 136.

Internally within the PAN this performance was viewed as one of consolidation and Clouthier's energetic, confrontational campaign as effective in holding the line in the face of a massive surge of support for Cárdenas. The PAN leadership, of course, claimed better results than those released by the government, but insisted that fraud had been committed not only by *priísta* officials, but also by *cardenistas* where they had access to the electoral machinery. The PAN's version of the final results, however, fell short of a claim of victory. It gave Salinas a narrow win with 34/35 per cent, Cárdenas a close second with 31/32 per cent and Clouthier breathing down their necks with 29/31 per cent.

In the new Congress the PRI no longer had the two thirds majority needed for constitutional change and the FDN and PAN deputies combined to delay the formal confirmation of Salinas as President for several months. The *impasse* was eventually broken when the PAN deputies broke their pact with the FDN in return for electoral reforms and what was widely rumoured to be the PRI's promise of free, untainted elections in the forthcoming gubernatorial contest in Baja California.

THE SALINAS *SEXENIO*

This decision to recognise the Salinas administration and a later decision to accept the 'governability' provisions in the new electoral law, which guaranteed 60 per cent of the seats in Congress for the party polling over 35 per cent of the votes, reactivated an old debate within the PAN. From the earliest days there had been members who cautioned against collaboration with an inherently illegitimate government. Even electoral competition was dangerous since the party's participation gave a veneer of respectability to an authoritarian and corrupt regime. That isolationist position had been abandoned by the 1980s, but was reactivated by a group led by Jorge Eugenio Ortiz Gallego who established the *Foro Doctrinario y Democrático* within the party in order to press for a policy of non-cooperation with a government that had so recently resorted to massive electoral fraud to secure its victory.

The *Foro* did not last long and its members were expelled in 1990. The party leadership was aware of the dangers of collaboration but the success of Ernesto Ruffo in the 1989 Baja California gubernatorial contest had given the party control over its first state. The PAN was in Ruffo's words now 'in government' and this was seen as an opportunity to demonstrate its talents. Rather than withdraw from contacts with the national *priísta* government the PAN now frequently found itself negotiating with it. The structure of federal financing meant that the Ruffo adminstration and, at times, the CEN had to make deals with ministries in Mexico City in order to claw back taxation revenue and to press for the full local implementation of national development projects. These deals did not always satisfy party activists but, once the strategy of participation within the system had been adopted, they were inevitable.[4]

In fact the party contested the 1991 mid-term congressional elections in good spirits. Salinas had begun to establish himself as a dynamic proponent of economic modernisation but his political strategy seemed more concerned with attacking the *cardenistas* than the PAN. Meanwhile, the PAN had worked to consolidate its position. Its membership had risen by 50 per cent over its 1988 figure of 49,000 and it had won 35 additional mayoralties and claimed to be 'governing' over five million voters (CEN del PAN, 1994a). In the elections this steady progress was maintained, with its share of the vote increasing slightly to 17.9 per cent and its number of votes rising by 25 per cent over its 1988 figures. Celebrations were muted, however, since the party saw its congressional representation drop from 101 to 90 and the overall poll increase by 33 per cent. In regional terms its vote continued to be heavily concentrated in the northern states and Yucatán, where its vote averaged 24.6 per cent. In the southern states its vote averaged a modest 5.2 per cent.[5]

The most dramatic result of the elections was the collapse of the *cardenista* vote. The PRD, which had become the main vehicle for Cárdenas' ambitions with the dissolution of the FDN, became the focus of attention for the PRI. Its local organisations, particularly in Cárdenas' home state of Michoacán, were short of finance and experience and had frequently been intimidated, including the assassination of several activists. *Caciques*, who had deserted the PRI for the FDN in 1988, had been wooed back into the *priísta* fold by the funds made available through Salinas' new social development programme PRONASOL. The result was a drop in the share of the vote for the FDN affiliates from the 1988 figure of 30.7 per cent to 16.3 per cent and a net loss of 47 seats in Congress. In absolute terms this represented a fall of 25 per cent from its 1988 poll when the overall poll had risen by 33 per cent.

The PRI, on the other hand, improved on its 1988 *debâcle*. Its share of the vote increased from 51 to 64 per cent and the number of people voting for its candidates rose from 9.25 to 14.1 million, a rise of 53 per cent and well over

---

4 See Vicencio this volume for an account of the relations between Ruffo administration and the Salinas government.

5 The seven northern states are Baja California, Baja California Sur, Coahuila, Chihuahua, Nuevo León, Sonora and Tamauilpas. The seven southern states included are Campeche, Chiapas, Guerrero, Oaxaca, Quintana Roo, Tabasco and Veracruz.

the national expansion of the electorate of 33 per cent. In Congress it now had a clear majority with 321 seats – a net gain of 58 on 1988.

In sum, the most important features of the 1991 elections were interrelated – the rise of the PRI's support and the slump in the former FDN's support. The PAN was able to hold on to most of its 1988 gains, but was unable to gain much outside Baja California from the FDN's decline. The following tables indicate that although the PRI made gains across the country it had greater success in mobilising its vote in states where the FDN had polled well, i.e. over 20 per cent, in 1988 than in those where the PAN had polled at similar levels. The PRI's average rise in the *cardenista* 'strongholds' was 142 per cent, compared with an average of 43.1 per cent in the PAN's. It is unclear whether this means that the PRI put less effort into fighting the PAN or that the PAN vote proved to be firmer than the FDN's. Interviews with *panista* activists in the 'stronghold' states, however, do not suggest that there was any noticeable pulling of punches by their opponents.

The PAN leadership was reasonably satisfied with this performance and within a year had gained two additional governorships in Guanajuato and Chihuahua and had increased its number of mayoralties to 98, allowing it to claim that it was now responsible for 'governing' 12.6 million Mexicans. Ideologically the party was less fractious. With the death of Clouthier in a car accident in 1989, the CEN, headed by Luis Alvarez, returned to more cautious policy programmes, which stressed the traditional principles of a limited but benevolent State within a free enterprise system. Ernesto Ruffo was thought to have shared some of Clouthier's more libertarian ideas, but

Table 8.1: PRI's performance in PAN 'strongholds' (Over 20% of the vote) 1988-91

	1988	%	*1991*	%	*% Change in PRI turnout*
Aguascalientes	83 498	51	137 627	66	+64.8
Baja California	169 137	41	261 140	46	+55.1
Baja California Sur	47 623	58	59 950	64	+25.8
Chihuahua	283 888	56	414 397	58	+45.9
Durango	191 098	60	201 861	62	+5.6
Federal District	740 423	28	1 519 157	46	+97.1
Guanajuato	317 778	45	622 707	53	+95.9
Jalisco	508 816	44	940 413	63	+88.7
Nuevo León	497 221	72	400 162	68	-19.5
Querétaro	150 419	65	213 066	70	+41.6
San Luis Poltisí	241 763	68	328 895	64	+36.0
Sinaloa	322 366	62	415 645	67	+28.9
Sonora	282 474	71	333 226	60	+17.9
Yucután	205 833	69	226 250	61	+9.9

Table 8.2: PRI's performance in FDN 'strongholds' (Over 20% of the vote) 1988-91

	1988	%	*1991*	%	*% Change in PRI turnout*
Federal District	740 423	28	1 519 157	46	97.1
Mexico	693 980	31	1 608 441	53	131.7
Michoacán	152 547	26	507 788	53	232.8
Morelos	93 622	37	194 988	65	108.2

his experience of governing Baja California seemed to have convinced him of the need for a State with considerable powers in the fields of economic and social development. The removal of the *Foro* group had also silenced the debate on whether the party should participate in an inherently corrupt system. Diego Fernández de Cevallos, the PAN's presidential candidate for the 1994 elections, and Carlos Castillo, the party's national president, were firmly committed to an electoral strategy and refused to follow the more extreme line of the Clouthier campaign. This may have been the product of their philosophical disposition but was more likely to reflect their desire to appeal to a wider spectrum of voters than in 1988. In the search for support beyond its traditional strongholds, and/or its mainly middle class image, the PAN had to attract more votes in the poorer states and from lower income groups. A demand that such people should 'pull themselves together' was not seen as an obvious vote-winning slogan.

THE 1994 ELECTIONS

Salinas' rising popularity and a series of good economic results in 1992 and 1993 caused problems for the PAN and PRD alike. The regime seemed committed to political reform and the President had chosen, Luis Donaldo Colosio, as his successor as candidate of the governing party. Colosio had a reputation as a moderniser, openly in favour of a more democratic, competitive political system. Economically he was committed to the neoliberal policies of Salinas but as the former Minister of Social Development responsible for the PRONASOL programme, which had helped to re-establish the PRI in many low-income areas, he was also well acquainted with the clientelistic capacity of the State machine.

The PAN's platform did little to challenge the direction of economic reform. In proposing a 'Social Market Economy' it was argued only that monetarism must be subjected to moral scrutiny and that economic decision-making should be 'less discretionary and less arbitrary than before'. As befitted a party with experience of 'government' in three states it also suggested specific areas in which economic efficiency could be improved, such as stricter budgetary controls, more integrated information systems and clearer taxation schemes. It also raised the vexatious issue of financial relations within the federal system. PRONASOL and its agrarian counterpart PROCAMPO were attacked for their direction by *priísta* 'viceroys', not for their functions. They would be better administered by local officials in the *municipios*. On the question of the continuing problem of the country's debts, PAN suggested that those who had contracted the loans be held responsible for them and that the performance of the funds borrowed be judged against the declared objectives of the loans (CEN del PAN, 1994b).

The main emphasis of the PAN's programme, however, was on political reform, which it described as having 'primacy'. The demand for increased electoral probity was central. The changes required were a mixture of new procedures and an insistence on the implementation of existing regulations. They therefore favoured a fuller, more accurate electoral roll, with each voter issued with photocredential cards similar to those the Ruffo administration had distributed in Baja California; more independent observers in polling booths and on local electoral commissions; greater safeguards against the falsification of results at local and national levels and a national electoral institution staffed with non-party officials and directed by a body on which all political parties were fully represented. Easier access to the media and better state funding for the opposition parties were also on the agenda along with a demand that the PRI be prevented from unofficially using State resources for its own political purposes. The party was less sure on what to do if these demands failed to be met. The CEN, in its wish to be 'responsible', was embarrassed but not swayed by those, particularly in San Luis Potosí and Chihuahua, who spoke of the need for civil disobedience in the face of fraud.

In Congress, the PAN was looking for an increase in the number of seats to be allocated through proportional representation. They also argued for an increase in its powers, especially in budgetary matters and in foreign policy, both of which were currently dominated by the presidency. Their support for the 'governability' reform of 1989 which guarantees a congressional majority to the largest party was more controversial.[6]

The experience of Governors Ernesto Ruffo in Baja California, Carlos Medina in Guanajuato and Francisco Barrio in Chihuahua introduced a new

---

6 The PAN's proposal built on those made in the *Iniciativa de Código Electoral de los Poderes Legislativo y Ejecutivo de la Unión* published in 1989.

concern for decentralisation. They had found that their scope for action was limited. Although formally a federal system, state governments were heavily dependent on the central authorities for finance. This was seen as not only illegal and inefficient but also, and perhaps more importantly, as a way in which the PRI could paralyse their initiatives. They were also concerned to decentralise PRONASOL, which had become a major source of development projects during the Salinas *sexenio.* On corruption, a traditional plank of *panista* platforms for the past forty years or so, the party muted its muck-raking style of the last two decades and, in the spirit of 'responsibility' and 'experience of government', suggested specific methods for making public authorities more accountable. In sum, the PAN challenged the PRI in 1994 much more on political than economic grounds. These political issues had been present in earlier platforms, but the PRI's occupation of its ideological space on economic reform left it few options but to change its emphasis.

In the event, the defining issues in the 1994 elections had little do with the economic debate and more to do with the character of the political system, and in this sense the PAN was able to benefit from this shift in strategy. The year started dramatically with reports on New Year's Day of the occupation of the Chiapas town of San Cristóbal de las Casas by a group of armed insurgents which called itself the *Ejército Zapatista de Liberación Nacional* (EZLN). Its leaders condemned the regime for its lack of concern for the indigenous peoples of that state and demanded radical change. Timed by the *zapatistas* to coincide with the inception of the North American Free Trade Agreement (NAFTA), which had become a corner-stone of Salinas' export-led economic strategy, the insurrection was a worrying development for the government. Troops were despatched to Chiapas and, after a series of skirmishes in which a number of lives were lost, a cease-fire was eventually arranged and a Peace Commission appointed under the leadership of Manuel Camacho, a former cabinet member and *presidenciable*. The spokesman for the EZLN, *subcomandante* Marcos, soon emerged as an embarrassingly articulate critic of the regime and the Salinas government was forced into admissions of mistakes and malpractices by its local politicians. It insisted, however, that violence was an unacceptable form of political expression and stressed that its response to the rebellion would be one of negotiation. Meanwhile it tried to isolate the rebels and encircle them with troops.

Two months later on 22 March the government was rocked again by the assassination of the PRI's presidential candidate, Luis Donaldo Colosio, in Tijuana, Baja California. Rumours about the killing included suggestions that it had been arranged by elements within the PRI who were concerned by his commitment to political reform. The fact that such rumours gained credibility suggested that there was a belief that the governing party was riven by splits and that the modernisation of the PRI was far from complete. Talk of political crisis and instability became common and President Salinas moved quickly to appoint Colosio's campaign manager and former Minister of Education, Ernesto Zedillo, as the party's new candidate. Government statements stressed the need for calm and a commitment to institutional politics. Opposition parties were similarly discomforted by these events. While the PRD had obvious sympathies with the *zapatistas*, too close an identification with their cause could threaten its appeal to urban voters, particularly the more prosperous ones. Nor could it make too much capital out of the assassination of Colosio without risking a backlash. The PAN, with its insistence on the electoral route to change was quick to condemn these developments. It had little sympathy with the substance of the *zapatista* demands, although it criticised the government for having created the conditions which caused the trouble. It was also disturbed that Colosio's assassination had occurred in a state which it governed and which may have involved some local officials. Its main concern was that the PRI's commitment to political reform might die with Colosio.

From March onwards the presidential campaign was contested largely on political issues. The personalities of the candidates also began to appear as factors. In this respect the PAN appeared to have an advantage over the other parties. Diego Fernández de Cevallos' flamboyant style and sharp oratorical skills made him an excellent television and platform performer. In contrast, Zedillo appeared cold and awkwardly inexperienced, particularly in public meetings, and Cuauhtémoc Cárdenas a low key, faltering performer, especially when faced with questions about his *priísta* past. Indeed, after the televised debate in May between the candidates polls suggested that 'Diego' was closing fast on the 'official' candidate. The party machines, however, were unevenly matched. The PRI had vastly greater resources, in the shape of both finance (official and unofficial) and experienced personnel. In contrast the PAN and the PRD had regional gaps in their coverage of the republic and, despite grants from the *Instituto Federal Electoral* (IFE), had access to more limited funds.[7]

The election of the 21 August proved to be less traumatic than feared and more successful than had been hoped for. The turnout was the largest in Mexican history at 77.7 per cent of the electorate, with over twice as many

7 The PRI received over 68 million pesos from the IFE in contrast to the PRD 11 million pesos (reported in *El Porvenir*, 28 August 1994: 13). These sums are additional to the funds raised by the parties themselves. The opposition parties also claim that the PRI illegally used public funds for electoral purposes.

Mexicans voting than were reported in the elections in 1988. The 34 million votes were also cast in conditions regarded by most commentators as the cleanest on record. Over 80 000 registered observers, local and foreign, and unprecedented press coverage made electoral fraud more difficult than ever before and there were remarkably few instances of the type of serious disturbances which had occurred previously. The events were supervised by the IFE, on which all the parties were represented and which met in public and the results were published quickly. Irregularities were recorded but they were few relative to the numbers involved. The main cause for opposition complaint was the situation in the voting booths which had been created for voters in transit or working away from home (*casillas especiales*). Fearing that the PRI might use the 'difficult to trace' ballots in these booths to inflate its support, the PRD had insisted on a limit of 300 ballots per voting station. In fact this proved to be too few and there were numerous instances of the stations running out of ballots before the close of polling. There were undoubtedly other cases of voting irregularities but the scale of malpractice was significantly lower than previously.

By the early hours of the following day the exit polls (*conteos rápidos)* were predicting a Zedillo victory, with Fernández de Cevallos second and Cárdenas third. Within a few days the IFE was confirming this result and giving the candidates, 50.2, 26.7 and 17.1 per cent respectively. In the Senate elections the PRI's candidates had a clean sweep of all 64 of the simple majority seats available, with the PAN and PRD limited to 26/27 and 5/6 of the proportionality, list-based seats. Since the PRI already had 31 and the PAN 1 sitting members the new Senate was overwhelmingly *priísta.* The PRI was also in a dominant position in the new Congress. Only 23 of the 300 simple majority seats were won by the opposition parties; the PAN 18 and the PRD 5. Of the list-based seats the PAN was awarded 101, the PRD 66, the PRI 23 and the PT 10. This gave the PRI 300 or 60 per cent of the seats. This is not the place for a detailed breakdown of the PRI's victory, but a brief analysis of the PAN's performance is necessary.

PAN'S RESULTS

In overall terms the PAN increased its share of the presidential vote from its 1988 17.1 per cent to 26 per cent. In absolute numbers this meant a 185 per cent increase in support. This exceeded the PRI's 85 per cent gain and the PRD's more or less stable support. In the context of an overall national rise in the number of voters of 82 per cent, the PAN can be said to have performed well and the results are a vindication of the leadership's strategy of pressing for, and thereby benefitting from, cleaner elections.

Although unable to win a majority for its presidential candidate in any one state the PAN edged significantly closer to the PRI's vote in several. In 1988 Clouthier was within 20 per cent of Salinas in six states. In 1994 Fernández de Cevallos increased this to ten states, including three where the gap was less than ten per cent. At the other end of the scale the PAN also improved its performance in states where it had been traditionally weak. In 1988 it had won less than ten per cent of the vote in twelve states. In 1994 it dropped below this level only in Tabasco.

The Regional Dimension

The North

The regional distribution of PAN's strength shifted slightly in 1994. In the northern states, with the exception of Chihuahua, which will be referred to below, its share of the presidential vote increased over its 1988 figures – on average by 12 per cent (Table 8.3). This swing to the PAN, however, was insufficient to produce any majorities for Fernández, despite falls of six and nine per cent in the shares of the *priísta* and *cardenista* candidates respectively. It does mean that the PAN is now firmly re-established as the main opposition with the PRD back in third place, 22 per cent behind. It would seem that the interlude of tripartism in 1988 has reverted back to the old PRI>PAN bipartism, but with an average gap between the two parties reduced to 16 per cent. In two states, Sonora and Nuevo Leon, the gap is less than ten per cent but the PAN must be concerned that the two states it governs, Baja California and Chihuahua, were the only ones in the region in which the

Table 8.3: Presidential Votes in Northern states, 1988-94

	1988			*1994*					
	PRI	*PAN*	*FDN*	*PRI*		*PAN*		*PRD*	
	%	%	%	%	change	%	change	%	change
BC	36.66	24.39	37.19	50.07	+13.41	37.07	+12.68	8.55	-25.64
BC South	54.02	19.00	25.87	56.18	+2.16	32.62	+13.62	6.63	-19.24
Coahuila	54.27	15.34	29.95	49.67	-4.60	31.34	+16.00	12.90	-10.05
Chihuahua	54.58	38.19	6.76	60.40	+5.82	28.28	-9.91	6.23	-0.47
Nuevo León	72.08	23.70	3.88	49.17	-22.91	40.63	+16.93	3.01	-0.84
Sonora	68.59	20.85	9.78	42.67	-25.92	38.95	+18.10	13.21	+3.23
Tamaulipas	59.33	9.91	30.15	47.64	-11.69	27.31	+17.40	19.11	-11.14
Average	57.03	21.62	20.50	50.83	-6.24	33.73	+12.11	9.94	-9.59

Figure 8.1: PAN vote by state in 1988 Presidential Election

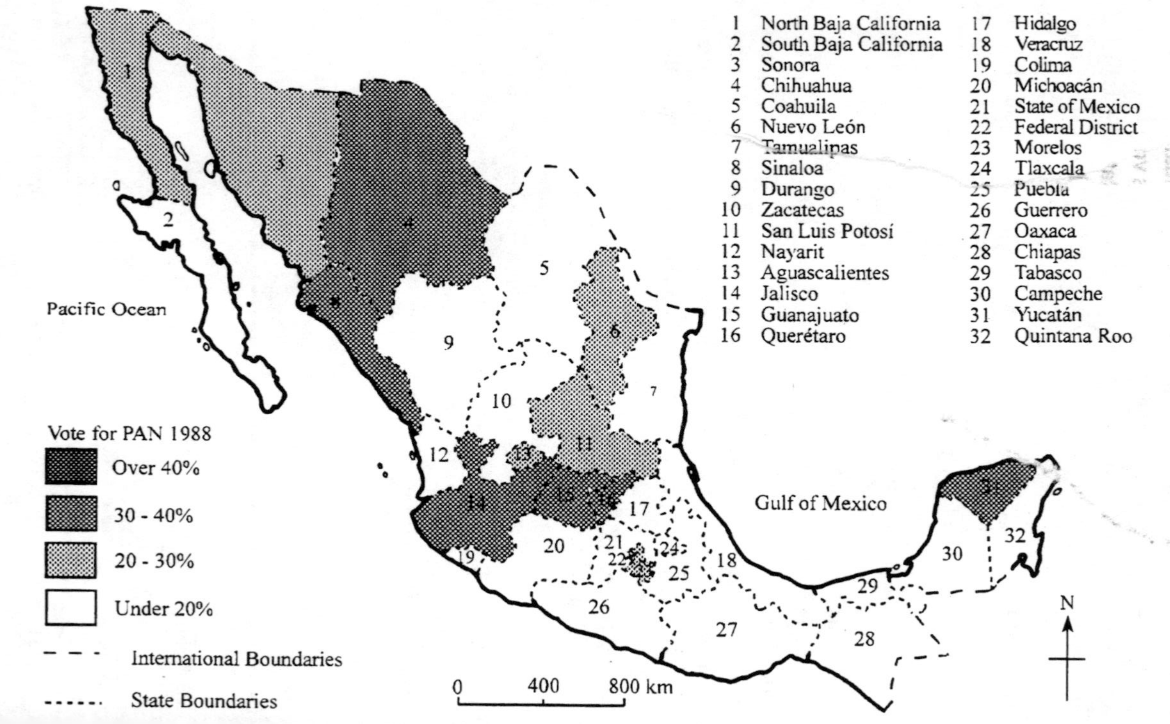

Figure 8.2: PAN vote by state in 1994 Presidential Election

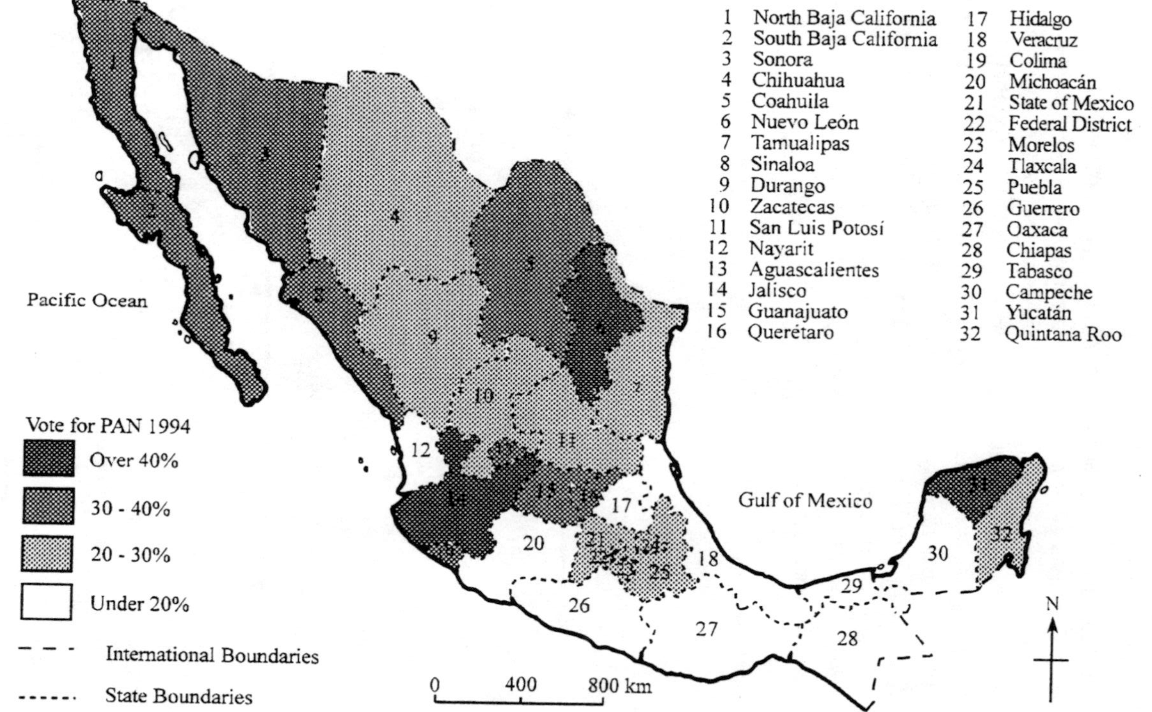

PRI increased its share of the vote. Voter allegiances appear to be less strong in this region than in any other.

The Centre-North

Table 8.4 illustrates the fortunes of the parties in the centre-northern states and suggests a significant improvement in the PAN's penetration of this region with its share of the vote increasing by an average of 8.6 per cent. In the state of Jalisco it moved to within two per cent of the PRI and took the Governorship in February 1995 with a 15 per cent margin. The PRI, while still winning a majority in all of the states, saw its share of the vote decline by an average of five per cent and the FDN/PRD a drop in share of ten per cent to leave it at less than ten per cent in all the states. The average gap between the PRI and PAN dropped to 20 per cent and in two states is less than ten per cent. While in 1988 this region exhibited a degree of PRI>PAN>FDN or PRI>FDN>PAN tripartism, in 1994 PRI>PAN bipartism had developed.

Table 8.4: Presidential Votes in Centre-North states

	1988			*1994*					
	PRI	*PAN*	*FDN*	*PRI*		*PAN*		*PRD*	
	%	%	%	%	change	%	change	%	change
Aguascalientes	50.21	28.42	18.67	47.14	-3.07	37.50	+9.08	8.76	-9.81
Durango	63.63	16.98	18.82	48.41	-15.22	27.63	+10.64	9.73	-9.09
Guanajuato	44.03	28.93	22.01	52.18	+8.15	27.63	-1.30	9.73	-12.28
Jalisco	42.57	30.76	23.87	44.14	+1.57	42.95	+12.19	7.10	-16.77
Queretaro	63.34	19.43	15.81	60.63	-2.71	31.49	+12.06	5.50	-10.31
S.Luis Potosí	68.25	21.15	8.81	58.32	-9.87	26.21	+5.06	9.82	+1.01
Zacatecas	66.17	10.71	22.31	51.41	-16.54	23.21	+12.45	9.09	-13.22
Average	56.88	22.34	18.61	51.74	-5.14	30.94	+8.60	8.53	-10.08

The Core

In the core region of the DF and the state of Mexico the combined number of votes for both PRI and PAN increased significantly, by 171.16 per cent and 121.84 per cent respectively. Their shares of the vote also improved by 16.98 per cent and 7.54 per cent. The clear loser was the FDN/PRD which saw its vote sink by 33.73 per cent and its overall share from 50.24 to 19.73 per cent. This decay of the FDN/PRD clearly helped the PRI more than the PAN. An element of tripartism still persists, but the ranking of parties has shifted strikingly, from FDN>PRI>PAN to PRI>PAN>PRD. Although the PAN has strong niche support in particular districts, it has yet to expand its

Table 8.5: Presidential Votes in the DF and the state of Mexico

	1988			*1994*					
	PRI	*PAN*	*FDN*	*PRI*		*PAN*		*PRD*	
	%	%	%	%	change	%	change	%	change
D.F.	27.25	22.01	49.22	43.42	+16.17	27.19	+5.18	20.91	-28.31
Mexico	29.79	16.33	51.33	47.59	+17.80	26.24	+9.91	18.56	-32.97
Average	28.52	19.17	50.27	45.50	+16.98	26.71	+7.54	19.73	-30.64

support widely enough to make an impact on the PRI's dominance. In the capital city's Representative Assembly (ARDF), for example, it succeeded in winning only two of the 40 simple majority seats.

The South

In the 1988 elections Clouthier did badly in the southern states. Only in Campeche did he poll more than ten per cent and his average in the region was 5.62 per cent. In 1994 Fernández de Cevallos improved significantly on this, raising the PAN's average share of the vote to 15.45 per cent and more than quadrupling its number of votes (Table 8.6). The PRI saw a fall in share in every state and a severe swing against it and to the PRD in Chiapas. In that state its actual poll dropped by almost 100 000 votes and the PRD's rose by over 300 000. Clearly the PRD was able to take advantage of the anti-PRI feeling generated by the *zapatista* rebellion, but must be concerned that it was unable to capitalise on this in the other states of the south, with the possible exception of Tabasco. The PAN, on the other hand, increased its share across the region, even overtaking the PRD as the main opposition party in Quintana Roo. While this does not mean that the PAN has usurped the

Table 8.6: Presidential Votes in the Southern states

	1988			*1994*					
	PRI	*PAN*	*FDN*	*PRI*		*PAN*		*PRD*	
	%	%	%	%	change	%	change	%	change
Campeche	70.88	11.60	16.30	65.42	-5.46	18.81	+7.21	21.46	+5.16
Chiapas	89.91	3.73	6.45	48.17	-41.74	12.50	+8.77	33.80	+27.35
Guerrero	60.53	2.24	35.80	50.20	-10.33	9.79	+7.55	34.90	-0.90
Oaxaca	63.81	4.97	30.25	52.24	-11.67	13.44	+8.47	28.34	-1.91
Quintana Roo	65.70	8.77	24.14	53.95	-11.75	29.75	+20.98	12.59	-11.55
Tabasco	74.30	5.35	19.94	56.76	-17.54	7.64	+2.29	33.18	+13.24
Veracruz	62.59	7.28	31.05	53.56	-9.03	16.27	+8.99	24.03	-7.02
Average	69.67	5.62	25.87	54.32	-12.85	15.45	+9.18	27.94	+3.48

PRD and is on the verge of a major breakthrough, it does give it a foothold in states where its previous representation has been meagre.

PROBLEMS FOR THE PAN

The major concern for the PAN after the elections must be its performance in states where it was in 'government', that is, the three states where it held the governorships. This could not only represent a verdict on the quality of service offered by the incumbent governors, but also an indication of how well they may do in forthcoming elections. Table 8.7 demonstrates that the PRI won the presidential elections in these states with an average increase in share of over ten per cent. In Baja California and Guanajuato the collapse of the *cardenista* vote and, in the case of Baja California, the local origins of Zedillo, seemed to have benefitted the PRI; but in Chihuahua there appears to have been a distinct swing away from the PAN to the PRI, reflecting the particular problems facing the governor or maybe that accountability in politics is not as popular as expected.

This experience is likely to have an impact on the PAN leadership. Much of its current strategy is based on the fact that it now has 'experience' of government, and that its governors are introducing new policies and making their administrations more accountable. It is accepted that they are doing so within a highly centralised political system dominated by a *priísta* government, but they argue, that by sensible negotiation and continuing support, they will be able change the 'rules of the game'. If, however, this produces only a series of short, one-term PAN governorships which, because of political *naiveté* or limited access to central funds, are replaced by the national governing party, this commitment to a negotiated form of transition from the single party state will be re-examined. 'Experience' in this sense can cause tension within the party.

Table 8.7: Presidential Votes in PAN Governed states

	1988			*1994*					
	PRI	*PAN*	*FDN*	*PRI*		*PAN*		*PRD*	
	%	%	%	%	change	%	change	%	change
Baja California	36.66	24.39	37.19	50.07	+13.41	37.07	+12.80	8.55	-28.64
Chihuahua	54.58	38.19	6.77	60.40	+5.82	28.28	-9.81	6.23	-0.54
Guanajuato	44.03	28.93	22.01	52.18	+8.15	27.63	-1.30	9.73	-12.28
Average	45.09	30.50	10.65	54.21	+9.12	30.99	+0.49	8.17	-2.48

EXPLANATIONS

On the whole, with the important exception of the states where it is currently in control, the PAN came out of the 1994 elections well. The explanations for this lie in a complex of structural and contextural factors. Among the former it is obvious that the political reforms of the last decade or so have helped all opposition parties to some extent. There can be doubts about the veracity of the electoral roll (*padrón)*, about the representational quality of the proportionality, list-based *diputados de partido* system, about the composition of the IFE, about the unfairness of treatment by the media and about the ways in which parties are financed, but the elections were clearly cleaner than ever before and the PAN has gained from it. This, however, might turn out to be a mixed blessing, since accusations of electoral corruption have been an important part of the PAN's complaint against the PRI, and a dramatic clean-up of the system might steal yet another of the PAN's political weapons. This situation has not yet arrived but the leadership of the PAN must be aware that political reform poses threats as well as opportunities.

Another general factor which seems to be working in the PAN's favour, is the long-term economic trend. The opinion pollsters' profile of the 'typical' PAN voter is younger, more likely to live in a town or city, better educated and better off than his 'typical' PRI counterpart (Basáñez, 1994). Recent trends suggest that the Mexican electorate is increasingly composed of young, urbanised voters. It is less clear that the electorate is becoming better educated and more financially secure, but the PAN must take heart from these trends.

In addition to these underlying factors, the PAN's performance in 1994 was a product of several recent or current developments. The atmosphere of looming political crisis after the Chiapas rebellion and the Colosio assassination clearly penalised the left, particularly in urban, middle class and many working class areas. The PRI's massive propaganda campaign stressed the need for stability and for a return to institutional politics and the PAN was able to benefit from this. It represented an alternative to the PRI, but an institutional one.

It is difficult to measure the impact of the personality of the candidates in the elections but it is commonly accepted that 'Diego', certainly in the early stages of the campaign, was more able to generate enthusiasm than Zedillo and Cárdenas. That his campaign lost impetus in the last few weeks is a matter of conjecture for both party activists and commentators alike.[8] It remains to

---

8 There was much speculation in the press and among *panistas* about the low-key style of 'Diego' in the later stages of the campaign. After the television debate, which he was judged by

be seen if PAN can find another such candidate for the next elections, although in Carlos Castillo, the party's president, and Ernesto Ruffo it has two ambitious and now experienced figures.

CONCLUSIONS

The PAN's loss of a good part of its traditional economic programme to the government party in the wake of the debt crisis caused introspection and divisions in the party in the 1980s. An old debate on the role of the State was revisited and, in the 1988 campaign at least, resolved in favour of an enabling, slimmed-down State shorn of most of its social functions. The party also committed itself to full, but critical participation in the electoral process in the hope/expectation of achieving political responsibility. Although the former shift proved to be short-lived, and was abandoned after the death of Clouthier in favour of a State which had a concern for the welfare of the community as a whole and which could curb the excesses of the free market-driven system, the political tactics, reinforced by a spate of mayoral and gubernatorial victories, remained much the same in the lead-up to the 1994 elections. Indeed the party stressed the primacy of politics in its propaganda and concentrated much of its efforts on demanding and negotiating political reforms.

The results of these tactics have, on the whole, been good, but not spectacular. In sub-national elections the PAN has continued steadily to gain posts and experience. In national contests it has consolidated its position in traditionally sympathetic states, significantly increased its support in states where its representation had earlier been mediocre and established a foothold in states where it had previously been weak. In these gains it has clearly benefited from an improvement in the conduct of elections and from the collapse of the *cardenista* vote.

It would, however, be dangerous to assume that these positive trends will persist. The regime's commitment to political reform is under pressure from

---

most commentators to have won and which produced a sharp rise in the PAN's showing in the polls, he was thought to have toned down his attacks on Zedillo and to have lost much of his enthusiasm for the hustings. His acknowledgment of the PRI's victory early in the morning after the elections and his acceptance of the overall probity of the conduct of the elections,despite numerous cases of irregularities, disturbed many of his followers. The reasons offered for this change in style range from his illness and/or exhaustion, a fear of actual victoryand a secret deal with the government which will allow the PAN to win a number of governorships during the Zedillo *sexenio*.

within the governing party and the 'clock can be turned back'. Moreover the change towards bipartism at state levels in 1994 might mean that in the future the government party machines will be able to concentrate their considerable resources on one party rather than two. Having disposed of the PRD it could next concentrate its considerable resources on the PAN. The *panista* leadership must also be concerned about the 1994 vote in the states in which it holds the governorships. 'Experience in government' is a vital part of the party's plan to win voter credibility. An inability to retain posts, unless explained as the results of electoral malpractice, will slow down, if not derail, the party's transition from an opposition role.

9 The Opposition and the 1994 Presidential Elections in Mexico[1]

Jorge Regalado

The political process of the 1994 Mexican presidential elections cannot be explained without considering the events of July 1988 when the crisis, centred on the state party which has governed Mexico continuously for over 70 years, began. From then it was clear that the PRI would have great difficulties in maintaining power. The political events which snowballed during 1994, combined with the slowness of the political governing classes to find adequate and efficient solutions to the new emerging reality, forced many to consider the strong possibility that the PRI would be beaten and, more importantly, that a political transition was inevitable. Society, generally speaking, would like to see substantial political changes in Mexico, with or without the PRI in power, as long as it signified the advent of democracy. This process advanced at full speed thanks to the growing response and participation of society in the public sphere, as well as both the strengthening and subsequent crisis of the social movements[2] and party political opposition,[3] but above all, it is due to the fact that the State party was not only incapable of incorporating itself into the process, but was indeed trying to stall it.

By the beginning of the summer of 1994 it became apparent that there was an increasing possibility of a victory for the PAN's Diego Fernández de

1 Translated by Jasmine Gideon and Nikki Craske.

2 Social movements which were highly active during 1980s slumped into a crisis resulting in a loss of initiative and their political identity as social movements. Many of them today appear tightly linked to the political parties, making the difference between the parties and movements hard to detect.

3 The main opposition parties are the *Partido Acción Nacional* (PAN) and the *Partido de la Revolución Democrática* (PRD). In a contradictory manner, the number of sympathisers grew and at the same time they have suffered internal divisions. These problems affected the decisions and positions taken by the parties.

Cevallos. However, a series of political events modified the scenario which led observers to comment of a *concertacesión*[4] between the PRI and the PAN. These observations were given credence when the PAN apparently slowed down its campaign after its success in the televised debate on 12 May 1994 and when Fernández de Cevallos conceded defeat so quickly on 22 August despite the 1 279 complaints presented to the *Instituto Federal Electoral* (IFE).[5] On the other hand, there was also movement on the left where two acts were becoming increasingly relevant: a) the resurgence of the *cardenista* campaign after the mass meeting at UNAM and, b) the interest reawakened by the EZLN calling for a National Convention for Democracy for 6-9 August.

There were many doubts about what would happen on and around 21 August, yet what could not be doubted was the extent of the protest throughout the country indicating that, whoever won, s/he would have to prove that s/he had done so legitimately and in addition would have to construct a plural government and orchestrate substantive political changes. In this sense, it was clear that the triumph of a general democratic approach was assured before the 21 August. That the possible defeat of the official candidate was seriously acknowledged even by *priístas* and President Salinas, was in itself a great victory. It only remained to be seen if the people would choose the democratising process promoted by the PRI or if they would prefer that proposed by the opposition. Superficially, the decision seemed easy but given the characteristics of the Mexican political system and the unpredictability of the process, it was not. Both another victory for the PRI and an opposition victory posed great risks and challenges, that is the risks and challenges of democracy, and this became the central issue. The question was whether to take up the challenge.

THE STALLING OF EVENTS

Before 1994 the electoral process was, for a number of reasons, a highly anticipated political event and it was felt that it would reach high levels of competitiveness. However, it was difficult to foresee the build up of events

4 *Concertacesión* refers to a form of pacted agreement outside the results of the ballot box based on actions, pressures and post-electoral blackmail.

5 446 of these pertained to the presidential elections and the rest to congressional and regional elections. The PRD made 85 per cent of the complaints.

which continually modified the political scene, nine of which are worth mentioning here:

- the armed uprising in Chiapas on 1 January and the subsequent leadership of two characters, Manuel Camacho Solís, the Commissioner for Peace, and the guerrilla *subcomandante* 'Marcos' who, excitingly, renewed a type of struggle now unheard of in Mexico and considered overcome in Latin America;
- the assassination of the PRI's presidential candidate, Luis Donaldo Colosio, on the 24 March 1994 in Tijuana;
- the designation, now by presidential '*videodazo*' of his 'successor', Ernesto Zedillo Ponce de León;[6]
- the nationally transmitted television debate between the three main candidates on 12 May, for the first time in Mexican political-electoral history, and subsequently, on the 30 May, between the PRD representative on the IFE, Samuel del Villar and Carlos Almada, director of the Federal Register of Electors;
- the consensus between the PRI, PAN and PRD regarding the appointment of respected citizens as Citizen Advisers;
- the support and recognition by the United Nations of a diverse range of non-governmental organisations (NGOs), to undertake electoral observations and to be ready to hold a 'rapid count' on the night of the elections to provide an indication of the trend of the results;[7]
- the resignation of Commissioner for Peace Manuel Camacho Solís (16 June 1994) in open disagreement with Zedillo over the events in Chiapas;
- the threatened resignation of the *Secretario de Gobernación* (Interior) Jorge Carpizo MacGregor (24 June 1994) arguing that political party 'pressures' were stopping him from carrying out his duties;
- the ELZN's call to hold a *Convención Nacional Democrática* only a few days before the elections.

---

6 This refers to the manner in which Ernesto Zedillo was nominated; a large number of governors, deputies and Cabinet members were called together by Salinas to watch a video in which Colosio, while still alive, spoke positively about Zedillo, who had acted as his campaign coordinator. Nothing more was necessary, everyone understood who would be the new candidate.

7 Out of all the recognised NGOs the one which stood out was the so-called *Alianza Cívica 1994* which grouped together around 400 civic groups nationwide. There was also the emergence of another group of intellectuals and political leaders who were known in the press as the *Frente Amplia* and later as the *Grupo San Angel* where initially Camacho participated.

These political events all came together; as one was dealt with, another emerged. Soon it was a question of what would happen next.

The electoral process took place in a different Mexico, one almost uncoupled by decree from its revolutionary history. The political Constitution and institutions created by the Mexican Revolutionary State had been modified to establish the neoliberal and privatisation model (see Powell, this volume). And so, in August 1994, 'two processes of change were to coincide, one foreseen and timely – the change of president the other unforeseen and of longer gestation which began at least a dozen years ago, – the change of the development model' (Meyer, 1993: 49). But not only that, by August the efforts made since 1988 by both civil society and opposition parties materialised in the direction of a peaceful, Mexican path to democracy.

THE FAILING POLITICAL SYSTEM

During his six years in power, Salinas de Gortari made a substantial attempt to transmit the image of a new modern Mexico to the outside world: neoliberal, open to investment, with commercial opportunities and a globalised economy. However, this modernity, notable in productive activities, has not been reflected in an improvement in the living conditions of the majority and provides a stark contrast to the outmoded political system.

Modernity, even for the current neoliberals, is synonymous with democracy. Yet it is democracy which is substantially lacking in Mexico, as well as jobs, housing, decent salaries and social security. Any form of modernisation of the political system cannot be contemplated whilst certain characteristics persist:

- presidentialism more firmly entrenched than ever where 'the Congress, Judicial Power and public arena belong to the President' (Monsiváis, 1993:5), and 'the basic political decisions are taken by closed groups' (Arizpe, 1993:28);
- when *el tapadismo* is maintained as the best sign of pre-modernity;[8]
- when the symbiosis between government and official party remains and as a consequence 'the needs of government are subsumed to the interests of the PRI and functionaries are moved from .... a Ministry to the official

8 This is the literal uncovering of the presidential candidate when the incumbent indicates his choice of successor.

party'[9] and illegal use is made of the public treasury for the campaign of the government party candidate;

- when the government maintains control of the electoral process and the electoral officials are mainly members of the government party, and fraud is well established, notwithstanding the technological innovations in the compilation of the electoral register (it must be the only case in the world where the voting card carries a photograph);
- where the electronic media are controlled and information is manipulated.[10]

The lack of modernity in Mexico is such that the process of presidential change is still referred to as the presidential 'succession'. The word *succession* conveys an idea of continuation and sequence, descendency, heritage and patrimony. We speak of 'transformation and reconfirmation of the summit of political power, but not of simple mechanisms, clear and recognised' (Cordera, 1993: 30) to bring about political change. The procedure which is followed is not well understood and therefore there is speculation over whether a decision is made by those 'belonging to the most inner circle of power' (Cordova, 1993: 32) or if 'the president makes the decision alone and the night before only a few people know about it' (Fernández Christlieb, 1993: 37). Whatever the case, what is certain is that the orthodox manner in which Colosio was first nominated represented a backward political step in that it 'prevented what would have been a more open and democratic political game between the seven precandidates of the official party' (Esther Kravoz in *El Financiero*, 24 December 1993); 'precandidates', it is worth noting, who were never publicly recognised as such in that none of them ever stated that he was looking for the candidature of the PRI. Zedillo's nomination similarly followed traditional practices.

The above merits emphasis in the sense that the Mexican presidency has made the development of a political class capable of thinking and acting independently impossible. Whilst this has had an effect on the opposition, those most affected are the governing political classes themselves for whom it is unthinkable to criticise the president, let alone oppose him. Deputies, senators, municipal presidents, governors and secretaries of State do not dare, or are not allowed, to think for themselves. They always interpret, or they

9 Porfirio Muñoz Ledo, President of the National Executive Committee of the PRD interviewed in *El Financiero*, 16 December 1993.

10 Televisa is a case in point. It is a private television company but a powerful news organisation where information in favour of the official candidate was slowly and systematically released.

assume they do, the thoughts of the president. This explains the 'tough and evident dislike that the President displayed towards Cárdenas and Muñoz Ledo for their boldness' (Monsiváis, 1993: 5) – that is, daring to question him and trying to speak to him as equals. In this sense, the attitudes and stands taken by Camacho Solís as Peace Commissioner and Carpizo as Secretary of State for *Gobernación* stood out, notwithstanding the distance between them.

Considering the way in which this scenario was fashioned it was neither an exaggeration nor out of context to contemplate a PRI defeat and government by one or more parties. Nothing was certain, but optimism grew because society showed signs of rapid political development and the country filled with 'civic initiatives with a fervour that was reminiscent of the last years of Porfiriato' (Gabriel Zaid in *Siglo 21*, 26 December 1993). On the other hand the opposition parties had strengthened and represented viable and credible alternatives to the governing PRI. As a result, analysts agreed that 1994 would be one of the most interesting electoral processes in the history of Mexico, the most closely scrutinised and the most competitive.

However, despite these advances there were also problems since modern political practices were not fully established. Exemplifying modernity were sectors of society in Mexico City which, totally independently of the government, demonstrated their capacity of organising and successfully executing a plebiscite which allowed people to express their opinion over the preferred form of government. Yet, alongside this, there are also examples not only of pre-modernity but of barbarity where in the short life of the PRD 260 of its militants have been assassinated. In addition, in some regions of the country, to participate in, or simply vote for, the opposition can mean risking life. It is therefore not surprising that in an investigation carried out by the Civic Alliance 94, a high percentage of citizens were worried about the possibility of violence and non-governability resulting from the election process.[11] This, and the behaviour of the official party and government, made it impossible to imagine that after August 1994 the democratic wave would reach Mexico. Furthermore, the events in Chiapas acted as a reminder that a large part of the country is closer to the poverty of Central America than the wealth of the First World. Nevertheless in his six-year report the *Secretario de Hacienda* (Treasury), Pedro Aspe Armella, insisted on stressing that poverty in Mexico is a myth since, according to him, what was really happening was 'the reduction of the rate of price increases to the consumer to the level of

11 This poll was carried out with 9 507 respondents from 20 states published in *La Jornada*. 30.6 per cent of the population considered that violence and ungovernability could occur and 35.5 per cent that a situation of violence with repression could occur (*La Jornada*, 30 June 1994).

recuperation of salaries, the increase in jobs and the reduction in the number of homes in extreme poverty' (*La Jornada*, 13 July 94).

THE OPPOSITION IN MEXICO

Opposition parties of both left and right have existed for many years in Mexico, as many registered as illegal. However, the opposition is not, nor ever has been, represented solely by political parties. Social movements, guerrilla groups and non-registered political organisations have also played their part. Although, given the type of political system in Mexico, for the opposition to play a role in electoral politics and aspire to government, it had to comply with a series of requisites imposed by the government. That is to have a place in the system, they must be recognised by a register drawn up by the same government they intend to oppose. This compels unregistered parties, social movements, organisations and individuals which want to participate in the electoral process, to form alliances with recognised parties. Whilst continuing to question these limitations, the opposition in general agreed to participate in the 1994 elections.

The population's increasing demands for democracy did not go unnoticed and gauging its potential, the problems and limitations of parties within an authoritarian political culture notwithstanding, the opposition tried to respond to this challenge. This provides a marked contrast to previous elections when a number of parties and social organisations together agreed to abstain from voting and some in this group believed, and indeed continue to believe, that violent revolution is the only way forward. In 1994 there was no party or democratic movement which remained at the margins. Even the EZLN had to recognise the importance of electoral participation; despite its decision not to accept government proposals, they decided to extend the truce until the elections had passed. All social and political forces were calling people to vote and not all were against the PRI.

The Mexican opposition of 1994 was not the same as it had been in 1988. One result of the changes and political advances that the country was experiencing was that the opposition also entered a process of political and ideological redefinition which resulted in ruptures and unexpected alliances. The combined opposition forces were so heterogeneous that it could include a modern guerrilla movement like the EZLN proposing, not the taking of power, but a democratic revolution, but which in the medium term also wanted to ensure that the elections of 21 August were transparent and credible.

Despite, indeed including the events in Chiapas, it is clear that the opposition and much of Mexican society continue to accept the peaceful and constitutional route to making social changes. Nonetheless, the government and its party decided to continue with the obstacles delaying democratic advances. Mexico represents one of the last systems in the world where 'the idea of alternation in power is unacceptable' and therefore 'today it remains an exception to the democratizing wave due to the efficiency of its political structures in concentrating of power' (Meyer, 1993: 49).

Although the opposition has been in existence for decades, it was not until 1988 that it began to acquire a real dimension and develop its vocation for power, thus becoming a risk for the PRI. This began following the internal rupture of the PRI and the departure in 1987 of the leaders of the *Corriente Democrática* (CD) led most notably by Cuauhtémoc Cárdenas, Porfirio Muñoz Ledo and Ifigenia Martínez Navarrete, who subsequently established the *Frente Democrático Nacional* (FDN). Later the *Partido de la Revolución Democrática* (PRD) emerged, made up of members of the CD and other left-wing parties and political organisations.

The PRI learnt some lessons from its bitter experience of 1988 and as a result, always counting on the support of the PAN, reformed the electoral law to prohibit alliances and party coalitions from presenting a common candidate for the Presidency of the Republic in 1994. The PAN following its electoral triumphs in Baja California and Chihuahua, operated on the grounds of being a 'co-governing' party with the conviction that it alone could secure victory in the elections. This conviction grew following the televised debate; prior to this the PAN lacked any real possibility of winning.

Prior to 1988 the opposition was content with governing any municipality, however small, or with leading a union, neighbourhood or *ejido*. It is true that their stated objective was to win power but, in reality, they did not believe that they could achieve this through the electoral process. Consequently, their real goal was to form the second electoral force, but recognising in advance that this position would not place anyone on the verge of power. This vision changed during the Salinas administration; the opposition as a whole governed approximately 230 municipalities in Mexico (10 per cent of the total), including a number of important cites.

The PAN, unaided, won the governorship of Chihuahua and Baja California and 'negotiated' that of Guanajuato. However, these experiences have not demonstrated any radically different tendencies or practices to those of the PRI, except perhaps in the case of Baja California where certain democratising processes have been seen with changes of power in municipalities and the local congress, the separation of powers and decentralisation of state power in favour of the municipality (cf. Vicencio this volume). However, due to inexperience of government, the PAN has had to accommodate businesspeople in government. In this sense the PRD is no better off than the PAN; it has not even had any experience of state government, but it has participated in municipal government, most notably in the state of Guerrero.[12] Before the new law prohibiting joint candidates, the possibility was briefly considered of an alliance that would prove lethal to the PRI – a common candidate for the PRD and the PAN. However, the differences between these two parties grew considerably and naturally, the PRI did all it could to encourage this. The distinctive attitude that the PRI adopted towards the two parties is widely acknowledged. The intense relationship between the PRI and PAN bought the latter both positive and negative political consequences. Its best power positions, governorships and some mayoralties, were, in general, gained through means of *concertacesión*. This was the case of the city council of Mérida, Yucatán, where, in late 1993, elections were held which were plagued with irregularities. The PRI claimed victory, the PAN agreed that it did not have proof of winning but neither did it believe the PRI's victory and called for the annulling of the whole electoral process, threatening not to participate in any civic pact for the 1994 federal process and to initiate civil resistance. Surprisingly, a few days after the election and the official declaration of PRI victory, it was retracted and most unusually, without modifying the electoral results, triumph was conferred on the PAN candidate with the argument that he had won second place and naturally he accepted. Such compromising situations resulted in a critical current at the centre of the PAN, called the *Foro Democrático y Doctrinario* later the (unregistered) *Partido del Foro Democrático*. It was comprised of distinguished *panistas* identified with the traditional, democratic and oppositional beliefs of the party who were disenchanted with such events (cf Stansfield this volume). Similarly, public opinion had grown increasingly sceptical about the current role of the PAN as a real opposition party. Such splits and reorganisations led to a new opposition geography.

With different strategies and tactics, the local government experience and new relations with the government, the Mexican opposition, even before Chiapas, found itself ready and willing to challenge the power of the PRI. This was not an easy goal to achieve but now there was talk of the possibility

12 Data and certain ideas in this paragraph are taken from Peter Ward's paper 'Governments of Opposition in Mexico' presented in Guadalajara, December 1993.

that in the next presidential cabinet there would be space for a member of the opposition.[13] Independently of who won the elections, many thought the terms of the coexistence between the political parties would have to change.

THE PARTIES AND THEIR CANDIDATES

The following is an analysis of the opposition candidates of left and right, with the exception of the PAN. Given the impossibility of nominating a single candidate for an alliance or interparty coalition, there were nine parties and candidates. With the opinion polls indicating that abstentionism seemed to be in decline, a bigger problem was taking shape; the possible fragmentation of the opposition vote. This question was more worrying since it was always clear that many opposition groups never had the chance of carrying out a real campaign, less achieve victory. Consequently, the electorate concentrated on three candidates: Luis Donaldo Colosio and to a lesser degree Ernesto Zedillo for the PRI, Cuauhtémoc Cárdenas for the PRD-*Alianza Democrática Nacional* (ADN) and Diego Fernández de Cevallos for the PAN. Nearer to 21 August, Cecilia Soto, the *Partido del Trabjo* (PT) candidate, was put in fourth place by the opinion polls but there were many questions about her political past and above all about the propriety with which she carried out her electoral campaign; on more than one occasion candidates of the PAN and PRD had seen teams from the PRI replacing one of their posters or placards with one of Zedillo and another of Soto.

So, the real competition was between the PRI, the PAN and the PRD. However, many thought that in reality there were only two options since there were no substantial differences between the PAN and the PRI. In an equally simplistic manner, it was claimed that Cárdenas wanted to return to the populist and statist past whilst others defended him as the only one who represented the possibility of democracy or change. It was never doubted that Colosio or Zedillo symbolised the continuity of the neoliberal project which began in Mexico in 1982 during the de la Madrid mandate. The project of the PAN coincided with that of the PRI, so much so that they insisted that the PRI had stolen its programme, and Diego Fernández, even before becoming a candidate, devoted his time to opposing Cárdenas. The extent of his anti-*cardenista* vocation was demonstrated in the televised debate. It was

13 This idea was popular when it was assumed that the PRI would win and the PAN come second but the question became: would the PRI be prepared to have a PRD cabinet member if it were the second electoral force and would the PRD be prepared to accept such an offer?

made clear that for both the PRI and the PAN, Cárdenas was the opponent to defeat. The other parties and candidates who were involved in the contest were the federal deputy Cecilia Soto for the *Partido del Trabajo* (PT); Marcela Lombardo Otero for the *Partido Popular Socialista* (PPS); Rafael Aguilar Talamantes for the *Partido Frente Cardenista de Reconstrucción Nacional* (PFCRN); Pablo Emilio Madero for the *Partido Demócrata Mexicano* (PDM)-*Unión Nacional Opositora* (UNO); Jorge González Torres for the *Partido Verde Ecologista* and Alvaro Pérez Trevino for the *Partido Auténtico de la Revolución Mexicana* (PARM). Even an un-registered, independent candidate carried out a campaign; Alejandro Gascón Mercado for the *Partido de la Revolución Socialista* (PRS).

In the 1988 elections, Cárdenas was supported by a number of these parties: the PPS, the PARM, the PFCRN and the *Ecologistas*. The PDM, now UNO, presented its own candidate and did not secure the minimum national vote necessary to maintain its registration. In 1994 it returned to participate with conditional registration and a new name and emblem. The PRS was never registered and in 1988 it did not put forward a candidate nor, as on this occasion, make an alliance. In reality it was always a totally marginal party. It is worth noting that, despite their slim chances of winning, two women were nominated as candidates which at least had a symbolic impact. The pattern, first started in 1982 and repeated in 1988 by Rosario Ibarra de Piedra seems to have become institutionalised.[14]

Their Possibilities

In 1988, three parties, the PFCRN, the PPS and the PARM, were on the crest of the *cardenista* wave and were central protagonists of that movement. As a result of this a good number of its deputies entered Congress. It is acknowledged that Cárdenas allowed them to receive more votes in this election than they had obtained in their entire history, however they declined the invitation to join the PRD. In 1994 they not only played a different role but had to resolve considerable problems that threatened their entire existence. The opposition has on various occasions been described as fictitious; sustained by votes of the government granted to them when they are in a

14 Rosario Ibarra de Piedra was the presidential candidate for the first time in 1982 registered with the *Partido Revolucionario de los Trabajadores* (PRT) and supported by a broad range of political and social groups and organisations. She has stood out in Mexico and at an international level for her activities in favour of political prisoners, the disappeared, the persecuted and political exiles and, more generally, in defence of human rights. The recognition of her work resulted in her nomination for the Noble Peace Prize. In 1988 she was newly nominated for the PRT but many of those who supported her in 1982 decided to back Cárdenas. In the 1994 elections Ibarra publicly declared her sympathy and support of Cárdenas.

position to administer them discretionally. However, in 1994, the situation was more complicated; the government and official party were more concerned with securing themselves enough votes than distributing votes to minor parties. Also, the divide-and-rule tactics were less effective against a solid opposition and a more politically aware electorate. It was soon evident that the smaller parties were not contemplating success in 1994, but were more concerned with conserving their registration and having some deputies elected. However, with the degree of campaign competitiveness it was obvious that for some their registrations were jeopardy.

The PFCRN had internal differences which resulted in various leaders and grassroot members abandoning it. Some promptly affiliated themselves to another party and others set up a new party.[15] This group were always ready to negotiate with the government in return for little. They delivered an anti-*cardenista* speech and have always proudly professed to being the first left-wing electoral force, without ever having been tested at the ballot box. The leader, Rafael Aguilar Talamantes, has demonstrated his cunning and political opportunism; in 1988 with a sense of foresight he rapidly changed the name of his previous party (PST) to that of the *Frente Cardenista* which was sufficient to make it the party with the greatest number of votes within the FDN. In 1994, however, things did not work out for him. He was heavily discredited by his unsolicited offering, two days into the Chiapas uprising, to act as civil ambassador and representative of the EZLN – it's surprising that he didn't change the name of the party to the PFZRN (*Partido Frente Zapatista de Reconstrución Nacional*)!

Although the ecological problem in Mexico is extremely serious, the *Ecologistas* has not had the same success as similar parties in Europe. The party, although small, has also experienced internal struggles over who should be leader. Its candidate was conspicuous as an employee of *Gobernación* and, as a result, the main ecological groups did not join the party and nor did they support its candidate. As in the case of the PFCRN, local leaders have left the party, some with the aim of obtaining local party registration.

The PARM has been immersed in a severe internal crisis resulting from corruption. For various reasons, its long-standing leader, Carlos E. Cantu Rosas, was dismissed. Consequently he, along with seventeen other leaders, was definitively expelled from the party. Although the party recognised that

15 For example, in Jalisco as a result of corruption problems related to the legalisation foreign vehicles, the leaders left the party together and soon formed the *Partido Popular Jaliciense* (PPJ) and requested registration as a local party. They decided to support Cecilia Soto which resulted in Cesar Humberto González Magallon and Miguel Pelayo Lepe, principal leaders of the PPJ, being candidates for federal plurinominal deputy and senator respectively.

it could only hope to receive between 2.3 and 2.5 per cent of the national vote (*El Financiero*, 26 November 1993), with the new candidate it was difficult to be more optimistic and things worsened after the nomination. In Sonora for example, several municipal committees defected to offer their support to Cecilia Soto.[16] If this were not enough, at the beginning of March, the state, municipal and district leaders in twenty states announced both their resignation and their intention to form the *Partido de la Auténtica Democracia* (PAD) and join UNO.[17]

The PDM emerged in the 1970s, yet its ideology belongs to a long political tradition in the country, especially in the west and the Bajío. In 1988 it lost its registration and the experience, it was hoped, would lead them towards 'important changes in its direction and even in its practices' (Alonso, 1989: 15). The changes were such that to participate in 1994, the PDM was disbanded and its members joined other little known political organisations to form the UNO. Pablo Emilio Madero, nephew of the apostle of democracy in Mexico, Francisco I. Madero, was nominated as the presidential candidate.[18]

The above events clearly marked Cárdenas as the principal candidate of the democratic left-wing opposition. In general he was seen to be the major critic of the system and before the presidential debate he was considered the most likely to beat the PRI. However, events changed after his meeting with the members of UNAM. Soon it became apparent that the best he could hope for would be for both his personal and the PRD's standing as the main opposition party to continue, especially given the closed and aggressive contest fought by the Salinas government. Despite the importance acquired in its few years of existence, the future of the PRD is not clear, given that it has been called into question for failing to be open to popular demands and for having reproduced the old system of parties, groups and power quotas. It can justifiably be said that Cárdenas suffered the most political attacks; Diego

16 It must be pointed out that, at the time of being nominated as presidential candidate for the PT, Cecilia Soto was federal deputy for the PARM in Sonora. Patricio Estévez Nenninger, state leader of the party, is married to Soto.

17 The mass resignation occurred in Jalisco, Aguascalientes, Campeche, San Luis Potosí, Tlaxcala, Veracruz, Zactecas, Guerrero, Michoacán, Nayarit, Nuevo Leon, Oaxaca, Baja California, Colima, Distrito Federal, Guanajuáto, Chihuahua and Quintana Roo. The resignations were as a result of their failure to have Javier Garcia Paniagua nominated as PARM presidential candidate (*Siglo 21* 6 March 1994).

18 Madero had been presidential candidate for the PAN in 1982 and leader of the *Partido del Foro Democrático* a position he later abandoned after his disagreement with the decision of the party to support the candidature of Cárdenas.

Fernández de Cevallos, Cecilia Soto and Rafael Talamantes spent a large part of their campaigns attacking him and on many occasions with more vehemence than that shown to the two official party candidates. However, given that it was only awarded 17.1 per cent of the vote, it will have to reassess its opposition role over the next six years.

ALLIANCES AND CONVERGENCES

During the Salinas Administration a number of key events led to the emergence of new groupings that were not characterised by a strict ideological definition; political leaders of diverse tendencies left various political parties then joined together to create new organisations and political leaders abruptly abandoned their parties to become candidates of others. This represented something novel about the 1994 campaign. It is not that this type of manoeuvring had not existed before but the novelty was the extent to which this happened. In 1982 alliance formed around the candidates of the left, Rosario Ibarra de Piedra and Arnoldo Martínez Verdugo, in 1988 in a broader way but still within the left, they were found around Cárdenas, however in 1994 the alliances and convergences surpassed these experiences; here are two examples of distinct political tendencies and possibilities.

The *Unión Nacional Opositora* (UNO)

This alliance emerged from the ashes of the PDM but also included the Liberal Democrats, the Christian Democrats and the *Federación de Partidos del Pueblo*, parties with little profile, but with all their hopes and goals of gaining registration and of winning a few deputies resting on their presidential candidate, the ex-*panista* Pablo Emilio Madero. UNO brought together many groups and civic organisations in this quest. A challenge was whether UNO would be able to go beyond the PDM's achievements. However, whatever the outcome, the need for change within the PDM was obvious after its poor showing in 1988.

The *Alianza Democrática Nacional* (ADN)

The broad support that Cárdenas would receive began to take shape shortly after the start of 1994. On the 29 January in Ciudad Juárez, Chihuahua, 'political organisations and local civic groups formed the Coordinating Committee for the Support of the Cuauhtémoc Cárdenas Campaign. Among the group participants were the *Frente de Orientación Ciudadana* led by Sergio Hayen, who had been state president for the PAN until 1992; *Destacamento del Pueblo* an organisation affiliated to the PT; the Democratic

Teachers and the *Foro Democrático*.' (*La Jornada*, 30 January 1994). To gain the widest possible support, Cárdenas was proposed as the citizens' candidate before becoming the PRD's candidate and gradually a diverse group of political and social organisations showed their allegiance. The ADN was formally constituted as a political front on the 5 February 1994 in the Federal District with the aim of making Cárdenas the President of the Republic. The participating groups included unregistered parties, both national and regional, urban popular movements, peasant groups, professional associations and civic organisations.

Various elements contributed to make such a convergence possible: a) the tense political situation that the country was experiencing and the general crisis in which the PRI found itself, b) the ability to unite and the political and moral confidence which Cárdenas characterised and c) the offer that 50 per cent of the candidatures would go to non-PRD affiliated citizens. In this way various social and political leaders and members of citizens organisations were registered as candidates for deputy and senator.

Nevertheless, as the PRD recognised, despite its importance this alliance would not be sufficient to guarantee success especially since a large majority of the population was disorganised and, above all, it was uncertain whether the people would have the enthusiasm or commitment to turn up at the ballot box. Consequently, the fight for a peaceful transition to democracy became an essential part of the process thanks to both the events in Chiapas and to the civic initiatives that came from unaligned organisations and individuals who, without openly declaring their political sympathy, were most concerned with promoting the largest possible attendance at the ballot box to ensure a credible electoral process and a legitimate winner.

CONCLUSION

The 1994 electoral process has given us reasons to be both optimistic and pessimistic. From the start certain elements stood out: a) with the enforced change of candidate the PRI showed itself to be weaker and that it had entered politically the final road as the single party in power; b) the opposition was developing systematically to the level of becoming a viable alternative; c) the population was showing increasing levels of politicisation and did not, on this occasion, wish to remain on the margins of the electoral process; d) interest in the electoral process was demonstrated by the various groups of electoral observers – notably the Civic Alliance 1994 and e) the private television companies were obliged to provide free space for the opposition candidates, albeit at the last moment, not at prime viewing time and without neglecting to show their preference for the official candidate.

Thus, not withstanding the huge advantages of the PRI, there was electoral competition. It was highly significant that neither of the official candidates were seen as the certain future presidents. Society had developed politically and showed its capacity to distinguish and decide between the proposals and the candidates. This was partly demonstrated in the televised debate between the main candidates. Candidates and parties were obliged to improve and clarify their offers and had to 'de-ideologise' the competition.

In sum, society generally showed itself disposed towards peaceful political change, however it also showed show signs of turning to civil insurrection if the vote was again not respected. At least this was the indication given by their sympathy for the *zapatista* guerrillas and their interest in participating in the *Convención Nacional Democrática* convened by the EZLN. On the other hand, the PRI government showed few signs of trying to change at the same pace as society, much less accept that society would now set the tone. Zedillo's campaign was characterised by the traditional practices of busing in 'supporters', the use of the corporative vote, its unhealthy relationship with the government and the control of the electronic media.

The major social concern had been whether the PRI would insist on fraudulent practices and the use and abuse of State resources, or, should the unresolved Chiapas conflict have coincided with a non-credible election, whether it would be prepared for post-electoral conflict and social tension. Given the character of the Mexican political system, the possibility of peace and violent conflict depended, in the first instance, on the attitude of the government and its party. In the event, the results were accepted by large sections of the population, the protests of the PRD notwithstanding, however the volatility of the situation was underlined when the PRI's general secretary, José Ruiz Massieu, was assassinated on 28 September 1994. Identified with the modernising wing of the party, this indicated continued tensions within the party itself.[19]

In the elections between 1988-94 (including 6 July) the fundamental problem was the population's disbelief in the results. This problem is intimately linked to the question of the legitimacy of the future government[20] and possibly Colosio's comments tried to answer this, 'the PRI does not need (nor want) even a single vote at the margin of the law'; this was never

19 Tensions which have continued to grow, particularly after the arrest of Raúl Salinas in February 1995 accused of the intellectual murder of Ruiz Massieu.

20 See the series of essays published in *Cuadernos de Nexos* No.67 January 1994.

reiterated by Zedillo. This and the way in which Zedillo was 'nominated', showed again that Salinas and the PRI were not disposed to adopt completely the risks of democracy.

It was clear that the credibility and legitimacy of President Zedillo depended on a clean and transparent electoral process, the PRI had to 'understand that the verdict about the cleanliness of an election is not in their hands, but in the hands of the opposition' (Molinar Horcasitas, 1994: xviii). In this election it was not only the PRI which could judge the process, the EZLN, the electoral observers, the Citizens' Councils of IFE, the National Democratic Convention and also international public opinion watched the final results.

Perhaps the greatest lesson on 1994 for everyone, in particular for academics and analysts, is the proof of how much we lack an understanding of the profound political sentiments felt by the Mexican people. Self-critically we must recognise that Mexican political science has failed to analyse adequately the most important presidential elections this century, those of 1988 and 1994.

10 The State, the Countryside ... and Capitalism

John Gledhill[1]

The modification of Constitutional Article 27 by the administration of Carlos Salinas de Gortari seemed to mark a watershed in the history of rural society in post-revolutionary Mexico. Wayne Cornelius judged *ejido* reform 'probably the most politically audacious step to be taken by Carlos Salinas during his presidency thus far', given the role of the *ejido* in the maintenance of political control over the peasantry, suggesting that the constitutional amendments 'passed with only the feeblest of dissents', not simply because the political opposition was weak but because there was 'widespread recognition, even among the most fervent defenders of the *ejido*, that something had to be done to modernise and stimulate this sector of Mexican agriculture' (Cornelius, 1992: 3).

Given the regime's adeptness at engineering consent from the leaders of peasant organisations, such a conclusion might seem premature *a priori*, and doubly so in the wake of the Chiapas uprising. Nevertheless, the heterogeneity of Mexican rural society guarantees diversity in the way that *ejidatarios* view the implications of the reform and respond to it. As Zendejas and Mummert (1994) observe, in some local contexts the *ejido* is much more than an economic institution and may have a social and political value to people who are not themselves *ejidatarios*. There are certainly local contexts where more commercially successful elements within *ejidos* are already pushing for full land privatisation. Yet even where something approaching the neoliberal ideal of how *ejido* reform should be conducted in areas of high commercial potential enjoys politically effective local backing, responses will still be influenced by the wider effects of economic policy and the expectations they engender.

As Cornelius rightly argues, there are a number of good structural reasons why a massive sell-up of peasant land is not likely to occur in the near future,

1 I gratefully acknowledge the support of the Wenner-Gren Foundation for Anthropological Research and the Central Research Fund of the University of London for the collection of field data used in this paper.

ranging from the fact that the new legislation largely gives *de jure* legitimacy to *de facto* practices on tenure and alienation to the limited interest of modern agribusiness in land ownership as such (1992: 7). Yet the other side of the new agrarian law, the removal of the legal basis for most petitions for new land redistribution and extension of new guarantees to owners who convert pasture land to arable, has deeper implications than Cornelius acknowledges: it impedes struggles by the rural poor to wrest subsistence resources from existing latifundists and expansionary cattle ranchers, undermining the viability of semi-proletarian modes of life. How ordinary peasants view the matter is important, since the reform of Article 27 is a *symbol*, adding to other experiences shaping perceptions about the future.

However much pro-regime intellectuals like Octavio Paz (*El País*, 7 January 1994) may wish to dismiss the rebellion as an atavism, the uprising in Chiapas not only demonstrated the continuing difficulties confronting those who wish to exorcise the ghost of *agrarismo* (Gledhill, 1991) but the consistency between longstanding popular projects and the new politics of identity in a postmodern world of globalised mediascapes (Appadurai, 1990) and late capitalist marginalisation (Bartra, 1992). Yet at the more mundane but no less significant level of individual strategies, the changing pattern of international migration from both rural and urban areas of Mexico during the 1980s, reflected a general sea-change in perceptions of life chances within Mexico (Cornelius, 1991; Escobar Latapi, 1993). The geographical and social composition of international movements widened to a point where we can talk about the transnationalisation of the opportunity structure of the Mexican 'popular sector' as a whole (Escobar Latapi, 1993: 75–7).

Against this backdrop, it makes little sense to talk about 'modernising the *ejido*' in abstraction from the international political economy of food production, particularly in the case of Mexico, which has long been integrated into transnational systems of production *and* social reproduction. From this point of view, the *ejidos* as they exist today are already 'modernised' and have played an important role in the evolution of transnational class relations which link rural poverty in Mexico to rural and urban poverty in the United States. The issues are complex, involving not merely political economy, but the cumulative effects of the social strategies pursued by a diverse group of actors, in both Mexico and the United States, and also political processes reflecting the differing organisational capacities of different social and ethnic groups. In this discussion I will restrict myself to two issues. The first is the way that the Salinas regime's apparent 'audacity' on the question of *ejido* reform has been accompanied by a less decisive approach to agricultural policy as a whole. I then go on to argue that improvisation is an inadequate response to the real problems posed by a continuously evolving bi-national political economy of food production.

CAMPESINISTAS AND TECHNOCRATS

Cornelius notes that the *ejido* reform itself is not without contradictions. He ascribes this to divisions within the regime between the *campesinista* faction led by Gustavo Gordillo and Arturo Warman and 'modernising technocrats'. For the former, State tutelage over the *ejidos* was a dead hand which inhibited potential capital accumulation by sections of the land reform peasantry capable of producing commercial surpluses (Gordillo, 1988). The leap of faith which this diagnosis invites us to make when it is wedded to neoliberalism is that peasants can reorganise themselves as effective market agents in production and commercialisation within a system which is dominated economically by transnational corporations and remains subject to politically reinforced structures of private economic power domestically. In practice, the model only appears plausible with continuing indirect State intervention to regulate markets and control the use of non-economic power for economic ends.

The *campesinista* perspective does, however, embody an important truth which distinguishes it from the technocrat position. Producers sowing marginal land which is of no interest to capitalist farmers have been able to supplement family income deriving principally from off-farm activities, wage employment and migration. Nothing would be gained from eliminating such 'marginal' production. The labour expended on it and resources used by it have no competing uses in the short and medium term. It makes low rural wages sustainable and restrains permanent out-migration.

The technocratic viewpoint focuses on the fiscal costs of producer subsidies and the need to make Mexican agriculture more competitive internationally. Salinas proclaimed early in the *sexenio* that food policy would be qualified by the principle of comparative advantage:

> ... the country's food policy has as its fundamental objective to attain *food sovereignty*, which is understood to be the *the efficient use of comparative advantage* which the country possesses for agricultural and forestry production. (Appendix to *Ley Federal de Reforma Agraria*, 1991: 741–3; author's translation and emphasis).

This proposition sounded alarm bells for Salinas critics, notably José Luis Calva (1991a). Calva predicted a massive flight of population from rural areas as peasant farmers faced an insuperable 'cost-price squeeze' following the withdrawal of subsidies and the liberalisation of imports.

Looking at the aggregate figures for the disparity between US and Mexican average productivity figures for maize (4.35:1), many commentators concluded that this meant that Mexico would deepen its food dependency on imports. According to the figures supplied by the *Scretaría de Alimietnos y Recursos Hidraúlicos* (SARH) in the NAFTA negotiations, less than eight per cent of Mexico's corn farmers were competitive at international prices in 1990, and only 35 per cent were growing maize at a profit with the existing domestic price. The issue of food dependence was central to the debates about Mexican agriculture long before Salinas became president (Barkin and Suárez, 1985), but Salinas approach provoked renewed debate around the long-term economic and political dangers of abandoning real 'food sovereignty' (Barraclough, 1992). Many technocrats have argued that Mexico should meet its maize needs from imports, concentrating agricultural development efforts on fruit and vegetables for export, an argument which Cornelius suggests only makes sense if the 'safety-valves' of migration to the United States and the urban informal sector in Mexico remain open (Cornelius, 1992: 5–6).

At first sight, some of the fears expressed in the first half of Salinas *sexenio* appear exaggerated. Escalating dependence on basic food imports was reversed in 1991 and 1992. Moreover, the regime has moved to a system of direct producer subsidies, *Programa de Apoyos Directo al Campo* (PROCAMPO), which includes marginal corn farmers (see below). And, contemporary patterns of out-migration from rural communities are complex, and movement to the United States is continuing to increase. Yet it was the medium-sized cities of the centre, west, and northern border which became the foci of internal migration during the 1980s (Escobar Latapi, 1993: 74). The real issue is what kind of infrastructure and job opportunities smaller urban centres will be able to provide in the 1990s. Many towns which remain dependent on the prosperity of an agricultural hinterland have been devastated by agricultural recession combined with the collapse of public sector salaries and employment, and if we look more closely at underlying trends in the farm sector, the picture remains disturbing.

What happened over the Salinas *sexenio* suggests the absence of any coherent strategy for 'agricultural modernisation'. Mexican agriculture is not perceived as a core sector in the technocratic project of export-led development and economic integration with the United States. Nor is it central for the Mexican transnational capitalist interests with most to gain from NAFTA. The reason that policy appears improvised, is not, however, so much a reflection of factional conflicts within the regime as a consequence of strong objective constraints, both political and economic.

FROM STRUCTURAL ADJUSTMENT TO PROCAMPO

The agricultural situation which Salinas confronted on entering office was dismal. The absolute volume of national production of basic grains for human consumption fell by over 20 per cent between 1981 and 1988, whilst the per capita harvest declined by a third (Calva, 1991b: 41–2). Gross public fixed investment in agriculture fell 68.2 per cent between 1982 and 1986, prejudicing even the maintenance of existing infrastructure. The irrigated area fell by 22 per cent between 1981 and 1988. The real value of credits offered by the State development banks and commercial sector declined below that of the early 1970s, and the previously subsidised or even negative real interest rates the development banks charged rose to 'usurious real levels' (Calva, 1991a: 6). Deflated by the index of agricultural input prices, the real guaranteed price of maize fell 43.7 per cent between 1982 and 1988, and that of beans by more than 50 per cent (Solís Rosales, 1990: 931–3). Input subsidies for fertiliser fell from a total of 9756 million pesos in 1982 to 7069 million in 1988, and those for irrigation water from 4581 million to 1308 million, measured at 1980 price levels (Escalante, 1993). Producers therefore faced a serious deterioration in the relationship between the real prices of agricultural outputs and the real price of inputs. By the end of 1988, 750 000 cultivators of basic grains were unable to cover the costs of their credit from the proceeds of their harvests. Small producers were hardest hit, but this was not simply a crisis for the *campesinos*. The falling sales of tractors and fertilisers reflected erosion of the profitability of capitalist farming (Calva, 1991b: 9–10).

Per capita production also fell in the meat and dairy industries, but the impact of declining grain production was particularly severe for the economy as a whole, since supply shortfalls had to be made up by unprecedented levels of importation. By 1990 the deficit in the country's trade balance in agricultural, pastoral and agroindustrial products had reached $US 1530 million (Alcocer, 1991: 38). The deficit was aggravated by the removal of protection which meant that Mexican farmers who had crops like sorghum and rice to sell in 1990 found the market flooded with cheap imports. In many cases, the imports had been released from US reserves, so that Mexican producers were asked to compete with imports priced at the costs enjoyed by American farmers four years earlier.

The 1989 price of sorghum in the Ciénega de Chapala region of Michoacán was 350 000 pesos a ton (equivalent to the national average rural price). This fell to a new low of 280 000 pesos in November 1990, when regional *acaparadores* (buyers) refused to honour the *precio de concertación* (negotiated price) of 414 000 pesos per ton established by agreement between the government, the *Confederación Nacional Campesina* (CNC) and the private sector buyers after this crop was removed from the system of guaranteed prices.[2] Even at the better market prices achieved in the region of La Piedad, 360 000 pesos per ton, a producer with 3.5 hectares who achieved a harvest of six tons per hectare in 1990 still had to cope with a 100 per cent increase in production costs relative to 1989, and could expect to receive a net income little higher than the minimum wage for six months of farm labour. This miserable situation was, however, idyllic in comparison with that faced by sorghum farmers in the Ciénega de Chapala, who earned even less on average yields of between 3 and 3.5 tons per hectare. Although US sorghum farmers, on average, have a productivity advantage over the Mexican producer, the difference is slight, at ten per cent, and the irrigation districts of Michoacán figure in the ranks of the most productive zones nationally (Martínez Fernández, 1990: 939). The crucial difference between American and Mexican sorghum growers was that between 1982 and 1989 the former received subsidies to the tune of 32 per cent of their total income (Alcocer, 1991: 38). Yet sorghum imports to Mexico were unrestricted and free of duty in 1989 and 1990.

Producers of rice in Veracruz and Colima experienced similar difficulties with cheap US imports, again a reflection of a higher rate of subsidy on the American side, which the *Secretaría de Agricultura y Recursos Hidráulicos* (SARH) estimated at $US 85 per metric ton. The recently privatised sugar mills of Los Reyes, Michoacán, found themselves equally uncompetitive against imports despite extracting a record quantity of sugar from the cane cut in the 1990–1 harvest (Powell, forthcoming). In the spring of 1991, milk producers were repeating the complaints of the arable farmers in the face of declining prices and demand for their product on the part of a national dairy industry increasingly meeting its needs from powdered milk imports. Roads were blocked to traffic and milk poured onto the highway. The official response was that imports had been increased to cope with an expected shortfall in domestic supply, but no promises were made on future prices and small producers were left with the problem of feeding cows whose milk could not be sold outside the village.

---

2 There may be wider lessons to be learned from this experience. Dependence on *precios de concertación* as a means of creating and stabilising regional markets for agricultural products remains a cornerstone of current policies.

Government liberality towards imports wiped out much of the benefit which might have accrued to the nation from the fact that 1990 was a year of good rainfall, a factor which reversed the contraction of gross physical farm output of the previous two years. All farms producing grains were hit by the cost-price squeeze but peasant farmers who failed to secure an income sufficient to cover their debts to credit institutions were worst affected, given the State's eagerness to run credit policy on more 'commercial' lines.

The 1990 rainy-season cycle coincided with the end of administration of agricultural insurance by the parastatal *Aseguradora Nacional Agrícola y Ganadera SA* (ANAGSA). On the basis of personal observation, I would have to say that the way its successor, AGROASEMEX, operated in its first year made it virtually impossible for peasants to receive indemnification and there were press reports of complaints against AGROASEMEX from many regions. Denied indemnification, a majority of *ejidatarios* inevitably defaulted on the loans provided to them by BANRURAL. This gave the Bank the pretext needed to close seven of its sixteen branches in Michoacán in July 1991, declaring that its diminishing resources would be concentrated on those who had proved their capacity to repay in recent cycles.

The ideological justification for these developments centred on 'ending paternalism' and promoting 'responsibility' on the part of credit recipients. The old system managed by ANAGSA was certainly riddled with corruption and encouraged peasants to cooperate in fraudulent transactions from which bureaucrats were the primary beneficiaries (Gledhill, 1991). Yet as Gustavo Gordillo demonstrated in the writing of his militant phase, the root of the problem was the State's own strategies for inhibiting peasant empowerment, strategies which Salinas himself has exploited with consummate skill throughout the *sexenio* in engineering consent to his reforms and dividing potentially recalcitrant forces through selective deployment of federal patronage. Peasant views of the problem of their debts to BANRURAL in Michoacán mirrored Marilyn Gates's account of the conviction of a broad spectrum of commercial and subsistence producers in Campeche that:

> ... ejidatarios should not be held in default, either specifically in terms of debts owed to the credit bank for failing to produce in misguided government projects or more generally as scapegoats for the failure of State policies. Rather, ejidatarios believe that the government has defaulted on its constitutional contract with the peasantry to deliver social justice in the countryside ... (Gates, 1993: 7)

The policy shift carried through in the period 1990 to 1991 was a 'wager on the strong', redirecting the remaining public resources targeted at agriculture towards the most viable commercial producers, but leaving it to private capital to fill the gap created by the overall reduction in State support.

At first sight, the policy appeared viable. National production of six of the ten principle crops, including wheat, rice and soya, continued to decline through 1991 and 1992, but maize and beans production improved significantly, enabling the country to cut back its imports of these basic staples to insignificant levels (Escalante, 1993). This turnaround reflected the impact of a deliberate policy to preserve a guaranteed price for maize and beans whilst prices of other crops were allowed to fall to international levels. Although the maize and beans prices set in 1990 were not modified in the ensuing years, they remained at a level double international prices, fostering a process of crop substitution. Nationally, some 1.6 million hectares were switched to maize from other crops, and this shift included a substantial amount of movement out of wheat and forage crops by the most heavily capitalised irrigated commercial farms in northern Mexico. Fruit and vegetable production also increased and private sector investment did compensate for some of the reduction in State funding. But this 'success' was deceptive.

In December 1992, I sat in the office of the SARH in Sahuayo, Michoacán, interviewing the director, accompanied by an *ejidatario* friend who came from the same village and had known the official since childhood. After delivering a brief homily on the end of paternalism and the need for *campesinos* to pay attention to prices in the Chicago futures market, the director turned to my companion and urged him to sow maize and beans, since these were obviously the best bet commercially. Since my friend, along with his two neighbours in the *ejido*, had rented half his own land to a commercial grower for a planting of beans in the previous cycle, and was now surrounded by maize fields sown by another group of renters from Zamora, the point was not lost on him, though it was hardly of much relevance, since his only source of finance for cultivation was remissions from a migrant son in the United States. The raw data for the irrigation district provided to me by the SARH for the spring-summer cycle of 1991 showed that maize was the most significant irrigated crop in all but one of the *municipios* within the district. Maize and beans combined occupied 50 per cent of the irrigated area, compared with the 28 per cent sown in sorghum, a major change relative to the situation a decade earlier, when sorghum was the predominant crop.

Some of the maize sown represented peasant production, and some of it represented a peasant sowing only a fraction of the land holding to meet family subsistence needs, the rest remaining unsown or being rented to a third party. The overall picture in 1991 and 1992 confirmed, however, that the increase in national production of maize and beans in these years came principally from commercial producers. Yet many of these producers were essentially speculators able to benefit from the inability of *ejidatarios* to exploit their land, including former public sector employees whose capital represented the illicit fruits of the era of statisation. Others were long-term US migrants who had cash to invest in agriculture. Few represented a new flowering of enterprise in the countryside or produced yields superior to the peasant farmers they displaced, some of whom were hired at day-labourer rates for their technical expertise. Even fewer made substantial profits.

By 1993 it was becoming clear, however, that the use of price support for maize and beans was a transitional measure designed to help cushion the impact of liberalisation, with the added attraction of providing a short-term rebuttal of the argument that the government favoured food dependence on the United States. Its impact on peasant farmers was limited by the difficulties many had financing production. On 4 October 1993, Salinas formally announced a new policy, based on direct cash subsidies to producers, which it was claimed would extend government support to 2.2 million peasant farmers excluded from existing programmes and cost 11 700 million new pesos in the calendar year 1994.

Official literature promoting PROCAMPO belatedly recognises disequilibria in the international grain market arising from the producer subsidies enjoyed by farmers in metropolitan countries, and, indeed, stresses that the scheme will bring the level of State support received by Mexican farmers in line with that enjoyed by farmers in the USA and Canada in terms of percentage of GDP. Equally belated is its recognition that policies based on price support are regressive from the standpoint of low income consumers. At the same time, the regime justifies PROCAMPO as an extension of policies designed to remove domestic market distortions by encouraging competitive commercialisation and establishing prices reflecting regional comparative advantage. The introduction of direct subsidies to producers is, however, to be accompanied by a progressive reduction in the indirect subsidies provided by the guaranteed price system. It therefore offers only a cushion to help producers weather the negative effects of NAFTA implementation. Any farmer – title-holder or usufructuary – who is registered in the agricultural census as a producer of maize, beans, sorghum, wheat, rice, soya or cotton will receive a cheque for 330 new pesos ($US 103) per hectare for the 1993–4 season, to be paid in March 1994 (a provision which is not helpful to the cash-starved). The subsidy will increase gradually until the autumn-winter cycle of 1994-5 and thereafter be maintained at a constant real value until the eleventh year of the programme, which will mark the beginning of its progressive elimination over five years. Farmers are not obliged to continue sowing grains, and another claim made for the programme is that it will encourage abandonment of grain cultivation on forest land where it causes erosion, promoting an ecologically desirable diversification of rural production.

In practice, the introduction of PROCAMPO subsidies has reinforced the existing tendency for commercial producers to switch to growing staple crops during the first year of the scheme's operation, producing an unwelcome national surplus of maize and additional pressures on prices. PROCAMPO was, however, specifically designed also to include *campesinos* who produced mainly for subsistence and would represent something of a windfall for farmers in this category. This, the anti-poverty side of PROCAMPO, may be its most significant aspect in political terms. Calculations made by Neil Harvey suggest, however, that the subsidy offered cannot compensate small farmers for whom market sales of maize are a significant component of income for the combined negative effects of declining output prices and rising input costs and it does not offer them sufficient financial resources to switch to more profitable crops. Given that 67 per cent of the maize grown by the social sector is marketed, even in Chiapas, PROCAMPO's ability to halt rural impoverishment should clearly not be exaggerated (Harvey, 1994: 14–17).

Despite the protestations of Agriculture Secretary Carlos Hank González that PROCAMPO was a logical development of earlier policies, it required an effort of will to ignore the significance of the 1994 presidential elections for what appeared to be a straightforward attempt to give some income back to a peasantry being marginalised by ongoing neoliberal 'reform'. Disbursement of PROCAMPO funds is reserved for the SARH, through its network of *Centros de Apoyo al Desarrollo Rural* (CADER), although other agencies and state government offices can act as intermediaries in the inscription process. Peasant organisations (including the CNC) have been explicitly excluded from playing any role. Nevertheless, past experience, including experience of the political manipulation of PRONASOL funds in rural areas, does not encourage optimism concerning the impartial and transparent administration of the programme.

Given the chaotic nature of land registration, opportunities abound for manipulating the system at the inscription stage for a variety of ends, despite the control apparatus established to accompany the programme, much of which is also pertinent to the *ejido* reform. Local practice appears to vary on the question of whether the implementation of PROCAMPO should be linked to what is supposedly the voluntary entry of *ejidos* into the programme for overhauling and regularising land tenure, *Programa de Certificación de Derechos Ejidales y Titulación de Solares Urbanos* (PROCEDE). In practice, however, establishing a linkage seems utopian in the light of the Herculean task facing the PROCEDE bureaucrats, who face the prospect of confronting foot-dragging and delaying tactics by opposition groups even within *ejidos* which enter the programme (Pisa, 1994), and thus far seem to have avoided problems by beginning with *ejidos* where potential for conflict seemed minimal (Carlos *et al.*, 1994). Given the size of the existing backlog of unresolved land petitions (*rezago agrario*) in many regions – much of it a legacy of previous strategies for political control over the peasantry as well as a product of peasant struggles against *caciquismo – and the extreme gaps between juridical theory and actual land tenure practice which have long characterised many ejidos*, this new State bureaucratic intervention in agrarian affairs is likely to be deflected into the same pragmatism and accommodation with local power relations which has characterised the entire history of agrarian reform. PROCEDE apart, however, functionaries are in a good position to use allocation of PROCAMPO funds as a means of political manipulation and wealthier members of the community may well benefit disproportionately.

Although it is true that PROCAMPO, like PRONASOL, is structured in a way which should reinforce central government control relative to local and regional power holders, its implementation is likely to reflect the way that centralisation is compromised in practice by continuing dilemmas of maintaining political control in rural regions under sustained crisis conditions, in a society in which it has never been convenient to establish a genuine rule of law. Symptoms of such necessary compromise to date include the resurgence of distinctly 'traditional' ways of doing politics around current gubernatorial regimes in states like Michoacán and Guerrero, and still closer associations between politicians and the less reputable kinds of regional economic elites, developments which have already triggered serious local splits within the PRI itself. It is difficult, for example, to believe that income subsidies will have a great impact on forest conservation whilst the directing hands behind the continuing destruction of forest resources are those of persons whose illicit economic power arises from a political untouchability guaranteed from Mexico City. States like Michoacán and Guerrero may be extreme cases, although they are highly pertinent to the pretensions of PROCAMPO to address the problem of rural poverty, along with regions like Chiapas, where the hidden compromises underlying the political success of *salinismo* reinforced the potential for violence by giving the green light to the *caciques*. Yet partial dismantling of the old, more inclusionary, infrastructure of State clientelism has more widespread regionalising consequences, which a strategy of targeting remaining resources directly to selected clienteles via federal-run programmes cannot wholly eliminate.

One feature of PROCAMPO is particularly striking. Cutting out peasant organisations as intermediaries between the State and the *campesinos* places each claimant in the position of confronting the apparatus as an individual. Those, like Cornelius, who see the role of the *comisariado ejidal* as a local power broker able to regulate access to land and resources as one of the principal failings of the old system, are forgetting that the leverage such agents acquired arose from the fact that they handled the internal distribution of resources to beneficiaries who were deliberately individualised (Martínez Saldaña, 1980; Gledhill, 1991: 309–10). PROCAMPO cuts out the go-between only to restore the dependence of *campesinos* on bureaucratic agents and increases their vulnerability to manipulation (or exclusion) by those controlling local levers of political and economic power.

There are therefore ample reasons for being sceptical about the kinds of claims made for PROCAMPO as a social and environmental policy. Even if the programme is implemented according to the letter of its norms, the actual economic effects of putting cash in the hands of rural people are quite unpredictable: the subsidy might, for example, be used to finance migration, which might or might not have a beneficial long-term effect on agricultural production. Yet PROCAMPO did seem to be a policy U-turn, which drew fire from technocrats and free-marketeers as well as from the political left. Its survival beyond the Salinas *sexenio* is not, of course, guaranteed, and at the time of writing, speculation about an increasingly uncertain future is less important than a more rigorous assessment of what caused the regime to embrace it.

THE CRISIS CONTINUES

Commitment to the NAFTA encouraged the government to maintain an overvalued currency and a budget surplus even though this caused growth to slow (and unemployment to rise) during 1993. The primary sector, including agriculture, fishing and forestry, but excluding mining and crude oil extraction, has continued to be the worst performer in the entire economy. Its contribution to GDP contracted throughout 1992, and whilst the economy as a whole showed dismal growth of 1.3 per cent in the first half of 1993, the primary sector declined by 1.5 per cent. The bulk of foreign capital inflows into the Mexican economy under Salinas have been destined for the financial sector, but agriculture seems to remain particularly unattractive to those few foreigners who are willing to invest in production. Domestic investment in the sector was clearly not encouraged by the uncertainty surrounding the NAFTA negotiation and ratification process and sectoral confidence was not enhanced by the particularly extensive concessions Clinton made to the farm lobby in the course of securing ratification. Then came the Chiapas rebellion, an event which stimulated a significant increase in local agrarian conflicts throughout southern Mexico during 1994 and reinforced investors' doubts about the regime's ability to resolve the country's agrarian problems.

The improving balance of agricultural trade since 1990 reflects an increase in fruit and vegetable exports as well as a reduction in maize and beans imports. Once again, however, it is necessary to ask what this modest improvement in the aggregate picture actually represents. Since the 1960s, the Ciénega de Chapala has been an important area for the commercial production of tomatoes, onions, potatoes, cabbage, lettuce and other vegetables, sown on private ranches and on rented *ejido* land. The data I gathered from within the *ejidos* in 1990–91 and 1992 show significant changes in the structure of production. First, there is a considerable amount of land of commercial quality being left fallow, up to half the land in some *ejidos* in the 1992–3 winter cycle, despite the plentiful supply of irrigation water. Second, there has been a shift from production of fruit and vegetables towards maize and beans on the part of many of the smaller-scale commercial growers. Better-off *ejidatarios* who owned machinery and rented the land of others have been forced by rising costs and a shortage of capital to shift downward in the hierarchy of commercial production and switch from vegetables to grains. Some have passed land they rented to outsiders with whom they have commercial relationships, generally of the small-scale, speculative variety. There was also a notable diminution of activity by growers who were sub-contracted by the wholesalers in the *mercados de abastos*. No tomatoes were sown at all in the rains of 1993, depriving the local communities of the wage-incomes generated by labour intensive production.

These data suggest that substantial regional variation in the fortunes of commercial agriculture is disguised in aggregate figures. Some major regional agroindustries are in decline, the Michoacán centre of strawberry production, Zamora, being a notable case in point. Some branches of export agriculture which are, in principle, capable of substantial expansion, in particular the Michoacán avocado industry, are prevented from doing so in the US market because the fresh product remains excluded on phytosanitary grounds (Cook *et al.*, 1991: 143). The continuing problems afflicting commercial agriculture are clearly problems of profitability in the face of escalating non-wage costs, some of which, in particular the rising cost of water, are a direct consequence of government policies.[3] It is not simply the *campesinos* who have *carteras vencidas* (unpaid overdrafts). In 1993,

3 The reorganisation of water distribution, another project initiated by Gustavo Gordillo when he was Undersecretary of Agriculture, with arguably laudable intentions, is a paradigm case of the inadequate assessment of both the technical and economic parameters of reform which has characterised the administration. Implementation of the programme is behind schedule in many districts and farmers have suffered an enormous increase in costs without receiving any of the (debatable) benefits of decentralisation of control to the users.

Guadalajara and the Bajío agricultural cities witnessed another summer of farmer protests, which on this occasion reflected the mounting private sector debt of those medium sized commercial producers whom free-market policies were supposedly to galvanise. The private sector farmers who formed the original core of the *El Barzón* movement which organised these protests had mostly been PRI loyalists until they found themselves facing ruin and foreclosure. But the movement's militancy increased further after its leaders were subjected to repression following their attempt to mount tractor protests in Mexico City on the day of the *destape* of the new presidential candidate of the PRI. This has facilitated a considerable broadening and diversification of the groups which identify with the *barzonistas*. The movement readily provided disgruntled *ejidatarios* in western Mexico with another symbol of resistance, although many peasant producers remain sceptical about the value of allying themselves with farmers whose class position remains radically distinct to their own and intensely fearful about accepting any form of credit which would involve putting up their land or homes as collateral. Nevertheless, the case shows that peasants were not the only victims of the agricultural policies of the Salinas period. When one considers that more than half of the increase in the private external debt of $US 40 billion recorded up to August 1993 was borrowed by Mexican banks to cover overdue domestic loans, the true costs of negotiating the NAFTA for an economy in which domestic savings actually fell by three per cent of GDP in the first four years of the Salinas *sexenio* become apparent.

Ejido reform was intended to provide agricultural entrepreneurs with the kinds of guarantees they lacked under the old tenurial regime, enable more prosperous *ejidatarios* to finance cultivation via the private banking system and make a reality of the kind of associations between private capital and *ejidos* first propounded by López Portillo's singularly unsuccessful *Ley de Fomento Agropecuario*. It remains, however, for the next administration to lay a basis for recapitalising the *ejido* sector and Mexican agriculture as a whole. The problem facing the *ejido* reformers is not the imminent prospect of a return of the *latifundios*, but the continuation of a situation in which in a rag-bag assortment of 'people with money' scavenge over an increasingly impoverished countryside.

WHY THE COUNTRYSIDE MATTERS: RURAL POVERTY AS A BINATIONAL PROCESS

From the technocratic point of view, none of this may seem of great moment in the long-term. Statistical observations of the following kind are now commonplace. The 27 per cent of the Mexican population which still lives in rural areas accounts for 70 per cent of the nation's poverty, but the 21 per cent of the economically active population engaged in agriculture contributes only 8.9 per cent of GDP. The 2.5 per cent of the US labour force which works in agriculture (3.5 million people) produces an output of $US 28 500 per capita per year, as against the $US 3345 per capita output of 5.5 million Mexicans (*Mexico and NAFTA Report* 93-10: 7). There are, however, two flaws in this comparison.

Firstly, a proportion of measured Mexican peasant farm output (along with much that is statistically invisible) must be seen as sustaining the reproduction of labour power in a wider economic system. Secondly, approximately 90 per cent of the farm labour force for California agribusiness was of Mexican origin or descent by the early 1980s (Palerm, 1991: 14). Male and female Mexicans are working today in less familiar places, picking mushrooms in Pennsylvania, dressing chickens in Atlanta, Georgia, and packing meat in towns on the High Plains, as agro-industries which remain labour-intensive despite mechanisation seek to cut costs by displacing established local workforces in favour of immigrant minorities (Stull, 1993). As Palerm and Urquiola (1993) point out in an analysis of the relationship between the evolution of capitalist farms in California and peasant farms in the Valle de Santiago region of the Bajío, the relationship is a systemic one, which dates back to the 1940s but has undergone progressive transformation in a way which forces us to re-evaluate the 'inefficiency' of the 1980s *ejido.*

Developments in the Bajío resemble those I have described for the western zone of Michoacán (Gledhill, 1991). The official agricultural policies of the Díaz Ordaz and Echeverría periods promoted transformations which deepened the integration of local farmers into a transnational system of agricultural production – as consumers of industrialised farm inputs as well as producers – and also reinforced involvement of *ejidatario* households in international migration (see also López Castro and Zendejas Romano, 1988: 58). Even well-to-do *ejidatario* families in the Bajío were drawn towards participation in international migration because the replacement of their capital stock in the form of tractors and pumps required a dollar income (Palerm and Urquiola, 1993: 345). During the crisis of the 1980s, population boomed in the Valle de Santiago as high fertility coincided with return migration from devastated Mexican cities and commuter migrants to Bajío industrial centres lost their jobs. Bajío farms were unable to absorb the growing labour surplus and US migration both intensified and transformed. Individuals stayed for longer periods in the North, more spouses accompanied husbands and true binational households were established (ibid.). At the same time, the composition of the migrant stream changed, drawing in people displaced from urban jobs and rural professionals in significant numbers.

Similar tendencies are manifest in the Ciénega de Chapala and Escobar notes that one of the effects of unrestricted rice imports was to drive once-prosperous (and fully technologically modernised) rice farmers from Colima back into the migration process, along with manual workers from Guadalajara and lower middle-class urban professionals who saw little future even in turning to small business within the country (Escobar Latapi, 1993: 76–7). Nevertheless, the overall social composition of international migration in the 1980s was transformed by the addition to the flow of relatively uneducated urban migrants and people from more marginal rural areas who would previously have moved internally, including young male and female migrants from indigenous communities with little past tradition of international movement.

The increased social heterogeneity of international migration has significant implications for both Mexico and the United States, but it is important not to lose sight of the role of the *ejido* in the process. Palerm and Urquiola (1993: 347) conclude that in the context of sustained international migration, the *ejido* farm of the 1980s continued to perform an essential social reproductive function, holding the extended family together, maintaining those left behind and enabling those who were now absent for an extended period to survive on what were absolutely low wages in US terms. At the same time:

> ... *modernised but cash-starved and overpopulated* peasant/ejido farms continue to provide labour hungry California agribusiness with a steady, reliable and growing supply of immigrant and migrant workers, giving agricultural entrepreneurs *the confidence needed to intensify farming operations* to produce a cornucopia of goods which are devoured avidly by national and international markets. (Palerm and Urquiola, 1993:347, emphasis added)

The irony of this situation is, as writers like Martin (1988) and Palerm (1991) have shown, that Mexican governments pursued rural policies which provided California agribusiness with the labour force they required to sustain a shift out of low-value field crops and dairy farming towards high-value fruit and vegetable crops. Despite mechanisation, the growing world surpluses brought by the 'Green Revolution' and spiralling costs of production set in train by the oil crisis made field crop production and dairying unprofitable. The period 1975 to the present has seen a massive switch towards fruit and vegetable products which are not merely labour intensive, but augment the demand for workers who will remain year round in the region and possess specific skills (Palerm, 1991: 78–80). This shift has been accompanied by an increasing domination of corporate over owner operated farms and, through the 1980s, by the growth of Mexican-dominated rural enclaves which have become sites of poverty as significant as those of the inner cities.

Palerm argues that rural enclave formation reflects the growth of direct migration to urban centres from Mexico and Central America in the late 1970s and 1980s, which choked off an earlier process of two-stage migration by which farm workers tended with time to shift to urban employment, requiring a constant replenishment of the farm labour force through new migration (Palerm, 1991: 34–5). As rural to urban migration by migrants already in California became less viable, rural and urban migrant networks bifurcated, and farm workers began to settle in rural locations. The process was reinforced by growing inner-city blight, rising costs and deteriorating wages, which reduced the comparative advantage of urban areas.

A major (and ultimately political) factor to consider here is how 'white flight' to the edge-cities and the collapse of the fiscal base for public services in inner city cores during the Reagan-Bush years exacerbated problems of urban living for immigrants, notwithstanding the diverse demands of the 'global city', yuppies, and lower class households with working parents for the services they provide (Sassen, 1986; Davis, 1993a). As Anglo 'nativism' intensifies in the face of California's economic decline, and inter-ethnic hostility escalates among the subalterns of the inner-city core itself, disenchantment with cities is unlikely to diminish. Yet Palerm demonstrates that the *same* kinds of problems now afflict some Mexican rural enclave settlements as non-Latino medium-to-high income residents move out, along with local agroindustries, turning the now Mexican 'town' from 'a relatively prosperous, self-contained and diverse farm community into a depressed farm worker bedroom community' (Palerm, 1991: 21).

The urban earnings and employment situation has, however, continued to deteriorate in recent years, not merely as a spin-off from the devastation wrought to California's military industries by the end of the Cold War, but because of the ascendancy of neoliberalism in Mexico. A considerable number of jobs have been lost in non-durable, non-military manufacturing in sectors in which Latino workers predominated, since movement of production to *maquiladoras* south of the border did not wait for the ratification of the NAFTA to put the formal seal on the transformations initiated by Mexico's entry into the GATT. Male unemployment in the predominantly Latino manufacturing districts where urban migrants from the regions of Michoacán in which I have worked are concentrated, like El Monte, was running between 15 and 25 per cent by the end of 1992 (Davis, 1993b: 46). In the light of these developments, it is not surprising that a substantial proportion of the migrants who secured legalisation under the Special Agricultural Worker programme of the Immigration Reform and Control Act

(IRCA) chose to remain in the rural sector, although they are under no legal obligation to do so. The IRCA has, however, made its own specific contribution to the emerging situation.

My studies of the impact of the IRCA in the Ciénega de Chapala indicate that some (poorer) villages continue to specialise almost exclusively in rural-rural international migration, although such communities are participating in a general trend towards family migration. Particularly illuminating, however, are the data on a large community which has evolved a diverse pattern of occupational and geographical distribution. In 1990–1 only 54 per cent of its current migrants were employed in the rural sector. If one singles out the group of 57 young men who secured legalisation under the Special Agricultural Worker programme using falsified documentation purchased from intermediaries, without having entered the USA previously as undocumented migrants, only 52 per cent chose farm work or agroindustry as their employment. Yet two-thirds of the 56 new undocumented migrants I recorded in December 1992 who made their first trip North that year worked in agriculture. Far from discouraging migration, the IRCA stimulated it and flooded the farm labour market (Palerm, 1991: 113). It has brought new undocumented migration in the wake of legalised migration (through the undocumented movement of wives and children of SAW migrants, and latterly, the undocumented movement of male and female siblings and other kin and family friends of legalised migrants). The sanctions IRCA introduced against employers hiring undocumented labour have fostered a greater reliance on labour contractors, at least in Southern California and the Central Valley. These trends have broken the stability in farm employment produced by sedentarisation and created social tensions between 'old' and 'new' migrants and workers and employers. The oversupply of rural workers is now contributing to the processes making Mexican enclaves in rural California enclaves of rural poverty.

CONCLUSION

The negative impact of new migration on the prospects of the established Chicano and previous generation sedentarised migrant population is not restricted to the rural context (Escobar Latapi, 1993: 79–80), but it is essential to recognise the continuing importance of rural migration and its contribution to a growing problem of rural poverty in the United States. The implications of these trends for rural Mexicans are bleak. California agribusiness is continuing to evolve by focusing production investment on the highest-value food commodities, leaving its Mexican competitors behind technologically and feeding off Mexican immigrant labour. Further growth of Mexican migration is evidently not particularly desirable from the point of view of Mexicans. Treating it as a 'safety-valve' today is the height of complacency. Yet what are the realistic alternatives?

The development of additional Mexican export production capable of competing directly on US markets with US products outside seasons when domestic production is inadequate to meet demand is premised on a variety of imponderables, not least of which is the real commitment of the US to agricultural free trade, though questions of quality control, the monopoly power of brokers and cartels and other factors of long-standing significance enter the equation. This kind of agricultural restructuring would be labour intensive, but the fact that it would generate rural employment would not necessarily improve rural welfare, since international competitiveness would demand continuing repression of wages. It is conceivable that US corporate capital might eventually be induced to invest more in Mexican agriculture, although there is unlikely to be much direct investment in production even of the highest-value commodities, and wage costs would have to remain very low for such a move to make sense in the light of the scale of non-wage costs in total costs and conditions prevailing elsewhere in Latin America.

In practice, international market forces and the responses of ordinary people to solving problems for themselves have been directing events more strongly than Mexican government policy for three decades. We are now in a better position to analyse the social, political and economic processes which have shaped the evolving transnational relationship between Mexican regions and the United States. If the Mexican State is not yet ready to embrace political democracy, it might at least begin to dedicate a modest portion of the resources currently squandered on political control to utilising research for planning purposes and make a more coherent attempt to guide the market. If it fails to do so, critics of the NAFTA who argue that it is a means for transnational corporate capital to press home an attack on the working people of three countries are likely to be proved right.

11 Dismantling the *Ejido*: A Lesson in Controlled Pluralism

Gareth A. Jones[1]

Images of the countryside are inherent to Mexico's national identity and the land reform programme represents probably the most enduring achievement of the Revolution (1910-17). Article 27 of the 1917 Mexican Constitution established a system of land reform based on agricultural communities known as *ejidos* – since 1917, 29 951 *ejidos* representing over 55 per cent of the Mexican land area have been created. The term *ejido* virtually defies a simplistic definition (Cymet, 1992; Needler, 1982: 103). It refers to a juridically defined system of land tenure as well as the community of peasants with rights over the land. Moreover, the *ejido* has become closely bound up with the PRI. The affiliation of the 3.5 million *ejidatarios* to the *Confederación Nacional Campesina* (CNC) forms one of the three key components to the corporate structure of the PRI, serving to create political passivity in the countryside and currently the longest period of uninterrupted one-party rule in the world. As Fox and Gordillo (1989: 131) observe, the *ejido* is simultaneously 'a state apparatus of political control and an organ of peasant representation'. Given the degree of inter-connection it came as some surprise that in the space of under three months, from 6 November 1991 to 26 January 1992, 75 years of agrarian reform were overwritten.[2] Will the reform undermine the conventional stability of state-*ejido* relations? What will the political landscape of Mexico look like post reform?

---

1 I would like to thank Peter Ward for advice and comments on earlier versions of this chapter. Research was funded by a grant from the Nuffield Foundation. Fieldwork was conducted during four months in 1994. Interviews were held with national, state and municipal-level planners, agrarian agencies, political parties and private real-estate operators. In-depth interviews were conducted with representatives of *ejidos* and *non-ejidatarios* living in *ejido* settlements for a number of communities in Puebla and Cholula.

2 The timing of the reform was dictated by the PRI's 1991 mid-term success which raised the number of deputies from 263 to 319, securing with only 15 votes from other parties the two-thirds majority needed to change the Constitution.

The reform of Article 27 is a generic term to describe three related pieces of legislation. These are the new Article 27 of the Mexican Constitution (*Diario Oficial*, 6 January 1992), the new Agrarian Law (*Diario Oficial*, 26 February 1992, hereafter *Ley Agraria*) and the new Agrarian Law Regulations (*Diario Oficial*, 6 January 1993, *Reglamento de la Ley Agraria en Materia de Certificación de Derechos Ejidales y Titulación de Solares*, hereafter *Reglamento*). Together these pieces of legislation establish four changes which inform the direction of this chapter (see also Cornelius, 1992). The first change is the enhanced autonomy of decision-making of the *Asamblea General* (general assembly of *ejidatarios* in a community). The second change is the right to convert land 'use' rights into individual parcels in a market restricted to *ejidatarios*. Subsequent land sales will treat the parcels as private property and require the authorisation of a notary public and a formal valuation (*UnomásUno,* 9 February 1992). The third change is to promote the right to transfer *ejido* land to private companies for up to 30 years or to set up joint partnerships, including with foreign firms (Article 127, *Ley Agraria*). Finally, the new *Ley Agraria* and accompanying *Reglamento* establish new methods of land tenure regularisation (Austin, 1994).

The principal problem that the reforms sought to address was the well rehearsed shortcomings of agrarian production (Cornelius, 1992; Gledhill, this volume). By the 1980s productivity in agriculture had declined to levels below those encountered in 1965, such that some commentators were able to argue that most peasants in Mexico complemented their wages with agriculture (Bartra, 1993). According to the view of both opposition parties and dissident elements in the PRI and the CNC, this situation was heightened by State intervention which had drawn the *ejido* into a growing reliance on resources and credits from banking institutions (Gates, 1993; Gordillo, 1992). Simultaneously, an important body of research was beginning to indicate that under a different set of organisational and technological conditions, or through a greater reliance on cash crop exports rather than staples, Mexican agriculture could be turned around (Heath, 1992; López, 1992). For Salinas and the technocrats within government, a radical reform of the *ejido* appeared to offer a range of attractive opportunities: a more productive agrarian sector would allow more to be done with fewer resources; and, greater autonomy and less 'political management' would permit a more efficient targeting of these resources – a view supported by the World Bank (Corro and Correa, 1991). Politically too, there was pressure to change. As Cornelius *et al.* (1989: 13) point out, in 1988, the peasant sector 'represented neither a vital nor a promising asset that could be used to advantage in the more critical battles likely to be fought in the near future'. While Salinas and the PRI had fared particularly badly in urban areas and among middle-income constituents, voters in the countryside were also less than consistently supportive. Seen in its political context, rather than breaking the traditional interconnection between countryside and PRI, and between state and *ejido*, the reform might be regarded as one method to rejuvenate these relations.

In place of firm prognosis on the likely impacts of the reform of Article 27 and the dismantling of the Mexican State, however, this chapter wishes to forward a number of theses. The first thesis is that the reform of Article 27 represents a new ideology for the countryside, albeit one with a clear precedent in political discourse at least as far back as the 1970s. The adoption in the legislation and institutional framework of this ideology marks an important shift in government and PRI thinking and, in particular, a convergence of PRI and PAN rhetoric on this issue. The second thesis is that the reforms may produce a political opening, both by default and by design. Insomuch as this opening is by design then the chapter develops the case that the outcome will be, in Lorenzo Meyer's phrase, 'controlled pluralism' (Meyer, 1989). The third thesis is to forward a link between the *ejido* reform and the demise of corporatism, to be replaced with Salinas's own brand of neo-corporatism, more broad based and inclusive than before, but highly controlled nonetheless. The persuasiveness of this argument hinges on the faith one is willing to place in the contention that Mexico's stability is not the result of avoiding change, but by allowing change in order to produce continuity (Molinar Horcasitas, 1991). Thus, the undermining of corporatism is permissable only in as much as it permits neo-corporatism to emerge in its place. The final thesis is that reform of Article 27 is illustrative of a new federalism in Mexico which on paper promises decentralised autonomy but in practice delivers enhanced powers to the president. What is interesting is the skilful means by which the new federalism does not contradict the drive for neo-corporatism.

None of these arguments should be regarded as exhaustive of the possible angles on this topic. Rather, the aim is to identify the layers of complexity which cross-cut the issue of *ejido* reform. Moreover, in so far as a sensitive reading of the agrarian structure of Mexico requires close attention to the regional and local levels, the potential scenarios drawn here should not be regarded as general hypotheses which can be tested at the national scale. Indeed, the arguments are immediately qualified by the limitation that the discussion is informed by fieldwork in *ejidos* surrounding the city of Puebla, and it is not the intention to cover what is happening or going to happen in *ejidos* throughout Mexico. The urban dimension, however, is illuminating for two reasons. First, because by formally setting out the means to transfer *ejido* decision-making and eventually ownership to the *ejidatarios* the reform appears to resolve one of the critical problems of urban growth; namely, the confusion over whether the *ejido* is property of the nation or of the *ejidatarios* (Cymet, 1992). This issue is at its most striking in the urban context where it has contributed to the production of illegality and a situation whereby as much as 60 per cent of urban growth has been conducted by means of the alienation of *ejido* land (Varley, 1985a; Ward, 1986). Second, because the Mexican state has consistently established highly innovative methods to intervene in urban *ejidos*, particularly through mechanisms designed to regularise land tenure (Varley, 1993).

A NEW IDEOLOGY: FROM *REFORMA AGRARIA* TO *LEY AGRARIA*

The clearest indication of the ideological underpinnings to Article 27 is the dropping of the word 'Reform' from the new *Ley Agraria.* This change represents the outcome of at least twenty years debate within the Mexican state in which the advocates of a populist alternative for the countryside have been defeated (Bartra, 1993). As part of this internal struggle one can witness a continuity between the present proposals and past policies. Article 27, for example, draws to a close land redistribution in Mexico. Yet, the claim of 'no more land' to distribute was made at least as early as 1976 by López Portillo (1976-82) and repeated by de la Madrid (1982-8) (Grindle, 1986). Other provisions of the reform, such as the recognition of renting *ejido* land to private companies in joint ventures, were permitted by the 1981 *Ley de Fomento Agropecuario* (Agricultural Development Law). The greater commercialisation of the *ejido* was an explicit element of the *Sistema Alimentario Mexicano* (Mexican Food System) and in de la Madrid's drive for the reorganisation of the *ejidos* into 'efficient and productive units' (Barry, 1992: 156; Goodman and Redclift, 1981). Furthermore, mechanisms to allow the internal sale of *ejido* parcels were mooted during the López Portillo *sexenio* (Foley, 1991) and state-level plans for partnerships to develop the *ejido* for urban purposes came from SEDUE (*Secretaría de Desarrollo Urbano y Ecología*, now part of SEDESOL) and the SRA (*Secretaría de la Reforma Agraria*).[3] What is new is that these proposals have been packaged for the first time into a single policy position.

Moreover, there would appear to be a marked shift in the conventional State and PRI thinking on the subject of the *ejido*, and a convergence with earlier positions adopted by the PAN. Between 1971 and 1975 the PAN

---

3 In Puebla, in 1988, a plan was struck between the SRA, the state government and selected *ejidos* to permit, albeit clandestinely, the 'purchase' of land by the state and its subsequent subdivision in return for a share of the profits. Interview, *delegado* SRA-Puebla, 9 May 1988.

forwarded the idea that the *ejido* be divided into individual land holdings (Galarza, 1991). A refined version of this idea, now with specific mention of the right to sell *ejido* land for urban development (when this was the most economic option available), formed part of the PAN electoral agenda in 1988 (Centeno, 1991: 37). In 1991 the PAN published a position document in the run up to the mid-term elections entitled *El Estado al Servicio de la Nación* (The State at the Service of the Nation). On the subject of the *ejido* it stated the aim of:

> granting the freedom to decide upon the form of land tenure that each producer considers to be appropriate and open up the possibility of obtaining full land ownership in order to allow efficient production and to satisfy basic needs; to promote the free association between agricultural producers and other national and foreign sectors in order to form economically viable production concerns (cited in Galarza, 1991: 11; author's translation).

These and similar statements from the PAN mirror closely those of Salinas and influential figures such as Gustavo Gordillo (1992). The discourse promoted by Salinas in his third State of the Nation address illustrates a drive for productivity, liberty and justice, transformation and flexibility. However, rather than seeing this discourse as a description of an undisclosed longer term aim of privatisation, I would contend that it genuinely is the object that it pretends to describe. Instead, Salinas has adopted the traditional stance of both the PRI and Mexican political system toward ideology; namely, that it is a resource to be manipulated rather than adhered to (Purcell and Purcell, 1980: 226).[4] This is consistent with the observation that the systematic manoeuvring by Salinas during the *sexenio* is neither radical nor utopian, but pragmatic (Garrido, 1989; Meyer, 1989). Thus, instead of incipient privatisation, as argued by Calva (1993) and others, an alternative thesis is that the reform represents a change of emphasis in terms of where the *ejido* fits into Salinas' vision of a modern Mexico.

In reality, therefore, the proposals fall short of advocating the break-up of the *ejido* and the sell-off to business interests or the *ejidatarios*. Although Salinas has been an ardent supporter of the privatisation of the Mexican State (Lustig, 1992; Vera Ferrer, 1991), the reform of Article 27 does not represent a straightforward attempt to disestablish or privatise the *ejido*. Indeed the abolition of an *ejido* is a complicated and lengthy procedure which requires

4 This is quite clearly the case with welfare expenditure in Mexico during the Salinas *sexenio*. Despite the neo-liberal ideology and rhetoric concerning a desire to 'roll back the state' programmed cut-backs in public expenditure in urban areas have been few and countered by the establishment of safety-nets (Dresser, 1991; Jones *et al.*, 1993).

an *Asamblea General* to initiate and validate the termination process.[5] This is not the end of the *ejido*, however. The *fundo legal* (core area of the *ejido*), plots designated for community amenities including the school, youth and women's institutions, and areas for collective agriculture such as grazing and forestry will continue to remain part of the *ejido*. The difficulty of disestablishing the *ejido* is born out by the direct opposition of many *ejidos*, such that up to December 1994, only two *ejidos* had opted and completed the procedure for the abolition of their rights and a further 20 had received individual property titles to land parcels.

Furthermore, as I argue in the following section, Salinas had no intention of individualising the *ejido* such that it moves beyond the control of the State, nor of granting it autonomy of decision-making without setting out the requirements of State sanction. In order to safeguard the ability of the State to intervene, the ambiguity over whose rights are held in *ejido* property has been continued. In my view, the reform of Article 27 is not in the strict sense an attempt to destroy the *ejido* as a form of land tenure, but to destroy the social and economic relations which surround it. Such an aim means that a convergence of political and economic ideology and practice must remain incomplete for the time-being. What implications does this have for political opening in Mexico?

THE POTENTIAL FOR POLITICAL OPENING

The inter-connectedness of the *ejido* to the political system and the aforementioned discourse on liberty and justice provided by Salinas, if taken at face value, should infer an opportunity for political opening in Mexico as a result of the reform of Article 27. Indeed, Salinas argued explicitly that the reform of Article 27 is evidence of democracy in Mexico (Salinas de Gortari, 1991: 1097).[6] This democratisation will take place through two processes: first, through increased productivity and the well-being of a property-owning *ejido* sector; and second, through decentralisation of decision-making away from

5 On first reading, a vote by two-thirds of the *ejidatarios* in an *Asamblea*, where a quorate 75 percent of the *ejido* is present, can terminate the legal status of an *ejido*. If an agreement or quorate is not reached a second meeting can terminate the *ejido* by a two-thirds majority with only half the community plus one *ejidatario* present.

6 'The reform sets out to restore to the peasant the freedom to decide upon, under adequate conditions, the destiny of his land holding. For this reason the reform is a proposal in support of democracy'. (Salinas de Gortari, 1991: 1097; author's translation).

federal and *ejido* authorities to the individual *ejidatario*. Both of these processes, however, are deceptive.

The nature of the first process sets out a fairly conventional link between *ejido* reform, property ownership and democracy. However, what Salinas's scheme appeared to offer is property ownership as a feature of an already enhanced democracy. Salinas's message was that an ability to make decisions on one's property represents a strengthening of the democratic practice. The intention is not to make Mexico more democratic but to confirm that it is democratic, otherwise it would be unable to deliver such a reform. The second process, the decentralisation of decision-making, is more deeply enshrined in the reform of Article 27 (Cornelius, 1992). Supposedly, the reform grants an *ejido* greater autonomy from the intervention of the agrarian ministries by establishing the *Asamblea General* as the maximum authority. Yet, both in theory and practice confusion reigns. On the one hand, the preamble to the reform of Article 27 firmly states that 'the *ejido* is property of the *ejidatarios*, and to them fall the decisions about its management' (*Presidencia de la República,* 1991). On the other hand, the preamble to the *Ley Agraria* establishes the *Asamblea* 'not as the principal authority in the initiative but as organs of representation and execution' – a point forcefully established during interviews with the *Procuraduria Agraria* (Agrarian Ombudsman).[7] Having established the *ejido* as property of the *ejidatarios* with autonomy to control internal affairs democratically, the new agrarian law sets about removing this autonomy and the *Nueva Ley de Asentamientos Humanos* (New Human Settlements Law, *Diario Oficial*, 21 July 1993) re-establishes that all land in Mexico is subservient to the nation and subject to State control. This allows the State to circumscribe the autonomy of the *ejido* by a host of rules and regulations which permit intervention.

In practice too, the autonomy of the *ejido* is curtailed by the limited experience of equal voting, participation and agenda-setting. These caveats may allow greater scope for political manipulation, from either inside or out of the *ejido*, rather than the emergence of transparent democratic practices. As Knight observes in an historical referent, 'Mexican history is littered with examples of political and economic reforms wrecked on the flinty rocks of *caciquismo*' (Knight, 1990b: 97). Thus, while on paper, the reforms suggest greater transparency and flag calls for grassroots democracy, the wider experience of internal organisation in *ejidos* is for the *Comisariado Ejidal*, the body of elected representatives constituted to organise *ejido* affairs, and more directly its president, to perform critical decision-making functions

---

7 Interview, *delegado* Procuraduria Agraria-Puebla, 28 July 1994.

(Austin, 1994). Just as the reform promotes the disappearance of State institutions in the *ejido* by exerting the role of the *Asamblea General*, it simultaneously confers greater powers and legitimacy on the *Comisariado Ejidal*. As a *delegado* (official) of the *Procuraduria Agraria* summarised it, in reality, 'a *Comisariado Ejidal* may still get away with anything'. The reform fails to guarantee the rights of the individual *ejidatario* over the *Comisariado*. Such an omission may fuel *intra-ejido* conflict which prior to reform was already reported to affect nearly one half of *ejido* communities (DeWalt and Rees, 1994). Taking the reform at face value as a technocratic solution to an economic problem may be to miss the space it creates for enhancing and prolonging the life of rural *políticos*, who might have come to expect a very different fate had a truly transparent democratic structure transcended to the local level.

Indeed, the reform appears to offer greater scope for political intervention in the *ejido*; first, by changing the internal political dynamics of the *ejido*; and second, by altering State-*ejido* relations. Both of these processes can be seen with respect to the future role of the municipality in the *ejido*. The apparent promotion of the *ejido*'s right to make autonomous decisions within its territory contradicts the aim of recent Mexican presidents of enhancing the powers of the municipality. Although not legally recognised as such, in many municipalities it is the *ejido* which has traditionally functioned as the local government (Azuela, 1994). It is to the *ejido*, for example, that *avecindados* (*non-ejidatarios* working 'to the use of the community' (Article 93)), conventionally turn for access to services which have often been acquired through direct negotiation between the *Comisariado* and the appropriate federal agency. As Azuela documents, the subsequent management of the services is often conducted by the *ejido* (ibid.). This traditional autonomy for the *ejido* has meant that both the municipality and the *avecindados* have been excluded from the decision-making process even where the latter are the majority.

The opening of the political structure of the *ejido*, supposedly to confirm its autonomy, may offer ways for the municipality and *avecindados* to exert a greater control over local affairs. The new laws, for example, establish *Juntas de Pobladores* (neighbourhood councils) in each *ejido* made up of both *ejidatarios* and *avecindados* to administer management issues and the acquisition of services (*UnomásUno,* 10 February 1992). This permits the *avecindados* a greater say in the affairs of the community than hitherto. Although the power of the *juntas* is firmly controlled, they can press for improved services but are not given the means to acquire them, the reform does appear to herald the enhanced politicisation of community demands.

The most practical method for these demands to be met is through the intervention of the municipality. This might take many forms, but in urban areas the use of *Convenios de Desarrollo Social* (Social Development Agreements) have appeared in order to translate neighbourhood demands into action. The *convenios* establish a direct contract between the local inhabitants, which may consist of both *avecindados* and *ejidatarios*, the municipality and the servicing agency. The *convenios* may extend as far as the regularisation of land tenure and a number of municipalities have encouraged the *juntas* to become *Comités de Regularización* in order to request the introduction of land-ownership regularisation programmes through the offices of the *Procuraduria de Colonias*.[8] In such cases, the intervention of the municipality in conjunction with the *juntas* marginalises the power of the *ejidatarios* within the *ejido*.

Parallel to these changes is the formation or strengthening of political agents which have the capacity to intervene in the *ejido*. The most important is the *Movimiento Territorial Urbano Popular* (Popular Urban Territorial Movement) of the PRI. The *Movimiento* has targeted settlements on *ejido* land for the setting up of community-based committees, although its success is difficult to gauge (see Craske this volume).[9] At any given moment, these committees can convert themselves into *Comités de Regularización* or *Comités de Solidaridad* (PRONASOL). This manoeuvre strengthens the routes by which settlements at the rural-urban fringe, which are often difficult for the PRI to 'capture', are drawn into the now familiar process of *concertación*.[10] Moreover, the committees provide the *avecindados* with a direct link to urban agencies and the municipality, at the expense of the *ejidatarios*.[11] Reforming Article 27 has shifted the balance of power in urban settlements on *ejido* land toward the *avecindados* and has offered the State a matrix of intervention opportunities.

The potential for political opening as a result of changes to Article 27 seem likely to occur by default rather than design. The reform is designed to

8 The *Procuraduria de Colonias* is a municipal office established to form *Comités de Regularización-Solidaridad* in low-income settlements

9 Interview, *Movimiento Territorial Urbano Popular-Puebla*. 17 November 1994.

10 Again, one might note that *concertación* is not new. The *Pacto de Ocampo* during the *sexenio* of Lopez Portillo tied the peasantry to the State through agreements in return for public solidarity against *caciques* (local bosses).

11 One can only hypothesise whether the logical conclusion of reforms, which set up *juntas de pobladores*, would have been a less sectoral and more spatially directed political system known to be favoured by the assassinated presidential candidate, Luis Donaldo Colosio.

confirm the autonomy of the *ejido* and protect the rights of its members. In reality, however, the democratic nature of these changes are not guaranteed. By default, however, the reform would appear to open a series of new political spaces in the interstices between the *ejido*, State and society. In so much as these spaces may be occupied by *avecindados*, one might consider such an outcome to be a democratic step even if it is achieved at the expense of the *ejido*. Moreover, I would argue that it is the State which commands how these spaces are to be developed in the future and who may occupy them. The potential intervention of the municipality, the PRI, PRONASOL and a host of other agencies means that such 'openings' may be of principal benefit to the State. As so often with political reform in Mexico, the legal changes appear to be carefully setting out a series of constraints to the granting of enhanced rights and citizenship, which has allowed the state to occupy and to construct the 'grey areas' between clientelism and citizenship (see also Fox, 1994a).

THE DEMISE OF CORPORATISM AND THE RISE OF NEO-CORPORATISM

There is evidence to support the argument that Mexico's traditional corporatist model is breaking down (Wiarda, 1989; Cornelius *et al.*, 1994). During the 1980s it was becoming clear that the CNC, for example, was losing ground to independent agrarian groups, especially in *ejidos* located on the urban fringe (Hardy, 1984; Jones, 1991). A complementary argument is to propose that the breakdown is really closer to an implosion. Within the agrarian and labour organisations democratic currents have been emerging which cut across the corporate structure and have made discipline difficult to sustain (Foweraker, 1993). One consequence was the strain felt by corporate groups in delivering the vote in 1988 when pitched against an organised and committed opposition. As a result Salinas began his *sexenio* in an unprecedented position. Unlike most of his predecessors who ended their term of office lacking legitimacy and credibility, the Salinas *sexenio* began in this fashion. Salinas' response has been to seek support from groups excluded from the PRI machine: business and financial groups, non-affiliated urban groups (particularly the independent left); independent *campesinos*, *sindicatos blancos* (non-allied unions), small scale commerce and religious groups. The project of political regeneration, therefore, has come from within, not to rid the system of corporatism or its institutions, but to seek to renew these institutions and to devise new methods to allow them access to the system. Again, there is an historical precedent; setting up parallel systems of intervention is a common theme in Mexican political history which has not hitherto been labelled as neo-corporatist (Knight, 1990b; Ward, 1986). This argument would appear to be consistent with the new constitutional arrangements for *ejido* reform. Within the various aspects of the reform one can witness the setting up of new state agencies and the creation or formalisation of new methods of state intervention in *ejido* affairs.

New state agencies have emerged in many guises: *Tribunales Agrarios* (Federal Agrarian Tribunals) set up to resolve land disputes; the *Registro Agrario Nacional* (National Agrarian Register) to collate and publish agreed changes to the legal structure of an *ejido*; and the *Procuraduria Agraria* to oversee and give faith to the new laws in the *ejido* communities. Of these new agencies the most important is the *Procuraduria Agraria*. Set up in the words of the *delegado* in Puebla to 'have a presence' in the *ejido*, but not to be an 'authority', the *Procuraduria* oversees a comprehensive land title campaign called PROCEDE (*Programa de Certificación de Derechos Ejidales*, see below) and guarantees that decisions taken by the *Asamblea General* are properly arrived at. In principle, the *Procuraduria* has no designated power to uphold the law, to enforce decisions taken by the *Asamblea* or to resolve intra-*ejido* or inter-*ejido* settlement disputes. The only official recourse is to denounce transgressions to the *Tribunal Agraria*, but it is unable to insist that action be taken. Restricted to this procedure, the *Procuraduria*, again in the words of the *delegado*, is left 'between a rock and a hard place'. The moment the *Procuraduria* intervenes it is making a decision to take sides and contradicts the sensitive aim of removing the State as a patron of the countryside.

However, the reality is that the *Procuraduria* is both passively and actively interventionist. This intervention is evident in three ways. First, the *Procuraduria* is universally present in all *ejidos*. Unlike the CNC, which might be opposed by *ejidatarios* in preference for independent agrarian groups, the *Procuraduria* is obliged to have a 'presence' at most of the meetings in which key decisions are to be taken. To an extent also, the *Procuraduria* can provoke its own intervention by convening an *Asamblea* upon the petition of 20 *ejidatarios*.[12] This has led some critics of the *Procuraduria* to claim that it will become the new CNC for the year 2000.

12 In one *ejido* in Puebla, which opposed PROCEDE, an *Asamblea* was repeatedly convened by the *Procuraduria* at the behest of a sub-group of *ejidatarios* in favour of the programme. The argument of the *Comisariado*, who was forced into hiding in order not to be present at the signing of documentation should a vote in favour of PROCEDE ever be won, is that the *Procuraduria* had encouraged the rival group.

By virtue of the sanction which the *Procuraduria* has within its gift for key decisions, the second level at which it intervenes is as a negotiator between rival groups, and/or the *ejido* and the State (Baitenmann, 1994). The clearest example of the *Procuraduria* as negotiator is with the acquisition of *ejido* land for public projects. In contrast to the use of land expropriations which proved to be highly conflictive, politically unreliable and ultimately, in most instances, an unsuccessful method of land acquisition, Article 27 offers more consensual approaches from a menu of intervention options. First, government agencies can await the 'individualisation' of land holdings through PROCEDE and acquire these through purchase agreements. As the State has some control over the rate at which PROCEDE will distribute titles, there is some scope for the time-lag to be reduced where public land acquisition is pressing. Second, the government can buy *ejido* land in advance of the introduction of PROCEDE and tidy up the paperwork later. This seems to be the preferred option in Puebla. Third, land can be acquired through the recently created *Comisiones Estatales y Municipales de Desarrollo Urbano* (State and Municipal Commissions for Urban Development) which can establish joint ventures with federal, state and municipal authorities, and *ejido* communities (SEDESOL, 1993a). If the aim is land development the new regulations open the way for *Fraccionamientos* - PRONASOL (subdivisions) set up by *Inmobiliarias Ejidales de Solidaridad (ejidal* real estate companies) in which the *ejido* supplies the land and the public sector provides services. In all three cases, it is the *Procuraduria* which acts as the go-between in the acquisition process. As the new planning regulations dictate that compensation paid to the *ejido* is now calculated at commercial rates, the position of an agency with an obligatory 'presence' in the *ejido* is most useful.

Finally, the *Procuraduria* is interventionist in that its functions come under the auspices of the SRA and, therefore, the federal government (Baitenmann, 1994). The formal procedure for incorporation of *ejidos* into PROCEDE is controlled by the *Procuraduria*: Its remit, therefore, is to simultaneously defend the *ejido* and promote the programme which most threatens the *ejido*'s existence. Again, this promotes the *Procuraduria's* role as a negotiator and facilitator. To date, despite the progress claimed for PROCEDE, the programme's success has been overshadowed by the level of conflict and passive opposition it has provoked. Up to June 1993, 13 842 *ejidos* had apparently been contacted to join PROCEDE, although fewer than 4350 had held *Asambleas* to give consent to this process, and only 87 had held a further *Asamblea* to approve land holding distribution. In 229 *ejidos* incorporation into PROCEDE had been rejected and the programme was temporarily suspended in a further 295 (*Procuraduria Agraria*, 1993a). Furthermore, in the first two years the land title programme appeared to provoke new disagreements or kindle old ones (Stephen, 1994). Up to March 1993, 9515 complaints had been received concerning land holding delimitation and a further 1400 complaints were received against the role of the internal *ejidal* authorities, mostly the *Comisariado Ejidal (Procuraduria Agraria,* 1993b). One solution has been for the *Procuraduria* to offer greater incentives for incorporation. As PROCEDE is seen to be of benefit only to *ejidatarios* the *Procuraduria Agraria* has worked closely with PRONASOL to offer funds to women, sharecroppers and employees of the *ejido*. Many of these people, of course, will be relatives of *ejidatarios* with no claim to a land holding, thus drawing a relationship between incorporation into PROCEDE and the welfare of all groups in a community.

The argument to this section, then, is that the reform of Article 27 might be used to strengthen the political ties between the State and the countryside rather than act as a method of opening this space to non-corporate agents. Salinas' aim has been to draw a more heterogeneous agrarian sector under an umbrella of political control. Instead of opening new political spaces and allowing greater access to old ones, the new methods of intervention and the system of relations between agents and the State (so-called neo-corporatism) has brought greater levels of intervention. The result is neither more democratic, nor is it more transparent, and nor does it seem to restrict the PRI or the government's room for manoeuvre.

MESSAGES FOR *PRESIDENCIALISMO* AND FEDERALISM

On paper, Mexico possesses a well developed federal political and administrative structure. In practice, however, this federalism is cross-cut by system-based clientelism, *personalismo* and *caciquismo*, in-built corporatism and a lack of political and financial autonomy at lower levels of government. These conditions have prevailed despite policies adopted by the previous president, Miguel de la Madrid, toward decentralisation and Salinas' respect for opposition victories. In fact, Salinas has continued the centralisation of policy-making and power in the presidency – almost 91 per cent of proposed legislation has emanated from the cabinet, which is to say the president (Camp, 1993b: 261). Salinas has additionally found new methods to centralise resources in the executive office and more gradually at the federal level via programmes which seem to possess a strong decentralisation ethic (Rodríguez, 1993: 142). This is most obviously the case with PRONASOL which has been heralded as the most important decentralisation effort of the *sexenio*, in so far as it distributes funds directly to the municipality, but has simultaneously allowed Salinas to institutionalise clientelism and patronage at a time when the official economic and political line is toward more rational resource distribution (Dresser, 1991). Doubt has also been cast on the degree to which the greater responsibility placed on the municipality and the partisan conferment of resources represent true empowerment (Cornelius *et al.*, 1994; Rodríguez and Ward, 1991), particularly as recent research shows that the outcome of opposition parties winning local elections continues to depend in part upon decisions made high up (Rodríguez and Ward, 1992). The 'rosy romanticism' of those who foresee greater federalism or empowerment in civil society is to ignore the lessons of history and, one might add, the imbalance of power in the present (Knight, 1990b: 98). The fact remains that the old practices still dominate the Mexican political system.

Nevertheless, some observers have adopted a more optimistic reading of recent changes identifying a new federalism (Rodríguez and Ward, 1994a; Sánchez Susarrey, 1991), a feeling which has been continued with the reform of Article 27 (Austin, 1994). Against, this 'rosy' picture is the lack of consultation and speed which brought about the reform in the first place. The *Plan Nacional de Desarrollo (1989-94)* afforded scant attention to the modernisation of the countryside. The plan flagged the desire for greater producer autonomy and, in the only direct reference to the *ejido*, the need to recognise in law the reality of commercialisation and sub-letting. There was no indication of the pending reform, although the *Programa Nacional de Modernización Rural* (1990-4) tested the water by outlining the withdrawal of farm subsidies and the privatisation of CONASUPO (Correa, 1991). Even groups which might have expected some prior warning, notably the SRA and the CNC, appeared to be shocked by the reform and were invited to enjoin the debate only after the official policy had been outlined. The call for regional meetings to be held in order to forward recommendations to the *Cámara de Diputados* was a largely cosmetic exercise that produced no major changes. Objections from political parties also failed to have much impact.[13]

In practice too, optimism for a new federalism probably has to be tempered for the time-being. At the grassroots level, the new legal provisions grant extended powers to the *Comisariado Ejidal*, new roles to the municipality and the devolution of a number of federal agencies to the local level. However, considerable ambiguity persists: the new laws place such changes on the statute but do not guarantee them in reality. An example here, which draws together many of the issues raised in other sections, is the new provisions for land regularisation. The reform of Article 27 recognises that

13 Interestingly, the only major modification came from the PAN which argued for restrictions on foreign ownership.

the *ejido* is the property of the *ejidatarios* and would, therefore, appear to establish the right of an *ejidatario* to legally cede land to a third party. As if to partly confirm this interpretation, Article 81 of the *Ley Agraria* states that *ejidatarios* may adopt *domino pleno* (full control) on land holdings so long as the process is agreed in an *Asamblea* and witnessed by the *Procuraduria Agraria.*[14] Equally, Article 30 of the *Reglamento* and Article 39 of the *Nueva Ley de Asentamientos Humanos* confer powers on the *Asamblea General* to 'regularize the tenancy of plots in illegally established urban settlements'. A judicious reading of the new laws would appear to suggest the self-regularisation of land development or, in so much as all *ejido* settlements, new or old, have to be sanctioned by the municipality, a significant transfer of power to the lower levels of government (Austin, 1994; López Velarde and Rodríguez Rivera, 1994).

The reality, however, is more complex. Article 64 of the *Ley Agraria* confirms that *ejido* land designated for an urban settlement is 'inalienable, non-prescribable and non-removable', meaning that the State has the sole right to regularise tenure – a provision reaffirmed by the *Nueva Ley de Asentamientos Humanos* (also, Salinas de Gortari, 1991). One implication is that a reform which should pave the way for federal agencies such as the regularisation agency, *Comisión para la Regularización de la Tenencia de la Tierra* (CORETT) to be disbanded has enhanced its role. This is consistent with past practice. During the *sexenio* of de la Madrid a move to liquidate CORETT came to nothing and the original intention at the beginning of the Salinas *sexenio* to merge CORETT and *Secretaría de Deasrrollo Urbano y Ecología* (SEDUE) to allow greater planning control of the urbanisation of the *ejido* was quickly dropped. In fact, rather than lose its position, CORETT has been subsumed into a series of joint programmes with PRONASOL. On the eve of the reform to Article 27 Salinas announced ambitious new targets for land regularisation in full knowledge that in the lifetime of the programme the legal conditions of the land tenure situation would change radically. Overall, in the first three years of Salinas' government more land titles were distributed than during any other *sexenio* (*La Jornada*, 14 February 1992). As one observer has put it, the Salinas government rediscovered the political value of land tenure regularisation (Rébora, 1994: 40).[15] This inability to

14 The *Registro Agrario Nacional* can then be instructed to issue a land title and register the same in the *Registro Público de la Propiedad.*

15 Having regularised no more than 250 000 plots from 1975 to 1988, in the first three years of the Salinas *sexenio* CORETT regularised 1.2 million plots and had plans to regularise a further 1.25 million by 1994.

curtail federal powers over land regularisation runs counter to the spirit of new Article 27. The contradiction permits a dovetailing of potential outcomes, subsequent legal and political interpretations, and, of course, methods for State intervention.

CONCLUSION: THE GREATLY EXAGGERATED DEATH OF THE *EJIDO*

Most of the attention afforded to the reform of Article 27 has concentrated upon the issues of agrarian production and privatisation (Calva, 1993). By contrast, this chapter has displayed four alternative theses: the emergence of a new ideology for the countryside; a potential for political opening especially by default; the link to a more sophisticated neo-corporatism, and the implications for presidential and federal power. Such theses suggest the need for a broader and less economistic reading of the reform. All four have a common point of departure, namely, that the reform does not represent a further stage in the strategic withdrawal of the state. Around each thesis is the case that rather than contemplate the removal of the Mexican State, Salinas' aim is to revitalise it, give it greater legitimacy and freedom for action and to provide the means to design and implement other more efficient interventions.

This is the context of the argument that the reform of Article 27 opens new spaces for presidential and federal power through an invigorated neo-corporatism. It also seems likely that we are witnessing one more example of what Morris (1993: 203) has called 'adaptive authoritarianism'. This looks at reforms which appear to offer progress along a path to democracy as actually delivering a stronger potential position for authoritarianism. As the chapter has outlined, the new found belief in autonomy, participation and dialogue with the *ejido* may not represent, in practice, genuine steps along a path to democracy or a withdrawal of the State, as new methods of intervention are found, through new agencies and extended rather than curtailed rights of control over *ejido* affairs. The weakening of traditional corporatism and the emergence of new methods of inclusion are therefore just the necessities of this reformism. The result may be a political system which is more efficient. Contained within the reform is the means to deliver a blend of neo-populist and patronage-based politics centred on the Presidency and more sensitive and technocratic targeting based on selectively strengthened municipalities. This does not seem akin to the optimistic visions of a new federalism, but to a new form of governance which is occasionally but not rigidly less federal, and may simultaneously include features recognised by supporters of decentralisation and centralised patronage politics alike.

12 Delivering the Goods: Solidarity, Land Regularisation and Urban Services

Ann Varley

The *Programa Nacional de Solidaridad* (PRONASOL) offers fertile ground for the debate around change versus continuity which Stephen Morris (1993) identifies in interpretations of political reformism in Mexico. From its earliest days PRONASOL was promoted as 'a new style of social policy' giving 'a new dimension to public investment and social expenditure' (González Tiburcio, 1992: 4-5)[1] and seeking 'to create a new relationship between the people and the state' (Salinas, cited in Moguel, 1994: 167). The theme of a break with the past is stressed in PRONASOL publications such as *Solidarity in National Development: New Relations between Society and Government* (SEDESOL, 1993b)[2] and has been taken up, sometimes uncritically, by commentators in Mexico and overseas. Even the Programme's critics acknowledge the claim to newness, for example, by calling PRONASOL a '*neo*populist' solution to Mexico's neoliberal problems (Dresser, 1991). The Solidarity Programme thus epitomises 'the reverential cult of "the new" which now characterizes Mexican politics' (Cordera Campos, cited in Knight, 1994a: 29).

The 'optimistic' assessments of Solidarity-as-change are contested by 'pessimists' for whom any changes associated with PRONASOL are essentially a means to ensure continuity (Morris, 1993). For example, Denise Dresser (1991: 15) notes that 'Much of PRONASOL is not new; many of the program's strategies are streamlined versions of old populist formulas'. Those following this line of argument point to the existence since the 1960s

1 Translations from Spanish originals are by the author of this chapter.

2 English version of Spanish original entitled: *La Solidaridad en el Desarrollo Nacional: La Nueva Relación entre Sociedad y Gobierno*

of 'direct precursors of Solidarity' such as CONASUPO, PIDER, COPLAMAR and SAM (Knight, 1994a: 35; Fox, 1994b). And yet, as Alan Knight (1994a: 29) has argued, 'one of Solidarity's successes ... has been its capacity to cover its trail, to deny its political paternity'. The question then arises: why should those responsible for the Programme *wish* to deny its origins in this way?

In this chapter, I explore what was and what was not new about PRONASOL and related urban development policies under Salinas, with particular emphasis on one area of the Programme, land tenure regularisation, which has been mentioned but not examined in any depth in the literature to date. I briefly review the debate about the purposes of PRONASOL; explore the significance of examining the Programme in a specifically urban context; and present a national overview of regularisation achievements under Salinas, followed by a discussion of regularisation and services installation in two areas to the east of Mexico City, Ixtapalapa in the Federal District and the Valle de Chalco in the state of Mexico.

THE DEBATE ABOUT PRONASOL: POVERTY VERSUS POLITICS

While Salinas was still the PRI's presidential candidate, he chose Chalco as the setting for a widely-quoted speech concerning his intention to create a new 'social floor' guaranteeing equal opportunities for all Mexicans as regards nutrition, education, health, and housing (*Consejo Consultivo del Programa Nacional de Solidaridad*, 1994). This speech heralded the establishment of 'Solidarity ... as a Programme of immediate attention to the most pressing needs and demands of sectors of the population in conditions of extreme poverty' (ibid.: 57).

PRONASOL therefore had a material focus on poverty alleviation and the provision of infrastructure and services to accompany its institutional focus on creation of a new State-society relationship (Cornelius *et al.*, 1994). Critics have remained unconvinced that the Programme's institutional objective was to promote 'the democratic reform of the Nation' (SEDESOL, 1993b: 23), preferring to regard it as a strategy for recovering the PRI's electoral fortunes after the 1988 Presidential elections and as a mechanism for the renewal of presidentialism (Bailey, 1994; Piñeyro, 1992; Dresser, 1991). The twin objectives of PRONASOL have therefore been translated into a debate on 'poverty versus politics' as the driving force behind the Programme.

It is difficult to do justice to the breadth and depth of argument in the debate in a brief review. A wide range of material has been gathered together and perceptively summarised by Cornelius *et al.* in their (1994) edited collection *Transforming State-Society Relations in Mexico: The National Solidarity Strategy*. However, I believe it is worth making a few observations about the contrasting approaches of those taking up different positions in this debate. Those favouring the 'political strategy' argument tend to base their case on at best in-depth but at worst anecdotal analysis of the *processes* by which the Programme has operated in specific cases (Lomelí Meillón, 1993; Bailey, 1994; Craske, 1994; Dresser, 1994; Haber, 1994). In contrast, the researchers favouring the anti-poverty argument have used statistical data in a cross-sectional analysis comparing Solidarity expenditure patterns with poverty indicators or previous government spending. Even if the poorest do not appear to be the main beneficiaries, this may be explained by the (supposedly) demand-driven nature of the Programme: the poorest are also the least able to press their demands effectively (Lustig, 1994; Guevara, 1994). Moreover, although Molinar Horcasitas and Weldon (1994: 139) present impressive statistical evidence for 'the claim that PRONASOL is not only electorally driven, but ... also electorally effective', they concur with Alec Gershberg (1994) in interpreting this in terms of praiseworthy electoral responsiveness, portraying PRONASOL as an example of 'the pork barrel common to all electoral democracies' (Cornelius *et al*., 1994: 17).[3] The 'electoral responsiveness' argument has of course been favoured by those working with PRONASOL. As President of the Programme's Consultative Council, José Carreño Carlón argued that 'formulating policies which will be well received by the electorate cannot be taken as a criticism' (*El Sol de México*, 10 September 1991). The head of Alvaro Obregón *delegación* in Mexico City declared openly that PRONASOL funds were being used to buy votes for the PRI, adding aggressively that 'this is valid for any government ... any illegitimacy lies not in there being a political advantage [to those in power] but in a failure to undertake necessary projects' (*UnomásUno*, 13 March 1991).[4]

Whilst acknowledging the need to supplement what Molinar and Weldon (1994: 124) term 'fragmentary evidence from case studies' I think it is important to consider why other approaches may also be handicapped in their ability to capture the significance of PRONASOL. Using data aggregated to state level is not ideal when Solidarity projects operate mostly at the level of individual communities, leading to ecological problems in statistical analysis

3 This begs the issue of what happens to resource distribution once an area has returned to the fold in terms of voting for the PRI.

4 In the interests of clarity, I have expanded on the terse Spanish original: *'lo ilegítimo no es que hubiera una ventaja política, sino que no se realizaran las obras'*.

(ibid.). It is also difficult to distinguish between the impact on voting patterns of Solidarity spending and economic changes such as the reduction of inflation (Cornelius *et al.*, 1994). Certainly, the significance of economic conditions has been underlined in a recent analysis suggesting that inflation, the balance of payments and per capita income together account for nearly 85 per cent of the variation in the vote for the left in presidential elections from 1946 to 1988 (Brophy-Baermann, 1994), and it was the left which gained most from voter defection from the PRI in 1988 (Domínguez and McCann, 1992). On the other hand, analyses of opinion poll data suggest that it was 'changing public perceptions of *political* issues', rather than economic performance, which explained defection from the PRI in 1988 (ibid.: 220) – a point to which I shall return below.

Another issue concerns the extremely wide scope of the Programme. Not all elements of PRONASOL necessarily came with a price attached. The land regularisation programme is one example of the way in which 'Solidarity incorporates a number of activities for which it does not have its own economic resources, but rather takes advantage of the work of other institutions' (Méndez *et al.*, 1992: 63).[5] Nevertheless, there was clearly a major expansion in funding under the Programme, whose overall expenditure increased 247 per cent from 1989 to 1992 (*Consejo Consultivo del Programa Nacional de Solidaridad*, 1994: 39). Its contribution to public investment in social development grew from 33.3 to 49.3 per cent from 1989 to 1992 (ibid.: 48), leading to comments that it 'encapsulates ... virtually all the social programs of the federal and state governments' (Morris, 1993: 201) and 'fills virtually all policy space' in this area (Bailey, 1994: 110).[6] When dealing with such a sectorally and geographically wide-ranging programme, in a country of over 80 million people, it is hardly surprising if observations relating to one sector or region do not apply elsewhere.

This point is particularly important given that one of the main objections to claims about Solidarity's political and electoral logic has been the incon-

5 Solidarity expenditure does not include management and administrative costs since these are covered in the budgets of the other federal and local agencies involved in PRONASOL (*Consejo Consultivo del Programa Nacional del Solidaridad*, 1994).

6 The enormous variety of programmes involved has been reviewed elsewhere (Bailey and Boone, 1994; SEDESOL, 1993b). 'Social Welfare', just one of its three major areas of expenditure, involved 'providing health services, constructing schools, supporting literacy drives, regularizing and rehabilitating housing, electrifying rural and urban areas, and even (*sic*) establishing a program targeting women' (Morris, 1993: 201). Even the restoration of ten 16th and 17th century churches in the Yucatán was seen as an appropriate subject for PRONASOL funding (*La Jornada*, 14 March 1991).

sistency in explanations of how this logic operates. On the one hand, it is said that PRONASOL benefits have been withheld to punish communities voting for the opposition; on the other, that they have been targeted at opposition areas to undermine support for the PRI's rivals.[7] It is argued for example that PRONASOL funds were directed towards states which had voted for Cuauhtémoc Cárdenas in 1988 but away from states voting for the PAN's presidential candidate since 'PANistas are not as easily converted as Cardenistas, especially since many of the latter had once voted for the PRI, while the former have long voted for the opposition' (Molinar Horcasitas and Weldon, 1994: 135). Such diametrically opposed explanations may smack of 'damned if they do, damned if they don't', yet studies of the opposition vote support the logic of this argument (Davis and Coleman, 1994). In short, in a highly heterogeneous context, it seems only to be expected that such a broad and elaborate Programme will have operated in a variety of ways, whatever its aims. To demand a single line of reasoning about the political logic of Solidarity seems out of tune with a political system whose workings, whatever else they may be called, cannot be called simple.

The following account of urban land regularisation and servicing under Salinas is necessarily coloured by the perspective I have developed on this issue since first studying it in the early 1980s. I have argued elsewhere that regularisation of illegal settlements has obeyed a political logic, demobilising independent organisations in low-income areas and remobilising the urban poor within the limits of political activity consistent with the maintenance of the existing regime (Varley, 1993). As a first step towards exploring the role of regularisation in Solidarity, I wish to raise the issue of the extent to which PRONASOL has responded to urban rather than rural concerns.

URBAN BIAS IN PRONASOL?

It would be logical to expect that PRONASOL's primary focus was on rural areas, given that the Programme's stated priorities were, from the first, indigenous groups, peasants and the urban poor living in *colonias populares* (SEDESOL, 1993b). Two of these three categories are associated with rural areas, and the urban poor have always been mentioned as the third group - logically, since poverty is above all a rural phenomenon, with less than 30

7 Salinas and PRONASOL officials have emphasised that municipalities held by the opposition have benefited from Solidarity funds – 171 out of 176 such municipalities by 1991, according to PRONASOL's General Coordinator (*El Día*, 9 September 1991).

per cent of extremely poor households living in urban areas (Lustig, 1994; see also Cordera and Tello, 1984). If, therefore, PRONASOL was indeed primarily an anti-poverty strategy, we might expect it either to reflect the distribution of poverty between rural and urban areas in Mexico or to be biased towards the former. If, on the other hand, we find evidence of *urban* bias, this may suggest that PRONASOL (also) responded to other considerations.

Molinar and Weldon (1994: 128) found 'a clear antiurban bias' in Solidarity: spending was negatively correlated with the proportion of a state's population living in large cities. There could however still be a bias towards urban areas within states, and other commentators are inclined to see urban rather than anti-urban bias (Lustig, 1994; Dresser, 1991). Alec Gershberg (1994) finds a statistical correlation between Solidarity's educational spending and the percentage of a state's population in urban areas, though not that in cities of over 100 000 people, and a detailed evaluation of the Programme's operation in the state of Zacatecas has found that the state capital received the lion's share of resources without making a major contribution to the measure of poverty used in the study (Guevara, 1994).

One subject of comment in this context is the provision of 'urban' services (Lustig, 1994). From 1989 to 1993, drinking water and sewage systems accounted for 20.2 per cent of spending under the 'social welfare' heading representing 57 per cent of total Solidarity expenditure (*Consejo Consultivo del Programa Nacional de Solidaridad*, 1994). Official figures indicate that only 21.6 per cent of water and sewage systems installed under PRONASOL were directed to urban settlements (SEDESOL, 1993b). This suggests an anti-urban bias, given that towns and cities house over 70 per cent of the Mexican population. However, no urban/rural breakdown is given in official reports of related areas of expenditure such as 'urbanisation' (primarily street paving) and electrification: headings which together account for a further 22.8 per cent of Solidarity social welfare spending (*Consejo Consultivo del Programa Nacional de Solidaridad*, 1994). Moreover, resources could also be directed to service installation via PRONASOL's municipal funds and regional development programmes (ibid.). Thus, although we lack information about the urban/rural distribution of total expenditure on water, sewage, electrification and street paving, it seems likely that urban communities may have benefitted considerably more than might be expected.

The evidence, therefore, is inconclusive, but we cannot, I suggest, dismiss the hypothesis of a bias towards low-income urban settlements. We must then ask why such a bias might have come about. I limit myself to one observation here: between the 1960s and 1980s, there was an increasingly negative relationship between urbanisation and the PRI vote in elections, whereas the

Table 12.1: Expropriations of *ejido* lands for regularisation by CORETT 1973 - April 1994

President	*Decrees* (number)	(%)	*Area Expropriated* (hectares)	(%)
Echeverría, 1970-76	139	13.4	27 995.0	26.6
López Portillo, 1976-82	87	8.4	7 311.0	7.0
De la Madrid, 1982-88	210	20.2	18 835.0	17.9
Salinas de Gortari, 1988-94	605	58.1	51 226.7	48.7
All, 1970-94	1 041	100	105 367.7	100

Source: Calculated by the author from publications in the *Diario Oficial de la Nación* of expropriation decrees in favour of the Commission for the Regularisation of Land Tenure (CORETT), the federal agency responsible for regularisation of *ejido* lands.

relationship for other parties was consistently positive (Klessner, cited in Molinar Horcasitas, 1991: 168). Thus:

> ... if in 1960 the PRI benefited from the fact that the majority of the population displayed the characteristics which appeared to work to its advantage (low education levels, agricultural occupations, rural location), by 1980 the situation had been reversed ... the PRI saw these social changes occurring without adapting to them. In 1960 it was electorally advantageous to be the party of the rural population, or the illiterate population. By 1988, not so (ibid.: 169).

LAND TENURE REGULARISATION IN PRONASOL

The purpose of regularisation is to provide legal property titles for the Mexicans who have settled in their millions, illegally, on *ejido* or private lands around the nation's cities. Those unfamiliar with this process may be inadvertently misled into thinking that regularisation was one of Solidarity's innovations when, in fact, there have been federal programmes in this area since at least the 1940s, and the current federal programme for *ejido* lands dates from 1973 (Varley, 1993). It is clear, however, that there has been a massive expansion since 1988, with the Salinas administration accounting for almost half the area of *ejido* lands expropriated for regularisation up to May 1994 (Table 12.1). Not all of these expropriations were necessarily initiated under the same President, but the emphasis placed on regularisation by the different administrations may be gauged from Table 12.2. It is noteworthy that in spite of the speeding-up of the process under Salinas

Table 12.2: Time taken by expropriation for CORETT, 1973-94

President	*Mean time taken 'All'* (months)	Mean time taken *'Complete'* (months)	'Complete' expropriations as a percentage of all such expropriations[1]
Echeverría 1970-76	10.7	10.7	26.9
López Portillo 1976-82	36.3	35.0	9.3
De la Madrid 1982-88	54.8	29.9	12.7
Salinas de Gortari 1988-94	54.0	26.4	51.2
All, 1970-94	47.0	23.4	100
N	1029	506	506

Source: As Table 12.1. A few publications do not provide sufficient information for the expropriation to be included in this table.

Notes:

'All' - all expropriations completed from 1970 to April 1994.

'Complete' - all expropriations completed during the Presidency in which they were first requested.

[1] Expropriations requested and decreed during the Presidency indicated as a percentage of all expropriations requested and decreed during the same Presidency.

compared with his two predecessors, the Echeverría administration under which regularisation first became a national programme appears to have placed even greater emphasis on this policy, if the speed of expropriation is a reliable guide to its perceived importance. On the other hand, the Salinas administration accounted for the major share of expropriations carried out during the same Presidency as that in which they were requested.

Two questions arise with regard to regularisation's forming part of the package of 'social welfare' programmes under PRONASOL. First, why should land tenure regularisation be considered an appropriate part of an anti-poverty strategy? Second, what did PRONASOL have to contribute to a process that had been firmly established for at least fifteen years before Salinas came to power?

The Mexican government is not alone in depicting regularisation as an anti-poverty strategy. International agencies support regularisation on the grounds that it provides the security of tenure people require in order to invest in housing improvements, in particular because land titles can serve as security for loans. It has also been argued that regularisation plays an essential part in provision of urban services to illegal settlements. For example, the Mexican government cannot legally charge urban land taxes in *ejido* areas until they are regularised, and these taxes are needed to pay for the installation of services. Both arguments are cited in Solidarity publications. For example:

> The legal situation with regard to ownership of the land prevented [the low-income families] from having access to public services and credits for building or improving their housing (SEDESOL, 1993b: 103).

However, in practice the low-income population prefer to find ways of financing home improvements without recourse to formal loans; local governments have charged property taxes before regularisation; and the logic of the order in which settlements are serviced may have little to do with their legal status (Varley, 1985b, 1987). Thus, the argument that regularisation is an anti-poverty strategy, although convincing on paper, is far less so when examined in practice.

The need for PRONASOL's intervention in regularisation is far from self-evident. Regularisation of *ejido* lands is supposed to be self-financing. Compensation to be paid to *ejidatarios* is fixed legally at twice the agricultural value of the lands plus a share of the profits of regularisation. The value of the lands to be expropriated is decided by a commission belonging to the urban planning ministry (later SEDESOL). Representatives of the regularisation agency sit on this commission and this has helped to ensure that in practice the values assigned to expropriated land have allowed CORETT to carry out its work without making a loss. Moreover, although the cost of regularisation is not generally regarded as unreasonably high by residents (Varley, 1985b), it is well known that the process offers abundant opportunities for illicit personal enrichment on the part of agency officials. In short, the process does not apparently require significant (if any) additional funding to be viable. Why, then, should PRONASOL be involved?

One possibility is that PRONASOL funds have been used to buy off opposition from *ejidatarios*. In the past, a substantial proportion of expropriations have been the subject of injunctions by *ejidatarios* seeking to improve compensation levels. Although the Mexican courts are often regarded as unwilling to challenge government policies, these injunctions have imposed serious delays or, in some cases, required the whole process to be re-started from scratch as is acknowledged in PRONASOL and other government publications (concerning private as well as *ejido* lands) (SEDESOL, 1993b; DGRT, 1994b). Since the early 1970s the authorities have sometimes avoided the threat of injunctions by informally paying extra compensation to keep *ejidatarios* 'sweet' (Varley, 1985b).

In principle, PRONASOL funds could have been used for this purpose, although it is unlikely that this would be publicly acknowledged in practice.

Table 12.3: Mean compensation paid per hectare for expropriations in favour of CORETT, 1973 - April 1994

President	*Nominal Value* (thousands old pesos)	*Real Value* (thousands 1978 pesos)	*N*
Echeverría 1970-76	37	58.6	139
López Portillo 1976-82	51	32.8	87
De la Madrid 1982-88	164	4.8	207
Salinas de Gortari 1988-94	7 833	26.4	605
All, 1970-94	4 607	26.9	1 038

Source: As Table 12.1.
Note: Values in 1978 pesos calculated using the *Indice Nacional de Precios al Consumidor*.

Although formal compensation levels appear to have recovered from their low-point under de la Madrid, they do not match the levels offered under earlier presidents, although it must be borne in mind that the quality of the lands may have varied and that this would affect the compensation levels paid (Table 12.3).

The possible use of PRONASOL funds to grease the wheels of expropriation cannot, therefore, be proven. However, official publications concerning Solidarity's role in regularisation and interviews with CORETT officials indicate that PRONASOL's involvement concerned a later stage in the process, the provision of individual land titles, rather than expropriation:

> Solidarity's objective is to speed up the legalization process for land ownership in irregular settlements. Corett is supported so that it can fully carry out its functions. (SEDESOL, 1993b: 104).

In 1991, a CORETT representative claimed that within one year of expropriation, the agency was providing titles for 80 per cent of plot owners (*El Día*, 23 April 1991). A rate of 60 per cent within one year was claimed by a CORETT official in the Federal District.[8] Even allowing for exaggeration, this represents a considerable advance on previous achievements: it was not uncommon for such progress to take at least five or six years (Varley, 1985b). The acceleration reflected a strong top-down emphasis on speeding up existing procedures, plus some important innovations. PRONASOL publi-

8 Interview with CORETT official, 8 August 1991.

cations mention two specific changes. The first was that 'residents ... participate in mapping and compiling technical files' (SEDESOL, 1993b: 104); it is unlikely that this has had any great significance, given the technical complexities involved.[9] The second was that in nineteen states residents were totally exempted from payment of taxes incurred by the transfer of ownership: partial exemptions were granted elsewhere. This was a significant benefit for residents, which will have helped to speed up the process, but any 'citizen participation' involved had very little to do with residents or the Solidarity Committees which are the supposed cornerstone of the Programme's creation of new State-society relations.

The effort to speed up regularisation was successful. In 1988, there were reportedly 1.79 million plots waiting to be regularised by CORETT; the agency is recorded as having legalised 1.10 million plots from 1989 to 1993, compared with only 288 130 titles issued from 1974 to 1988 (*Consejo Consultivo del Programa Nacional de Solidaridad*, 1994: 221; SEDESOL, 1993b). However, in all 2.12 million plots are reported to have been regularised under Salinas, because CORETT's efforts have been supplemented by those of state governments legalising plots on private or government-owned lands.[10] In the state of Mexico, for example, renewed emphasis was placed on the work of the local regularisation agency, CRESEM. In the Federal District, the same applied to the work of the *Dirreción General de Regularización Territorial del Distrito Federal* (the DGRT) and the *Fideicomiso de Vivienda y Desarrollo Urbano* (FIVIDESU). The federal housing agency INFONAVIT undertook the regularisation of its housing projects in various states, and titles for former rental property purchased under the *Casa Propia* programme of the housing agency FONHAPO were also handed out in Solidarity events (*El Día*, 11 September 1992). The great increase in the number of plots regularised was thus achieved by: a) a strong central directive to speed up the process; b) procedural modifications; and, c) an extension of the regularisation initiative to other state and federal agencies.

---

9 Unless it is an oblique reference to the practice of using a block map as a basis for regularisation of individual plots (see below).

10 The speed with which regularisation was handled under Salinas led to accusations from opposition parties that documents handed out were not genuine land titles. This occurred in Tierra Blanca, Veracruz (*La Jornada*, 5-7 August 1991). The accusations were immediately and firmly denied and there was probably no substance in them.

SOLIDARITY IN MEXICO CITY: TWO EXAMPLES

a) Valle de Chalco, the cradle of Solidarity

As mentioned above, Salinas chose Chalco for his announcement of the policies which would give rise to Solidarity. For this reason, this area to the east of Mexico City, formerly one of the lakes surrounding the city and home to around half a million people, became known as 'the cradle of Solidarity'. It was the target of intense and sustained intervention by PRONASOL. As the most recent of the massive areas of illegal settlement formed in sudden bursts of urban growth around the capital, the municipalities of Chalco and Ixtapaluca housed one of the largest concentrations of urban poverty in Mexico (Hiernaux, 1991). Together with other municipalities in this part of the state of Mexico, they formed the subject of a special report prepared for Solidarity by the state government in the first year of Salinas' administration (Gobierno del Estado de México, 1989). As this report was being prepared, work was already underway on the first of the Programme's major investments, bringing electricity to the Valle. In January 1990, Salinas visited the area to 'switch on the lights' after electricians had 'worked like mules', 24 hours a day, to get things ready (*UnomásUno*, 17 January 1990). The visit was recorded, even in newspapers generally critical of the regime and by commentators long familiar with the nature of political spectacle in Mexico, in emotional language conveying the massive scale of the event and the enthusiasm of residents who a couple of years earlier had 'no longer believed in Presidents' but who now came to voice their thanks to Salinas (*La Jornada*, 18-22 January 1990; *UnomásUno*, 17 January 1990). Indeed, Salinas said that when he first visited Chalco, the tension in the air 'could be cut with a knife', but when he went there to 'switch on the lights', he was received with open arms (*La Jornada*, 22 January 1990). Much emphasis was placed on his spending the night in an ordinary home in Chalco, an act he was subsequently to repeat on at least two occasions (*El Día*, 20 March 1993). The President made a number of other visits, to inaugurate other PRONASOL Programmes and to celebrate the Third National Solidarity Week in September 1992. When PRONASOL was incorporated into the new Ministry for Social Development in early 1992, the newly-appointed Minister, Luis Donaldo Colosio, made his 'debut' in Chalco, again underlining the area's importance to the Programme and the PRI government (*Proceso*, 7 September 1992).

Electricity for domestic use and street lighting was followed by the provision of domestic water supplies (reportedly completed in 1993) and regularisation of 60 000 plots (*El Nacional*, 18 March 1993). Installing a sewage network and paving the main streets took longer and were accompanied by the construction of health centres and schoolrooms as well as rehabilitation of existing schools. Other areas of investment were planned to bring total expenditure to over 660 million new pesos by the end of 1994, according to PRONASOL calculations reported in the press (*El Universal*, 12 September 1993; *El Financiero*, 13 March 1993). Although there were continuing reports of delays, poor technical quality, and financial abuses, it is evident that under Salinas there was a tremendous push to improve the quality of life dramatically for the inhabitants of the Valle de Chalco, at least as far as urban services and regularisation were concerned.

Commentators have pointed out that in 1988 Salinas obtained scarcely one in four votes in Chalco, but the PRI recovered the area in an 'overwhelming' victory in the 1991 federal elections, in which Chalco was one of 121 (out of 123) municipalities won by the PRI in the state of Mexico, compared with only 41 three years earlier (*Proceso*, 7 September 1992; Dresser, 1991). But the significance of Chalco arguably goes beyond local political fortunes - a point to which I shall return below.

b) Ixtapalapa

Although the Federal District was not a major recipient of PRONASOL funds in the early years of the Programme, urban servicing and regularisation were brought under the Solidarity banner to highlight the administration's campaign against poverty. One of the main local targets of this campaign was Ixtapalapa, the District's largest *delegación*, with almost 1.5 million inhabitants in 1990. In the 1988 elections, Ixtapalapa was part of the band of poorer areas along the east of Mexico City in which over half the inhabitants voted for Cárdenas, with Salinas getting less than one-third of the area's votes and the PRI performing correspondingly badly in congressional elections (Ward, 1990). Over the next few years the *delegación* benefitted from a series of servicing and regularisation projects. There was much to be done: one half of all the Federal District's half million illegal plots were to be found in Ixtapalapa, constituting, according to the President, the major concentration of land tenure problems in the country (DGRT, 1994b; *La Jornada*, 3 August 1991). Moreover, unlike Chalco, most of the illegal development in Ixtapalapa was on private land: of the estimated 500 000 illegal plots in the Federal District, 180 000 were reported to be *ejido* and 320 000 on private land. (DGRT, 1994a). The *delegación* also had two-fifths of the capital's unpaved streets; one-third of its population reportedly lacked connection to the sewage system and one-sixth a domestic water supply (*El Nacional*, 14 October 1991).

Ixtapalapa provides a good example of the way in which the provision of services and land titles was heavily publicised in the run-up to the 1991 elections. In May 1990, Federal District Mayor Manuel Camacho Solís handed out 5800 land titles to residents. At the same time, *mitad y mitad* ('half and half') agreements were signed with residents of 20 settlements to formalise cooperation in the provision of materials and labour for the installation of services.[11] The Mayor was followed, in April 1991, by Manuel Aguilera Gómez, then head of the Federal District's internal affairs department, handing out over 2000 titles and reporting on progress in street paving. At the beginning of August, the month of the federal elections, 7000 titles were handed out by Salinas at a ceremony attended by 10 000 people. The President reported that a total of 82 000 Ixtapalapa families had benefited from regularisation since the beginning of his administration. A few days later his wife visited the *delegación* in connection with a micro-industries programme. Then, exactly one week before the elections, the Federal District Delegate to Ixtapalapa handed out a further 3000 titles at a ceremony where Solidarity banners decorated the platform and the following day, there were further public ceremonies to mark additions to the *delegación*'s fleet of rubbish collection trucks. The PRI recovered the area in the elections. In all, the area's authorities are said to have spent as much on servicing in the six months before the 1991 elections as they had in the previous three years.[12]

Perhaps the most interesting aspect of the policies adopted in Ixtapalapa were the modifications to the process of regularisation. Ixtapalapa had been the scene of a meeting, during Salinas' election campaign, to evaluate the government's achievements in regularisation and housing. The meeting delivered a clear message to the officials involved: people didn't trust the government.

> It was a question of endless to-ing and fro-ing: when people thought they'd finally got hold of a paper guaranteeing their right to their plot, it turned out that it was only a promise ... it gave an extremely bad impression of government actions ... (DGRT, 1994b: 8).

A particular problem had been the practice, in previous administrations, of what were known as *inmatriculaciones administrativas* of plots in the Public Property Register (DGRT, 1994b). This meant simply reserving a number in the Register for plots without a previously recognised owner; after five years,

---

11 This *mitad y mitad* system was a characteristic feature of Solidarity programmes, which formally took over the Ixtapalapa projects in September 1991, by which time one-quarter of the of the target figure for street paving had been achieved, various drainage systems had been completed, over 3500 houses had received electricity and 261 schools had been repaired (*El Nacional*, 14 October 1991).

12 Interview with official of Ixtapalapa *delegación*, 11 August 1991.

if there were no rival claims on the property, its residents could become the legal owners, but meanwhile their legal status remained undefined and the documents they held turned out not to guarantee their property rights. This practice had provoked widespread cynicism about legalisation on the part of Ixtapalapa residents.[13]

From the administrative point of view, the main problem had been the extreme legal complexity of regularisation on private lands. The problems were particularly acute in areas which had been the subject of inheritance, intra-family cessions and subdivisions as well as sales over a period of several generations, all without formal documentation. In these circumstances, the dangers of conflicts between rival claimants resulting in injunctions undermining the whole process were considerable (DGRT, 1994b).

The response was to extend the use of expropriation to these cases. This was a radical innovation. Expropriation had not been used for this purpose since the 1940s (Azuela, 1989), although the expropriation of properties damaged in the 1985 earthquake had shown how effective it could be. Experience gained by Aguilera Gómez in the housing agency FONHAPO led to the suggestion that the General Directorate of Land Regularisation (DGRT, a dependency of his own department) should adopt this strategy, on condition that prior approval was gained from residents and subdividers (ibid.). Between 1989 and May 1994, expropriation by the Federal District authorities led to the regularisation of 3324.7 hectares (DGRT, 1994a), compared with 2908.8 hectares expropriated by CORETT. Fifty five per cent of the DGRT area and 35 per cent of the *ejido* lands were located in Ixtapalapa.

Other changes introduced to complement this new strategy involved legal and administrative simplifications, including the measure exempting residents from taxes on the transfer of ownership (*Diario Oficial*, 5 April 1989). The DGRT's work was decentralised: four local offices were established to improve accessibility for residents (DGRT, 1994b). Finally, the problem of conflicts over the dimensions of individual plots which had been a major cause of delays was considerably reduced by getting the residents of a block to sign a plan showing the relationship between all the plots before any individual documents were produced. Together, these innovations led to a total of almost 116 000 titles being produced by the DGRT from 1989 to April 1994, half of them as a result of expropriation, and half of them in Ixtapalapa (DGRT, 1994a).

---

13 Interview with CORETT official, 8 August 1991.

What is particularly interesting about these innovations is that they were successfully transferred from the DGRT to CORETT's operations within the Federal District. DGRT methods and personnel were employed by CORETT's Federal District offices under the direction of a close associate of Aguilera Gómez. This was understood by those involved to be a 'concession' by Salinas to Mayor Manuel Camacho Solís, in the context of Camacho's ambitions to become the next presidential candidate and Aguilera Gómez's designs on the Federal District mayorship.[14] The price of the 'concession' was made clear in Aguilera Gómez' instructions to the CORETT delegate. She told her staff that he had given her one instruction to obey above all else: to improve the government's image. Above and beyond technical modifications to the regularisation process, improving the government's image meant, first, that meticulous attention was to be paid to the way in which CORETT officials dealt with the public, emphasising work 'on the ground' and personal contact between officials and residents, and second, that there were to be *no* corrupt practices by officials.[15] This was particularly important given that CORETT was (in)famous for corruption, inefficiency and the political nature of its activities.[16] Not that the new 'get it done and get it done fast' principle prevented a political logic from continuing to shape CORETT's actions at the micro-level. All sorts of tactics were used to simultaneously appease and undermine opposition groups active within the regularised areas. In Ixtapalapa, for example, when inaccurate surveying led to a substantial area being omitted from expropriations for both CORETT and the DGRT, it 'coincided' with an area in which the left-wing opposition enjoyed particular support and in which its local leaders lived. At the level of individual families, some agency officials would bend the rules (for example, allowing 'invasion' of an unclaimed plot) on condition that the beneficiaries participated in the ceremonies in which titles were handed out. And at these ceremonies, areas dominated by opposition groups were under-represented in the number of titles handed out. Some of their residents would

---

14 Interview with CORETT official, 8 August 1991.

15 The need for good public relations, and the considerable difficulties involved in achieving them, also emerged from a series of DGRT publications recording its work during the Salinas administration (DGRT, 1994a and 1994b). Personnel employed by CORETT in the Federal District are reported to have been paid unusually high salaries as part of the effort to avoid corruption by individual officials.

16 For example, CORETT had previously been overly concerned with getting residents signed up to start paying, without giving sufficient attention to legal or technical problems which would later made it difficult to produce titles for some plots.

receive titles, but many other titles would be held back until nearer or even after the elections to encourage residents to vote for the PRI. At the ceremony held in Ixtapalapa one week before the August 1991 elections, in which the main opposition group received 600 of the 3000 titles handed out, its representative commented ironically that although the final documents had in some cases been signed as early as March, 'they preferred to wait until now, a week before the elections [to hand out the titles] - I can't *think* why' (*La Jornada*, 12 August 1991).

Changes in the regularisation programme can therefore be understood in two contexts: one, the political ambitions of the Federal District's leadership and the other, the drive to recover the Federal District for the PRI. They were clearly two sides of the same coin. In spite of the 'Solidarity' label attached to the regularisation programme and associated ceremonies, PRONASOL as an agency appears to have had little to do with the process of regularisation in the Federal District; CORETT or the DGRT did the work and 'Solidarity' took the credit.

SOLIDARITY: CHANGE IN THE PURSUIT OF CONTINUITY

This discussion of land tenure regularisation and servicing under Salinas provides useful pointers for identifying what was and what was not new about PRONASOL. The scale of the efforts involved was clearly unprecedented. Salinas signed expropriation decrees for the regularisation of an area of *ejido* lands only marginally smaller than that expropriated by his three predecessors put together, and the number of titles issued by CORETT is reported to have been almost four times the number produced in the previous three administrations. PRONASOL predicted that by the end of 1994 the (total) population with access to drinking water and sewage services would have increased by 13.9 and 15.6 million people respectively, increasing coverage from 70 to 81 per cent and 49 to 63 per cent of the population since 1990 (SEDESOL, 1993b), and between 1989 and 1993 PRONASOL brought electricity to 11.5 million Mexicans (*Consejo Consultivo del Programa Nacional de Solidaridad*, 1994).

Such extraordinary achievements required a major financial commitment. But Solidarity also benefitted from some government actions, such as the dramatic acceleration in the delivery of land titles, for which no great financial investment was needed. What was required in such cases, if not funding, was a strong central directive to ensure that things happened. Such a directive is at odds with the portrayal of Solidarity as demand-driven - of improvements resulting from people and government working together to decide what their most pressing needs were and then finding ways of meeting them. In the case of regularisation at least, so much could not have been achieved in so little time if things had really worked that way.

The drive to achieve results on this scale was new. What was not new were some of the special features attributed to the Programme. For example, the much-lauded *mitad y mitad* system of cooperation between community and government in the installation of services was anything but new. Rather, it was a way of doing things long familiar to residents of illegal settlements. In the early 1970s, to cite one example, residents of municipalities in the north and west of Mexico City provided labour for the installation of water and sewage systems and street paving in the state of Mexico programmes *Operación Hormiga* (Operation Ant) and *Ejército del Trabajo* (Army of Labour) (Varley, 1985b).

Another widely-trumpeted feature of Solidarity was Salinas' own 'personal presence, commitment and activism' (Dresser, 1991: 30). The President was reported to spend one or two days a week on Solidarity, travelling 'incessantly to isolated communities to inaugurate Solidarity projects and to directly receive petitions' (Cornelius *et al.*, 1994: 14). During the National Solidarity Weeks, Salinas visited at least three towns a day and over ten states in the week (Dresser, 1994). However, although Dresser (1991: 30) cites these 'whirlwind tour[s]' to underline the difference between Salinas and Miguel de la Madrid, his 'ineffectual predecessor', a chronicle of de la Madrid's activities while in office show that he made working visits approximately once a fortnight, to an average of three states per month, during his first year in office (*Presidencia de la República*, 1984). As with Salinas, handing out land titles and inaugurating urban services provided a convenient rationale for de la Madrid's visits to low-income settlements during these *giras* (tours). And the emphasis on direct interaction between residents and President, with Salinas' receipt of petitions 'by the hundred' (*UnomásUno*, 17 January 1990) and frequent meetings with representatives of Solidarity Committees in Los Pinos (Braig, 1994) is strongly reminiscent of Luis Echeverría's open-door policies, designed to cultivate *colonos*' loyalty to the President himself rather than the welfare agencies he created to deal with their demands (Ward, 1981). The Solidarity Committees themselves raise questions about the newness of the Programme: the most credible explanation for the figure of 150 000 such committees supposedly formed by November 1993 is that many of them existed on paper only or that they represented a grafting of the Solidarity label onto existing organisational structures (Moguel, 1992; Contreras and Bennett, 1994).

In short, PRONASOL is indeed 'less innovative than its apostles have claimed' (Dresser, 1991: 30). Why, then, such emphasis on the new? The answer is that Solidarity must be interpreted primarily as a political response to the enormous shock of the 1988 election results. For the first time, there was a real challenge to the PRI that very nearly succeeded, and was only prevented from doing so at the cost of a dramatic loss of credibility for the regime. Any chances of recovering legitimacy depended on an ability to persuade the disaffected population that Salinas' government really had something new to offer Mexico, and that something was Solidarity.

That something new, moreover, had to be very closely associated with Salinas himself. It is sometimes difficult to remember just how unprepossessing a presidential candidate Salinas had seemed in 1988. Jorge Domínguez' and James McCann's (1992) analysis explains defection from the PRI in 1988 in terms of voters' views of the PRI's prospects of continuing as the party of the State and their opinion of Salinas' personal characteristics. Solidarity, therefore, had to convert a no-can-do candidate into a can-do President, lending him the charisma to fend off the challenge from Cárdenas.

For these reasons, I agree with those who argue that PRONASOL was 'a vehicle for reasserting presidential power ... in order to legitimize the regime' (Dresser, 1994: 160). The need to promote the authority of the President came before the need to strengthen the PRI itself or to maintain some well-established corporatist practices. Thus, although CORETT and its parent ministry continued to be the domain of the 'peasant' sector of the PRI, this was not allowed to interfere with the need to do things differently, as can be seen in the imposition of more efficient DGRT practices and staff on CORETT in the Federal District. The centralism involved was reflected in the nationwide modifications to regularisation procedures: whatever the origins of the idea of suspending taxes on property transfers, for example, the central imperative behind regularisation under Salinas can be seen in the adoption of the reform by at least nineteen states.

For PRONASOL to succeed in reasserting presidential authority, its work had to be familiar throughout Mexico, and this gave rise to the intense and highly successful publicity campaigns described by Braig (1994) and Dresser (1991, 1994). Understanding PRONASOL as a public relations campaign throws new light on the stress on Chalco, for example, since Chalco's symbolic significance was arguably more important than the voting patterns of local residents. One of the key points about Chalco was its visibility: it lay astride the main motorway exit from Mexico City for travellers to the east and south-east, giving them the opportunity to see the enormous scale of poverty in the area. The rapid expansion of settlement could be traced alongside the motorway from the early 1980s, as unfinished concrete-block houses gave way to temporary shacks and foundations and finally chalked-out plots and grass. Middle-class Mexicans who would never have reason to visit such areas could therefore get a glimpse of what life might be like for the residents. Chalco became a symbol of poverty in Mexico,[17] but Solidarity changed the meaning of that symbol. As the cradle of Solidarity, the Valle came to represent the fight against poverty, a symbol of hope that was underlined when the Pope visited Chalco in 1990 (at Salinas' invitation - Dresser, 1991).

Chalco was, then, a 'showcase' for Solidarity (Hiernaux, 1991) in the same way as San Bernabé in Monterrey (Bailey, 1994), and Colonia Jalisco in Guadalajara.[18] The existence of such showcases underscores the Programme's public relations component, directed at the middle classes and residents of other areas as well as the immediate beneficiaries. For the middle classes who had no personal need for Solidarity benefits, the point was to restore a sense of normality, of the viability of the political regime and its capacity to solve the country's problems, quelling the doubts which had been so important in defection from the PRI in 1988 (Domínguez and McCann, 1992). Although some of the middle classes would be long-term PAN voters, the 'labile' urban middle classes who had voted for the PRD in 1988 could be wooed in this way, and one 1991 opinion poll suggested that support for PRONASOL was inversely related to social class (Morris, 1993). But residents of other areas in need of Solidarity benefits could take hope from examples like Chalco, just as in earlier years the rural population could 'live in hope' that one day the agrarian reform programme would give them the patch of ground of which they dreamed (de la Peña, cited in Chevalier, 1967: 187).

This interpretation of Solidarity also throws new light on the question of urban bias in PRONASOL. The point about towns, and especially state capitals, is that they are regularly visited by non-residents. Consequently, well-signalled improvements in urban areas served to demonstrate how seriously the government was taking the need to combat poverty to a wider population. And there can be no doubt that PRONASOL achievements were well publicised in Mexico's cities. The emphasis on the state capital in PRONASOL's spending in Zacatecas has already been mentioned. At the time of the 1991 elections the results of Solidarity's work in Zacatecas were advertised on huge billboards alongside the main road approaching Zacatecas

17 For foreigners as well as Mexicans: images of Chalco featured prominently in a documentary about the debt crisis made by Susan George, for example.

18 In the mid 1980s Colonia Jalisco was a seemingly remote and inaccessible part of Guadalajara, but it can now be seen by anyone using the eastern ring-road, as the last section of the ring-road to be completed runs right through the settlement.

City, starting miles out and continuing into the city itself. The importance of the mass communication media is underscored by the poor performance of Cuauhtémoc Cárdenas in the 1994 presidential elections. Cárdenas has been criticised for failing to make effective use of the media to communicate effectively with the urban middle classes and the PRD vote amongst these groups declined from its 1988 level (*Proceso*, 5 September 1994). The Solidarity strategy reminds us of just how well versed Cárdenas' opponents were in using the means of mass communication to their best advantage.

In short, PRONASOL demonstrates how 'PRI elites remain far better positioned to define and symbolize the issues for the electorate than do opposition parties' (Davis and Coleman, 1994: 366, referring to Gómez Tagle). Urban areas are important in this process of symbolic definition because of their role in communications. They are also important because of the increasingly negative relationship between urbanisation and the PRI vote since the 1960s. Solidarity's activities in urban Mexico therefore had two 'constituencies': those who benefitted directly on the one hand and a far wider target audience for the demonstration effects of PRONASOL projects on the other. Changes were certainly made to the systems delivering benefits such as regularisation and services, but perhaps the most important changes were those wrought in public perceptions of the government's ability to deliver the goods. These changes paid off: access to PRONASOL benefits was significantly correlated with the PRI vote among lower-class voters surveyed at the time of the 1991 federal elections, and it was among these voters that the PRI registered its greatest gains compared with 1988 (Davis and Coleman, 1994). In general, voting was 'only indirectly affected by policy preferences' concerning, for example, NAFTA and economic liberalism, responding instead to 'satisfaction with the performance of the Salinas administration' (ibid.: 364). We may suggest that the public image of PRONASOL and of Salinas himself played a significant part in producing this satisfaction. In just three years, effective changes in government strategy towards the poor had made a major contribution to changing the popular assessment of Salinas' capacity to govern and in doing so had ensured continuity in the political regime by restoring the electoral fortunes of the PRI.

13 Towards a Pluricultural Nation: The Limits of *Indigenismo* and Article 4

Jane Hindley[1]

In 1991 Rigoberta Menchú warned that if national governments, particularly in Latin America, did not take indigenous rights seriously, there was a danger of armed indigenous rebellion. Quoting experts at the United Nations, she suggested that such an uprising could be imminent as indigenous peoples had learned from political experiences internationally (R. Rojas, 1991). By this point, mid-way through the *sexenio*, the Salinas administration had undertaken a series of reforms specifically relating to Mexico's indigenous peoples. These included ratification of new international norms for relations between states and indigenous peoples contained in the International Labour Organisation's (ILO) Convention 169; constitutional reform (Article 4); and new policies at the *Instituto Nacional Indigenista* (INI) oriented to promoting justice, training, self-reliance and the transfer of resources.

This chapter traces the political history of these reforms and analyses their limits. It discusses how the 'new indigenism' of the Salinas administration responded to the changing status of indigenous peoples and the establishment of indigenous rights internationally; and how the scope and meaning of these rights were subverted. In this way, I emphasise how the issue of indigenous rights was effectively harnessed to the Salinas project of modernising the Mexican state and the broader political context of ensuring neoliberal economic restructuring and regime maintenance. In order to understand how Salinas' indigenist reforms were deployed as legitimation strategies and how the government could proclaim its commitment to the indigenous cause, initially with some degree of credibility, it is necessary to examine the complex legacy of the Revolution.

---

1 I would like to thank the Centro de Investigaciones y Estudios Superiores en Antropología Social (CIESAS-México), the Economic and Social Research Council and the Center for US-Mexican Studies at the University of California-San Diego, for support at different stages of my research; and Gareth A. Jones for his editorial comments.

THE LEGACY OF THE REVOLUTION

In the regime that emerged in the wake of the Revolution, indigenous peoples were classified simultaneously in two ways: according to class (economic identity) as *campesinos*; and, according to ethnicity (socio-cultural identity) as *indígenas*. The former were the subject of political recognition, the latter of political negation. Revolutionary nationalism exalted the *mestizo* present and the glorious indigenous past while ignoring the (ignoble) indigenous present; and, though Zapata occupied a sacred place in the pantheon of revolutionary heroes, his Nahua identity was all but invisible. Within the Mexican Constitution *campesinos* were accorded economic rights within the agrarian regime: Article 27 recognised historic indigenous forms of land tenure (*tierras comunales*), provided grounds for their restitution and the redistribution of new lands in *ejidos*. On the other hand,

> the indígenas do not appear in any part [of the Constitution] as if the *constituyentes* (like the liberals before them in 1857...) could erase a socio-cultural reality they found uncomfortable. (Stavenhagen, 1988: 303; author's translation).

Later, with the formation of the ruling party, *campesinos* were recognised as political actors and their interests incorporated. *Indígenas*, however, became the objects of state practices and ideologies, closely related to anthropology and dominated by evolutionism that came to be known as indigenism, and by which the state would deal with the 'indigenous problem' (Knight, 1990c: 77).

This had two dimensions. First, it referred to the extreme poverty, exploitation and oppression suffered by indigenous peoples; but which were attributed to the cultural inferiority and the evolutionary backwardness of indigenous peoples and not to their position within the socio-economic or political system. Second, it referred to the dominant view that the existence of a large indigenous population with multiple languages and cultures constituted a positive obstacle to national unity and progress (Stavenhagen, 1988). In both dimensions, the causes of the problem were located in cultural difference. The solution was considered to lie in integration into national *mestizo* culture under State tutelage; namely, socio-cultural assimilation through education. In this way, assimilation was defined as in the interests of indigenous peoples (solving their poverty) and the nation (creating the socio-cultural homogeneity necessary for national development). The State, as the agent of development, was assigned the dual role of representing the nation's interests and indigenous interests. Henceforth, any resistance by indigenous peoples was considered a confirmation of their backward mentality.

The foundation of the *Instituto Nacional Indigenista* (INI) in 1948, as a dependency of the Ministry of Education, following other programmes such as Vasconcelas' cultural missions, responded to this logic: it assumed the task of educating and developing indigenous peoples as well as the paternalistic and authoritarian prerogative of representing their interests. The INI's first director, Alfonso Caso, confident of the inevitability of assimilation, predicted that the indigenous problem (and thus indigenous peoples) would disappear within 20 years (Warman, 1978: 143). However, the impact of the institutionalisation of indigenism lies not just in the programmes undertaken, but its role in legitimating racism and existing relations of exploitation and domination in society and the State. Moreover, the founding of the INI corresponded to the institutional marginalisation of the indigenous problem from the central issues of national debate and the central agencies of the State (ibid.: 142). In this sense, the existence of the INI both legitimised the marginalisation of indigenous peoples in society and isolated them from the resources of the State.

ACCUMULATING FORCES FOR CHANGE

Not only did Caso's predictions prove to be wrong, but, in absolute terms the indigenous population increased. Furthermore, from the late 1960s indigenous peoples began to emerge both in Mexico and internationally as political actors vindicating a specifically indigenous identity based on a common experience of domination and exploitation (internal colonialism).[2] Simultaneously, increasing international concern for the environment and the questioning of evolutionist development paradigms, contributed to the creation of a positive image of indigenous peoples as environmental custodians with a role to play in global conservation (Tennant, 1994: 16). As with the environmental movement, the emergent indigenous movement was not homogenous, but comprised local, regional, national and international organisations and networks with differing degrees of articulation, linked by a

2 The post-war period has witnessed successive movements of overt resistance, by those assigned to inferior sociopolitical and economic status, against regimes of domination based on evolutionist categories of innate racial or cultural inferiority. These include the colonial independence movements and the American civil rights movement. The indigenous movement is related to these and many date its emergence to the formation of the American Indian Movement in 1968.

common identity and set of demands. Together with diverse allies from among critical anthropologists and non-governmental organisations (NGOs), to progressive elements within the Catholic Church, these organisations started to denounce the historic and contemporaneous injustices suffered by indigenous peoples generally, and to challenge both the theoretical premises and ethnocidal consequences of assimilationism and development. From denunciation, indigenous movements began to make positive demands for the recognition and respect for their collective rights as the first peoples; that is, in the sense of nations with distinct languages, cultural, juridical and political systems. Their central demands were pluralism, autonomy and territoriality; explicit in these demands is a conception of land not just as an economic resource but as the space for social, cultural and political reproduction.

This movement succeeded in putting the question of indigenous peoples on the international political agenda. Discussion of the specific situation of indigenous peoples was initiated in the early 1970s at the United Nations, and by the mid-1980s the need to formally confer specific collective rights on indigenous peoples was gathering pace.[3] In Mexico, despite the unprecedented scale of indigenous (and *campesino*) mobilisation (Mejía Piñeros and Sarmiento Silva, 1987), indigenous demands had made little impact on the authoritarian structures of the State at the national level, a fact that is directly related to the regime's attempts to monopolise structures of representation and to disarticulate autonomous organisations, either through repression or cooptation. Although from the late 1970s the INI abandoned assimilationism and espoused the notion of 'participation', its limits were demonstrated by two events. First, when the *Consejo Nacional de Pueblos Indígenas* (CNPI) attempted to exercise autonomy in 1979, its efforts were consistently blocked and was subjected to divisionary tactics and it was finally re-incorporated into the CNC and the PRI under an imposed leadership (ibid.: 166-7).[4] Second, attempts by Salamón Nachmad, INI director at the beginning of the

3 In 1971 the United Nations Sub-Commission on the Prevention of Discrimination and the Protection of Minorities commissioned its first study on 'The Problem of Discrimination Against Indigenous Populations'. In May 1982 the UN Economic and Social Council authorised the Sub-commission on Prevention of Discrimination and Protection of Minorities to establish the new Working Group on Indigenous Populations (Sanders, 1989).

4 The National Council of Indigenous Peoples was created by the State in 1975 after the First National Congress of Indigenous Peoples held in Patzcuaro which followed 56 regional congresses begun in 1971. The Council was an attempt by the Echeverría administration to organise and incorporate the emerging indigenous movements and channel their demands. It also represents the institutional recognition of indigenous peoples as political subjects.

de la Madrid administration, to recognise and promote autonomous decision-making by turning over INI regional centres to existing indigenous organisations, were swiftly followed by his imprisonment amidst widespread protests from such organisations (ibid.). The State's response to these initiatives was to mark the limits of what was politically tolerable for subsequent administrations at the INI.

THE POLITICAL EXPEDIENCY OF REFORM

Until 1988, therefore, beyond the few policy changes at the INI, the revolutionary legacy of political negation of indigenous peoples in Mexico was largely intact: the demands for pluralism and indigenous rights had scarcely made an impact on public opinion or the political agenda. Although national-level indigenous organisations existed, with the exception of the *Coalición de Obreros, Campesinos y Estudiantes del Istmo* (COCEI) in Juchitán, Oaxaca, no major mobilisations of indigenous peoples, *qua* indigenous peoples, had punctured the political system nationally. In this context, it seems that rather than domestic mobilisation, events on the international political calender, notably the Quincentenary and the Earth Summit, were to provide the catalyst for putting indigenist reforms onto the political agenda of the incoming administration.[5] While both events were to provide foci for indigenous organisation and international networking, they also created an unprecedented historic conjuncture for international scrutiny on indigenous rights.

In the anticipatory build-up to the Quincentenary, Mexico, which had once prided itself on being the vanguard of indigenist policy,[6] was clearly lagging behind other Latin American countries: constitutional reform recognising the collective and individual rights of indigenous peoples had already been established in Costa Rica (1986); Nicaragua (1986); Brazil (1988); and Argentina (1985). Furthermore, the UN's Declaration on Indigenous Rights

---

5 Preparatory talks for the 1992 celebrations between the National Commissions of the Iberoamerican Community began in 1982. Mexican representatives had protested against the notion 'The Discovery of America' and proposed the alternative 'Encounter of two Worlds' to reduce the triumphalist tone of the Spanish authorities (Krafft, 1993: 46). However, the assertion of the indigenous component of the national identity by Mexican elites in relation to Spain has a long history (Brading, 1985).

6 This dates back at least to 1940 when the Mexican government hosted the First Interamerican Indigenist Congress in Patzcuaro, which led to the setting up of the Interamerican Indigenist Institute.

was due to coincide with the Quincentenary and human rights was a potential achilles heel of the Salinas administration. Recognising this, Salinas was often swift to act. When denunciations of human rights violations in Mexico from international non-governmental organisations seemed to hit deep, they received a rapid institutional response.[7] In view of these factors, and given Salinas' personal and the regime's general legitimacy deficit and concern for its international image, it had clearly become politically expedient to address the question of indigenous rights.

Two acts in the early months of the *sexenio* indicate the political will on behalf of the in-coming President. The first was the choice of Arturo Warman, a long-established critic of assimilationist indigenism and a proponent of pluralism and indigenous autonomy, as Director of the INI (Warman *et al.*, 1970; Warman, 1978). The second act was to create the *Comisión Nacional de Justicia para los Pueblos Indígenas* (CNJPI) as a consultative organ of the Institute on 7 April 1989. Its President and Technical Secretary were stipulated as the INI Director and the Director of the INI's new Programme of *Procuración de Justicia* respectively. Other members were drawn from indigenist intellectuals and bureaucrats, anthropologists and jurists, but significantly no indigenous representatives were included (Díaz Polanco, 1992b: 165).

The new Commission's tasks were to elaborate a legislative proposal addressing the specific question of constitutional recognition for indigenous peoples, and to make recommendations regarding the general condition of indigenous peoples in Mexico. The CNPJI's title represents an explicit reframing of the indigenous problem in terms of justice/injustice and signalled the direction of future acts. It was justice for indigenous peoples, not rights, that was to become the *leitmotif* of presidential initiatives towards indigenous peoples throughout the *sexenio*. In this sense, the naming of the Commission bears the hallmark of neoliberalism: in neoliberal discourse, justice generally occupies a central position, whereas collective rights are considered to be an obstacle to the free operation of the market.

---

7 Shortly after Americas' Watch (1990) report 'Human Rights in Mexico: A Policy of Impunity' was published, the government responded by setting up the *Comisión Nacional de Derechos Humanos* (CNDH).

RATIFICATION OF ILO CONVENTION 169

The incoming President's espousal of justice for indigenous peoples domestically was soon followed by an important opportunity for the Mexican government to demonstrate it's commitment to the indigenous cause in the international arena. Following agreement, in 1988, on the need to modify the assimilationist ethos of its Convention 107 on Indigenous Populations (1957), the International Labour Organisation (ILO) had drawn up a draft proposal for a new convention. According to existing ILO procedure the draft was sent out to national governments to consult with representatives of employer and labour organisations. In the Mexican case, this process of consultation meant the government was under the formal obligation to consult, not with representatives of indigenous organisations, but, with the CTM (Gómez, 1991). The lack of direct input from Mexican indigenous peoples into the new Convention was later (in the INI's annotated text) ascribed to 'the absence of a consolidated, national indigenous organisation which could produce a mobilisation and discussion around the draft' (ibid.: 20). Equally, the lack of input via trade unions was seen as 'a reflection of the weakness of Mexican indigenous organization' (ibid.: 20) rather than the authoritarian character of the former. The interests of Mexico's indigenous peoples, therefore, were represented only indirectly via revisions proposed by international indigenous organisations. However, when decision-making took place at the ILO in Geneva on 27 June 1989, representatives of these organisations were assigned 'observer' status. Despite the lack of consultation with indigenous groups in Mexico and the marginalisation of their representatives in Geneva, the outcome of the meeting was the agreement of Convention 169 on Indigenous and Tribal Peoples in Independent Countries. Convention 169 provided for improved new international standards for relations between states and indigenous peoples.

While this is not the place to describe Convention 169 in detail, several points should briefly be emphasised. First, the Convention constitutes a rejection of assimilationism as prescribed in ILO Convention 107 (1957) and a recognition of pluralism. Second, it marks a shift in the subject of rights from populations to peoples, albeit without the juridical connotations ascribed to peoples in international law. Third, it recognises the social inequality suffered by indigenous peoples contemporaneously and the systematic violations of their citizenship and human rights and prescribes that measures should be taken to redress this situation. Fourth, it recognises the intimate relationship between indigenous identities, land and natural resources, and introduces a weak conception of territory and habitat. Fifth, it assigns indigenous peoples status as political actors with rights to participate in the formulation, application and evaluation of legislation and policies that affect them, whether these be educational, social, economic, regional or national development (López Barcenas, 1994). In sum, Convention 169 represents a clear and detailed outline of specific collective economic, cultural, social and political rights for indigenous peoples and the obligations of states towards them. Moreover, it recognises the existence of two parties with distinct and possibly conflicting interests and attempts to redress the existing imbalance of power between them by making the interests of indigenous peoples visible and stipulating procedures for consultation and representation.

Despite protests by the indigenous observers that the new convention provided insufficient provisions for self-government and territory, it was approved by the majority of delegates: 328 votes compared to one against and 49 abstentions. However, ILO conventions are not binding on States unless ratified nationally and do not come into force until a year after ratification by two countries. Approval of Convention 169, was promptly followed by ratification in the Mexican Senate on 11 July and signed by the President on 3 August 1990, in line with Article 133 of the Constitution. A month later on 4 September Mexico notified the ILO that ratification was complete; it was the second country to do so, following Norway, and the first in Latin America. Thus, one year later the new normative framework for relations between States and indigenous peoples would enter into force simultaneously nationally and internationally.

The fact that Mexico was the first Latin American country to ratify Convention 169 was not lost on its neighbours, but, according to Magdalena Gómez (Subdirector of Juridical Anthropology at the INI), was a cause for surprise given that Mexico was among the last to recognise indigenous rights domestically (Rojas, 1991). Nor was Mexico about to abandon its espousal of the indigenous cause at an international level: it was Salinas who raised the issue of indigenous peoples at the Iberoamerican summit in Guadalajara in 1991; Mexico that organised the International Indigenous Dance Festival at Easter 1992 and the International Encounter of Indigenous Medicine in August of the same year; Mexico that sent indigenous children on the Quincentenary ship; and Mexico that celebrated the Nobel Peace Prize awarded to Rigoberta Menchú in October 1992 (Krafft, 1993: 47-8).

REFORMING ARTICLE 4

With ratification of Convention 169, the Mexican government assumed the responsibility to modify national legislation and indigenist action accordingly, an obligation anticipated with the creation of the CNPJI in 1989. By the time the Convention was ratified this process was well underway, the CNPJI had set in motion a process of extensive opinion surveys and consultations to prepare the ground for the legislative initiative with which it had been charged. According to then Director of Research and Cultural Promotion at the INI, José del Val, this period of consultation consisted of 136 meetings with different indigenous and non-indigenous groups, opinion leaders, jurists, anthropologists, as well as official unions, municipal presidents, federal deputies and state governors in different parts of the country (del Val, 1990: 16). So indigenous groups were just one among many actors consulted and their direct input into the decision-making process was clearly questionable. As one INI official told me,

> the existing information regarding indigenous demands is very old, and in this sense, well, even before sounding opinions, we knew what issues the *pueblos* were going to raise, they have been raising them for a hundred years or five hundred years. These demands go back a very long way.

Moreover, indigenous political organisations were not consulted and as already mentioned, there were no indigenous representatives on the Commission. Such exclusions are indicative of continued paternalism: the equivalent would be a commission on justice for women comprised solely of men.

However, surveys of opinion are politically useful in several ways: they identify those who support a political position and in conditions of unequal power make these demands visible. Also, they reveal and identify those who oppose a given position and the terms of such opposition. The reams of paper generated produce the appearance that 'something is being done'.[8] So it can be surmised that the surveys generated some public discussion and attempted to legitimise the legislative process as a truly plural enterprise with broad support. While aiming to accrue some political benefits from indigenous peoples and actors in civil society sympathetic to their situation, the surveys also served to garner support for the INI's position in negotiations within the State and political apparatus. It was here, within the State itself, that the real decision-making was to take place and where the initiative would encounter strong opposition. Del Val's comments in this respect are revealing:

---

8 2047 opinions were registered together with 88 written extended statements; approximately 6000 pages of information were open to public consultation and a synthesis of the process was presented in a document entitled *2da etapa de consulta pública informal sobre la propuesta de la reforma constitucional* (del Val, 1990: 16)

> The constitutional modifications are the result of complex processes and social struggles, of real subjects, of allies and concrete situations ... What social groups are represented in the congress, who in the last instance will have to approve, modify or reject the reform? We cannot, at the risk of taking these matters lightly, postulate reforms without taking this situation into account ... Any underestimation of the processes of struggle and concrete forces unfolding in the national scenario today is disastrous; so is any overestimation [of indigenous movements]. (del Val, 1990: 18; author's translation and parenthesis).

Such considerations of political pragmatism were echoed to me by another INI functionary who emphasised the difference between 'the wishes of the INI' in relation to indigenous peoples and what could be obtained 'in a complicated negotiation such as this'. The same functionary also informed me that negotiations were not just over content, where, for example, the Institute attempted and failed to get the notion of territory included, but also the position of the reform within the Constitution. Thus the terms of the reform reflect not the INI's position with regard to the extension of rights, but its political position within the State as the appointed representative of the weakest social force in society and the political conditions under which it was operating: one interviewee described the INI as a weak agency 'at the tail of the public administration'.

The outcome was an initiative to confer cultural rights on indigenous peoples. This was presented to the Chamber of Deputies by the President on 7 December 1990. In his speech, Salinas described the socio-economic marginalisation of indigenous peoples within Mexican society, emphasised the inequality and injustice suffered, and the need to demonstrate solidarity and promote justice. In fact, Salinas made direct reference to notions of justice/injustice at least 15 times, although the phrase 'rights of indigenous peoples' did not appear (Salinas, 1990). The presidential initiative was eventually passed unchanged, even if significant delays were achieved by elements of the PRI and the PAN in the Senate. On 28 January 1992, the *Diario Oficial de la Federación* published the long-promised constitutional amendment: a new first paragraph to be added to Article 4 of the Mexican Constitution. It read as follows,

> The Mexican Nation has a pluricultural composition, originally based on its indigenous peoples. The law will protect and promote the development of their languages, cultures, uses, customs, resources and specific forms of social organisation and will guarantee their members effective access to the jurisdiction of the State. In the agrarian judgements and procedures in which they are part, their juridical practices and customs will be taken into account in the terms established by the law.

INTERPRETING THE REFORM

An initial point to emphasise about the centrepiece of the constitutional reform is its location within the Constitution. Article 4 is contained within Chapter 1 of the First Section of the Constitution. This chapter is entitled 'Of Individual Guarantees' and immediately dilutes the concept of indigenous rights as collective rights. The new first paragraph is followed by five statements conferring a woman's right to equality; an individual's right to reproductive freedom; an individual's right to healthcare; a family's right to dignified housing; and the rights of minors. Such mandates make strange bedfellows with one that recognises 'the pluricultural composition of the Mexican nation'. Thus both the position of the reform within the Constitution and the context of the existing paragraphs of Article 4 effectively sever any connection between indigenous peoples and sovereignty, which might arise from their association with the Nation.

So what are the terms of the rights conferred in the reform of Article 4 and what does it represent in relation to post-revolutionary framing? There are four basic principles contained in the paragraph. The first establishes the pluricultural composition of the Mexican nation. It recognises the diversity of contemporary *cultures* that constitute the Mexican nation and therefore signifies an explicit rupture with the ideal of cultural homogeneity. But the phrase 'originally based on its indigenous peoples' represents continuity with revolutionary nationalism and significantly modifies the character of this rupture. Indigenous cultures, rather than peoples, are assigned the force of juridical recognition. Furthermore, the term 'peoples' in Spanish (*pueblos*) is problematic as it denotes a number of different subjects — peoples, communities, masses, towns and villages. The multiple meanings of the term opens it up to different interpretations which significantly shift the scope and subject of these rights and therefore have distinct political implications.

Second, insofar as the indigenous peoples are the bearers of cultural difference they are assigned rights to the protection, promotion and development of their languages, cultures, uses, customs, resources and specific forms of social organisation. Thus, in line with the recognition of cultural diversity, the law represents an explicit rejection of the State's past ambitions to assimilate and integrate indigenous peoples into the dominant hegemonic culture and society and stipulates the positive obligation to protect and promote social and cultural difference. The insertion of 'resources' at this point, however, is ambiguous as it is unclear whether it refers to natural and economic as well as social and cultural resources.

The third principle addressed by the new paragraph relates to the conferment of the right to effective access to the jurisdiction of the State for *individuals* belonging to indigenous peoples (as distinct cultures). This represents a recognition that while the State's action was premised on a notion of cultural homogeneity among its citizens, individuals from indigenous cultures, precisely because of their culture, were denied the possibility to exercise their basic citizenship rights. The modification of the Federal Penal Code in 1991 which established the right to translation for monolingual indigenous individuals, constituted one concrete legal step in this direction.

Fourth, the explicit stipulation that 'in the agrarian procedures and judgements in which they are part, their juridical practices and customs will be taken into account' is so vague as to leave interpretation wide open. It is unclear whether 'judgements and procedures' refer to a broad notion of agrarian matters which includes land tenure, or a narrow definition of dispute resolution. This vagueness is evident in the other principles, which all remit definitions to the secondary legislation.

What is particularly notable about the reform of Article 4, is that it represents an explicit reversal of the revolutionary legacy of assimilationism and the abandonment of the goal of creating a homogenous nation. At the same time the reform succeeds in containing the indigenous question within the parameters of culture: thus it reproduces the revolutionary nationalist framing of the indigenous problem as a *cultural problem*. The injustices and socio-economic marginalisation cited by Salinas are to be resolved at a constitutional level by mandates which confirm the recognition of cultural difference.

INDIGENOUS PEOPLES AND ARTICLE 27

A full appreciation of the limits of the indigenist reform programme is only possible if it is located in relation to the rural restructuring programme that formed part of the neoliberal macroeconomic structural adjustment project, and in particular the reform of Article 27. Whatever else, the reform of Article 27 clearly represents an end to the possibility of land redistribution, an ideological onslaught against communal land tenure and a statement about the dispensability of the rural population (Gledhill this volume; Barkin, 1994: 32). Moreover, in contrast to Article 4, the exclusionary way and speed with which the new agrarian legislation was formulated and passed was a clear demonstration of executive priorities and power (Jones this volume).

Unlike Article 4, this major reform was neither subject to broad consultation, nor did the INI participate in an institutional capacity in negotiations. This institutional marginalisation is a gauge of the weakness of the INI's position within the State apparatus, and constituted the exclusion of the principle representative of indigenous interests within the State from the central legislative initiative pertaining to rural matters in the *sexenio.* Fox (1994b: 213) notes that an INI internal study leaked to the press in October 1991, was the only official voice to highlight publicly the possible negative social impacts of the reform. He also points out the converse side of INI representation: that subsequently the INI attempted to generate support for the reform from its indigenous 'semi-clients'. However, individual functionaries did participate in a personal capacity and when Salinas introduced the reform initiative to the Chamber of Deputies in November 1991, his speech included the proposal to provide protection for the 'territorial integrity of indigenous peoples' (SISTA, 1993).

However, Article 27 and the Agrarian Law contain only three short references to indigenous lands. The second paragraph of fraction VII of Article 27 states that the 'law will protect the integrity of the lands of indigenous groups'. Article 106 of the Agrarian Law stipulates that,

> The lands that correspond to indigenous groups will/should (*deberán*) be protected by the authorities in the terms of the law that regulates Article 4 and the second paragraph of Fraction VII of Article 27 of the Constitution. (author's translation.)

Lastly, Article 164, second paragraph reiterates that,

> In the judgements that involve lands of indigenous groups, tribunals will take into account their customs, and uses, where these do not contravene the terms of this law nor affect the rights of third parties. Moreover, when necessary the tribunal will assure that the *indígenas* can call upon translators. (author's translation.)

The first point to note is the inconsistency and general weakening of the terminology employed by the legislation. The term 'peoples' established in Article 4 has been replaced by the weaker 'groups', and in the last case simply by *indígenas*, which has important juridical implications related to the status of indigenous peoples as collective or individual actors. Similarly, the presidential proposal to recognise 'territories' was replaced by a less defined reference to 'lands' in the final version. Second, the position of these provisions for indigenous lands is very significant. Had they appeared at the beginning of Article 27 and the agrarian law they would have signalled the recognition of a separate agrarian regime for indigenous peoples (Díaz Polanco, 1992b: 76). Instead they are hidden low on the agenda, among the detailed provisions for the privatisation of communal and *ejido* lands. Third, Article 164 of the agrarian law goes little further than restating in more detail the provisions of Article 4 for the resolution of agrarian disputes. It reiterates the State's obligation to provide translation services, but weakens the State's obligation to take into account indigenous laws and customs. to situations where they do not contravene the rights of third parties or the agrarian code. This suggests that the application of these provisions will be limited to the resolution of disputes between indigenous 'groups', and not those where the conflict is with powerful non-indigenous groups such as ranchers.

In sum, although the reformed Article 27 recognises the specificity of indigenous peoples' claims to protection of their lands, no positive provision is actually made for such protection. Article 27 refers the question to the agrarian law, while Article 106 of the agrarian law refers it to the still unwritten regulatory law of Article 4. The impression then is of a series of ad hoc additions to the main body of the new agrarian legislation. Any serious consideration of indigenous land rights would have included them either in the initial reforms of Article 4, Article 27 and the Agrarian law; or, the regulatory law of Article 4 would have been elaborated simultaneously (Díaz Polanco, 1992b: 76).

REGULATING ARTICLE 4

In Mexico, constitutional mandates are statements of principles that provide normative frameworks for State action. Constitutional amendments signify the intention to change the principles on which such action is premised. However, the political interpretation of these principles is provided by the regulatory laws. Furthermore it is through regulatory laws that new principles are given force, specific content, institutional and practical form; these define administrative structures, rules of operation and implementation, division and scope of powers. This is well illustrated by the reform of Article 27 which was swiftly followed by a host of secondary legislation and the setting up of new adjudicating structures such as the *Procuraduría Agraria* and the *Tribunales Agrarios* (Jones this volume). Without such regulatory laws, the constitutional norms are no more than statements of guiding principles which may do little to change practice. Thus, a regulatory law of Article 4 was clearly of paramount importance if indigenous rights were to be specified, the relationship between land and culture established in practice and a change to the form of State action forthcoming.

While on tour in Chiapas in early 1992, the President announced that the INI would initiate a new round of consultations designed to lead to a legislative proposal. By July, the PRD had forwarded a draft proposal drawn up by human rights and indigenous organisations. However, after October 1992, the international attention provided by the Quincentenary had dissipated. Although 1993 was the UN Year of Indigenous Peoples, there were no symbolic dates to commemorate, celebrate or contest, and unlike the Quincentenary, the Year received little publicity and minimal funding from its sponsor. The regulatory law was tabled and dropped from the government's political agenda and the reform process entered into limbo. In the absence of the regulatory law, the State was able to retain the prerogative to define what constitutes 'to protect', 'to develop', and 'to take into account' contained in Article 4. Moreover, practical changes in relations between the State and indigenous peoples were now delegated to the actions of the INI.

CHANGING INDIGENIST POLICY

From the beginning of the *sexenio*, with the appointment of Arturo Warman as Director of the INI, there appeared to be a reorientation of State policy toward a greater recognition of pluralism and 'the recent notion of indigenous peoples as a group with a future', effectively signalling the end of the whole indigenist debate about integration/assimilation (Warman, cited in R. Rojas, 1991). The amorphous principle of participation, inherited from the previous two administrations, was specified by the explicit aims of promoting the transfer of resources, self-reliance and training. But, following past practice, the INI's official position was neither to negotiate with indigenous political organisations, nor to include indigenous representatives in policy-making decisions (*ibid.*).

Although some pre-existing programmes such as the indigenous radios and videos were continued and their scope extended (INI, 1990b), the two major programmes to mark the Salinas administration, INI-Solidaridad and the Justice Procurement Programme, were new. INI-Solidaridad dealt with two types of projects, those aimed at promoting cultural development, and the Regional Funds which aimed to provide credit and technical support in order to strengthen the productive and commercial capacity of indigenous economic organisations. Within the Justice Procurement Programme there were a gamut of projects directed to promoting justice for indigenous peoples. First, there were initiatives to educate State workers and change their practices and conventions with some state governments and the *Procuraduría de la República* to provide translation and expert witness (*peritaje*). Second, research projects were set up designed to provide information for future policy formulation, such as how to reconcile indigenous 'customary' and national law and the situation of rural indigenous day labourers and urban migrants. Third, there were programmes designed to strengthen the capacity of indigenous peoples to defend their rights: including publications explaining the rights conferred by the Constitution (INI, 1990a), ILO Convention

169 (Gómez, 1991), the reform of Article 4 (Gómez, 1992); training for translators and support for NGOs advocating and defending indigenous rights. Fourth, the INI implemented programmes of direct advocacy such as the provision of lawyers, agrarian brigades to resolve existing land disputes between indigenous communities and a civil registration programme.

Thus, working with the policy parameters defined by executive power and in line with Article 4, reformists at the INI attempted to use programmes to empower indigenous peoples. So, for example, although the INI did not negotiate with indigenous political representatives, it worked with them as economic organisations as in the case of the *Frente Independiente de Pueblos Indios* (Fox, 1994b: 212), or provided resources for their meetings as cultural events as in, for example, the *Consejo Guerrerense de Quinientos Años*. More generally, the Regional Funds, by channelling resources through existing or new indigenous organisations, aimed to strengthen the organisational base irrespective of party of ideological affiliation. Conversely, the promotion of justice included a series of direct challenges to existing political agents and practices. Resource distribution via the Regional Funds, through working with independent indigenous organisations, aimed to circumvent existing corrupt channels of distribution (official unions, state and municipal government) and break the traditional *cacique* and clientelistic ties. As a consequence, in attempting to perform its new institutional role the INI was often brought into conflict with antagonistic forces within the PRI and government. Such resistance reduced the effectiveness of INI projects. So, for example, in Chiapas, the INI's work with independent indigenous organisations was consistently sabotaged by the de facto power of the state government. Significantly, INI functionaries, far from being successful in promoting a respect for rights, were themselves subject to repression and intimidation. In Chiapas, one regional director was forced to resign in 1990 and, in 1992, the state director and the director and treasurer for the Tzeltal region were imprisoned (Harvey, 1994: 19).

However, as INI officials interviewed emphasised, many of the attempts to promote justice were no more than pilot projects, and the INI's actions were a small step in the context of a deeply rooted racism and the historic structural inequalities suffered by indigenous peoples. Like the Regional Funds, the Justice Procurement Programme was a promotional and ameliorative programme and a substitute for more profound structural changes such as an overhaul of the public system for the administration of justice. Even so, both programmes represent an expansion of the INI's role within the State both in terms of the functions assumed and resources administered: Fox (1994b: 188) estimates that the INI budget increased 18-fold during the first three years of the Salinas *sexenio*. Furthermore, recognition of the Institute's redefined role came in May 1992 with a redefinition of its position within the State, moving away from the auspices of the Ministry of Education to the new *Secretaría de Desarrollo Social* (SEDESOL); thereby marking an end of the postrevolutionary conception of indigenist action as a predominantly educative task. Even if the Institute's political position remained all too often ambivalent, and support for the work of federal agents, as in Chiapas, was frequently lacking from either the President or the federal government, indicating a lack of political will to support justice for indigenous peoples in practice, the expanded and redefined role for the INI did constitute a political opening toward indigenous peoples. In supporting grassroots organisations and promoting information and debates about indigenous rights and issues, the INI's actions contributed to shifting the climate of opinion toward indigenous people in society, promoting a new ethic against which State action could be assessed, and thus the conditions for indigenous mobilisation and resistance.

CONCLUSIONS

The uprising of the indigenous forces of the *Ejército Zapatista de Liberación Nacional* (EZLN) on 1 January 1994 seems to vindicate Rigoberta Menchú's earlier warning regarding the political expediency of taking indigenous rights seriously. Despite the Mexican government's zeal to ratify ILO Convention 169 and to show its commitment to the indigenous cause internationally, the rights established in the new Convention were redefined, their legislative position relegated and their application postponed in a series of weak policy measures. Thus, although the reforms represented an explicit rupture with the revolutionary legacy of assimilationism and the notion of a culturally homogeneous nation, they were conditioned by the authoritarian of the State. Unlike Convention 169, the reform of Article 4 did not confer socio-economic or political rights on indigenous peoples and thus did it not directly address socio-economic or political inequalities. Rather, it reflected the minimalist notion of the State's responsibilities propounded by neoliberalism. Any rights which would entail the redistribution of wealth or power and which might interfere with the operation of the market or existing structure of political representation were excluded. Without a regulatory law for Article 4, the terms of consultation with indigenous peoples stipulated in Convention 169 remained subject to the contingencies of political conjunctures, pre-existing vertically accountable structures of representation rather than to institutionalised procedures and rules regulating the actions of involved parties. Rather than confer rights on indigenous peoples, the reform of Article 4 gave the INI the prerogative, contingent upon presidential will, to promote indigenous rights and cultures. Finally, the promise to protect agrarian lands contained in the reform of Article 27 remained just that, while the reform revoked one of the central rights obtained by indigenous peoples and *campesinos* through their revolutionary struggles - the redistribution of land.

Moreover, the government's response to the widespread indigenous and *campesino* mobilisation that followed the EZLN uprising outside Chiapas, demonstrated a determination to maintain the parameters of domestic reforms. In some regions the direct response was militarisation, in others, attempts were made to resolve existing material demands, or a combination of both. However, and despite the increased social polarisation and political mobilisation, as well as the calls for respect for Convention 169, the major executive response seemed to be a repeat of the initiatives which marked the beginning of the *sexenio*. On 19 January 1994, the *Diario Oficial* announced the setting up of the *Comisión Nacional de Desarrollo Integral y Justicia Social para los Pueblos Indígenas* (National Commission for Integral Development and Social Justice for Indigenous Peoples). It was headed not by the Director of the INI, but by an experienced PRI politician, Beatriz Paredes, the former governor of Tlaxcala, and later by Heladio Ramirez López, the former governor of Oaxaca. The Commission was composed, not of academics and jurists, but representatives of federal ministries and agencies. It was charged with two principal tasks: to examine the socio-economic needs of indigenous peoples, compile statistics and collate information, in order to emit recommendations to the President regarding measures to be implemented for the 'correct attention to the indigenous social problematic'; and, to formulate a legislative proposal for the regulation of Article 4 and the second paragraph of Fraction VII of Article 27.

In carrying out these objectives the Commission was instructed to consult indigenous intellectuals and representatives of indigenous organisations, as well as non-indigenous specialists. This took two forms. First, consultation fora were established in March 1994 in different regions of the country. These were unsuccessful in producing a consensus as many indigenous organisations challenged both the way the fora were organised and the premise of regulating a law they considered to be insufficient to address their principal demands. Second, Beatriz Paredes attempted to create a 'legitimate interlocutor' from among the representatives of the diverse indigenous organisations. In this she was more successful, as one indigenous representative commented to me 'she succeeded in her aim, she formed us as a group', known as the Plural Group. In July 1994, after months of negotiations, there emerged a proposal to form the *Consejo Nacional de Pueblos y Organizaciones*

Indígenas to coordinate indigenous representation at the municipal, state and national levels.

While such initiatives at the end of the *sexenio* may presage a concern for dealing directly with indigenous representatives, possibly with the aim of cooptation, it is more likely that they constituted another attempt to create the impression that 'something was being done' and to occupy indigenous leaders until the Chiapas crisis had passed. In this sense, they represent political strategies and form a part of a long-standing repertoire for diverting attention away from the real problems of socio-economic marginalisation, political exclusion, and human rights violations faced by indigenous peoples in Mexico, and to subvert their claims to exercise their rights as peoples.

14 Citizens with Dignity: Opposition and Government in San Luis Potosí, 1938-93

Wil G. Pansters[1]

La fuerza ficticia del cacique quedó pulverizada con el sólo recuerdo de sus víctimas y con la fuerza incontrastable de todo el Pueblo oprimido por su nefasta dictadura. (Ruben Rodríguez Lozano, 1938: 5)

It seems to me much too early to write the obituary of that most durable figure in the Mexican political landscape, the cacique. (Alan Knight, 1990b: 98)

Recent debates on social and political change in Mexico are strongly informed by major contemporary events, like the rise of strong opposition politics in northern Mexico, the controversial 1988 presidential elections, the rise of *neocardenismo* and, most recently, the uprising in Chiapas. Political scientists and sociologists may therefore be tempted to emphasise important ruptures with the past: a new State is discerned, as the old one is dismantled; civil society is seen to be emerging and increasingly emancipated; a new political culture is in the making and the opposition is finally reaching maturity; in sum, Mexico is said to be in a definite process of transition (to democracy).[2] It sometimes seems as if politicians and academics alike are caught up in the discourse of modernity. It is undoubtedly true that developments during the past ten years have redefined some of Mexico's most import institutional arrangements and policies. It is, however, precisely for this reason that it is worthwhile to go beyond a limited period of time and study political developments in historical perspective.

1 I am grateful to the Netherlands Foundation for the Advancement of Tropical Research for financing the research for this article.

2 An example of this trend is the publication of the four volume collection, *El nuevo estado mexicano* (Alonso *et al.*, 1992).

In this chapter I will analyse the major trends and events in the political history of San Luis Potosí by looking at three themes: the consolidation of regional elites and *caciques*; the conditions that allowed for the emergence of opposition movements in different historical periods; and the debate on popular movements, mainly in relation to the history of the *navista* movement. In conclusion, I will reflect on the issue of continuity and change in Mexican politics.

During the modern political history of the state of San Luis Potosí, the slogan *'el pueblo o el cacique'* has been applied on several occasions. On at least three historic moments it epitomised the political struggles in this important state. In 1938, during the heyday of *cardenismo*, the state was the scene of the last military uprising against the central government. Its defeat meant the end of the regional *cacicazgo* of Saturnino Cedillo, who had controlled the state since the early 1920s. Out of the ashes of *cedillismo* and under different political circumstances a new regional *cacicazgo* was consolidated, this time headed by former *cedillista* Gonzalo N. Santos. After becoming governor in 1943 he managed to construct a powerful regime and his puppets ran the state until the end of 1958. During that year an opposition movement arose that was to develop into a unique variant of political opposition in contemporary Mexico, and which is currently known as *navismo*. The demise of the *cacicazgo santista* inaugurated a prolonged period characterised by a fragile political equilibrium. At the beginning of the 1980s, yet another governor showed signs of turning San Luis Potosí into his own personal fiefdom. The authoritarianism and corruption of the government of union *cacique* Carlos Jonguitud Barrios revived the remnants of the opposition movement that had successfully driven Santos out of power in 1958. The year 1985 marked the start of a period of political instability that appears to have been resolved only a short time ago. Since the beginning of the 1980s, the state of San Luis Potosí, and more specifically the *navista* movement, were seen by many observers as a 'laboratory' of democratic transition and of the possibilities and limitations of political change in modern Mexico.

On all three occasions the organising principle of political discourse and practice was the struggle against regional strongmen (Cedillo, Santos, Jonguitud). Also, on all three occasions the result of these struggles was a significant shift, though in varying degrees, in the relation between political forces. Similarly, during the heights of the political conflicts under consideration, 'the people' appeared in political discourse as the main opposition actor. In spite of all similarities and despite the importance of accumulated experiences, there are significant differences that need to be addressed. In this paper I would like to focus on the conditions that made possible the emergence of apparently successful oppositional forces in *potosino* politics.

OPPOSITION AND THE DEMISE OF THE 'INDIAN' *CACIQUE*

Once a crucial support for the central State, Cedillo and his armed peasant following had become disfunctional for the federal state during the second half of the 1930s. Several developments had gradually undermined the political and military force of the *cacicazgo cedillista*. With the defeat of the Escobar rebellion and the *Cristero* revolt in 1929, the danger of military destabilisation of the country's political system was waning. The army was increasingly controlled by the federal government. One of the most important consequences of the slow but effective process of political and military centralisation was that the federal government came to depend less on powerful regional *caciques*, like Cedillo, and their armed followers and more on bureaucratic institutions. The foundation of the *Partido Nacional Revolucionario* (PNR) in 1929, and the growing influence of the nationally coordinated peasant and labour organizations contributed significantly to political centralisation and institutionalization. When Cedillo supported the candidacy of Lázaro Cárdenas for the presidency, and apparently conceded to the pressure of the left wing of the PNR to carry out more radical reforms, it seemed that the *cacique* from San Luis Potosí, who had ruled the state like a 'medieval baron' from his Palomas ranch, had once again secured his personal interests (Ankerson, 1984). However, the same PNR left wing was to be responsible for the eventual downfall of Cedillo. The PNR radicals had emerged strengthened from the conflict between Cárdenas and former president Calles in the summer of 1935. The labour sector, in particular, was able to profit politically from this crisis. If the peasants brought Cárdenas to power, organized labour mantained him there by reinforcing the alliance between the State and the working class to the detriment of the political clout of the peasants (Martínez Assad, 1990: 79). This situation harmed Cedillo to the extent that his main power base lay in the countryside. The foundation of the *Confederación de Trabajadores Mexicanos* (CTM) at the beginning of 1936 reinvigorated the rivalry between organized labour and Cedillo, which had its origins in Cedillo's harsh treatment of the teachers' movement in San Luis Potosí a few years before and in the strike of the Atlas textile factory in the *potosino* capital, which had attracted attention nationwide. After the 1935 Calles-Cárdenas crisis, the persistence of the regional fiefdom of Cedillo, which was perceived as a potential catalyst of opposition against the federal government, became an unacceptable political risk. From this time onwards an anti-*cedillista* campaign slowly came into being. At the same time Cedillo's regional dominance began to crumble from below. The organizations responsible for land reform established direct links between villages and peasants in San Luis Potosí and the federal bureaucracy. As a result

Cedillo's mediating role, which had been the cornerstone of his influence, was undermined.

While these processes marked a hidden disruption of Cedillo's power, the local elections in 1937 clearly pitted the general from Palomas against his most articulate adversary, the CTM. The union campaigned actively on behalf of well-known enemies of Cedillo. This led to one of Cedillo's rivals and a close associate of Cárdenas, Francisco Arrellano Belloc, becoming federal deputy for the northern electoral district of Matehuala. Backed by federal government patronage he led opposition to Cedillo within the state. Political conflict between the two groups culminated in a shoot-out on 3 October 1937 by *cedillistas* in Ciudad Valles in which several people were killed. Similar events took place in northwestern San Luis Potosí. Here, in most villages, two governments were installed after the elections, with the state government recognising the *cedillista* candidates. It was a clear strategy of Arrellano and his supporters in Mexico City to subvert the *cacicazgo* from below and to create problems for Cedillo and thus force him to make political mistakes, thereby drawing him into an open conflict with the federal government.

By the end of 1937, a multifaceted attack on Cedillo's stronghold began. Secretary of War Avila Camacho ordered changes of the military commanders in San Luis Potosí. The Agricultural Department embarked on a radical land distribution project at the end of 1937 supervised personally by the Secretary of Agriculture. Although widely publicized, the net effect of this operation was limited and its main impact political. It created a new balance of power which marginalized Cedillo's mediating role. Aspiring *ejidatarios* recognized the federal bureaucracy as the sole body able to carry out land reform, if necessary, rapidly. Cedillo's proven role as a patron thereby became obsolete. At the same time the CTM speeded up its anti-*cedillista* campaign, mainly as a consequence of violent encounters in Valles and San Luis Potosí (Ankerson, 1984: 171-7). Under attack, Cedillo began to plan an armed uprising which, despite attempts to reach an agreement with the President started after an uncompromising speech by Cárdenas in the state capital. However, the rebellion soon disintegrated as Cedillo's supporters surrendered to federal troops. The presence of the President and a considerable part of his cabinet in the capital of San Luis Potosí dramatically demonstrated the subordination of an anachronic regional power domain to the emerging bureaucratic central state, which was dominated by the figure of Cárdenas. Cedillo had been pushed to desperation and had refused to become politically neutralized. The significance of Cedillo's demise was the fact that it was actively sought by actors from outside the state. This does not imply that local groups were not responsive or willing to strive for political change, and many did join the anti-*cedillista* camp, but there can be no doubt that federal forces, not local ones, were decisive (although they emphasised that they were representing the 'peoples' will'). Thus a major difference with the movements opposing later *cacicazgos* is that the anti-*cedillista* campaign did not give rise to an independent protest movement, much less an organised one. The opposition against Cedillo originated in and was resolved within the revolutionary family. The long term effects were therefore limited. Many local *cedillistas* were replaced but others remained powerful in their local domains. The most telling case of a 'persistent oligarch' was Gonzalo N. Santos.[3]

THE RISE AND DEMISE OF THE 'WHITE *CACIQUE*'

The period immediately after the ousting of Cedillo was one of political instability and the battle for local political leadership was particularly fierce between 1939-41. A return to a stable, albeit authoritarian, regime came in 1943 when Santos became governor. Santos maintained excellent contacts with several presidents and PRI executives. This provided him with sufficient political backing for the imposition of his followers at all levels of government (local and federal deputies, senators, municipal presidents and important public officials). He was also able to control the choice of governor for two terms after his own, before opposition movements put an end to his pervasive grip on the state. The *cacicazgo santista* was a showcase of personal power with institutional underpinnings.

The degree to which the *santistas* managed to control local affairs, engendered opposition from different groups, from both inside and outside the PRI, during the 1950s. The narrowing circle of *santistas* who monopolised public office and local business marginalised several political groups.[4]

3 In his book *Persistent Oligarchs* Mark Wasserman (1993) analyses the way in which prerevolutionary elites managed to survive the Revolution and how they related to the new postrevolutionary elites. Although I am referring here to Santos' persisting influence in San Luis Potosí after he had held close ties to Cedillo throughout the 1920s, the parallels with Wasserman's arguments go much further. Santos belonged to an important *ranchero* family of *caciques* which had ruled part of the Huasteca since the middle of the 19th century. His brother Pedro Antonio had played a significant role in the *maderista* phase of the Revolution in San Luis Potosí and after his assassination Gonzalo entered postrevolutionary politics. He became local deputy at the age of 24 and spent many years in the federal chamber of deputies, of which he became a prominent leader. He also became senator and was one of the most important politicians in Mexico during the period of Calles.

4 Tomás Calvillo (1981) has observed that previous studies had mistakenly stated that the first

One opposition group, *Grupo Renovador Potosino*, in a report criticised the way in which Santos dominated the executive, legislative and judicial powers to the extent that these bodies could not act in a constitutional manner.[5] A key element was the manipulation of the electoral process which, along with control of the judiciary and finance ministry, resulted in Santos and a small group of intimates controlling the entire political process in the state. What was missing in the state's political process was 'the people':

> It is well known that the authorities represent the people and that their mandate derives and emanates from the people, however, as all the processes of their designation come from one man, it is the maximum *cacique* who controls all the official machinery, and has furthermore the unintended help of our leaders in the PRI, to enable him to control the whole process....[6]

This argument contains at least two elements that would inform the discourse and practices of future opposition to Santos and even beyond. First, it makes clear that the federal authorities and the central committee of the PRI cannot be held responsible for the situation in San Luis. The authority of the party system was not disputed, much less that of the President. Second, the question of legitimacy is addressed. With the help of government and partisan structures and a small clique of loyal followers, the *cacique* ruled the state without the consent of the people, or, for that matter, of *potosino* citizens.

The *Grupo Renovador* was not successful at the time, but many other opposition groups emerged, particularly around elections, whose significance would increase at the end of the 1950s when the various groups came together. By this time the *Grupo Renovador* had become the *Frente Reinvidicador de la Ciudadanía Potosina* (FRCP) led by two seasoned politicians (Márquez, 1987: 133). Another opposition group, the *Alianza Cívica Potosina*, was growing around the Ciudad del Maíz area and drew heavily on former *cedillistas*. However, both the *Alianza* and the *Frente* were largely made up of *priístas* who had previously had ties with Santos which reduced their political clout and left them open to accusations of political opportun-

---

efforts to bring down Santos developed after the presidential elections in July 1958. According to Calvillo, resistance was already discernible in 1957. In fact, opposition groups were active as early as 1954 and perhaps even before, albeit in an underground fashion.

5 Sympathisers of the *Grupo Renovador* were harassed, imprisoned and sometimes even murdered (Achivo General de la Nación AGN-DGG 2/311 DL (20)4, *Grupo Renovador* to Ruiz Cortines, 8 June 1954).

6 Archivo General de la Nación AGN-DGG 2/311 DL (20)4, letter from *Grupo Renovador* to Angel Carbajal, Minister of *Gobernación*, 18 June 1954, author's translation.

ism; a criticism which could not be levelled at a third group which emerged in 1958.

The *Comité de Profesionistas e Intelectuales* (CPEI) of San Luis Potosí state was founded in July 1958. They were not familiar with local or regional politics but with the local university which had been the scene of fighting between two factions; the *santistas* and the anti-*santistas* lead by Dr Manuel Nava. The struggles between the factions intensified after Nava's death and his brother, Salvador, became active within the CPEI. The organisation's objectives were simple and clear: to break the monopoly Santos had long held over the selection of candidates for public office. This was to be tested during the forthcoming municipal elections (December 1958). The means to this end was the PRI and to facilitate this the urban professionals had obtained the support of the CNOP committee in Mexico City. In ideological terms the CPEI, which was rapidly dominated by the figure of Salvador Nava, stood close to the other opposition groups which had emerged: Nava had declared that '*caciquismo* is the negation of the revolution' (cited in Calvillo, 1981: 40). The system in itself was not disputed; only *individuals* who abused the system, like Santos, should be removed by a civic movement. In this way personal favouritism and corruption would be overcome, and public morality and administrative honesty recuperated. The job could only be done by men who did not have dirt on their hands. Since the CPEI's direct aim was to conquer the administration of the city of San Luis Potosí, it also stressed the constitutional right of municipal autonomy (Granados Chapa, 1992: 40). Throughout Nava's campaign it was emphasised that his struggle did not represent sectoral, religious or class interests. Rather it represented a classless popular movement against Santos. Indeed, Nava himself recognised many years later that his first electoral campaign was ultimately founded on a critique of the *cacicazgo santista* and that it did not put forward a specific government programme (Borjas, 1992: 62). The central axis of opposition discourse and practices (alliances) was the mobilisation of 'the people' and the recovery of effective citizenship. In a local newspaper the activities of the *Unión Cívica Potosina*, a coalition of different opposition groups, were defined as '....essentially popular, more than political, as civic activities. It is the struggle of all of a people against all of a *cacicazgo*' (Borjas, 1992: 83, author's translation).

The emerging *navista* movement was ideologically underpinned by a variant of political liberalism but with conservative undertones. The leadership was dominated by the Catholic middle classes and concepts such as 'dignity' and 'decency' appeared regularly during the campaign, because the *cacicazgo santista* was held responsible for what was interpreted as the decay and degradation of *potosino* society. Santos and his followers had imposed ways and manners, which did not sit easily with the norms and values of the proud highland *potosinos*. Although Santos clearly represented the interests of the *criollo and mestizo ruling class in the Huasteca – Loret de Mola (1979: 13-73) called him the 'cacique blanco'* – it was his *ranchero* background with its concomitant violent methods that was perceived as disrespectful in the 'Porfirian' culture of the state capital (see Schryer, 1990: 142-5). Some writers have referred to the ideological underpinnings of the opposition movement as *potosinidad*. In sociological terms, the discourse of *potosinidad* expressed a sense of belonging to a community integrated through extensive (family) networks that cut through class divisions (Márquez, 1987: 144). The emergence of regional strongmen in the aftermath of the Revolution, who had their principal power base in 'peripheral regions' (Cedillo in Ciudad del Maíz, Santos in the Huasteca) and who did not share the socio-cultural outlook of the *capitalinos*, played a crucial role in the formation of a cohesive ideological and political opposition movement, underpinned by strong social and family ties within the state capital. In this sense, *navismo* provides a good example of a regional or local level political culture that mediates between national political processes and local specificities.[7]

By mobilising the population, appealing to citizen rights and by explicitly supporting the new federal government of López Mateos, the opposition movement had placed Santos and his puppet governor Alvarez in an awkward position. As I have argued elsewhere, the emergence of political pressure from below in combination with shifting alliances at the federal level has frequently been responsible for the fall of regional power groups (Pansters, 1990: 120-2; 143-7). Also the personalised and centralised nature of Mexican politics aided the opposition group since there had been tensions between López Mateos and Santos since 1929 when they were on opposing sides of the *vasconcelistas* repression. The change in the relations of forces at the national level provided the political space necessary for local dissident groups to come into the open and engage in a struggle against Santos. Nava's victory in municipal elections in the *potosino* capital forced the resignation of the santista governor, Manuel Alvarez, in January 1959. His remaining in office would, it was argued, be an insult to the 'dignity of the potosino people'. Despite Santos losing his grip on state power, he remained highly influential in the Huasteca region.

The in-coming Nava administration made massive changes, despite the fragmentation of the coalition which brought him to power. The new gover-

7 The importance of local political cultures is convincingly shown for Michoacán by Rob Aitken (forthcoming b).

nor, Francisco Martínez de la Vega, was a cousin of Nava and during 1959-60 Nava ruled the city according to three fundamental imperatives: honesty, legitimacy and accountability. His success as municipal president and his increasingly cordial ties with the political establishment in the state and Mexico City – he used every opportunity to express his gratitude towards the President, explicitly thanking him for having respected the popular vote at the end of 1958, thereby recognising the crucial influence of the federal authorities in local affairs – paved the way for his possible candidature for governor. Although Nava had received encouraging indications that another electoral campaign would be tolerated by the federal authorities, it soon became clear that the central committee of the PRI had other plans. At the beginning of 1961, Manuel López Dávila was put forward as candidate for governor. As the road to power through the PRI was blocked, Nava again decided to campaign as an independent candidate. From then the situation deteriorated steadily. The government, both in San Luis and in Mexico City, not only impeded the *navistas* from participating in the internal elections of the PRI, they were actually determined to exterminate the movement. Violence erupted when López Dávila was declared the winner. Nava was imprisoned though later released without charge. The municipal government was accused of having supported the opposition movement and dissolved. Attempts by the *navistas* to form a regional opposition party (*Partido Democrático Potosino*) failed and with the state and municipal administrations in the hands of loyal *priístas*, the *navista* movement seemed destined to become just another small obstacle to PRI dominance.

It is important to stress the different ways in which the *cedillista* and subsequently the *cacicazgo santistas* collapsed. The mix of local and external pressures was different. At the end of the 1920s it was the federal state and its local cronies which took the lead in the removal of the *cacicazgo*.Twenty years later opposition arose from below. The anti-*santista* forces had already acquired momentum when presidential candidate López Mateos opened Pandora's Box. The situation in San Luis Potosí provided the presidential candidate with the opportunity to project himself as a reformer and rid himself of one of the country's most powerful *caciques*. The recognition of Nava's victory could, therefore, be interpreted much more as compensation for his part in the demise of the *cacique*, than as proof of the regime's willingness to open up the system, as opposition leaders mistakenly believed. The success of the opposition movement led to its later suppression. The *navistas* discovered that challenging the federal authorities was different from ousting a regional *cacique* and that there was much truth in the words of the politician, Sánchez Vite, who had once declared that 'there is only one *cacique* in Mexico and he lives in Los Pinos!' (cited in Loret de Mola, 1979: 52). In

1961 the federal government was under pressure from many quarters and was unwilling to tolerate a challenge to the basic rules of the game.

OPPOSITION AND POPULAR MOBILISATION: A FIRST ASSESSMENT

The essential characteristics of the *potosino* opposition movement, which was soon consolidated as navismo, conform to the definition provided by Foweraker's recent work on popular mobilisation in modern Mexico. The opposition that emerged in 1958 was indeed a struggle to constitute 'the people' as a political actor (Foweraker, 1990: 5). It clearly sought to vindicate citizens' rights against the practices of imposition, personalism and the violation of municipal autonomy. The slogan 'el pueblo o el cacique' was never more true than during the second half of 1958, when the opposition pushed 'the people' onto the political stage. The opposition leaders strived to fight their way through the PRI, and only when this failed did they (temporarily) embark on an independent strategy, without breaking completely with the PRI. They welded alliances (horizontal linkages) that resulted in the formation of the Unión Cívica Potosina; a multi-class coalition that was sustained by the struggle against a common enemy. They also continuously appealed to the discourse of the incoming president. This seems to confirm what Foweraker has called the hallmark of popular political practice: institutionalism. By this it is understood that oppositional popular actors seek institutional recognition in order to get material or political benefits by employing political exchanges and gradualist strategies that involve negotiation with the government (Foweraker, 1993: 5). Evidently, the *potosino* opposition underscores the statement made by Foweraker that popular mobilisation is mainly directed against the particularistic relations of clientelism and caciquismo, since it arose explicitly in opposition to the pervading bossism of Gonzalo N. Santos. The first phase of navismo (1958-61) had an eminently political character as it focussed on electoral processes. Its basic operational terrain was citizen politics as opposed to mass politics.[8] It could be argued that Nava's victory during the 1958 municipal elections was 'tolerated' by the federal authorities precisely because the opposition's project was essentially limited to political reform.[9] Seizing the state govern-

8 This distinction was made by Arnaldo Córdova, as cited in Barry Carr (1991: 130).

9 It should be kept in mind that as municipal president Nava could, if necessary, be kept under control by the regional and national administration.

ment would have broadened the scope of navista influence to the realm of mass politics, particularly because links to organised labour and the popular sector of the official party already existed.

The basic weakness of the opposition movement was its organisational fragility. This is related to the characteristics of Mexico's political system, which has sliced up the population in sectoral or corporate groups, which are vertically linked to central power. Electoral opposition movements necessarily have to operate on this organisationally and institutionally fragmented terrain and reconstitute their (individually based) followings in different organisational formats. The difficulty in achieving this transition from economic-corporate representation and identities to individual-citizen representation is clearly illustrated by the *potosino* case: the Unión Cívica Potosina joined urban professionals, grouped in the Federación de Profesionistas e Intelectuales, peasants from the Ciudad del Maíz area organised in the Alianza Cívica Potosina, students grouped in the Frente Universtitario Germán del Campo, workers pertaining to the CROC and members of the Unión Nacional Sinarquista among others. The intention to transform this loose alliance of largely sectoral interest groups, after the mobilisations against Santos, into a political party with individual membership (Partido Democráta Potosino) failed, mainly as a result of government repression and cooptation. The organisational weakness, manifest from the beginning, and the necessity of some form of effective leadership paved the way for the consolidation of a movement that was headed by a powerful leader. Thus when the struggle between the people and the cacique generalised, a new strongman was born: Salvador Nava.

THE PHOENIX FROM THE FLAME: NAVA, THE UNION *CACIQUE* AND BEYOND

When lawyer Antonio Rocha assumed the governorship in 1967, the political situation in San Luis Potosí reached a new, though fragile equilibrium. This situation persisted during the government of Guillermo Fonseca Alvarez (1973-9). Both governors operated cautiously and strived towards political mediation. Since the once powerful opposition movement appeared to have been put to sleep, Nava's occupation of public non-political functions was not hindered.[10] No *navista* organisation was active during these years, but

10 He was active in several charity organisations and became director of the Medical Faculty of the local university in 1976, (see Granados Chapa, 1992: 58).

the civic experiences of the beginning of the 1960s, 'were built into society's political conscience' (Márquez, 1987: 136). Besides, Nava's professional activities as a doctor enabled him to remain in contact with a considerable portion of the *potosino* capital's population. This acquires additional importance if the demographic stability (insignificant immigration) and cohesiveness of the city of San Luis Potosí are taken into account.

When Carlos Jonguitud Barrios became governor in 1979, it soon became clear that the collective memory of ordinary citizens was stronger than that of the political elite. Jonguitud's power base lay not in his native state but in his absolute control of the national teacher's union (SNTE), which he had acquired in the shadow of President Echeverría. After Fidel Velázquez (CTM) and Hernández 'La Quina' Galicia (oilworkers), Jonguitud was probably the most powerful union *cacique* in the country at the time. Jonguitud's ruthless and rude methods and manners, which characterised his rule in the SNTE, soon came to offend the *potosinos*. His thirst for money led to widespread corruption. Popular discontent spread and channelled towards Nava's private home. The erstwhile civic leader was requested to assume, once again, the responsibility of mobilising the population, of which less than ten per cent had voted at the last elections in 1981. While the tragic events of 1961 were remembered, reasons to revitalise the movement abounded. The Frente Cívico Potosino (FCP) was founded and Salvador Nava was launched again as candidate for the forthcoming municipal elections. In a situation similar to that of the end of the 1950s, Nava appealed to the electoral promises of campaigning presidential candidate, Miguel de la Madrid, this time with respect to the latter's verbal crusade against corruption (moral renovation). In contrast to the first phase of navismo, however, no attempt was made to channel the opposition through the ranks of the PRI. The increased distance between the navistas and the PRI, if compared to the first phase of opposition, was clearly shown by a later statement by Salvador Nava in which he argued that, thirty years ago, he had fought against the cacicazgo of a single person, but now he confronted the cacicazgo of the PRI-system (Caballero, 1992: 48). With the support of the PAN and the PDM, Nava won the elections in December 1982, although he had to force official recognition, for which he also received the backing of several leftwing parties.[11] During the two years that Nava was in power, his government was

11 This differed from the situation more than two decades before, when the leftwing leaderships in Mexico City subscribed to official accusations of Nava being a representative of clerical and conservative forces. This assessment was obviously related to the Cold War that contributed crucially to the polarisation of Mexico politics in those years. Nevertheless, within San Luis Potosí, Nava managed to obtain the support of communist cells during the 1958 opposition

constantly in the stranglehold of the governor.[12] However, contrary to the earlier experience, the navista organisation (FCP) remained intact. With the onset of the economic crisis and the spread of electoral opposition, especially in the Mexican north, the navistas encountered a more fertile environment for survival. In 1985 the FCP and the PAN supported Guillermo Pizzutto in his bid to become mayor of the *potosino* capital.

In the meantime, a discredited Jonguitud had finished his term and had left the gubernatorial seat to Florencio Salazar.[13] Although a reconciliation between the *navistas* and Salazar seemed likely, problems soon emerged, mainly due to disagreements about the municipal elections. The state governor came under increasing pressure and was finally forced to resign in May 1987 after a violent prison uprising in which several inmates were killed. In order to capitalise on the renewed popular mobilisations, Pizzutto ran again for mayor in 1988, this time on a PAN ticket but with the support of the *navistas*. On this occasion he won. Nava's victory in 1982 and Pizzutto's in 1988 (and probably also in 1985), made the various opposition forces in San Luis believe that they stood a good chance of winning the gubernatorial elections that were to take place in 1991. After all, an opposition party, the PAN, had already managed to win in Baja California. Moreover, the issue of electoral democracy was on the national agenda when President Salinas announced further political reform. Finally, the coalition of leftwing parties organised in the PRD now fully recognised the civic potential of the *navistas* in San Luis Potosí. When different individuals and parties approached Nava as a possible candidate, the aged leader demanded that he would run only if he were nominated by several parties, a strategy that would enable him to secure for the *Frente Cívico Potosino* the maximum amount of political manoeuvrability.

---

movement against Santos. For the attitude of the left in 1961 (see Martínez Assad, 1985: 65).

12 The state government retained funds for the capital for a five month period and used all its influence with official unions and other organisations to cause problems for the city administration, which could not count on support of the federal authorities either. There was no communication between the governor and the municipal president. While Nava accused Jonguitud of political *revanchismo, the latter accused the former of provoking agitation against the state authorities. Both men only agreed on the fact that the political stalemate was utilised by politicians who wanted to become the PRI candidate for the next state government (Proceso,* 15 October 1984: 10-17). Nava left office a year before his term ended.

13 Florencio Salazar Martínez was the son of former leader of the CTM branch in San Luis Potosí and was well connected to the regional political elite. He had also served several missions as PRI delegate in different parts of the country.

The 1991 elections between the PRI candidate, Fausto Zapata, and the coalition (PAN, PRD, PDM) candidate, Salvador Nava, developed into a bitter struggle that acquired national importance.[14] Months before the polls the electoral machine of the PRI-government was paving the way for 'victory'. The electoral law of San Luis Potosí failed to incorporate the changes adopted by the new federal law giving the ruling party a considerable advantage. The local congress did, however, validate an amendment of the electoral law, which prohibited different parties from nominating the same candidate. This forced the opposition to form a coalition, leaving it with only one representative on the State Electoral Council instead of three. Voter registration was similarly biased towards vested interests. San Luis Potosí provides a classic example of a state in which the major urban area is dominated by the opposition, while the more backward rural areas, basically the Huasteca, deliver votes to the PRI. As was to be expected, the PRI-dominated areas achieved by far the highest levels of voter registration.[15] Throughout the campaign the PRI used its proven tactics to influence the vote: complete domination of the local media, excessive funds for propaganda, accusations against the *navistas* for provoking violence and so on.[16] Pre-electoral fraud was complemented by an even bigger fraud during the elections themselves. An independent report based on elections at 750 polling stations, concluded that in more than half some kind of irregularity had occurred.[17] It also registered fifty different types of fraud. The *navistas* also produced a document in which the electoral fraud was analysed. Despite the evidence of fraud and even before the polls had closed, the local press declared Zapata the winner. Although ample evidence of fraud existed, Nava declined to enter the judicial jungle of the electoral bodies. It was argued that the submission of hundreds of complaints would drag the *navistas* into a legal war of position with the authorities which they were unlikely to win. Instead, Nava announced his intention to pursue his case by emphasising his moral authority and

14 The most extensive coverage of these elections can be found in Caballero (1992); see also Granados Chapa (1992: 75-182) and Aziz Nassif (1992). I will draw on these texts to reconstruct the events.

15 While in the *potosino* capital little more than 70 per cent of the voting population had received adequate credentials, the district of Tamazunchale in the Huasteca almost reached 94 per cent, (see Aziz, 1992: 7 and Granados Chapa, 1992: 126). Both authors refer to a study by UNAM.

16 In the accounts of the electoral campaign the pronounced partiality of the *potosino* news media in favour of Fausto Zapata is emphasised. Nava therefore sought a forum in the national press.

17 Responsible for this study were the *Academia Mexicana de Derechos Humanos* and the *Centro Potosino de Derechos Humanos*, which is cited by Aziz (1992: 13).

legitimacy and to declare himself Governor on 31 August, the day on which the local parliament was supposed to validate Zapata's victory. Many *potosinos*, perhaps the majority, indeed considered Nava as their 'moral governor'. Consequently, Zapata was unable to take office. The navista municipal president of the state capital, Guillermo Pizzutto, announced that he would not recognise Zapata's government.

The tense situation in San Luis Potosí received an unexpected impulse when the PRI gubernatorial candidate in the neighbouring state of Guanajuato resigned after equally fraudulent elections and a *panista* assumed the post *ad interim*. If the federal government was willing or had been forced to sacrifice its candidate in Guanajuato, there were no reasons why it should not do so in San Luis as well. Meetings were held, a silent march was undertaken, roads were blocked and during the last address by the outgoing governor, female *navistas* made themselves heard by battering on their kitchen utensils while others started a permanent meeting in front of the government palace. As Nava travelled back and forth to Mexico City and catapulted himself onto a national platform, Zapata did not appear in public.[18] When, on 26 September Zapata officially took the oath as the new governor in the presence of the President, the aged and ill Nava embarked on the highly publicised *March of Dignity* to Mexico City, while a group of women impeded Zapata from entering his office. The demand: Zapata was to resign. Less than two weeks later he did so. Nava suspended his march and returned to San Luis Potosí, where he was welcomed as a hero. That same day the *priísta*, Gonzalo Martínez Corbalá, flew to the *potosino* capital to take over the government as interim governor.

'THE CAPITAL IS *NAVISTA*, NOT *PANISTA*'

The relationship between opposition movements and established political parties is one of the key elements in the debates on popular mobilisation and (new) social movements. On the one hand, it has been stressed that many contemporary popular movements enshrine a critique of political parties and their vested interests, but on the other hand it has been put forward that the establishment of alliances with other political actors, including political

18 During one of these meetings Nava was offered a compromise: either Zapata would become governor with Nava occupying an important position in his government, or Nava would become governor with *priístas* in crucial positions. Nava refused both proposals, (see Granados Chapa, 1992: 168).

parties, is the only viable alternative to political marginalisation. The case of *navismo* provides an excellent example of the possibilities and difficulties which popular opposition movements encounter in their strategies to influence the political process. The origins of the *navista* movement lay in a multi-organisational coalition formed in 1958 with initially close ties to the PRI. When the ruling party showed its intolerant side, the *navistas* participated as independents. In the early 1980s the *navista* strategy became more complicated. Nava's candidacy for municipal president in 1982 was supported by the PAN and the *Partido Demócrata Mexicano* (PDM). The latter had emerged from the *Unión Nacional Sinarquista* which had actively participated in the fall of Gonzalo Santos. The alliance between Nava and these conservative parties was primarily pragmatic, given the fact that there were important programmatic differences between them. The alliance provided the *navista Frente Cívico Potosino* with sufficient room for manoeuvre. During the post-electoral mobilisations left wing parties also participated and when Nava finally won, the majority of the municipal council were members of the *Frente Cívico*.[19] In the years to follow the relationship between the *navistas* and the PAN became closer. In 1985 and in 1988 both supported Guillermo Pizzutto for municipal president. These close ties, however, implied political risks for both. It was unclear whether the vote was *panista* or *navista*. Probably inspired by the growing influence of the PAN in Northern Mexico from 1985 and even more so after the unwritten agreements between their party leadership and President Salinas (*concertacesión*), the *panistas* in San Luis Potosí were confident that they had successfully absorbed the *navistas* and converted them into *panistas*. For the *Frente Cívico* it became increasingly difficult to maintain its political autonomy and leadership.

The ambivalent relationship between the *navistas* and political parties is also related to the former's ideological principles. According to leaders of the *navista* movement the establishment of alliances with political parties is a necessity, since the electoral law prohibits the participation of independent non-partisan organisations in elections for public office. *Navistas* argue that their main task is civic rather than electoral. Political parties, in contrast, are necessarily limited by electoral politics and the search for power.[20]

Navismo returned to its roots when Salvador Nava declared that he was only willing to run for governor if he could enjoy the support of different

19 The PAN had three councillors and the PDM two, despite the fact that the former had obtained several times the votes of the latter.

20 Separate interviews with Guillermo Pizzutto and Pablo Aldrete, the former *navista* campaign leader, San Luis Potosí, 17 March 1994.

parties. Building a new coalition was a difficult process, mainly because the PAN was initially unwilling to cooperate. In a clear attempt to subordinate the *navista* movement, the national leadership of the PAN proposed that Nava should run for governor on a PAN-ticket which other parties would join later.[21] Nava responded to this pressure by observing that he did not have much faith in political parties and that he was 'neither red nor white but just a simple doctor of the people' (Caballero, 1992: 43). When Nava left open the possibility of an alliance with only the PRD and PDM, the PAN finally gave in, aware of the fact that otherwise it would be marginalised. With such an arrangement it was the *Frente Cívico* and thus Nava, who would take the crucial decisions in the months to come. The *Frente Cívico* managed to withstand the pressures from the right and the left and followed its own path, that of the centre, without excluding the possibility of forging alliances with other political actors. As Martínez Assad has suggested, this was possible because of the presence of Nava himself, that is, his moral and political authority.[22]

The March of Dignity symbolised the struggle between the powerful 'institutional *caciquismo*' of the PRI and a civic opposition movement that achieved maturity in the shadow of a man of indisputable moral authority.[23] The outcome of the events was crucially influenced by the decision not to wage the struggle on the terrain defined by the government, that is, taking the protests to the electoral authorities, but instead to raise it to a level where the authorities proved to be extremely vulnerable. The reformulation of the post-electoral conflict in terms of dignity, legitimacy and honesty hampered the government machine. But above all, it was the presence of Salvador Nava, the appealing moral *caudillo*, that made it impossible for the government to withstand the pressure. The foundations of Nava's leadership were laid in the

---

21 Among the *panistas* who opposed the coalition were Abel Vicencio Tovar and Diego Fernández de Cevallos, presidential candidate of the PAN in 1994.

22 'Sheltered between the right (PDM, PAN) and the left (PSUM), the FCP has found itself with the dilemma of continuing on its own path, that of the centre – since it arose from this tendency – without losing any support, without damaging any alliance. This has been possible because of the presence of Nava. ....'(1985: 73; author's translation).

23 The importance of the concept of 'moral dignity' in the discourse and practices of the *navistas* is underlined by a text written by Salvador Nava shortly before he died in 1992: 'The installation of democracy cannot be delayed for long. The country demands it. This was demonstrated last year, when we began the March for Dignity from the city of San Luis Potosí. The principle of dignity brought together thousands of Mexicans without reservations about ideology or party. The dignity of the citizens has often been humilliated by power, violating the fundamental rights of Mexicans. It is because of this that today dignity demands the installation of democracy in Mexico.'(cited in Caballero 1992: 24; author's translation).

early 1960s and it strengthened during the 1980s. The way people personally requested him to return to the political arena bears resemblance to the way peasants called for Cedillo's personal intervention in order to resolve their needs. Of course, the demands and the times were different but the model is comparable.

Nava's challenge to Mexico's authoritarian regime shows perhaps even more resemblance to the way in which opposition movements and leaders have emerged in the former communist countries of Eastern Europe. The struggles of Solidarity in Poland (Walesa) and Czechoslovakia (Havel) finally rested on their attempts to reclaim the moral highground from socialist powerholders (Hann, 1993: 13). As Runciman (1985: 17-8) observed of the Polish case, the workers of Solidarity demanded to be treated by the authorities as they were entitled to be treated, and this did not mean taking over the government itself, but having their grievances properly recognised by those institutions. Equally, *navistas* have always emphasised that it is not their main objective to occupy the government palace but to create the conditions for a democratic transition. For that purpose people have to regain self-esteem and dignity and to demand that the authorities treat them like citizens.[24] Politics on such a basic level then become *cultural* politics: how do people perceive the authorities, the State and themselves, how do they act on these perceptions, and how can this be changed? The fundamental paradox of *navismo* is that, while it has been able to spread some kind of civic ethic, it has done so by reproducing the figure of the *caudillo*, Nava. In the words of Guillén Lopéz (1989), who analysed the case of *neocardenismo*, *navismo* represents a mix of traditional and liberal political culture. *Navismo* has until recently been successful in the mobilisation of popular support and in the construction of broad alliances, but it owes this largely to the revitalisation of the vertical and personalised links between *caudillo* and client.

Nava's importance in holding together an ideologically diverse coalition and in suppressing factional disputes within the opposition movement itself, became painfully clear after his death in May 1992. With new gubernatorial elections ahead, the 1991 coalition disintegrated and a struggle developed about the political heritage of the former leader, mainly between the PAN and the *navistas*, organised in the *Frente Cívico*. However, it was the PRI and the government which introduced new tensions into *potosino* politics,

---

24 The case of *acarreo*, in which hundreds, sometimes thousands of peasants and other PRI-clients are 'voluntarily' transported to electoral meetings in order to applaud the official candidate, stands as an example of the way human dignity is trampled on.Interview with Pablo Aldrete, *navista* leader, 17 March, 1994. Electoral fraud, corruption and the arbitrary use of the law are others.

when the priísta interim governor, Martínez Corbalá declared, in October 1992, his candidacy for the forthcoming gubernatorial elections.[25] It was, to say the least, an unfortunate choice for a state in which opposition groups had demonstrated great sensitivity to anything that vaguely smelled of imposition and arbitrary decision-making. The navistas joined forces with almost every political party in the state and immediately founded the Frente Antireeleccionista Nacional (FAN). Protest meetings were organised against the new interim governor and the local congress, which had approved the extraordinary decision. The banner of Francisco Madero was raised again in San Luis Potosí when Salvador Nava's wife, who was increasingly the main spokesperson of the opposition, declared that '..the reelectionist intent in San Luis Potosí violates the dignity of the Mexican people and despises the memory of more than one million compatriots who died for the demands of Effective Suffrage, No Reelection..' (Proceso, 19 October 1992: 16, author's translation). Although the PRI's national president declared that Martínez Corbalá's candidacy would be irreversible, he stepped down less than ten days after he had been 'elected'. This further complicated the situation since it provoked an outcry by enraged local priístas, who protested against the intervention of the central government. More than fifty mayors of the ruling party threatened to ask for leave of absence if Martínez Corbalá was to persist in his resignation. However, the decision had already been taken in Los Pinos and the threat was withdrawn.

The *navistas* were not satisfied with Martínez Corbalá stepping down, as their main programmatic issue, a new electoral law, was not yet resolved. In a clear attempt to keep the symbolism of Nava's March of Dignity alive, his wife resumed it exactly where it had ended little more than a year before, when Zapata resigned. In the end the *navistas* got what they wanted: for the first time in the history of modern Mexico, non-partisan citizens would form the majority in the state's electoral body.

The prominent role of Salvador Nava's wife, Concepción Calvillo, in the struggle against re-election, culminated in her selection as gubernatorial candidate of the *navistas*, a role she reluctantly accepted. This choice confirmed the fact that the 'moral capital' accumulated by the Nava *family* could only be transferred to one of its members. The importance of personalised authority was also recognised by the federal authorities, although indirectly. The choice of Horacio Sánchez Unzueta, who is married to a daughter of Salvador Nava, as the candidate for the PRI and who thus was to compete

25 It was widely rumoured that Martínez Corbalá's nomination was decided by Salinas who wanted to test the possible opposition to his own re-election.

with his mother-in-law, was perceived by the *navistas* as a clear attempt to divide the prestigious family and undermine its moral authority.[26] In order to participate in the elections the *navistas* founded, for the occasion, the *Nava Partido Político* (NPP), a decision which caused tensions within the *navista* camp, since some considered it was contrary to the movement's ideological principles.[27] While Concepción Calvillo de Nava later received the support of the PRD, PDM and the PT, the relationship with the PAN, formerly the most important ally, became conflictual. Both the NPP and the PAN disputed Nava's political heritage and accused each other of treason.[28] The tensions and distrust between the parties were the result of problems which had arisen around the municipal elections in 1991, of factional disputes and of the effects of national politics on San Luis Potosí: while the PAN was increasingly involved in a negotiation process with the PRI and the government at the national level, an apparently dominant faction within *navismo* was establishing more intimate ties with the PRD and Cuauhtémoc Cárdenas.[29] The death of Salvador Nava meant the end of a peculiar regional multi-party alliance and a 'nationalisation' of *potosino* politics.

CONCLUDING REMARKS ON CONTINUITY AND CHANGE

A review of the major developments in opposition and government in San Luis Potosí has shown that the debate on the evolution of Mexico's political system can best be understood as one of tensions between continuity and

---

26 Interview with Concepción Calvillo de Nava, 6 December 1993.

27 Former *navista* mayor Guillermo Pizzutto was among those who opposed the foundation of the political party. Interview with Guillermo Pizzutto, 17 March 1994.

28 The PAN candidate, Jorge Lozano Armengol, had previously been president of the FCP.

29 Before the municipal elections at the end of 1991, an agreement between the *navistas*, the PAN, PRD and PDM was reached about a boycott of the elections, due to the fact that the electoral law was considered to be inadequate. Local *panistas* were, however, forced by the national leadership to withdraw from the agreement and to participate in the elections. The *navistas* saw this decision as treason. The PAN candidate, Campos Leal, won the elections in the *potosino* capital in 1991. From that moment onwards relations between the navistas and the PAN have further deteriorated. The growing rapprochement between the navistas and the PRD (some even speak of neonavismo) can be explained also by the fact that Cárdenas's presidential campaign at the end of 1993 was inaugurated in San Luis Potosí. It was attended by all major navistas. The reconstruction of the recent events is based on articles in Proceso, 19 October 1992: 14-7; 26 October 1992: 29-31; 2 November 1992: 28-9; 22 April 1993: 20-3; also Fernández Menéndez (1993).

change, between tradition and modernisation. The argument in favour of change can be made with respect to the way in which opposition against regional strongmen has developed over the years. It could easily be argued that the case of San Luis Potosí illustrates the transition from a rural to a more complex, diversified and urbanised society, in which socio-demographic changes are increasingly reflected in processes of political differentiation, increasing electoral competition and decreasing margins for the ruling party. The struggle against Cedillo in 1938 originated within the revolutionary elite and was resolved within that elite. Opposition against Santos, twenty years later, was originally channelled through the ruling party, which implied that Mexico's political spectrum at the time did not allow for any significant political space for alternative projects. Finally, the rebirth of the *navista* movement at the beginning of the 1980s took place at a time when the regime had proved to be ineffective in channelling the effects of broad processes of socio-economic and political change. It could be argued that opposition in San Luis Potosí has matured during the last fifty years, in that it developed from elite controlled opposition (1938), through an opposition that arose from below but that did not dispute the essential characteristics of the system itself (1958), to an opposition movement from below, strongly informed by concepts such as effective citizenship, participation and democratisation (1982 and onwards). Moreover, the accumulation of popular experience in resisting authoritarian rule in a regional context, to be understood as a process of democratic learning, further adds to the argument in favour of change and political modernisation. All this is true: San Luis Potosí and Mexico as a whole have become more complex and differentiated. The conditions under which opposition to regional *caciquismo* emerged, as well as the nature of *caciquismo*, have changed. A highly personalised *caciquismo* which rested on an armed peasant following (Cedillo), was replaced by a *cacicazgo* with institutional underpinnings, and which no longer disputed the federal State's monopoly of violence (Santos). This was in its turn followed by what could be called a fully fledged institutional, almost absentee, union *caciquismo* (Jonguitud). Over the years *caciquismo* became increasingly interwoven with its direct institutional setting and context. *Caciquismo* adapted to it, was absorbed by it and, in the process, suffered transformations.[30] It should therefore not surprise us that opposition against such inherently arbitrary forms of power evolved from opposition against individuals who abused the system (*navismo* in the 1950s) to one that is directed against the system itself (*navismo* in the 1980s). But the emphasis on change and transformation could

30 Márquez (1988: 390) has called this the 'political metamorphosis of the forms of mediation'.

lead us to underestimate the continuity of *caciquismo*. How can it be explained that, less than five years after the euphoric victory on Cedillo, Santos was able to construct an equally strong *cacicazgo*? How can it be explained that in the 1980s, when the results of forty years of socio-economic development were clearly present in Mexico, a ruthless union leader yet again intended to dominate San Luis Potosí? And finally, what can be said about the paradoxical development of a civic opposition movement that simultaneously produced its own version of personalised power? The persistence of such political models appears to be the result of a deeply rooted set of cultural practices. Primordial ties and personal loyalties instead of institutional channels and programmatic consensus still pervade the capillaries of the Mexican political system, which finds its highest expression in presidentialism.[31]

The concentration of power in Mexico City and its ambivalent relationship with regional groups are also constant factors. Lázaro Cárdenas moved his office to San Luis Potosí to demonstrate the predominance of presidential power over regional dissidence. When opposition arose against Santos, it was successful because of the political opening provided by in-coming president, López Mateos. Even in the 1980s and 1990s, without wanting to downplay the importance of popular movements and political parties, the trump card still appears to be in the hands of the one who inhabits Los Pinos. The way the political crisis in 1991 was resolved demonstrates this: in a showcase of *concertacesión*, Guanajuato went to the PAN while San Luis Potosí remained with the PRI. Nava himself is said to have observed on several occasions that he was not sure who's game he was playing and who he was ultimately favouring.[32] What else could be on his mind, when a few days before he died, Salinas de Gortari visited him at home?

At the same time, it should be observed that regional and local elites and opposition groups always constituted a counterweight to the (ultimately) predominant central state. In this context the story of the many local and regional power groups, also during the so-called 'golden age' of the centralised PRI-government system, must be told. I have attempted to do so for San Luis Potosí, but the same holds for Puebla, Zacatecas and Nayarit, to mention just a few. All provide proof of the argument that there have been continuous negotiations between federal and regional power groups. It is therefore difficult to maintain the argument that the federal government in Mexico City has ceased to be (since 1982, 1985, 1988?) the only actor (Martínez Assad,

31 For an analysis of renewed presidentialism in recent years, see Dresser (1991: 37).

32 Interview with Concepción Calvillo de Nava, 6 December 1993.

1992: 157). It never was. In the words of Jeffrey Rubin (1990: 266), 'we should look at regional politics as continuations of long histories of conflict among popular movements, elites, and party and state actors over who gets what economically, politically, and culturally, as well as on what terms a centralised state is incompletely, ambiguously, and impermanently established.' The same holds for electoral competition. Although there has been an upsurge in electoral politics in recent years, it seems difficult to define it as a radical rupture. During the transition period between the fall of *cedillismo* and the rise of the *cacicazgo santista* (1938-43), municipal elections were, almost literally, a battle field for competing factions. Similarly, at the end of the 1950s municipal elections were bitterly contested. The (re)emergence of *navismo* in the 1980s must be understood in terms of this regional history.

On 28 October 1992, somewhere on the highway between Querétaro and Mexico City, two elderly women headed a protest march and talked about politics. One of them was Amalia Solórzano de Cárdenas, widow of ex-president Lázaro Cárdenas, one of the crucial architects of Mexico's modern political system. The other was Concepción Calvillo de Nava, widow of Salvador Nava, who had dedicated many years of his life fighting that very political system in San Luis Potosí. 'She is fighting for all of us and I came to tell her that she is not alone', Amalia Solórzano later declared (*Proceso*, 2 November 1992: 29). Is there a better metaphor for the coexistence of continuity and change in Mexican politics?

15 Opposition to PRI 'Hegemony' in Oaxaca

Colin Clarke

Mexico is currently experiencing, in an acute form, the dilemma faced by most Latin American countries: can economic liberalisation be made compatible with democratisation? Having signed the North American Free Trade Agreement (NAFTA) in 1992, Mexico in 1994 held Presidential and legislative elections that were scrutinised, as never before, for their efficiency, openness and fairness. To an outsider, this may seem strange, since Mexico claims to be a representative federal democracy, with elections, on various territorial scales, held on regular cycles since the 1920s. But, until recently, the *Partido Revolucionario Institutional* (PRI) has held office continuously at all significant levels of government. It is only in the last handful of years that the conservative *Partido de Acción Nacional* (PAN) has gained the governorship of Guanajuato by Presidential fiat and Baja California, Chihuahua and Jalisco by electoral victory, and that the PRI has been seriously challenged for the Presidency of Mexico – in 1988 and 1994.

Although the candidate of the PRI in the 1994 presidential election, Ernesto Zedillo, received slightly less than half the votes cast, and thereby extended the party's 'hegemony' over the Mexican State one *sexenio* (six-year presidential term) further, it would be wrong to conclude that challenges to the PRI's one-party 'democracy' were totally absent earlier. In 1988, for example, Carlos Salinas de Gortari received a bare majority of the vote, and it has been alleged that this small margin was itself rigged. Evidence for organised opposition to the PRI is particularly plentiful if the focus is shifted from the national to the local scale, in this instance to the communities of Oaxaca, in southern Mexico, one state 'in' from the Guatemalan border. At this level it is evident that, irrespective of whether the focus is grassroots movements or electoral competition, 'the accepted social science model of post-revolutionary Mexican politics as an inclusionary corporate system bears little resemblance to the politics of public office, economic production and daily life' (Rubin, 1994: 111).

Oaxaca was arguably the cradle of Mexican politics in the second half of the nineteenth century. Both Presidents Juárez and Porfirio Díaz were born there and inducted into its particular brand of Liberalism at the *Instituto de*

Ciencias y Artes del Estado. But in the first half of the twentieth century Oaxaca had become an economic and political backwater. While in colonial times it was the major source of cochineal, Oaxaca's internationally-orientated economy was undermined during the nineteenth century by Guatemalan competition and the development of synthetic dyes. An important factor in the political demise of Oaxaca was its preoccupation with a sovereignty movement during and after the Mexican Revolution (1910-17), which marginalised it from the main currents and arenas of military activity. Thus Oaxaca had almost no leverage in national politics from the 1920s until the 1970s, when radical groups emphasised their opposition to PRI control, and federal intervention became essential.

During the fifty years prior to these protest movements, ushered in by the government's massacre of students in Mexico City on the eve of the Olympic Games in 1968, national political authorities had gradually established control over Oaxaca, and the rest of Mexico, through the consolidation of a *de facto* one-party system after 1929 when the predecessor of the PRI was founded. The PRI spawned a host of affiliates through which it penetrated different sectors of Oaxacan (and Mexican) society: the *Confederación Revolucionaria Obrera y Campesina* (CROC), *Confederación Revolucionaria de Obreros de México* (CROM), *Confederación de Trabajadores de México* (CTM), the *Liga de Comunidades Agrarias y Sindicatos Campesinos del Estado de Oaxaca* (LICASCEO), linked to the *Confederación Nacional Campesina* (CNC), and the *Confederación Nacional de Organizaciones Populares* (CNOP). As a result, from its formation to the end of the 1980s, the PRI did not lose a single presidential, gubernatorial or senatorial election; and because of the centralisation of government, despite the national federal structure, the PRI was able to control most local governments, too. For example, in Oaxaca City, no one other than a PRI candidate has been president of the municipality since 1929 – unpopular figures have simply been replaced by other PRI nominees.

This chapter opens with an account of the rise of radicalism in Oaxaca among workers, peasants and students in the aftermath of the massacre at Tlatelolco in Mexico City in 1968. This precipitated a series of social and political crises in Oaxaca culminating in the events of 1977 in Oaxaca City, at which point the federal government used the military to suppress the activists. Attention is then shifted to the national political 'opening' of the late 1970s, which permitted teachers' protests in Oaxaca and the election of a 'socialist republic' in the municipality of Juchitán (1981-3). The final section details struggles within the PRI over the 1986 nomination for the Oaxaca governorship, and examines the municipal elections of the same year, which resulted in 15 out of 570 being taken by the opposition. Although the focus is Oaxaca, changing national styles of leadership and presidential attitudes to 'democracy' and dissent will be alluded to, since they provide vital contexts for events at the state and local scale. The conclusion briefly traces Oaxaca politics into the 1990s, and extrapolates the lessons to be drawn from long-run events in the state to the federal level.

Oaxaca is particularly interesting in relation to the nature of, and the challenge to, PRI 'hegemony', since the struggles of the period 1968 to 1994 ran the gamut from peaceful grassroots opposition via street violence to electoral competition (from both the left and right). Indeed, the events in Juchitán, which encompassed all these aspects, were accorded such significance that some were even reported in British newspapers (see *The Guardian*, 28 December 1983). Moreover, because the state of Oaxaca, with three million inhabitants, has 570 *municipios*, or more than one-quarter of all those in Mexico, there is the basis for an enquiry into the emergence of a voting opposition at a small-scale.

It will, however, be clear that neither the extra-electoral opposition of radical elements to the PRI, nor the 'socialist republic' in Juchitán were successful; that they existed is significant, but in each case they were stifled or contained by PRI manipulation or repression. Furthermore, scrutiny of the electoral results in, and since, 1986 scarcely provides evidence for the demise of the PRI in Oaxaca, though there are signs that its position may be weakening. In 1988, when Salinas' share of the national presidential vote was 50.36, it was 63.81 in Oaxaca, less than two percentage points behind what the PRI recorded in the election for state deputies that year. By 1991 the Salinas administration had been sufficiently successful to lift the PRI vote for deputies, nationally, from 51.11 per cent in 1988 to 61.4 per cent; in Oaxaca it was 73.4 per cent. By 1994, however, the PRI vote for the Presidency in Oaxaca slumped to just under 50 per cent – still a winning margin, despite a massive increase in the turn-out from 46 (in 1988) to 71 per cent.

The burden of this chapter, therefore, is to show that PRI 'hegemony' has not gone uncontested at the state or municipal level. But that is different from arguing that the 1988 emergence of Cuauhtémoc Cárdenas and the *Frente Democrático Nacional* (FDN) has changed Mexican politics for all time; it does not imply that democratic uncertainty has broken out or that the PRI is on the verge of losing the electoral and overall political dominance it has enjoyed for the last 65 years. My point of departure is essentially consistent with that of Rubin, when he writes: 'states do not arise uniformly across the physical and social geographies of peoples and nations;...recent grassroots struggles, while new in some ways, are the continuation of long histories of resistance, rebellion and accommodation' (1994: 111).

Figure 15.1 Oaxaca: major regions and towns

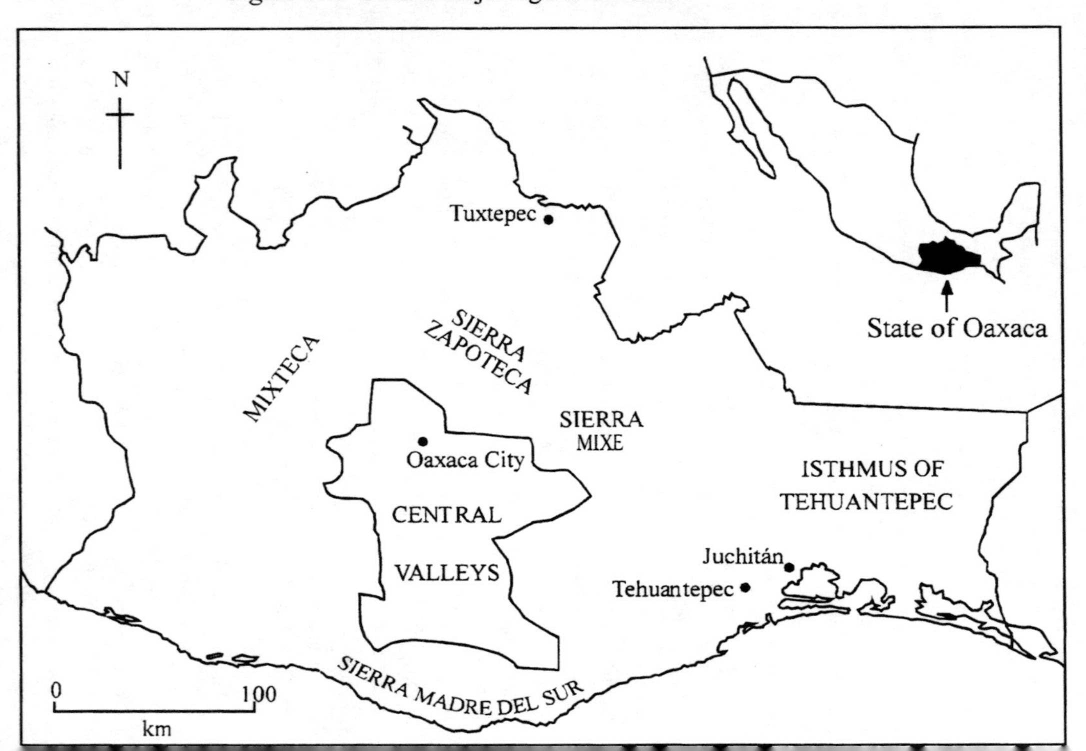

STUDENT RADICALS: THEIR OPPONENTS AND THEIR ALLIES (1968-80)

Since the World War II, urban-based *comerciantes*, many of whom are also engaged in small-scale industry and construction, have displaced the *hacendados*, scaled down by the post-Revolutionary land reform, as the leading economic element in Oaxaca. Although the political elite is a separate entity, there is some overlapping membership with the business group; for example, Bravo Ahuja, elected governor in 1968, came from a powerful Tuxtepec family, and several of Oaxaca's 57 elite business clans have had members serving in Oaxaca City's municipal government or in different state cabinets (Basáñez E. 1987 and Martínez Vásquez, 1990). For decades, the political leadership of the PRI has been drawn, in order of importance, from the Central Valleys, the Isthmus of Tehuantepec and Tuxtepec, the most dynamic areas of the state (Figure 15.1).

Shared membership of the political and economic elites is especially typical of the Central Valleys, where the *vallistocracia política* is noted for its multiple and diverse contacts with the *vallistocracia económica*. They share a certain amount of business; they are brought together through godparenthood, marriage, school attendance, professional services – law, medicine, accountancy; politicians provide merchants with support and construction work and the latter reciprocate. There is also the case of politicians who become businessmen, though it is difficult to detect because of concealment by the use of third parties in ownership registration (Martínez Vásquez, 1990: 107).

Even where the membership of these two elite groups does not coincide, both entities are usually, but not wholly, mutually supporting; and the PRI is expected to reinforce the social *status quo*, and to supply the business group with lucrative contracts (Martínez Vásquez, 1990: 85-108). Occasionally, however, the PRI has to respond to national rather than regional objectives and to use techniques of social control that seem too 'soft' to the *vallistocracia económica*.

Prior to 1968, the PRI adopted a heavy-handed approach to dissent in any form. But, after the 1968 student protests in Mexico City, inspired by similar outbursts in Europe, and, ultimately, by the Cuban Revolution of 1959, a different approach was adopted. PRI repression led to a sense of guilt, and to an acknowledgement of the need for greater political openness. This policy was initiated under the presidency of Luis Echeverría (1970-6), the minister in charge at the time of the Tlatelolco killings, and largely coincided with Oaxaca governorships of Bravo Ahuja (1968-70) and his associate, Gómez Sandoval (1970-4), who succeeded him when he became Minister of Education. Both governors, in turn, reflected national policy, and tolerated opposition to a degree unacceptable to the Oaxaca economic elite.

Tension in Oaxaca, after 1968, was fomented by radicalised students, workers and peasants opposed to the *vallistocracia*, to the allegedly undemocratic, permanent government of the PRI and to its suppression of popular dissent. Land grabs, including one or two urban squats, the creation of independent trade unions – independent of the formal links to the PRI that characterised most syndicates – and strike action at the university were the oppositional tactics adopted. The elite commercial sector, as the leading element among conservative forces, persistently urged repression of the militants on successive governors (González Pacheco, 1984; Martínez Vásquez, 1990). The response, when it came under the Governorship of Zárate Aquino, involved dispersal of squatters and strikers and, for the leadership, imprisonment and maltreatment.

The Oaxaca student movement, which had been spawned by the events of 1968, had strong left-wing, even Marxist affiliations. It demanded a far greater say, through democratic elections, in university affairs and argued for the autonomy of the *Instituto de Ciencias y Artes* from the state government. In addition, it seized upon a series of socio-economic disputes that were already occurring in Oaxaca, each of which brought it into conflict with either the *vallistocracia política* or the *vallistocracia económica*. Squatter invasions, the result of cityward migration and the inability of Oaxaca City to employ and house the population in formal circumstances, were a constant challenge to the authorities, as was the recrudescence of land disputes between peasants and bosses in rural communities. Members of the inflated urban labour market pressed for unionisation, better pay, or reduced outgoings. Peasant vendors in the Saturday market, many of whom were illegal, were subject to pressure from city-centre merchants who wished to monopolise the retail trade. The student body, which numbered about 300 in the late 1940s, 2000 in 1968, and 20 000 in 1988 (Martínez Vásquez, 1992a: 5), became less elitist in composition and more radical and militant with time. In 1968, it proceeded to enter the fray against the business class and their political associates in a series of overlapping and intertwining actions.

The *Federación Estudiantil Oaxaqueña* (FEO), which had been founded to stimulate social activities among the students at the *Instituto de Ciencias y Artes*, (in 1971 converted under dissident pressure into the *Universidad Autónoma 'Benito Juárez' de Oaxaca* or UABJO), rapidly took on a political role. Confronted by a conservative *Directorio Estudiantil* in 1970, it found itself locked in a violent struggle over the university buildings that resulted in the army's intervention, the death of a member of the FEO and the long-term imprisonment of Castillo Viloria, the FEO leader. This entire episode was essentially a re-run of the events of 1968, which had led to the imprisonment of González Pacheco; it was also a harbinger of the even more extreme circumstances that were to break out in 1976-7.

The FEO began to equip itself for the struggle ahead. Its new leadership drew to itself the students at the *Instituto Tecnológico*, the *Escuela Normal Urbana* and the *Escuelas Normales Rurales* at Reyes Mantecon and Tamazulapam, as well as a variety of dissident urban and rural groups. A coalition of workers, peasants and students was formally inaugurated in 1972 with the acronym of COCEO (*Coalición de Obreros Campesinos y Estudiantes de Oaxaca*) (Yescas Martínez, 1982). Key elements in the coalition, in addition to the FEO, were the *Partido Comunista Mexicano*, the marxist *Bufete Popular Universitario*, which was based on the Faculty of Law and was to provide legal advice to left-wing groups in Oaxaca throughout the decade, the *Central Campesina Independiente*, and two militant working-class unions, operating quite independently of the PRI, the *Sindicato Unico de Trabajadores Electricistas de la República Mexicana* and the *Movimiento Sindical Ferrocarrilero*. An explicit objective of COCEO was to 'achieve the socialist transformation of the country'(Martínez Vásquez, 1990: 133 fn.11). Later, in 1976, it was to join other movements to create the *Frente Campesino Independiente*, which linked peasant movements in Tuxtepec, where it was most active, with those in the Central Valleys and the Isthmus of Tehuantepec (Basáñez E, 1987: 79).

In 1969 and 1970, FEO had organised successful resistance to increases in Oaxaca City bus fares – a perennial issue in a state capital with burgeoning peripheral shantytowns. It then proceeded to stimulate vendors' resistance to the merchants' attempts to relocate the peasant market from the centre to the periphery. The *Federación de Mercados*, representing larger-scale merchants, 'argued that the smaller vendors were unhygienic, the old market was too crowded and too Indian, and that tourists were repelled by all these features' (Murphy and Stepick, 1991: 114). But their principal aim was more selfish – to capture a larger share of the retail market by banning their small-scale competitors. Plans for the new market were drawn up in the early 1970s and by 1974 the buildings were complete. The smaller marketeers, organised by student leaders, resisted the move; the government stalled; and it was not until the repression of 1978 that the *Federación de Mercados*, manoeuvred by the *priísta*, Genoveva Medina, was able to achieve sufficient leverage to move the Saturday market to a new site on the *periférico*. However, the central market buildings were not raised to the ground, as planned, and a substantial number of market sellers with permanent stalls stayed behind.

Government reaction in the early 1970s, though muted compared to its later response, exacerbated factionalism among the students and the FEO was banned. Part of the student movement went underground, notably *La Liga Comunista 23 de Septiembre* and the *Unión del Pueblo*, and planted bombs in symbolic locations, including an English-language library (Martínez Vásquez, 1990: 136). COCEO, however, continued its activities, helping to organise two land invasions by *campesinos* who were trying to recapture property seized by large land owners, notably at Tlalixtac de Cabrera, Zimatlán, Santa Gertrudis, la Ciénaga, Santa Catarina Quiané and Xoxocotlán in the Central Valleys, and supporting residents in land disputes in Oaxaca City at San Martín Mexicapan and Santo Tómas Xochimilco (Zafra, 1982).

Student radicals also pressed for political prisoners to be released, not only their own leaders, but others, such as Esteban Oviedo Escareño, an Indian from Jamiltepec, who had been jailed for opposing the brutal *cazicazgo* of the Iglesias Meza family. COCEO's anti-establishment activities reached a peak in 1974, when the high rate of inflation triggered widespread strikes in Oaxaca City, and it seized the opportunity to organise independent unions of bus drivers, auto mechanics, university workers, municipal workers, bakers, social workers at the *Instituto Nacional Indigenista* and employees in the city slaughterhouse. With recognition of their status came substantial pay rises and fringe benefits that effectively transferred union members into the formal sector of the economy (Murphy and Stepick, 1991).

These achievements were terminated in December 1974, with the inauguration of the new governor, Zárate Aquino, backed by the *Grupo Oaxaca*. COCEO was immediately identified as the enemy: 'to dismember and annihilate it would be the fundamental objective for property owners and the political regime'(Martínez Vásquez, 1990: 158). The Governor ordered the army to impose order in those *municipios* where opponents of the PRI had claimed that recent elections were fraudulent – Zimatlán, Zaachila, Santa Gertrudis, Xoxocotlán, Juchitán and others in the Isthmus of Tehuantepec. Explosions were attributed to COCEO (though the latter denied involvement), the student underground movement was targeted, the PRI pumped funds and personnel into opposing the radical student movement and the unions of bus drivers and auto mechanics were decertified and disbanded. In 1975, a massive land invasion involving 5000 people (Martínez Vásquez, 1990:174) – in which COCEO played no part (but for a contrary view see Basañez E, 1987:78) – took place on either side of the Pan American Highway on the outskirts of Oaxaca City and was dispersed by the army at the instigation of the governor (Murphy and Stepick, 1991). Although a small proportion of invaders who were able to pay for basic lots were eventually settled at Santa Rosa, repression of the urban poor began in earnest thereafter, and was completed by 1977.

The main focus of dissident activity in the late 1970s was the *Universidad Autónoma 'Benito Juárez' de Oaxaca* in Oaxaca City, and within it the recently formed *Centro de Sociología.* In 1975 the university was paralysed by conflicts over the voting rights of students in elections to the directorships of the various schools; since many part-time professors were also public officials, this issue rapidly spilled over into local politics and it was resolved, temporarily, only by local and federal mediators. The fragile truce was broken by elections to the rectorship in 1976, occasioned by the resignation of García Manzano. This produced two title-holders, one chosen by majority vote and validated by the *Secretaría de Educación Pública,* Martínez Soriano of the *Frente Democrático Universitario* and Tenorio Sandoval an ex-deputy and President of the Oaxaca Municipality imposed, so it has been argued, by the state government (Martínez Vásquez, 1992:39). Probably 90 per cent of the students were *democráticos,* but both they and the *restauradores* seized university buildings, from which the two groups sniped at, and killed, one another (Lozano, 1984). Throughout 1976 the university factions battled both the state and federal governments in actions that embroiled the campus, the city and the state (Santibáñez Orozco, 1982). In Juchitán, in the Isthmus of Tehuantepec, it was alleged that non-PRI candidates had been excluded from municipal office; in Oaxaca City, disputes over increased bus fares resulted in numerous arrests.

Conservative forces, many represented by organised business groups, such as the local *Cámara de Comercio* (CANACO), the *Consejo Coordinador Empresarial* (CCE), the *Cámara de la Industria de la Transformación* (CANACINTRA) and the *Centro Patronal* (CP), now combined: merchants, landowners, service clubs and the PRI formed the *Fusión Cívica de Organizaciones Productivas de Oaxaca* (FUCOPO), to oppose subversion and press for peace and stability. As Martínez Vásquez shrewdly observed, FUCOPO 'turned itself into a binding agent and organizer of the actions of the bourgeoisie, the corporate apparatus of the state and the governor'(1990: 188). Moreover, at the national level, FUCOPO was backed by the powerful *Grupo Monterrey,* while Zárate Aquino himself received the support of the Federal Deputies for Oaxaca, among them Heladio Ramírez López and the Senator for Oaxaca, General Eliseo Jiménez Ruiz. At the end of February 1977 FUCOPO announced the closure of all business houses for two days, on the second of which its supporters clashed in the markets with student radicals. Student demonstrators massed at the School of Medicine in the north of the city and marched on the *zócalo* (main square). Just short of the city centre they were dispersed with considerable violence by the state police;

during the night, federal troops took control of the streets. The next day, 3 March, Governor Zárate Aquino flew to Mexico City and formally asked President López Portillo for leave of absence. By the evening a new governor, General Eliseo Jiménez Ruiz, the Senator for Oaxaca, had taken command.

General Jiménez Ruiz was known nationally for his anti-communism and his successful military campaign in the state of Guerrero against the guerrilla Lucio Cabañas. Under his rule, Oaxaca experienced, for two years, a phase of fierce but selective military repression which fragmented COCEO and demobilised the masses politically. The university problem remained, however. Martínez Soriano and Tenorio Sandoval both stepped down in favour of the new regime's nominee, Fernando Gómez Sandoval, the interim Governor of Oaxaca in the early 1970s. But Tenorio refused to hand over the central building of the university in the core of the city; Gómez Sandoval, still unpopular with the *vallistocracia* withdrew; and in mid-March the federal government imposed a solution over the heads of the Oaxaca elite by placing the army in complete control of Oaxaca City and the most important settlements in the state: the central university building was emptied and placed under armed guard (Lozano, 1984).The *restauradores* abandoned the UABJO, and founded the *Universidad Regional del Sureste.* Oaxaca remained under military control until the next major elections, which, in 1980, brought Pedro Vásquez Colmenares, the former managing director of one of the two State airlines, to the governorship. As a mark of federal approval and support, the President of the Republic, López Portillo, witnessed his inauguration.

Events were not entirely to the liking of the commercial elite, who had backed Zárate Aquino until his governorship became untenable. They found the interim government of General Jiménez Ruiz unsympathetic, even if he was local. This was largely because he had to create sufficient freedom from the *Grupo Oaxaca* of Zárate Aquino to respond to policy emanating from Mexico City, notably from *Gobernación* (Interior) and *Defensa Nacional.* In particular, the commercial elite distrusted the general's Mexico City associates, the *Grupo México*, whom they called '*los gitanos*'. A figure soon to be associated with the '*oaxaqueños ausentes*' was Heladio Ramírez López, from the Mixteca, later to be dubbed by his business opponents, '*tercermundista*'. The *vallistocracia* feared that the departure of Zárate Aquino had produced a vacuum that was being filled alarmingly rapidly by the federal government, without reference to themselves, as the military occupation of the university confirmed. Moreover, Jiménez Ruiz's repression, though frequently resorting to violence, was more specific and less general than they wanted (for its targeted victims on the left it entailed gaol, torture or death).

The *vallistocracia* split into a hardline faction bent on repression of COCEO, headed by Juan José Gutiérrez Ruiz, and a group led by Carlos Hampshire Franco, which favoured a negotiated settlement of what came to be known, nationally, as *el Caso Oaxaca*. The Hampshire Franco element was more closely aligned with the PRI, but in the event lost support from the Oaxaca CANACO, leaving the José Gutiérrez faction in the ascendant – where it has remained. However, the latter had eventually to accept the Governor's strategy, backed as it was by the López Portillo administration in Mexico City (Basáñez E, 1987: 158). Splits among the student body were even more dramatic and fatal. In-fighting between different factions of the left reduced COCEO to giving legal advice to peasants and labour organisations, while the guerrilla activities of *el Güero Medrano* in the mountains near Tuxtepec were merely an excuse for blanket military operations in the region.

Intervention by the federal government was civilian as well as military (see Basáñez E, 1987: 142 for a list of federal institutions located in Oaxaca). Federal agencies increased their staff after 1977, often importing bureaucrats from other states. State infrastructure was improved and the housing agency, INFONAVIT, undertook the development of a new neighbourhood to the north of the state capital, specifically to house federal employees. The PRI, as the national government, aligned itself even more explicitly than before with Oaxaca's elite and, additionally, used the army to break the radical student opposition; but, through these actions the federal government emerged as an actor at the Oaxaca state level with the capacity and intent to nullify the isolationist tendencies of the commercial elite, which slipped into a more clientelist role facilitated by government construction contracts. Thus, the 'commercial elite, without the resources to overcome the external influences, no longer battled external elites directly as they had done in the 1950s and before the Revolution. As the old elite's control slipped away, its members complained that the outsiders were condescending, insensitive and prone to misjudge local needs' (Murphy and Stepick, 1991: 120-1).

The final phase of non-electoral dissent in the late 1970s was played out by teachers in Oaxaca through the *Movimiento Magisterial Democrático* (MMD) in their attempt to confront section 22 of their union, the *Sindicato Nacional de Trabajadores de la Educación* (SNTE). They joined colleagues, notably from Chiapas, to try to establish, at state level, democratic procedures over their union's exercise of power within the educational system, monopolised by a PRI-related clique, the *Vanguardia Revolucionaria*. They also wished to protest at the low wages handed out to teachers by the government; as the Mexican oil-boom of 1978-81 raised inflation to unprecedented levels, teachers found their living standard halved. Street protests, including sit-ins and a silent march in which 12 000 teachers participated, took place in Oaxaca City in 1980, backed by COCEO and parents of pupils; news of the 'insurgency' was broadcast through the newspapers, radio and television (Martínez Vásquez, 1990: 234).

In early June protesters from various states, including Oaxaca, camped out opposite the offices of the *Secretaría de Educación Pública* in Mexico City, as a result of which they were threatened and later promised a resolution of their grievances. But once they had withdrawn from the capital, the gains turned out to be far less satisfactory than the teachers had expected (Yescas Martínez and Zafra, 1985: 170-1). This was to be only the first step in a conflict that was to run on, repeating itself with seemingly endless ramifications, until the end of the 1980s, eluding all attempts by Oaxaca's governors to control it (Sorroza Polo, 1992).

Hostility, reminiscent of that voiced by the Oaxaca teachers opposed to PRI indifference and/or interference in the late 1970s and early 1980s, was already being expressed by a broad coalition of social groups in Juchitán. The issues and actors had been present much earlier in Juchitán; but it was the political reform of 1980 that provided the opportunity for dissent to take on the urgent electoral dimension that it did in 1983.

THE 1980 REFORM AND THE 'SOCIALIST REPUBLIC' OF JUCHITÁN

Towards the end of the 1970s an attempt was made at the national level to improve the image of Mexican democracy by allowing more space to opposition political parties, including those of the far left. Cynically, it might be said that the previously 'constrained democracy' presided over by the PRI was now to be slightly relaxed (*reforma política*), but only on (the undeclared) condition that the paramount position of the party was not seriously challenged. This provided an exceptional opportunity for left-wing dissidents in the turbulent *municipio* of Juchitán in the Isthmus of Tehuantepec. Now, according to the constitutional reforms, their movement had the political space to take part in a local election in alliance with a nationally-registered party, to compete with the PRI and to take power.

Opposition to the PRI in the isthmus was spearheaded by *Coalición de Obreros Campesinos y Estudiantes del Istmo* (COCEI), an affiliate of COCEO founded in 1974. The success of COCEI as a political force hinged on its appeal to Zapotec and regional identity in contradistinction to the PRI, which was seen, locally, as an alien force; and on its ability to whip up grassroots support by backing small cultivators and agricultural labourers in their struggles against large landowners and the State (Doniz and Monsivais, 1983). According to Rubin, COCEI 'is one of the strongest and most militant grassroots movements in Mexico, in large part because Zapotec Indians in Juchitán transformed their courtyards and fiestas into fora for intense political discussion, gathered in the streets in massive demonstrations and, in the course of the past two decades, redefined the activities, meanings and alliances of their culture' (1994: 110).

The conflicts in which COCEI intervened so successfully in Juchitán had their immediate origin in the late 1950s, when so-called 'communal lands', which were used for maize and sesame cultivation and cattle rearing, were the subject of dispute between large and small proprietors. To resolve these disagreements and to provide the infrastructure for agricultural development, communal land in adjacent *municipios* was taken into state control in 1964 by the president, López Mateos, and re-allocated as *ejidos* (land-reform properties), 54 000 hectares of which were irrigated from the newly constructed Benito Juárez dam. Large landholders persuaded small proprietors to join them in protest: the situation was returned to the *status quo ante*, except that the government exacerbated tensions further by providing credit for irrigated land, the bulk of which went to large landholders, though they, too, still lacked legal title. The majority of small-scale cultivators received no credit and were forced back into their traditional role as agricultural labourers. It was the combination of rural social inequality with differential access to irrigation and credit that provided the students at the *tecnológico* with the rural support that validated COCEI's reiteration of demands commonplace in Juchitán's political circles since the late 1960s.

COCEI was formed during President Echeverría's *apertura democrática* (political opening); it had his tacit backing and that of several government ministries. The movement won widespread support for marches, strikes, occupations of government offices and Zapotec cultural and artistic activities. Through these campaigns, improved living and working conditions were achieved for peasants and workers in and around Juchitán. In view of these successes, COCEI was attacked by the right wing of the PRI, by paramilitary groups and the local and state police, and more than 20 deaths were registered between 1974 and 1977 (Rubin, 1994: 122).

During the electoral reform of the early 1980s COCEI formed an alliance with the *Partido Socialista Unificado de México* (PSUM) – which the constitution now permitted - to secure a place on the ballot. COCEI's poll at the 1980 election, was sufficiently close to that of the PRI for it to cry 'fraud' and embark upon mass mobilisation in support of its claim to victory. Much of its success was, of course, due to the prominent position it gave to the land issue and other facets of social inequality (Prévot-Shapira and Rivière D'Arc,

1983). COCEI was eventually confirmed in government through a further close-run election which it won by the narrowest of margins in early 1981.

The success of COCEI's strategy of mass mobilisation, which involved the 'capture' of the *palacio municipal* and extended to occupations in Mexico City and Oaxaca City, was to become the model for opposition groups in other disputed elections throughout the 1980s. However, a crucial contributory factor in COCEI's victory was a split in the PRI in Juchitán (Martínez López, 1985). Juchitán became 'the first and only city in the country with a leftist government' (Rubin, 1994: 123), and COCEI-PSUM transformed the face of the town through the implementation of a form of participatory democracy. 'They were collecting money and signing referenda, as well as securing agricultural credit, payment of minimum wages and benefits, and long-absent municipal services. Juchitecos were literally speaking a language (Isthmus Zapotec) that was foreign to their government, a language rich in puns, evocations of local history and fidelity to local experiences and needs' (ibid: 112).

That Juchitecan activities under COCEI were in marked contrast to their experiences under the PRI is made patently clear by Rubin.

> Ordinary people in the city's neighbourhoods stated clearly – with new urgency, drawing new connections among their experiences, and with new kinds of actions – that they were poor people (*los pobres*) and that they were exploited in specific ways by local commercial enterprises and government agricultural programmes. They said that they...[had been]...ruled by a municipal government imposed through fraudulent elections and military force, that they supported COCEI because it fought unequivocally for their well-being, and that they participated in politics - attended meetings and marched in the streets, voted, joined communal work projects, and contributed financially – in order to carry on this struggle (1994: 121).

The tangible benefits of the COCEI government were a literacy programme, creation of a library and preparatory school (as a prelude to entry to university), a teachers' training college, a radio station, health centres and a book-publishing programme.

How were the PRI to topple this 'socialist republic', given that COCEI was able to mobilise and deploy so many historical facets of a distinct and self-aware community? (Aubague, 1985). The state government under the 'democratic' regime of Vásquez Colmenares, found itself in a cleft stick: on the one hand it was continuously pressured to oust COCEI by the local branch of CANACO, whose members carried out a series of strategic strikes; on the other, it felt constrained by the political reforms favouring the opposition that had been enacted by the López Portillo government.

Vacillating though the state government of Oaxaca was – not a surprising situation in view of the events in Oaxaca City in 1977 – it still had several levers it could operate as and when it chose: control of the municipal budget, manipulation of rumour and violence by local PRI militants, and the presence of large state-funded projects that had come on stream during the late 1970s, notably, the oil refinery on the Pacific at Salina Cruz and the sugar factory, López Portillo, at Espinal eight kilometres from Juchitán. Each of these projects drew labour from outside the isthmus – mostly from the oil and sugar areas of Veracruz. These were the bastions, impervious to COCEI, from which the 'reconquest' of Juchitán was to be carried out by the state government during the summer of 1983, in the last resort using force provided by the army (Prévot-Shapira and Rivière d'Arc, 1983). By this time, Miguel de la Madrid had replaced López Portillo as President of Mexico, the oil boom had degenerated into an economic crisis and the USA, confronted by left-wing revolutionaries in Central America, was pressing for the removal of the 'socialist republic' of Juchitán from the sensitive region of the isthmus.

Rubin, who arrived in Juchitán in August 1983, witnessed the aftermath of COCEI's expulsion from office (*desconocimiento*) by the Oaxaca state government.

> [Twenty-five thousand] Juchitecos gathered in the town square to defend the *Ayuntamiento Popular*, the People's Government. Large Juchiteca women surrounded the City Hall with their fists in the air, dressed in traditional embroidered blouses and gold jewellery, with red confetti streaming over their thickly braided hair. Everything they wore was outlined, ribbonned, or bannered in red, the colour of COCEI.In raucous, angry voices, they chanted slogans in defence of COCEI and its mayor, Leopoldo de Gyves, and vilified the official party, the Partido Revolucionario Institucional (Rubin, 1994: 111).

The Mexican government responded to the ousting of COCEI from Juchitán, and the PRI's ensuing electoral victory in November, with a broad spectrum policy of military involvement, support for the more moderate element in the local PRI, investment in municipal services, electoral competition and comparative freedom of organisation for COCEI.

> By stopping short of outright repression, policymakers in Mexico City hoped to resolve Juchitán's political conflict through what they called economic and political modernisation: with massive investment, they would put an end to the pervasive lack of basic services in the city and provide the infrastructure for commercial and urban development; at the same time, national and state leaders would press for the definitive ascendance of well-educated businesspeople and professionals to positions of municipal authority (Rubin, 1994: 123-4).

These machinations by the PRI to re-take and hold the ideologically high-profile *municipio* of Juchitán indicate the strict limits that the federal and state governments were to impose on the *reforma política*. In insignificant municipalities the PRI was prepared to lose, if the opposition was determined and there were not too many instances of defeat. Even so, electoral fraud and co-optation might be tried, culminating in manipulation of the electoral roll or of the hours of opening of polling booths, perhaps even the deployment of violence where the stakes were defined as being sufficiently high – as they were, notoriously, in Juchitán. The implications of these conclusions must now be set against the state-wide elections held in Oaxaca in 1986.

THE 1986 OAXACA ELECTIONS

The 1986 elections are of importance not only because of the opportunity they provided for 'the extension of the struggle to democratise the *municipio*' (Martínez Vásquez, 1990: 245), but because the municipal poll coincided with the hustings for state deputies and the governorship. Moreover, in-fighting within the PRI leadership gave rise to tensions that impacted at the community level. By the second half of 1985 two contenders for the governorship had emerged: Heladio Ramírez López, a former youth leader of the PRI in the Federal District, ex-federal deputy, former President of the PRI in Oaxaca and the state's senator, whose local base was in the rural sector; Jésus Martínez Alvarez, a former municipal president of Oaxaca City and member of the state bureaucracy with strong links to the PRI's 'Popular' Sector.

This, in a nutshell, demonstrates the complex interrelationships, on a variety of scales, between the PRI, its affiliated organisations and the membership of various government administrations in recruitment to, and selection for, political office. The two competitors, representing distinct power blocks within the Oaxaca PRI, jockeyed for position (Basañez E, 1987: 20), Heladio Ramírez (*Grupo Heladio*) consolidating his position nationally, while Jésus Martínez Alvarez (*Grupo Oaxaca*) focussed on his regional connections, particularly within Oaxaca.

In the autumn of 1985, the Governor, Pedro Vásquez Colmenares, was nominated Director of Federal Security in the *Secretaría de Gobernación* (Interior) and resigned his state post. With undue haste, the Oaxaca legislature voted Jésus Martínez Alvarez, locally perceived as the stronger of the two candidates, to the interim governorship, thereby making him constitutionally ineligible to compete for that position in 1986 (Yescas Martínez, 1991). Outmanoeuvred by Ramírez, Martínez tried, in turn, to block his rival's candidature for the governorship. When, eventually, Heladio Ramírez was nominated, 'the election of municipal presidents became the arena for resolving their political differences' (Díaz Montes, 1992: 46). However, the brief spell that Jésus Martínez had in the state palace, gave him only limited scope for achieving his aim. Moreover, neither politician had a free hand in choosing candidates, since so many intervening actors – outgoing municipal presidents, local deputies and various PRI officials with their own axe to grind – were involved.

It is conventional wisdom that the governor intervenes in the selection of PRI candidates in key urban *municipios* (such as Oaxaca City) and sensitive localities (such as Juchitán). Yet in the vast majority of municipalities this was unnecessary because in 1986 there was no organised opposition: non-PRI parties put up a total of only 150 candidates in 121 out of 570 *municipios*, though that was a substantial increase on the 87 contested in 1983 (Martínez Vásquez, 1990: 248). As Díaz Montes observes:

> There is an important number of rural and Indian *municipios* in which the selection of candidates is made by the community itself through communal assemblies, without much governor's interference. There are also some *municipios* in which the governor does not intervene, because they are controlled by *caciques*. The relative autonomy of these *municipios* is permitted by the governor and his party, since it represents no danger whatsoever for the system (1992a: 68).

Sometimes PRI officials imposed candidates on *municipios*, at the behest of *caciques*, notably in Chahuites, Etla, San Juan Mazatlán and Santa Catarina Juquila (Martínez Vásquez, 1990: 249). But in 521 instances, locally-chosen candidates were simply validated by the PRI as their own, in 27 cases there were primary elections for *priístas* (often giving rise to factionalism and later to opposition to official candidates), and in 14 urban localities the PRI held elections among its affiliated sectors.

Among parties opposed to the PRI in 1986, the only one with a long-run presence in the state was the PAN, characterised, nationally, by its conservative platform and its orientation to business needs. Its influence had been greatest in the Mixteca (Figure 15.1), an impoverished, highland region to the north-west of Oaxaca City, where, in 1980, it had won the major *municipio* of Huajuapan de Leon. The *Partido Socialista Unificado de México* (PSUM), *Partido Revolucionario de los Trabajadores* (PRT), and the *Partido Mexicano de los Trabajadores* (PMT), all of which had just been legalised, combined with COCEI to form the *Coalición Democrática* (CD), with the *Partido Auténtico de la Revolución Mexicana* (PARM), the *Partido Popular Socialista* (PPS) and the *Partido Socialista de los Trabajadores* (PST) forming additional opposition elements. Whereas the PRI contested

Figure 15.2 Oaxaca: Municipal Elections - Solutions to disputed results

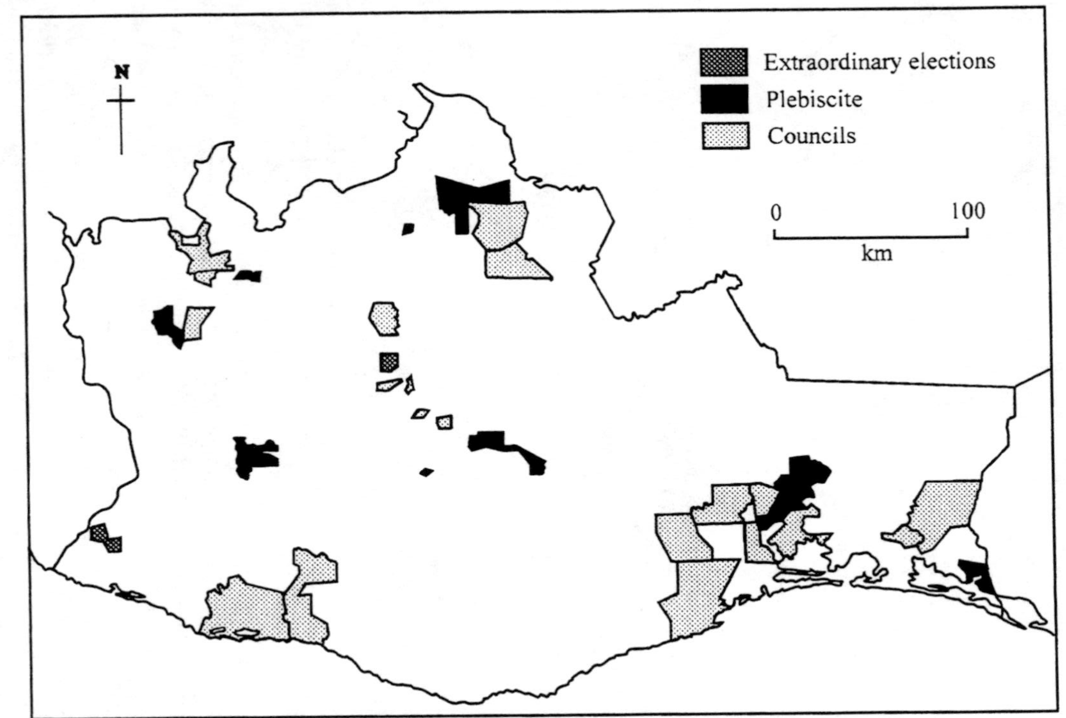

all 570 *municipios*, the CD competed in 32, the PAN in 39, the PARM and the PPS in 35, and the PST in 14.

In both 1983, when the turn-out was just over 500 000, and 1986 when it rose to 625 000, the PRI received 90 per cent of the vote cast. However, in 1986, the level of abstentions was high (47.4 per cent), especially where there were no opposition candidates, though lower than it had been in 1983 (51.5 per cent) or 1980 (49.7 per cent). Urban areas were notorious for their association with abstentionism, the rate rising to 70 or 80 per cent in and around Oaxaca City, where the masses remained disaffected from the political parties (Martínez Vásquez, 1990:255). Votes cast in *municipios* where the election was not annulled were: PRI 89 per cent, PAN 3.6 per cent, PPS 2.4 per cent and CD 1.9 per cent. Such was the dispute over the results that, during the month while the *Comisión Estatal Electoral* was reviewing the figures, the opposition parties joined forces to create the *Frente Cívico para la Defensa del Voto Ciudadano*. To keep up the pressure on the PRI, it organised various meetings and hunger strikes on the *plaza* in Oaxaca City (Díaz Montes, 1992a: 55).

On 14 September, the electoral commission pronounced its verdict: the PRI had taken 537 *municipios* against five for the CD, three for the PAN and one for the PST. In thirteen *municipios* the election was declared null and void, and in eleven more no decision was reached. Opposition parties decided to occupy certain municipal palaces to prevent the new regimes from taking possession. On the 15 September, 36 such buildings were invaded, and the municipal presidents took office in private houses (Díaz Montes, 1992a: 56).That pressure on the PRI was growing may be inferred from the fact that in 1983, only 24 municipal buildings had been invaded by opposition parties.

Some 50 *municipios* remained in dispute after 15 September, when the electoral commission closed. At this point the incoming administration of Heladio Ramírez, who had won 91 per cent of the vote cast for the governorship, became dominant, setting up special commissions involving one representative of the executive, one of the legislature and one of the PRI – panels heavily weighted in favour of the dominant party. Although these commissions met on various occasions with the groups in conflict, they managed to resolve only a handful of cases, either because the solutions were unacceptable or initial agreements were rejected (Díaz Montes, 1992a: 57). After Heladio Ramírez was installed as Governor on 1 December 1986, opposition pressure continued and resulted in three plebiscites and six new municipal councils being established to resolve the disputes.

All together, according to Díaz Montes, 73 *municipios* recorded conflicts over the electoral results, leaving 497 (490 recorded PRI victories) undisputed. Out of these 73 contested results, two were settled by new elections,

Figure 15.3 Oaxaca: 1986 Municipal Elections Municipios won by opposition parties

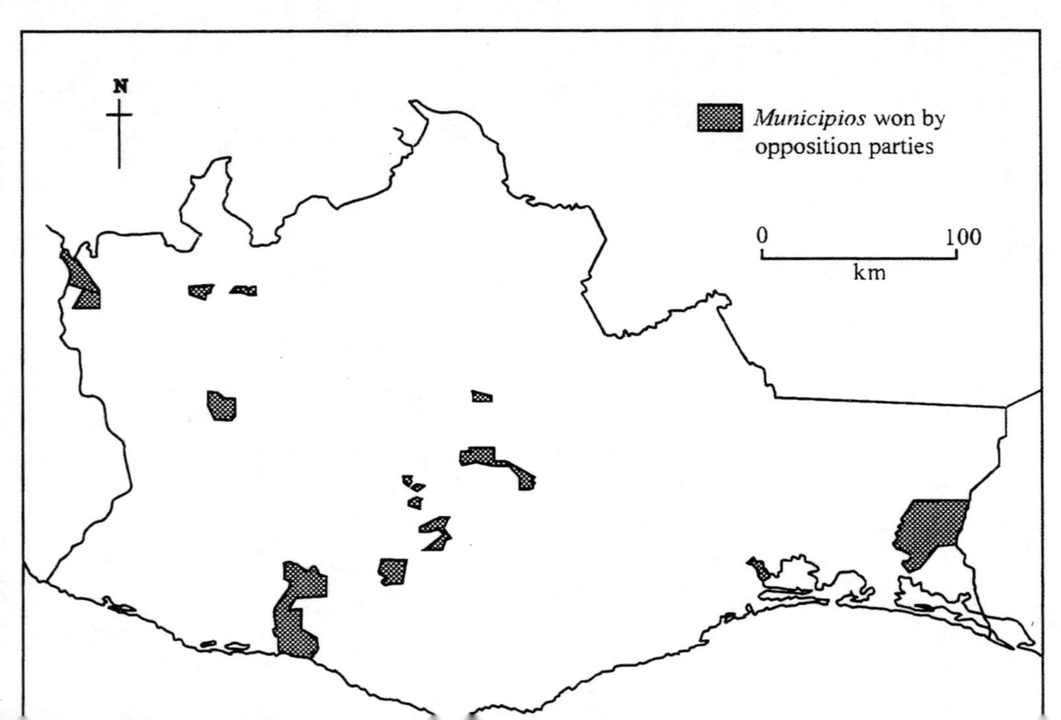

ten by plebiscites, 29 by municipal councils and 32 by incorporating opposition *regidores* (appointed municipal councillors) in the local government on the basis the votes cast for them. Disputed elections were widely scattered across Oaxaca, though plebiscites and councils tended to concentrate in the Central Valleys around Oaxaca City and in the Isthmus of Tehuantepec, where dissident activities had occurred in the 1970s and 1980s (Figure 15.2). In the case of the extraordinary elections, both were PRI victories; out of the ten plebiscites, seven were won by the PRI or PRI dissidents, one by the PAN and two by the CD. Deliberations in the 29 municipal councils resulted in control of nine being given to PRI dissidents (therefore not shown on Figure 15.2), with two going to the PAN and one to the PPS. All the remainder resulted in PRI dominance, as did 30 out of the 32 cases of incorporation. However, in eight *municipios* the PRI was forced into acknowledged coalitions with the PPS (five cases), the PAN, the PARM and the PST (Díaz Montes, 1992a: 64, Table 3.5).

The final result, which was arrived at only in January 1987, was that the PRI won 555 out of 570 *municipios*, the PAN six, the PPS one, the PST one, the PARM none, and the CD seven. Out of the 15 'opposition' victories, only seven were achieved in the election, the remainder coming from plebiscites and post-electoral pressure – the PRI rarely refused to acknowledge opposition victories unless they were particularly significant. Similar results had obtained in 1983, when the PRI gained 559 *municipios*, and 1980 and 1977 when its tally had been 552 and 561, respectively.

The *'reforma politica'* of 1980 seemed more apparent than real, the major up-turn in opposition fortunes in the *municipios* coinciding with the six-yearly elections to the state governorship. Examination of the spatial pattern of the 15 *municipios* won by opposition parties in 1986 suggests no simple interpretation, though they formed three concentrations in the Mixteca, Central Valleys, and the Isthmus of Tehuantepec (Figure 15.3). Given that they comprised fewer than three per cent of all Oaxaca's *municipios* and were split between four political parties or groupings, difficulty in providing a clear-cut interpretation of their distribution is hardly surprising.

Díaz Montes has produced an interesting statistical analysis of Oaxaca's *municipios*, in which he showed that a large population (urbanisation), high literacy and a low proportion of the population actively involved in agriculture could be taken together to distinguish conflictive cases, based on whether elections were disputed or not. Ability to speak a non-Hispanic language was shown not to be significant in a model framework that emphasised the crucial role of modernisation in electoral competition and conflict in Oaxaca (Díaz Montes, 1992a: 81-94). It must be borne in mind, however, that there was a significant difference between disputed elections in urban places (Figure

15.2) and opposition victories which were, with the exception of Tlacolula in the Central Valleys (Díaz Montes, 1992a: 113-44), rural and located in *municipios* of little consequence (Figure 15.3). In addition, there were a number of ethnic-ecological disputes in the early 1980s in the Sierra Zapoteca, north of Oaxaca City, and in the Mixteca Alta, but they were pursued largely outside the electoral arena (Basáñez E, 1987).

Juchitán, then, was clearly distinctive within Oaxaca, in that it was an urban *municipio* with a Zapotec-speaking population in which dissidence had taken on an electoral dimension. Drawing upon this ethnic identifier, COCEI, against the odds, was able to mobilise thousands of supporters throughout the 1980s. Taking advantage of PRI factionalism, it emerged from a period of repression in and after 1983 to continue mobilising support on agricultural and urban-workplace issues. In 1986 it joined a coalition municipal government in Juchitán headed by a *priísta*, in an arrangement presided over by the new governor, Heladio Ramírez. This link between urbanisation, ethnicity and electoral participation was to give a special flavour and durability to COCEI. According to Rubin, 'it demonstrates, contrary to most analyses of Mexico, the continuous importance of electoral competition in post-revolutionary Mexican politics' (1994: 124). But is this judgement correct, when one considers the specificity of Juchitán? One elected, left-wing *municipio*, however significant symbolically, scarcely confirms that Mexico is either democratic or socialist.

CONCLUSION

Rubin has recently proposed a framework for understanding Mexican politics, which abandons the idea of PRI hegemony in favour of an approach which emphasises competitive variations over time and space. He points to the decline of post-revolutionary regional *cacicazgos* during the 1950s and 1960s as a crucial starting point, arguing that:

> national and regional patterns of economic change transformed many of the economic arrangements upon which these regional power structures had been based, and elite and popular mobilisations directly challenged prevailing political procedures. In this context, as the bosses aged and died, conflicts ensued in the 1960s over how politics would be conducted. In many places, the PRI and its affiliated mass organisations barely existed or had only begun to forge procedures for political mediation. Movements for electoral competition, clean government, local cultural identity, and progressive social change met with some successes, but considerable hostility and repression (1994: 135)

In this chapter I have taken a wider brief than Rubin, who devoted himself to Juchitán in the early 1980s, covering the whole state of Oaxaca and the period since 1968. My findings confirm his generalisation that 'Mexican regions thus experienced a common pattern of political crises, different from those put forth by state-centred analysis; however, these crises occurred in a panoply of contexts, with the result that political beliefs and power relations consistently varied across geographic regions, economic sectors, and cultural arenas' (Rubin, 1994: 135).

Whether one is focussing on the PRI and internal struggles to obtain the Oaxaca governorship, examining relations between certain governors and the *vallistocracia*, or looking at dissident grassroots movements such as COCEO and COCEI within and outside electoral contexts, one cannot but be struck by the fact that, in Rubin's words, 'power in Mexico is much more diffuse and hegemony more contested than conventional accounts acknowledge. The regime's longevity results not from centralisation and corporatism, but from the way in which such diffusion and contestation reproduce broad patterns of power' (Rubin, 1994: 135).

However, Rubin overstates his case. Concentrating as he does on Juchitán, it is easy to do so. Yet the advantage of looking at the whole state of Oaxaca is that it puts Juchitán into its unique context, in which urbanisation, social inequality and ethnic identity have meshed in ways unparalleled in other areas. Moreover, conditions in Oaxaca give some pointers to the political diversity likely to be encountered in different parts of Mexico. In general, in Oaxaca, the contestation between the PRI and opposition political parties is much weaker and more sporadic than it has been in Juchitán, and PRI dominance, despite post-electoral disputes, is generally secure. Non-electoral competition from COCEO and COCEI, while intense in the past, has inevitably and universally led to PRI manipulation, co-optation and outright repression. There is little scope for democratic elections in which the PRI might be defeated on a sufficiently large scale, by either the left or the right, to cause the loss of the governorship of Oaxaca or the defection of the majority of *municipios* in Oaxaca. Indeed, the PRI has always tried to win back lost *municipios*: in 1983 it re-captured 15 out of the 18 it lost in 1980, and in 1986, it re-took eight of the 11 forfeited in 1983 (Martínez Vásquez, 1990: 251).

The elections for the governorship in 1992 served not only to re-emphasise the strength of the PRI, but the continuing tussle between the established power groups within it. For example, the two PRI, candidates, Luis Martínez Fernández del Campo and Diódoro Carrasco Altamirano, the state senator (Díaz Montes and Yescas Martínez, 1992), were backed, respectively, by ex-governor Martínez Alvarez and Governor Heladio Ramírez, rivals in the mid-1980s. Diódoro Carrasco, a former state official with advantageous connections to President Salinas' *Programa Nacional de Solidaridad* (PRONASOL), became the official candidate and eventually took 77 per cent of the vote against ten per cent for the *Partido Revolucionario Democrático* (PRD), whose candidate had resigned from the PRI, and five per cent for the PAN (Díaz Montes, 1992b). It is a measure of the co-optive power of the PRI and of the frustrations of those opposed to it, that many of the officials in Diódoro Carrasco's administration had been university activists in the 1970s.

Between the Oaxaca gubernatorial elections of 1986 and 1992, the PRI vote dropped by 14 per cent, the *Coalición Democrático*-PRD poll increased by eight per cent and that of the PAN by one per cent. Even more disturbing for the PRI was the increase in the level of abstentions from 40 to 60 per cent, and its comparatively weak showing in the urban centres, notably Oaxaca City, where the PAN has a minor power base among professionals (Martínez Vásquez, 1992b), Huajuapan and Tehuantepec (Díaz Montes, 1992b). Nevertheless, it was a measure of the effort made by the PRI in Oaxaca in the presidential election of 1994, that 390 000 more voters turned out than six years previously, so reducing abstentions to just under 30 per cent of the roll, compared to 54 per cent in 1988.

This chapter, though devoted to Oaxaca, suggests several generalisations that are of nation-wide significance in Mexico. The PRI may not be hegemonic and grassroots movements may have considerable scope at the local level, but it has a capacity for contesting every political turf in a way that no other Mexican political party can at a municipal, state and federal level. Moreover, it has had sufficient *de facto* leverage over the electoral process, despite substantial modification of the law in 1990 (Ward, 1994), to hold on to most *municipios* and virtually all states, as well as national power. The PRI's control becomes more uniform and complete as the spatial scale is increased to embrace the entire federal entity, where, of course, the political significance of its dominance is greatest.

Bibliography

N. Abercrombie, S. Hill and B.S. Turner, *The Dominant Ideology Thesis*, (London: Allen and Unwin, 1984)

C. Acosta, 'Sin Precedente en el Mundo, a la Apertura Comercial Mexicana, Washington Ha Respondido con Más Barreras', *Proceso*, 760 (1991) p.6-7.

L. Adler-Lomnitz and M. Perez-Lizaur, *A Mexican Elite Family, 1820-1980: Kinship, Class and Culture*, (Princeton: Princeton University Press, 1987).

L.F. Aguilar Villanueva, 'Solidaridad: tres puntos de vista', in C. Rojas (ed.), *Solidaridad a debate*, (México DF: El Nacional, 1991).

R. Aitken, 'Privatización, Autonomía y Género: aspectos de internalización e identidad en Ciudad Lázaro Cárdenas, Michoacán', in H. González Chavez (ed.), *Internacionalización e Identidad en el Occidente de México*, (Guadalajara: University of Guadalajara, forthcoming a).

R. Aitken, 'Political culture and local identities in Michoacán', in W.G. Pansters (ed.), *Descending the Pyramid? Essays on Mexican Political Culture and Politics*, (Wilmington: Scholarly Resources, forthcoming b).

J. Alcocer V., 'Alarma agropecuaria', *Proceso*, 763 (1991) pp.37-9.

A.M. Alonso, 'Progress as Disorder and Dishonor: Discourses of Serrano Resistance', *Critique of Anthropology*, 8 1 (1988) pp.13-33.

J. Alonso, *El PDM movimiento regional*, (México: Universidad de Guadalajara, 1989).

J. Alonso, A. Aziz and J. Tamayo (eds.) *El nuevo estado mexicano*, (México DF: Nueva Imagen, 1992).

L.H. Alvarez, 'Political and Economic Reform in Mexico: The PAN Perspective', in R. Roett (ed.), *Political and Economic Liberalization in Mexico: At a Critical Juncture?*, (Boulder, Colorado: Lynne Rienner Publishers, 1993) pp.143-7.

America's Watch, *Human Rights in Mexico: A Policy of Impunity*, (New York: Human Rights Watch, 1990).

B. Anderson, *Imagined Communities. Reflections on the origin and Spread of Nationalism*, (London and New York: Verso, 1991).

R. Anderson, 'Mexican Workers and the Politics of Revolution', *Hispanic American Historical Review*, 54 (1974) pp.94-113.

D. Ankerson, *Agrarian Warlord. Saturnino Cedillo and the Mexican revolution*, (DeKalb: Northern Illinois University Press, 1984).

A. Appadurai, 'Disjuncture and difference in the global cultural economy', in M. Featherstone (ed.), *Global Culture: Nationalism, Globalisation and Modernity*, (London: Sage, 1990) pp.295-310.

K. Appendini, 'Agriculture and Farmers Within Nafta: a Mexican perspective', in V. Bulmer-Thomas, N. Craske and M. Serrano (eds.), *Mexico and the North American Free Trade Agreement: who will benefit?*, (London: Macmillan and The Institute of Latin American Studies, 1994) pp.59-75.

L. Arizpe, 'El nuevo oficio político del ciudadano y del Presidente', *Nexos*, XVI 188 (1993) pp.28-30.

A. Arreola Ayala, 'Atlacomulco: la antesala del poder', in C. Martínez Assad (ed.), *Municipios en conflicto*, (México DF: Universidad Nacional Autónoma de México, 1985) pp.75-132.

J. Arroyo Alejandre and S.D. Morris, 'The Electoral Recovery of the PRI in Guadalajara, Mexico, 1988-92', *Bulletin of Latin American Research*, 12 1 (1993) pp.91-102.

T. Asad, 'Conscripts of Western Civilisation', in C. Gailey Ward (ed.), *Civilization in Crisis: Anthropological Perspectives*, Volume 1 of *Dialectical Anthropology: Essays in Honour of Stanley Diamond*, (Gainsville: University of Florida Press, 1991) pp.333-51.

L. Aubague, *Discurso político, utopía y memoria popular en Juchitán*, (Oaxaca: Instituto de Investigaciones Sociológicas, Universidad Autónoma 'Benito Juárez' de Oaxaca, 1985).

Austin, 'The Austin Memorandum on the Reform of Article 27, and its Impact upon the Urbanization of the Ejido in Mexico', *Bulletin of Latin American Research*, 13 1 (1994) pp.327-35.

A. Aziz Nassif, 'San Luis Potosí: la repetición de un agravio', *Eslabones: Revista semestral de estudios regionales*, 3 (1992) pp.6-19.

A. Azuela, *La ciudad, la propiedad privada y el derecho*, (México: El Colegio de México, 1989).

A. Azuela, *Ciudadania y gestión urbana en los poblados rurales de Los Tuxtlas*, (Mimeograph, 1994).

J. Bailey, 'Centralism and political change in Mexico: the case of National Solidarity', in W.A. Cornelius, A.L. Craig and J. Fox (eds.), *Transforming State-Society Relations in Mexico: The National Solidarity Strategy* (San Diego: Center for US-Mexican Studies, University of California, 1994) pp.97-119.

J. Bailey, 'Fiscal Centralism and Pragmatic Accommodation in Nuevo León', in V.E. Rodríguez and P.M. Ward, (eds.), *Opposition Government in Mexico: Past Experiences and Future Opportunities*, (Albuquerque: University of New Mexico Press, 1995) pp.173-87.

J. Bailey and J. Boone, 'National Solidarity: a summary of program elements', in W.A. Cornelius, A.L. Craig and J. Fox (eds.), *Transforming State-Society Relations in Mexico: The National Solidarity Strategy*, (San Diego: Center for US-Mexican Studies, University of California, 1994) pp.329-38.

M. Bailón, *Conflictos municipales, una historia no tan nueva: elecciones locales en Oaxaca, 1920-70*, Paper presented at XVII International Congress of the Latin American Studies Association, Los Angeles, 24-27 September (1992).

H. Baitenmann, 'Lo que no Procede: Las irregularidades en el programa de certificación ejidal', *La Jornada del Campo*, 6th September (1994).

Banco de México, *The Mexican Economy*, (México DF: Banco de México, 1993).

Banco de México, *Indicadores Económicos*, (Mexico DF: Banco de México, various numbers).

A.A. Bantjes, 'Burning Saints, Molding Minds: Iconoclasm, Civic Ritual and the Failed Cultural Revolution', in W.H. Beezley, C.E. Martin and W.E. French (eds.), *Rituals of Rule, Rituals of Resistance: Public Celebrations and Popular Culture in Mexico* (Wilmington, Delaware: Scholarly Resources Books, 1994) pp.261-85.

D. Barkin, 'The Specter of Rural Development', *NACLA Report on the Americas*, XXVIII 1 (1994) pp.29-37.

D. Barkin and B. Suarez, *El fin de la autosuficiencia alimentaria*, (México DF: Centro de Ecodesarrollo and Ediciones Océano, 1985).

S. Barraclough, 'Algunas cuestiones sobre las implicaciones del TLC en el México rural', in C. González (ed.), *El Sector Agropecuario Mexicano Frente al Tratado de Libre Comercio*, (México DF: Universidad Nacional Autónoma de México and Universidad Autónoma de Chapingo, 1992) pp.13–39.

E. Barragán López, 'Identidad ranchera. Apreciaciones desde la sierra sur "jalmichana" en el occidente de México', *Relaciones*, 43 (1990) pp.75-106.

T. Barry, (ed.) 1992. *Mexico: A Country Guide*. (Albuquerque: Inter-Hemispheric Education Resource Center, 1992).

R. Bartra, *The Imaginary Networks of Political Power*, (New Brunswick: Rutgers University Press, 1992).

R. Bartra, *Agrarian Structure and Political Power in Mexico*. (Baltimore: John Hopkins University Press, 1993).

M. Basañez E., (ed.) *La composición del poder: Oaxaca*, (México DF: Instituto Nacional de Administración Pública, 1987).

M. Basáñez E., *El pulso de los sexenios*, (México DF: Siglo XXI, 1990).

M. Basañez E., 'Opinion Poll Tracking in 1994: A Success Story', in P.M. Ward (ed.), *Mexico's Electoral Aftermath and Political Future*, (Austin, Texas: The Mexican Center, ILAS, University of Texas, 1994) pp.49-52.

I. Bizberg, 'Modernisation and Corporatism in Government-Labour Relations', in N. Harvey (ed.), *Mexico: Dilemmas of Transition*, (London: British Academic Press and The Institute of Latin American Studies, 1993) pp.299-317.

A. Blok, *The Mafia of a Sicilian Village 1860-1960*, (Oxford: Basil Blackwell, 1974).

A. Borjas, *El tratamiento periodístico de la información del movimiento político denominado navismo*, (Universidad Iberoamericana: Unpublished dissertation, 1992).

D. Brading, *The Origins of Mexican Nationalism*, (Cambridge: Centre of Latin American Studies, 1985).

M. Braig, *Continuity and change in Mexican political culture: the case of PRONASOL*, Paper presented at conference, Descending the Pyramid: Mexican Political Culture, University of Utrecht, 28-9 April (1994).

V. Brailovsky, R. Clarke and N. Warman, *La Política del Desperdicio*, (México DF: Universidad Nacional Autónoma de México, 1990).

M. Brophy-Baermann, 'Economics and elections - the Mexican case', *Social Science Quarterly*, 75 (1994) pp.125-35.

A. Caballero, *Salvador Nava. Las últimas batallas*, (México DF: La Jornada, 1992).

J.A. Calderón Salazar, 'Contribution to discussion in the Cámara Pública, 4th December 1991', in E. Valle Espinosa (ed.), *El Nuevo Articulo 27. Cuestiones*

Agrarias de Venustiano Carranza a Carlos Salinas, (México DF: Editorial Nuestra, 1992).

J.L. Calva, 'Política económica para el sector agropecuario', in J.P. Arroyo Ortiz (ed.), *El sector agropecuario en el futuro de la economía mexicana*, (México, DF: Universidad Nacional Autónoma de México, Facultad de Economía, 1991a) pp.3–13.

J.L. Calva, 'Funciones del sector agropecuario en el futuro de la economía nacional', in J.P. Arroyo Ortiz (ed.), *El sector agropecuario en el futuro de la economía mexicana*, (México DF: Universidad Nacional Autónoma de México, 1991b) pp.40-52.

J.L. Calva, *La Disputa por la Tierra: la reforma de Articulo 27 y la nueva Ley Agraria*, (México DF: Distribuciones Fontamara, 1993).

T. Calvillo Unna, *San Luis Potosí 1958*, (El Colegio de México: Unpublished dissertation, 1981).

R.A. Camp, *Politics in Mexico*, (Oxford: Oxford University Press, 1993a).

R.A. Camp, 'Political Modernization in Mexico: Through a Looking Glass', in J.E. Rodríguez, *The Evolution of the Mexican Political System*, (Wilmington, Delaware: SR Books, 1993b) pp.245-62.

R.A. Camp, 'The PAN's Social bases: Implications for Leadership', in V.E. Rodríguez and P.M. Ward (eds.), *Opposition Government in Mexico: Past Experiences and Future Opportunities*, (Albuquerque: University of New Mexico Press, 1995) pp.65-80

M.L. Carlos, J.J. Gutiérrez and G. Real, *An assessment of processes and outcomes of Mexican ejidal reform: ejidal communities of the state of Querétaro in a comparative ethnographic analysis*, Paper presented at XVIII International Congress of the Latin American Studies Association, Atlanta, 10-12 March (1994).

J. Carpizo, *El Presidencialismo Mexicano*, (México DF: Siglo XXI, 1972).

B. Carr, 'Labor and the left in Mexico', in K.J. Middlebrook (ed.), *Unions, workers and the state in Mexico*, (San Diego: Center for US-Mexican Studies, University of California, 1991) pp.121-52.

E.H. Carr, *What Is History?*, (Harmondsworth: Penguin Books, 1964).

J. Casar, C. Marques, S. Marvan, G. Rodríguez, and J. Ros, *La Organización Industrial en México,* (México DF: Siglo XXI, 1990).

H. Castro and M. Cantú, *Proceso Electoral en Baja California (Primera Parte)*, (Mimeograph, 1992).

CEN del PAN, *Información Básica sobre Acción Nacional*, (México DF: Espessa, 1994a).

CEN del PAN, *Plataforma Política 1994-2000*, (México DF: Partido Acción Nacional, 1994b).

M.A. Centeno, *Mexico in the 1990s: Government and Opposition Speak Out: Mexico in the 1990s*, (San Diego: Center for US-Mexican Studies, University of California, 1991).

M.A. Centeno, *Democracy within Reason: technocratic revolution in Mexico*, (Pennsylvania: Penn. State Press, 1994).

M. Centeno and S. Maxwell, 'The Marriage of Finance and Order: Changes in the Mexican Political Elite', *Journal of Latin American Studies*, 24 1 (1992) pp.57-85.

J. Chabat, 'Mexico's Foreign Policy in 1990: Electoral Sovereignty and Integration with the United States', in J. Heine (ed.), *Anuario de Políticas Exteriores Latinoamericanos: Hacia unas relaciones internacionales de mercado?*, (Caracas: Nueva Sociedad, 1991).

F. Chevalier, 'The *ejido* and political stability in Mexico', in C. Veliz (ed.), *The Politics of Conformity in Latin America*, (London: Oxford University Press, 1967) pp.158-91.

B. Clariond Reyes-Retana, *Primer Informe de Gobierno*, (Mimeograph, 1992).

B. Clariond Reyes-Retana, *Segundo Informe de Gobierno*, (Mimeograph, 1993).

L.D. Colosio, 'Why the PRI Won the 1991 Elections', in R. Roett (ed.), *Political and Economic Liberalization in Mexico: At a Critical Juncture?*, (Boulder, Colorado: Lynne Rienner Publishers, 1993) pp.155-65.

S. Commander and T. Killick, 'Privatisation in Developing Countries: A Survey of the Issues', in P. Cook and C. Kirkpatrick (eds.), *Privatisation in Less Developed Countries,* (Brighton: Wheatsheaf, 1988) pp.91-124.

Consejo Consultivo del Programa Nacional de Solidaridad, *El Programa Nacional de Solidaridad: Una Visión de la Modernización de México*, (México DF: Fondo de Cultura Económica, 1994).

O. Contreras and V. Bennett, 'National Solidarity in the northern borderlands: social participation and community leadership', in W.A. Cornelius, A.L. Craig and J. Fox (eds.), *Transforming State-Society Relations in Mexico: The National Solidarity Strategy* (San Diego: Center for US-Mexican Studies, University of California, 1994) pp.281-305.

R. Cook, C. Benito, J. Matson, D. Runsten, K. Shwedel and T. Taylor, *Implications of the North American Free Trade Agreement (NAFTA) for the US Horticultural Sector*', Volume IV, (Park Ridge, Illinois: American Farm Bureau Research Foundation, 1991).

M. Corden, 'Protection and the Real Exchange Rate', in M. Corden (ed.), *Protection, Growth and Trade*, (Oxford: Basil Blackwell, 1985) pp.302-10.

R. Cordera Campos, 'Ecos y recuerdos de La Sucesión Presidencial', *Nexos*, 188 (1993) pp.30-2.

R. Cordera Campos and C. Tello, (eds.) *La Desigualdad en México*, (México DF: Siglo XXI, 1984).

A. Córdova, 'Los estrechos marcos de la sucesión', *Nexos*, 188 (1993) pp.32-6.

W.A. Cornelius, 'Contemporary Mexico: A Structural Analysis of Urban Caciquismo', in R. Kern (ed.), *The Caciques*, (Albuquerque, University of New Mexico Press, 1973) pp.135-50.

W.A. Cornelius, 'Los migrantes de la crisis: The Changing Profile of Mexican Migration to the United States', in M. González de la Rocha and A. Escobar (eds.), *Social Responses to Mexico's Economic Crisis of the 80s*, (San Diego: Center for US-Mexican Studies, University of California, 1991) pp.155-94.

W.A. Cornelius, 'The Politics and Economics of Reforming the Ejido Sector in Mexico: An Overview and Research Agenda', *LASA Forum*, XXIII 3 (1992) p.3-8.

W.A. Cornelius, 'Mexico's Delayed Democratization', *Foreign Policy*, 95 (1994) pp.53-71.

W.A. Cornelius and A.L. Craig, *The Mexican Political System in Transition*, (San Diego: Center for US-Mexican Studies, University of California, Monograph Series 35, 1991).

W.A. Cornelius, J. Gentleman and P.H. Smith, 'The Dynamics of Political Change in Mexico', in W.A. Cornelius, J. Gentleman and P.H. Smith (eds.), *Mexico's Alternative Political Futures*, (San Diego: Center for US-Mexican Studies, University of California, 1989) pp.1-51.

W.A. Cornelius, A.L. Craig and J. Fox, 'Mexico's National Solidarity Program: an overview', in W.A. Cornelius, A.L. Craig and J. Fox (eds.), *Transforming State-Society Relations in Mexico: The National Solidarity Strategy*, (San Diego: Center for US-Mexican Studies, University of California, 1994) pp.3-26.

G. Correa, 'El ejido sobrevive, de nombre, pero se acerca la privatización', *Proceso*, 783 (1991) pp.13-5.

S. Corro and G. Correa, 'La Reforma del Articulo 27 se apega a recomendaciones del Banco Mundial', *Proceso*, 788 (1991) pp.22-3.

D. Cothran, 'Budgetary secrecy and policy stratgey in Mexico under Cárdenas', *Mexican Studies/Estudios Mexicanos*, 2 1 (1986) 35-58.

A.L. Craig, *The First Agraristas*, (Berkeley: University of California Press, 1983).

N. Craske, *Corporatism Revisited: Salinas and the Reform of the Popular Sector*, (London: Institute of Latin American Studies, Research Papers 37, 1994).

D. Cymet, *From Ejido to Metropolis, Another Path: An Evaluation on Ejido Property Rights and Informal Land Development in Mexico City*, (New York: Peter Lang, 1992).

R. Damatta, *Carnivals, Rogues and Heroes: an Interpretation of the Brazilian Dilemma* (Notre Dame and London: Notre Dame University Press, 1991).

C.L. Davis and K.M. Coleman, 'Neoliberal economic policies and the potential for electoral change in Mexico', *Mexican Studies/Estudios Mexicanos*, 10 (1994) pp.341-70.

M. Davis, 'Who killed LA? A political autopsy', *New Left Review*, 197 (1993a) pp.9–28.

M. Davis, 'Who Killed LA? Part II: the Verdict is Given', *New Left Review*, 199 (1993b) pp.29–54.

L. Demery and T. Addison, 'Stabilization Policy and Income Distribution in Developing Countries', *World Development*, 15 12 (1987) pp.1483-98.

B. DeWalt, and M.W. Rees, (with A.D. Murphy), *The End of Agrarian Reform in Mexico: Past Lessons, Future Prospects*, (San Diego: Center for US-Mexican Studies, University of California, Transformation of Rural Mexico Series 3, 1994).

DGRT (Dirección General de Regularización Territorial, Departamento del Distrito Federal), *La Regularización Territorial en la Ciudad de México: Soluciones de un Gobierno Solidario*, (México DF: Departamento del Distrito Federal, 1994a).

DGRT (Dirección General de Regularización Territorial, Departamento del Distrito Federal), *Programas de Regularización del Suelo en la Ciudad de México: PROGRESSE*, (México DF: Departamento del Distrito Federal, 1994b).

F. Díaz Montes, *Los municipios: la disputa por el poder local en Oaxaca*, (Oaxaca: Instituto de Investigaciones Sociológicas, Universidad Autónoma 'Benito Juáraz' de Oaxaca, 1992a).

F. Díaz Montes, 'Elección de gobernador en Oaxaca', *Cuadernos del Sur*, 2 (1992b) pp.113-28.

F. Díaz Montes and I. Yescas Martínez, 'Elecciones federales y sucesión gubernamental en Oaxaca', *Cuadernos del Sur*, 1 (1992) pp.5-24.

H. Díaz Polanco, 'Los pueblos indios y la Constitución' *México Indígena*, 15 (1990) pp.9-13.

H. Díaz-Polanco, 'Cuestión Etnica, Estado y Nuevos Proyectos Nacionales', in C. Noriega Elio (ed.), *El Nacionalismo en México* (Zamora: El Colegio de Michoacán, 1992a).

H. Díaz Polanco, 'El Estado y los indígenas', in J. Alonso, A. Aziz and J. Tamayo (eds.), *El nuevo estado mexicano*, (México DF: Nueva Imágen, 1992b) pp.145-70.

H. Díaz Polanco, 'Autonomía, territorialidad y comunidad indígena. Las reformas de la legislación agraria en México' *Cuadernos Agrarios*, 5-6 (1992c) pp.62-79.

J.I. Domínguez and J.A. McCann, 'Whither the PRI? Explaining voter defection in the 1988 Mexican Presidential elections', *Electoral Studies*, 11 (1992) pp.207-22.

R. Doniz and C. Monsivais, *H Ayuntamiento Popular de Juchitán*, (Oaxaca: H. Ayuntamiento de Juchitán, 1983).

R. Dornbusch, *Open-Economy Macroeconomics*, (New York: Basic Books, 1980).

R. Dornbusch and L. Tellez Kuenzler, 'Exchange Rate Policy: Options and Issues', R. Dornbusch (ed.), *Policy Making in the Open Economy*, (New York: Oxford University Press, EDI Series in Economic Development, 1993) pp.91-126.

D. Dresser, *Neopopulist Solutions to Neoliberal Problems: Mexico's National Solidarity Program* (San Diego: Center for US-Mexican Studies, University of California, 1991).

D. Dresser, 'Bringing the poor back in: National Solidarity as a strategy of regime legitimation', in W.A. Cornelius, A.L. Craig and J. Fox (eds.), *Transforming State-Society Relations in Mexico: The National Solidarity Strategy*, (San Diego: Center for US-Mexican Studies, University of California, 1994) pp.143-65.

L. Dumont, *Essays on Individualism: Modern Ideology in Anthropological Perspective*, (Chicago and London: University of Chicago Press, 1986).

S. Eckstein, *The Poverty of Revolution*, (Princeton: Princeton University Press, 1988).

S. Eckstein, 'Formal versus Substantive Democracy: poor people's politics in Mexico City', *Estudios Mexicanos/Mexican Studies*, 6 2 (1990) pp.213-39.

S. Edwards, *Exchange Rate Misalignment in Developing Countries*, (Washington DC: The World Bank, World Bank Occasional Paper 2, 1988).

C. Elizondo, *The State and Property Rights in Mexico Since the Revolution*, (Oxford University: Unpublished D.Phil. dissertation, 1993).

E. Elorduy, *Las Haciendas Estatales ante el Reto de la Modernidad*, Paper presented at XXIII Reunión Nacional de Funcionarios Fiscales, Acapulco, 26-9 July (1991).

R. Escalante, *La agricultura mexicana en los noventa*, Paper presented at FAO Seminar on Structural Adjustment and Agriculture in Latin America in the Eighties', Institute of Latin American Studies, London, 22-4 September (1993).

A. Escobar Lapati, 'The Connection at its Source: Changing Socioeconomic Conditions and Migration Patterns', in A.F. Lowenthal and K. Burgess (eds.), *The California-Mexico Connection*, (Stanford: Stanford University Press, 1993) pp.66–81.

V. Espinoza and T. Hernández, 'Tendencias de Cambio en la Estructura Corporativa Mexicana: Baja California, 1989-92', *El Cotidiano*, (1993).

F. Fajnzylber and T. Martínez, *Las Empresas Transnacionales*, México DF: Fondo de Cultura Económica, 1975).

F. Fernández Christlieb, 'Otro avatar sexenal', *Nexos*, 188 (1993) pp.37-8.

J. Fernández Menéndez, 'San Luis Potosí: ¿lejos de la estabilidad?', *Nexos*, 184 (1993) pp.49-52.

M.W. Foley, 'Agenda for Mobilization: The Agrarian Question and Popular Mobilization in Contemporary Mexico', *Latin American Research Review*, 26 2 (1991) pp.39-74.

J. Foweraker, 'Popular movements and political change in Mexico', in J. Foweraker and A.L. Craig (eds.), *Popular movements and political change in Mexico*, (Boulder, Colorado: Lynne Rienner Publications, 1990) pp.3-20.

J. Foweraker, *Popular Mobilization in Mexico: The Teachers' Movement 1977-87*, (Cambridge: Cambridge University Press, 1993).

J. Foweraker, *Measuring Citizenship in Mexico*, Paper presented at Beyond Economic Reform: Mexico under Zedillo, The Institute of Latin American Studies, London, 17-18 November (1994).

J. Fox, 'The Difficult Transition from Clientelism to Citizenship: Lessons from Mexico', *World Politics*, 46 2 (1994a) pp.151-84.

J. Fox, 'Targeting the poorest: the role of the National Indigenous Institute in Mexico's Solidarity Program', in W.A. Cornelius, A.L. Craig and J. Fox (eds.), *Transforming State-Society Relations in Mexico: The National Solidarity Strategy*, (San Diego: Center for US-Mexican Studies, University of California, 1994b) pp.179-216.

J. Fox and G. Gordillo, 'Between State and Market: The Campesino's Quest for Autonomy', in W.A. Cornelius, J. Gentleman and P.H. Smith (eds.), *Mexico's Alternative Political Futures*, (San Diego: Center for US-Mexican Studies, University of California, 1989) pp.131-72.

G. Galarza, 'Hace 20 Años la Mayoria PRIista Insultó al PAN por Proponer lo Mismo que Salinas', *Proceso*, 784 (1991) pp.10-11.

L.J. Garrido, 'The Crisis of Presidencialismo', in W.A. Cornelius, J. Gentleman and P.H. Smith (eds.), *Mexico's Alternative Political Futures*, (San Diego: Center for US-Mexican Studies, University of California, 1989) pp.417-34.

L.J. Garrido, 'Reform of the PRI: Rhetoric and Reality', in N. Harvey and M. Serrano (eds.), *Party Politics in "An Uncommon Democracy": Political Parties and Elections in Mexico*, (London: The Institute of Latin American Studies, 1994) pp.25-40.

M. Gates, *In Default: Peasants, the Debt Crisis and the Agricultural Challenge in Mexico*, (Boulder, Colorado: Westview Press, 1993).

GEA (Grupo de Economistas y Asociados), *Los Comicios de Nuevo León*, (México DF: Mimeograph, 1991).

G. Germani, *Authoritarianism, Fascism and National Populism*, (New Brunswick: Rutgers University Press, 1978)

A.L. Gershberg, 'Distributing resources in the education sector: Solidarity's Escuela Digna program', in W.A. Cornelius, A.L. Craig and J. Fox (eds.), *Transforming State-Society Relations in Mexico: The National Solidarity Strategy*, (San Diego: Center for US-Mexican Studies, University of California, 1994) pp.233-53.

D. Ghai and C. Hewitt de Alcántara, 'The Crisis of the 1980s in Africa, Latin America and the Caribbean: An Overview', in D. Ghai (ed.), *The IMF and the South. The Social Impact of Crisis and Adjustment*, (London and New Jersey: Zed Books, 1991) pp.11-42.

A. Gilbert and P.M. Ward, *Housing, the State and the Poor: Policy and Practice in Three Latin American Cities*, (Cambridge: Cambridge University Press, 1985).

A. Gilly, *Cartas a Cuauhtémoc Cárdenas*, (México DF: Ediciones Era, 1989).

J. Gledhill, *Casi Nada: A Study of Agrarian Reform in the Homeland of Cardenismo*, (Albany: Studies in Culture and Society, Volume 4, Institute for Mesoamerican Studies, State University of New York at Albany, 1991).

J. Gledhill, *Power and its Disguises: Anthropological Perspectives on Politics* (London and Boulder: Pluto Press, 1994).

Gobierno del Estado de México, *Solidaridad - Programa para el Oriente del Estado de México: Programa Especial para el Valle de Chalco*, (Toluca: Gobierno del Estado de México, 1989).

M. Gómez, *Derechos Indígenas. Lectura Comentada del Convenio 169 de la Organización Internacional del Trabajo*, (México DF: Instituto Nacional Indigenista, 1991).

M. Gómez, *Derechos Indígenas: Los Pueblos Indígenas en la Constitución Mexicana (Artículo Cuarto, Párafo Primero)*, (México DF: Instituto Nacional Indigenista, 1992).

S. Gómez Tagle, 'Electoral Reform and the Party System, 1977-90', in N. Harvey (ed.), *Mexico: Dilemmas of Transition*, (London: British Academic Press and The Institute of Latin American Studies, 1993) pp.64-90.

S. Gómez Tagle, 'Electoral violence and negotiations', in N. Harvey and M. Serrano (eds.), *Party Politics in "An Uncommon Democracy": Political Parties and Elections in Mexico*, (London: The Institute of Latin American Studies, 1994) pp.77-92.

P. González Casanova, *Democracy in Mexico*, (New York: Oxford University Press, 1970).

C. González Pacheco, 'La lucha de clases en Oaxaca 1960-1970', in R. Bustamante V., F.J. Cuautémoc González Pacheco, M.L. Ruiz Cervantes, F.A. Silva Millán Echegaray (eds.), *Oaxaca una lucha reciente: 1960-83*, (México DF: Ediciones Nueva Sociología, 1984) pp.31-73.

E. González Tiburcio, 'Seis tesis sobre el Programa Nacional de Solidaridad', *El Cotidiano*, 49 (1992) p.3-7.

D. Goodman and M. Redclift, *From Peasant to Proletarian: Capitalist Development and Agrarian Transitions*, (Oxford: Basil Blackwell, 1981).

G. Gordillo, *Campesinos al asalto del cielo: una reforma agraria con autonomía*, (México DF: Siglo XXI and Universidad Autónoma de Zacatecas, 1988).

G. Gordillo, *The Ejido and the Reform of Article 27 of the Mexican Constitution*, Paper presented at Center for US-Mexican Studies, University of California, 29 January (1992).

M.A. Granados Chapa, *¡Nava sí, Zapata no! La hora de San Luis Potosí: crónica de una lucha que triumfó*, (México DF: Grijalbo, 1992).

T. Grennes and B. Krissof, 'Agricultural Trade in a North American Free Trade Agreement', *World Economy*, 16 4 (1993) pp.483-502.

M.S. Grindle, *State and Countryside: development policy and agrarian politics in Latin America*, (Baltimore: John Hopkins University Press, 1986).

G. Guadarrama, 'Entrepreneurs and Politics: Businessmen in Electoral Contests in Sonora and Nuevo León,' in A. Alvarado (ed.), *Electoral Patterns and Perspectives in Mexico*, (San Diego: Center for US-Mexican Studies, University of California, 1987) pp.81-110.

A. Guevara, *Economic aspects of PRONASOL*, Paper presented at The Institute of Latin American Studies, London, 1 November (1994).

T. Guillén López, 'The social basis of the PRI', in W.A. Cornelius, J. Gentleman and P.H. Smith (eds.), *Mexico's Alternative Political Futures*, (San Diego, Center for US-Mexican Studies, University of California, 1989) pp.243-64.

T. Guillén López (ed.), *Frontera Norte: Una Década de Política Electoral*, (Tijuana: El Colegio de la Frontera Norte, 1992).

T. Guillén López, *Baja California 1989-1992: Balance de la Transición Democrática*, Paper presented at El Colegio de la Frontera Norte, February (1993).

P. Haber, 'Cárdenas, Salinas and the Urban Popular Movement', in N. Harvey (ed.), *Mexico: Dilemmas of Transition*, (London: British Academic Press and The Institute of Latin American Studies, 1993) pp.218-48.

P. Haber, 'Political Change in Durango: The Role of National Solidarity', in W.A. Cornelius, A.L. Craig and J. Fox (eds.), *Transforming State-Society Relations in Mexico: The National Solidarity Strategy*, (San Diego: Center for US-Mexican Studies, University of California, 1994) pp.255-79.

C.M. Hann, 'Introduction. Social anthropology and socialism', in C.M. Hann (ed.), *Socialism. Ideals, Ideologies and Local Practice*, (London: Routledge, ASA Monograph 31, 1993) pp.1-26.

C. Hardy, *El estado y los campesinos: la Confederación Nacional Campesina (CNC)*, (México DF: Nueva Imagen, 1984).

N. Harvey, *The New Agrarian Movement in Mexico, 1979-1990*, (London: The Institute of Latin American Studies, 1990).

N. Harvey, (ed.) *Mexico: Dilemmas of Transition*, (London: British Academic Press and The Institute of Latin American Studies, 1993).

N. Harvey, *Rebellion in Chiapas: rural reforms, campesino radicalism and the limits to Salinismo*, (San Diego: Center for US-Mexican Studies, University of California, Transformation of Rural Mexico Series 5, 1994).

O. Havrylyshyn, 'Trade Policy and Productivity Gains in Developing Countries', *World Bank Research Observer*, 5 (1990) pp.1-24.

J.R. Heath, 'Evaluating the impact of Mexico's land reform on agricultural productivity', *World Development*, 20 5 (1992) pp.695-711.

D. Hiernaux, 'Ocupación del suelo y producción del espacio construido en el valle de Chalco, 1978-1991', in M. Schteingart (ed.), *Espacio y Vivienda en la Ciudad de Mexico*, (México: El Colegio de México and Asamblea de Representantes del DF, 1991) pp.179-202.

G. Hufbauer and J. Schott, *NAFTA: An Assessment*, (Washington DC: Institute for International Economics, 1993).

S.P. Huntington, *The Third Wave: Democratization in the Late Twentieth Century*, (Norman: University of Oklahoma, 1991).

INEGI (Instituto Nacional de Estadística Geografía e Informática), *Sistema de Cuentas Nacionales de México 1988-1991*, (México DF: INEGI, 1993).

IFE (Instituto Federal Electoral), *Memorias del Proceso Electoral Federal de 1991*, (México DF: Instituto Federal Electoral, 1994a).

IFE (Instituto Federal Electoral), *Resultados Definitivos de 1994*, (México DF: Instituto Federal Electoral, Dirección Ejecutiva de Organización Electoral, 1994b).

INI (Instituto Nacional Indigenista), *Conoce Tus Derechos Para Exigir Su Respeto*, (México DF: Instituto Nacional Indigenista, 1990a).

INI (Instituto Nacional Indigenista), *Hacia un video indio*, (México DF: Instituto Nacional Indigenista, 1990b).

I. Jacobs, 'Rancheros of Guerrero: the Figueroa brothers and the Revolution', in D. Brading (ed.), *Caudillo and Peasant in the Mexican Revolution*, (Cambridge: Cambridge University Press, 1980) pp.76-91.

W. James, 'Migration, Racism and Identity: The Caribbean Experience In Britain', *New Left Review*, 193 (1992) pp.15-55.

G.A. Jones, 'The Commercialisation of the Land Market? Land Ownership Patterns in the Mexican City of Puebla', *Third World Planning Review*, 13 2 (1991) pp.129-53.

G.A. Jones, E. Jiménez and P.M. Ward, 'The land market in Mexico under Salinas: a real estate boom revisited?' *Environment and Planning A*, 25 (1993) pp.627-51.

G. Joseph and D. Nugent, 'Popular Culture and State Formation in Revolutionary Mexico', in G. Joseph and D. Nugent (eds.), *Everyday Forms of State Formation: Revolution and the Negotiation of Rule in Modern Mexico*, (Durham and London: Duke University Press, 1994) pp.3-23.

B. Kapferer, *Legends of People, Myths of State. Violence, Intolerance and Political Culture in Sri Lanka and Australia*, (Washington and London: Smithsonian Institution Press, 1988)

M. Kiguel and N. Liviatan, 'When do Heterodox Stabilization Programs Work?', *World Bank Research Observer*, 7 1 (1992) pp.35-57.

A. Knight, 'El liberalismo mexicano desde la reforma hasta la revolución (una interpretación)', *Historia Mexicana*, 35 (1985a) pp.59-91.

A. Knight, 'The Mexican Revolution: Bourgeois? Nationalist? Or Just a "Great Rebellion"?', *Bulletin of Latin American Research*, 4 2 (1985b) pp.1-37.

A. Knight, *The Mexican Revolution. Volume 1, Porfirians, Liberals and Peasants* (Lincoln and London: University of Nebraska Press, 1990a).

A. Knight, 'Historical Continuities in Social Movements', in J. Foweraker and A.L. Craig (eds.), *Popular Movements and Political Change in Mexico*, (Boulder, Colorado: Lynne Rienner Publishers, 1990b) pp.78-102.

A. Knight, 'Racism, Revolution and *Indigenismo*: Mexico, 1910-1940', in R. Graham, (ed.), *The Idea of Race in Latin America*, (Austin, Texas: University of Texas Press, 1990c) pp.71-102.

A. Knight, 'The Peculiarities of Mexican History: Mexico Compared to Latin America, 1821-1992', *Journal of Latin American Studies*, 24 (Quincentenary Supplement) (1992) pp.99-144.

A. Knight, 'State Power and Political Stability in Mexico', in N. Harvey (ed.), *Mexico: Dilemmas of Transition*, (London: British Academic Press and The Institute of Latin American Studies, 1993a) pp.29-63.

A. Knight, *México manso, México bronco: Mexico's Civic Culture Reconsidered*, Paper presented at conference, Changing Political Traditions in Mexico, Tulane University, 13-4 September (1993b).

A. Knight, 'Solidarity: historical continuities and contemporary implications', in W.A. Cornelius, A.L. Craig and J. Fox (eds.), *Transforming State-Society Relations in Mexico: The National Solidarity Strategy*, (San Diego: Center for US-Mexican Studies, University of California, 1994a) pp.29-45. [VARLEY, change to 1994a]

A. Knight, *Habitus and Homicide: Political Violence in Twentieth-Century Mexico*, Paper presented at conference, Descending the Pyramid: Mexican Political Culture, University of Utrecht, 28-9 April (1994b).

A. Knight, 'Cardenismo: Juggernaut or Jalopy?', *Journal of Latin American Studies*, 26 (1994c) pp.73-107.

J.L. Krafft, 'Indigenismo post (y después)' *Ojarasca* 24 (1993) pp.45-50.

A.C. Laurell, 'Democracy in Mexico: Will the First be the Last?', *New Left Review*, 194 (1992) pp.33-54.

D. Lindauer and A. Valenchik, 'Government Spending in Developing Countries: trends, causes and consequences', *World Bank Research Observer*, 7 1 (1992) pp.59-78.

S. Loaeza, *Clases Medias y Política en México*, (México DF: El Colegio de México, 1988).

L. Lomelí Meillón, 'Gobernantes y gobernados: una reflexión política', in C. Padilla and R. Reguillo (eds.), *Quién nos hubiera dicho: Guadalajara, 22 de abril*, (Guadalajara: Instituto Tecnológico y de Estudios Superiores de Occidente, 1993) pp.219-54.

C. Lomnitz-Adler, *Exits from the Labyrinth. Culture and Ideology in the Mexican National Space*, (Berkeley: University of California Press, 1992).

F. López Barcenas, 'Los derechos indígenas en México y el convenio 169 de la OIT', *Ojarasca*, 33-4 (1994) pp.43-6.

G. López Castro and S. Zendejas Romero, 'Migración internacional por regiones en Michoacán', in T. Calvo and G. López (eds.), *Movimientos de población en el occidente de México,* (Zamora: El Colegio de Michoacán and Centre d'Études Mexicaines et Centramericaines, 1988) pp.51–79.

J. López G., 'The potential of Mexican agriculture and options for the future', *CEPAL Review*, 47 (1992) pp.137-48.

O. López Velarde and C. Rodríguez Rivera, *Urbanization del Ejido: El Impacto de la Reforma del Articulo 27 Constitucional*, Paper presented at conference, The Urbanization of the Ejido: The Impact of the Reform to Article 27 upon Real Estate Development and Regularization Policies, University of Texas at Austin, 3-5 February (1994).

C. Loret de Mola, *Los caciques*, (México DF: Grijalbo, 1979).

M. Lozano, 'Oaxaca: una experiencia de lucha', in R. Bustamante V., F.J. Cuautémoc González Pacheco, M.L. Ruiz Cervantes, F.A. Silva Millán Echegaray (eds.), *Oaxaca una lucha reciente: 1960-83*, (México DF: Ediciones Nueva Sociología, 1984) pp.75-219.

M. Luna, *Los empresarios y el cambio político. Mexico 1970-87*, (México DF: Ediciones Era, 1992).

N. Lustig, *Mexico: The remaking of an economy*, (Washington DC: Brookings Institution, 1992).

N. Lustig, 'Solidarity as a strategy of poverty alleviation', in W.A. Cornelius, A.L. Craig and J. Fox (eds.), *Transforming State-Society Relations in Mexico: The National Solidarity Strategy*, (San Diego: Center for US-Mexican Studies, University of California, 1994) pp.79-96.

D. Mabray, *Mexico's Acción Nacional: A Catholic Alternative to Revolution*, (Syracruse: Syracruse University Press, 1973).

F. Mallon, 'Reflections on the Ruins: Everyday Forms of State Formation in Nineteenth-Century Mexico', in G.M. Joseph and D. Nugent (eds.), *Everyday Forms of State Formation. Revolution and the Negotiation of Rule in Mexico*, (Durham: Duke University Press, 1994) pp.69-106.

E. Márquez, 'El movimiento navista y los procesos políticos de San Luis Potosí, 1958-1985', in S. Loaeza and R. Segovia (eds.), *La vida política mexicana en la crisis*, (México DF, El Colegio de México, 1987).

E. Márquez, 'Gonzalo N. Santos o la naturaleza del "tanteómetro político', in C. Martínez Assad (ed.), *Estadistas, caciques y caudillos*, (México DF: Universidad Nacional Autónoma de México, 1988) pp.385-94.

P.L. Martin, *Harvest of Confusion: Migrant Workers in US Agriculture*, (Boulder, Colorado: Westview Press, 1988).

C. Martínez Assad, 'Nava: de la rebelión de los coheteros al juicio político', in C. Martínez Assad (ed.), *Municipios en conflicto*, (México DF: GV-Editores and Universidad Nacional Autónoma de México, 1985) pp.55-74.

C. Martínez Assad, *Los rebeldes vencidos. Cedillo contra el estado cardenista*, (México DF: Fondo de Cultura Económica, 1990).

C. Martínez Assad, 'El despertar de los regiones', in J. Alonso, A. Aziz and J. Tamayo (eds.), *El nuevo estado mexicano*, (México DF: Nueva Imágen, 1992) pp.157-71.

B. Martínez Fernandez, 'Los precios de garantía en México', *Comercio Exterior*, 40 10 (1990) pp.938–42.

F. Martínez López, *El crepúsculo del poder: Juchitán, Oaxaca 1980-1982*, (Oaxaca: Instituto de Investigaciones Sociológicas, Universidad Autónoma 'Benito Juárez' de Oaxaca, 1985).

T. Martinez Saldaña, *El costo social de un éxito político: la política expansionista del estado mexicano en el agro lagunero* (Chapingo: Colegio de Postgraduados, 1980).

V.R. Martínez Vásquez, *Movimiento popular y política en Oaxaca: 1968-1986*, (México DF: Consejo Nacional para la Cultura y las Artes, 1990).

V.R. Martínez Vásquez, *El movimiento universitario en Oaxaca (1968-1988)*, (Oaxaca: Instituto de Investigaciones Sociológicas, Universidad Autónoma 'Benito Juárez' de Oaxaca and the Dirección de Comunicación Social del Gobierno del Estado de Oaxaca, 1992a).

V.R. Martínez Vásquez, 'Información y comportamiento electoral en la ciudad de Oaxaca', *Cuadernos del Sur*, 1 (1992b) pp.117-26.

S. Maxfield and R. Anzaldúa Montoya, *Government and Private Sector in Contemporary Mexico*, (San Diego: Center for US-Mexican Studies, University of California, 1987).

M.C. Mejía Piñeros and Sarmiento Silva, *La lucha indígena un reto a la ortodoxia*, (México DF: Siglo XXI, 1987).

L. Méndez, M.A. Romero and A. Bolívar, 'Solidaridad se institucionaliza', *El Cotidiano*, 49 (1992) pp.60-6.

J. Meyer, *The Cristero Rebellion: the Mexican People between Church and State, 1926-29*, (Cambridge: Cambridge University Press, 1976).

L. Meyer, 'Democratization of the PRI: Mission Impossible?', in W.A. Cornelius, J. Gentleman and P.H. Smith (eds.), *Mexico's Alternative Political Futures*, (San Diego: Center for US-Mexican Studies, University of California, 1989) pp.325-48.

L. Meyer, 'México 1994 o el difícil camino de un cambio sin reglas', *Nexos*, XVI 188 (1993) pp.48-55.

J. Moguel, 'Cinco críticas *solidarias* a un programa de gobierno', *El Cotidiano*, 49 (1992) pp.41-8.

J. Moguel, 'The Mexican left and the social program of Salinismo', in W.A. Cornelius, A.L. Craig and J. Fox (eds.), *Transforming State-Society Relations in Mexico: The National Solidarity Strategy*, (San Diego: Center for US-Mexican Studies, University of California, 1994) pp.167-76.

J. Molinar Horcasitas, 'The Future of the Electoral System', in W.A. Cornelius, J. Gentleman and P.H. Smith (eds.), *Mexico's Alternative Political Futures*, (San Diego: Center for US-Mexican Studies, University of California, 1989) pp.265-90.

J. Molinar Horcasitas, *El Tiempo de la Legitimidad: Elecciones, Autoritarismo y Democracía en México*, (México DF: Cal y Arena, 1991).

J. Molinar Horcasitas, 'Una ojeada a las campañas', *Cuadernos de Nexos*, 67 (1994) pp.xvii-xviii.

J. Molinar Horcasitas and J.A. Weldon, 'Electoral determinants and consequences of National Solidarity', in W.A. Cornelius, A.L. Craig and J. Fox (eds.), *Transforming State-Society Relations in Mexico: The National Solidarity Strategy*, (San Diego: Center for US-Mexican Studies, University of California, 1994) pp.123-41.

C. Monsivaís, 'Aproximaciones y reintegros. (Notas sobre el presidencialismo III)', *El Financiero*, 26 de diciembre (1993).

Monterrey, *Cuenta Pública de la Tesorería Municipal*, (Monterrey: H. Ayuntamiento de Monterrey, various numbers).

B. Morris, *Domesticating Resistance: The Dhan-Gadi Aborigines and the Australian State*, (Oxford, New York and Munich: Berg, 1989).

S.D. Morris, 'Political Reformism in Mexico: Salinas at the Brink', *Journal of Interamerican Studies and World Affairs*, 34 1 (1992) pp.27-57.

S.D. Morris, 'Political reformism in Mexico: past and present', *Latin American Research Review*, 28 2 (1993) pp.191-205.

S.A. Mosk, *Industrial Revolution in Mexico*, (Berkeley, University of California Press, 1950).

A.D. Murphy and A. Stepick, *Social inequality in Oaxaca: a history of resistance and change*, (Philadelphia: Temple University Press, 1991).

J. Nash, 'Mexico: Adjustment and Stabilization', in V. Thomas, A. Chibber, M. Dailami and J. De Melo (eds.), *Restructuring Economies in Distress*, (New York: Oxford University Press, 1991) pp.494-515.

M.C. Needler, *Mexican Politics: The Containment of Conflict*, (New York: Praeger Press, Hoover Institution Series, 1982).

D. Nugent, 'Mexico's rural populations and "La Crisis": Economic Crisis or Legitimation Crisis', *Critique of Anthropology*, 7 3 (1988) pp.95-112.

D. Nugent, *Spent Cartridges of Revolution: An Anthropological History of Namiquipa, Chihuahua*, (Chicago and London: University of Chicago Press, 1993).

A. Nuncio, *El PAN*, (México DF: Nuevo Imagen, 1986).

J. O'Connor, *Accumulation Crisis*, (New York: Basil Blackwell, 1984).

H. Pack, 'Industrialization and Trade', in H. Chenery and T. Srinivasan (eds.), *Handbook of Development Economics*, (Amsterdam: New Holland, 1988) pp.333-80.

J-V. Palerm, *Farm Labour Needs and Farm Workers in California, 1970 to 1989*, (Sacramento: Employment Development Department, 1991).

J-V. Palerm and J.I. Urquiola, 'A Binational System of Agricultural Production: The Case of the Mexican Bajío and California', in D.G. Aldrich and L. Meyer (eds.), *Mexico and the United States: Neighbours in Crisis*, (San Bernadino: The Borgo Press, 1993) pp.311–67,

W.G. Pansters, *Politics and Power in Puebla: The political history of a Mexican state, 1937-1987*, (Amsterdam: CEDLA, 1990).

PRI (Partido Revolucionario Institucional), *En Pie de Lucha, Crónica del Fraude*, (Mexicali: Comité Directivo Estatal en Baja California, 1992).

M. Pastor Jr, *The International Monetary Fund and Latin America: economic stabilization and class conflict*, (Boulder, Colorado: Westview Press, 1987).

J. Petras and M. Morley, *US Hegemony under Siege: Class, Politics and Development in Latin America*, (London and New York: Verso, 1990).

G. Pfefferman and M. Madarassy, *Trends in Private Investment in Developing Countries 1993*, (Washington DC: International Finance Corporation, Discussion Paper 16, 1992).

J.L. Piñeyro, 'El Pronasol ¿nueva hegemonía política?', *El Cotidiano*, 49 (1992) pp.58-71.

R.A. Pisa, *Popular response to the reform of Article 27: state intervention and community resistance in Oaxaca*, Paper presented at XVIII International Congress of the Latin American Studies Association, Atlanta, 10-12 March (1994).

K. Powell, (forthcoming) 'Cambio Socio-Económico y Cultura Política en la Región Cañera de Los Reyes, Michoacán', in V.G. Muro (ed.), *Estudios Michoacanos*, (Zamora: El Colegio de Michoacán).

Presidencia de la República, *Las Razones y Las Obras: Gobierno de Miguel de la Madrid. Crónica del Sexenio 1982-1988: Primer Año*, (México DF: Presidencia de la República, 1984).

Presidencia de la República, 'En Marcha, La Reforma que Necesita el Campo Mexicano', *Proceso*, 784 (1991) Supplement.

M-F. Prévot-Shapira and H. Riviere D'Arc, 'Les Zapoteques, le PRI et la COCEI. Affrontements autour des interventions de l'état dans l'isthme de Tehuantepec', *Amerique Latine*, 15 (1983) pp.64-71.

Procuraduría Agraria, 'III Reunion Nacional de Delegados', *Espacios*, 3 (1993a) pp.19-24.

Procuraduría Agraria, *Primer Informe de Labores*, (Mimeograph, 1993b).

Procuraduría de los Derechos Humanos y Protección Ciudadana de Baja California y Academia Mexicana de Derechos Humanos, *Baja California 92: Ensayo Democrático*, 4 August (1992) Mimeograph.

C. Puig, 'Conclusión de Negroponte: con el Tratado de Libre Comercio, México quedaría a disposición de Washington', *Proceso*, 758 (1991).

S.K. Purcell and J.F.H. Purcell, 'State and Society in Mexico: Must a Stable Polity be Institutionalized?', *World Politics*, 32 (1980) pp.194-227.

I. Ramírez, 'El sistema no renuncia a sus vicios: rasuramiento del padrón, acarreos de votantes, falta de boletos, urnas desaparecidas...', *Proceso*, 929 (1994) pp.8-12.

A. Rébora, *Notas sobre la accion gubernamental en el combate al precarismo urbano en terrenos ejidales*, Paper presented at conference, The Urbanization of the Ejido: The Impact of the Reform to Article 27 upon Real Estate Development and Regularization Policies, University of Texas at Austin, 3-5 February (1994).

J. Reyes Heroles, *El liberalismo mexicano, 3 vols.* (México DF: Universidad Nacional Autónoma de México, 1957-61).

J.L. Reyna and R. Weinert, *Authoritarianism in Mexico*, (New York: Inter-American Politics Series, 1977).

A. Riding, *Distant Neighbors*, (New York: Vintage Books, 1986).

S. Rizzo García, *Estrategias del Pacto Nuevo León*, (Monterrey: Gobierno del Estado de Nuevo León, 1992a).

S. Rizzo García, *Primer Informe de Gobierno, Nuevo León*, (Monterrey: Gobierno del Estado de Nuevo León, 1992b).

S. Rizzo García, *Segundo Informe de Gobierno, Nuevo León*, (Monterrey: Gobierno del Estado de Nuevo León, 1993).

V.E. Rodríguez, 'The Politics of Decentralization in Mexico: from *Municipio Libre* to *Solidaridad*', *Bulletin of Latin American Research*, 12 2 (1993) pp.133-45.

V.E. Rodríguez, 'Municipal Autonomy and the Politics of Intergovernmental Finance: Is it Different for the Opposition?', in V.E. Rodríguez and P.M. Ward (eds.), *Opposition Government in Mexico: Past Experiences and Future Opportunities*, (Albuquerque: University of New Mexico Press, 1995) pp.153-72.

V.E. Rodríguez, *Decentralization in Mexico: The Facade of Power*, (Boulder, Colorado: Westview Press, forthcoming).

V.E. Rodríguez and P.M. Ward, 'Opposition Politics, Power and Public Administration in Urban Mexico', *Bulletin of Latin American Research*, 10 1 (1991) pp.23-36.

V.E. Rodríguez and P.M. Ward, *Policymaking, Politics, and Urban Governance in Chihuahua: the experience of Recent Panista Governments*, (Austin, Texas: LBJ School of Public Affairs, US Mexican Policy Report 3, 1992).

V.E. Rodríguez and P.M. Ward, 'Disentangling the PRI', *Mexican Studies/Estudios Mexicanos*, 10 1 (1994a) pp.163-86.

V.E. Rodríguez and P.M. Ward, *Political Change in Baja California: Democracy in the Making?*, (San Diego: Center for US-Mexican Studies, University of California, 1994b).

V.E. Rodríguez and P.M. Ward, (eds.) *Opposition Government in Mexico: Past Experiences and Future Opportunities*, (Albuquerque: University of New Mexico Press, 1995).

R. Rodríguez Lozano, *San Luis Potosí en su lucha por la libertad*, (México DF, 1938).

D. Rodrik, 'Closing the Productivity Gap: Does Trade Liberalization Really Help?', in G. Helleiner (ed.), *Trade Policy, Industrialization and Development*, (Oxford: Clarendon, 1992) pp.155-75.

C. Rojas, 'Solidaridad en México', in C. Rojas (ed.), *Solidaridad a debate*, (México DF: El Nacional, 1991).

R. Rojas, 'Los indios, trás 499 años de guerra en su contra' *Perfil de La Jornada*, 12 October 1991.

J. Ros, 'Free Trade Area or Common Capital Market? Notes on Mexico-US Economic Integration and Current NAFTA Negotiations', *Journal of InterAmerican Studies*, 34 2 (1992) pp.53-91.

J. Rubin, 'Popular mobilization and the myth of state corporatism', in J. Foweraker and A.L. Craig (eds.), *Popular movements and political change in Mexico*, (Boulder, Colorado: Lynne Rienner Publications, 1990) pp.247-67.

J.W. Rubin, 'COCEI in Juchitán: grassroots radicalism and regional history', *Journal of Latin American Studies*, 26 1 (1994) pp.109-36.

E. Ruffo, *Tercer Informe de Gobierno*, (Mexicali: Gobierno del Estado de Baja California, 1992).

W.G. Runciman, 'Contradictions of state socialism: the case of Poland', *The Sociological Review*, 33 1 (1985) pp.17-8.

C. Salinas de Gortari, *Iniciativa de decreto que adiciona el artículo 4 de la Consitución Política de los Estados Unidos Mexicanos para el reconocimiento de los derechos culturales de los pueblos indígenas*, (México DF: Instituto Nacional Indigenista, 1990).

C. Salinas de Gortari, 'Diez Puntos para la libertad y justicia en el campo', *Comercio Exterior*, 41 11 (1991) pp.1096-100.

J. Sánchez Susarrey, *La Transición Incierta*, (México DF: Vuelta, 1991).

D. Sanders, 'The UN Working Group on Indigenous Populations', *Human Rights Quarterly*, 11 (1989) pp.406-33.

P. Santibáñez Orozco, 'Oaxaca: la crisis de 1977', in R. Benítez Zenteno (ed.), *Sociedad y política en Oaxaca 1980*, (Oaxaca: Instituto de Investigaciones Sociológicas, Universidad Autónoma 'Benito Juárez' de Oaxaca, 1982) pp.309-29.

S. Sassen, 'New York City: Economic restructuring and immigration', *Development and Change*, 17 (1986) pp.85–119.

F. von Sauer, *The Alienated 'Loyal' Opposition: Mexico's Partido Acción Nacional*, (Alburquerque: University of New Mexico Press, 1974).

P. Schmitter 'Still a Century of Corporatism?', in P. Schmitter and G. Lehmbruch (eds.), *Trends towards Corporaitist Intermediation*, (London: Sage) pp.7-52.

F.J. Schryer, *Ethnicity and Class Conflict in Rural Mexico*, (Princeton: Princeton Univesrity Press, 1990).

J.C. Scott, *Domination and the Arts of Resistance*, (New Haven: Yale University Press, 1990).

SEDESOL (Secretaría de Desarrollo Social), *Programa de 100 Ciudades*, (México DF: SEDESOL, 1993a).

SEDESOL (Secretaría de Desarrollo Social), *Solidarity in National Development: New Relations between Society and Government*, (México DF: SEDESOL, 1993b).

Secretaría de Finanzas, Gobierno de Baja California, *Estudio del Comité Facilitador Sobre las Participaciones al Estado de Baja California*, (Mexicali: Gobierno del Estado de Baja California, 1993).

SHCP (Secretaría de Hacienda y Crédito Público), *El Nuevo Perfil de la Economía Mexicana*, (México DF: SHCP, 1991).

W.C. Sellar and R.J. Yeatman, *1066 And All That*, (London: Methuen, 1930).

SISTA, *Législación Agraria*, (México DF: Editorial SISTA, 1993).

H. Sobarzo, 'A General Equilibrium Analysis of the Gains from trade for the Mexican Economy of a North American Free Trade Agreement', *World Economy*, 15 1 (1992) pp.83-100.

R. Solís Rosales, 'Precios de guarantía y política agraria: un analisis de largo plazo', *Comercio Exterior*, 40 10 (1990) pp.923–37.

C. Sorroza Polo, 'Sociedad y política en Oaxaca 1970-90', *Cuadernos del Sur*, 1 (1992) pp.99-116.

R. Stavenhagen, *Derecho Indígena y Derechos Humanos en América Latina*, (México DF: El Colegio de México and Instituto Americano de Derechos Humanos, 1988).

L. Stephen, *Viva Zapata! Generation, Gender, and Historical Consciousness in the Reception of Ejido Reform in Oaxaca*, (San Diego: Center for US-Mexican Studies, University of California, Transformation of Rural Mexico Series 6, 1994).

D. Story, *Industry, The State, and Public Policy in Mexico*, (Austin, Texas: University of Texas Press, 1986).

D.D. Stull, *Of Meat and (Wo)men: Beefpacking's Consequences for Communities on the High Plains*, Paper presented at 92nd Annual Meeting of the American Anthropological Association, Emerging Heterogeneity in Rural US Communities, Washington DC, 18 November (1993).

P. Tandon, *Mexico*, Paper presented at conference, Welfare Consequences of Selling Public Enterprises, Country Economics Department, Washington DC: The World Bank (1992).

A. Ten Kate, 'Trade Liberalization and Economic Stabilization in Mexico: Lessons of Experience', *World Development*, 20 (1992) pp.659-72.

C. Tennant, 'Indigenous Peoples, International Institutions and the International Legal Literature from 1945-1993', *Human Rights Quarterly*, 16 (1994) pp.1-57.

G.P.C. Thomson, 'Bulwarks of Patriotic Liberalism: The National Guard, Philharmonic Corps and Patriotic Juntas in Mexico, 1847-1888', *Journal of Latin American Studies*, 22 1 (1990) pp.31-68.

G.P.C. Thomson, 'Popular Aspects of Liberalism in Mexico, 1848-1888', *Bulletin of Latin American Studies*, 10 3 (1991) pp.265-92.

A. Ugalde, 'Contemporary Mexico: From Hacienda to PRI, Political Leadership in a Zapotec Village', in R. Kern (ed.), *The Caciques*, (Albuquerque: University of New Mexico Press, 1973) pp.119-34.

J.M., del Val Blanco, 'El discreto encanto del maximalismo', *México Indígena*, 15 (1990) pp.14-8.

A. Valderrábano, *Historias del Poder: El Caso de Baja California*, (México DF: Editorial Grijalbo, 1990).

A. Varley, 'Urbanization and Agrarian Law: the case of Mexico City', *Bulletin of Latin American Research*, 4 1 (1985a) pp.1-16.

A. Varley, *Ya somos dueños: ejido land development and regularisation in Mexico City*, (University College London: Unpublished Ph.D. dissertation, 1985b).

A. Varley, 'The relationship between tenure legalization and housing improvements: evidence from Mexico City', *Development and Change*, 18 (1987) pp.463-81.

A. Varley, 'Clientilism or technocracy? The politics of urban land regularization', in N. Harvey (ed.) *Mexico: Dilemmas of Transition* (London: British Academic Press and The Institute of Latin American Studies, 1993), pp.249-76.

C.G. Vélez-Ibáñez, *Rituals of Marginality*, (Berkeley: University of California Press, 1983).

O.H. Vera Ferrer, 'The Political Economy of Privatization in Mexico', in W. Glade, (ed.), *Privatization of Public Enterprises in Latin America*, (San Fransisco: ICS Press, 1991) pp.35-57.

P.M. Ward, 'Political pressure for urban services: the response of two Mexico City administrations', *Development and Change*, 12 (1981) pp.379-407.

P.M. Ward, *Welfare Politics in Mexico: papering over the cracks?*, (London: Allen and Unwin, 1986).

P.M. Ward, *Mexico City: The Production and Reproduction of an Urban Environment*, (London: Belhaven Press, 1990).

P.M. Ward, 'Mexico's electoral aftermath and political future', in P.M. Ward (ed.), *Mexico's Electoral Aftermath and Political Future*, (Austin, Texas: The Mexican Centre, ILAS, University of Texas, 1994) p.1-4.

P.M. Ward, 'Policy Making and Policy Implementation Among Non-PRI Governments: The PAN in Cd. Juárez and in Chihuahua', in V.E. Rodríguez and P.M. Ward (eds.), *Opposition Government in Mexico: Past Experiences and Future Opportunities*, (Albuquerque: University of New Mexico Press, 1995) pp.135-51.

A. Warman, et al. (eds.) *Eso que llaman antropologia mexicana*, (México DF: Nuevo Tiempo, 1970).

A. Warman, (1978) 'Se ha creido que el indigenismo es un apostolado, no una acción política', in INI (ed.) *El Instituto Nacional Indigenista Treinta Años Después*, (México DF: Instituto Nacional Indigenista) pp.141-4.

M. Wasserman, *Persistent Oligarchs. Elites and politics in Chihuahua, Mexico, 1910-1940*, (Durham and London: Duke University Press, 1993).

S. Weintraub, *A Marriage of Convenience. Relations Between Mexico and the United States*, (New York: Oxford University Press, 1990).

J. Weiss, *Industry in Developing Countries*, (London: Routledge, 1990).

J. Weiss, 'Trade Liberalisation in Mexico in the 198Os: Concepts, Measures and Short-run Effects', *Welswirtshaftliches Archiv Band*, 128 4 (1992a) pp.711-26.

J. Weiss, 'Export Response to Trade Reform:Recent Mexican Experience', *Development Policy Review*, 10 (1992b) pp.43-60.

J. Weiss, 'Trade Policy Reform and Performance in Manufacturing: Mexico 1975-88', *Journal of Development Studies*, 29 1 (1992c) pp.1-22.

J. Weiss, 'Mexico: Comparative Performance of State and Private Industrial Corporations', in P. Cook and C. Kirkpatrick (eds.), *Post-Privatization Policy and Performance*, (Brighton: Wheatsheaf, 1994).

K. Weyland, *Neopopulism and Neoliberalism in Latin America: Unexpected Affinities*, Paper presented at American Political Science Association, New York, 1-4 September (1994).

H.J. Wiarda, 'Mexico: The Unravelling of a Corporatist Regime?', *Journal of Inter-American Studies and World Affairs*, 4 (1989) pp.1-28.

The World Bank, *Poverty and Income Distribution in Latin America*, (Washington DC: The World Bank, Latin America and the Caribbean Technical Department, Regional Studies Program 27, Human Resources Division, 1993).

I. Yescas Martínez, 'La Coalición Obrero Campesino Estudiantil de Oaxaca: 1972-74', in R. Benitez Zenteno (ed.), *Sociedad y politica en Oaxaca 1980*, (Oaxaca: Instituto de Investigaciones Sociológicas, Universidad Autónoma 'Benito Juárez' de Oaxaca, 1982) pp.289-308.

I. Yescas Martínez, *Política y poder en Oaxaca*, (Oaxaca: Gobierno del Estado, 1991).

I. Yescas Martínez and G. Zafra, *La insurgencia magisterial en Oaxaca, 1980*, (Oaxaca: Instituto de Investigaciones Sociológicas, Universidad Autónoma 'Benito Juárez' de Oaxaca, 1985).

G. Zafra, 'Problemática agraria en Oaxaca 1971-75', in R. Benítez Zenteno (ed.), *Sociedad y política en Oaxaca 1980*, (Oaxaca: Instituto de Investigaciones Sociológicas, Universidad Autónoma 'Benito Juárez' de Oaxaca, 1982) pp.331-49.

S. Zendejas and G. Mummert, *Respuestas locales a reformas gubernamentales en el campo mexicano: el ejido como forma de organización de prácticas políticas de grupos locales*, Paper presented at XVIII International Congress of the Latin American Studies Association, Atlanta, 10-12 March (1994).

Index

p. 201 - continuation of practices

p. 203 dont expect much to change in the ejido

p. 206 debate about solidarity.

p. 208 summary of view of solidarity.

p. 223 on solidarity.

p. 224 CSG use of indigenist strategy.

p. 265 continued importance of caciquismo

p. 269 -> long history of Revolution.

p. 290 historical view of hegemony

distribution of moneys
p. 118

p. 128-29 judgement on
PAN in BC

p. 132 PAN ideology

p. 148 problem of the PAN
in 1994.

p. 158 great quote from
Aspe.

p. 171 nice summary of
CSG assumption.

p. 172 good on key to CSG
success

p. 197 good on CSG
beginning +
end of corporatism

p. 4 - Social liberalism as ideology.

p 20 a new capitalism in Mexico would not necessarily favour democracy.

p. 20 books has lots of stuff on Allegreism.

p. 23 contours of fate of Salinato

p. 28 Salinismo threatened identities.

p. 38 contradictions in Salinas ideology

p. 41 ideological resistance problem of creating a viable ideological project

p. 61 nice analysis of different forms of budget deficits.

p 63 centrality of external capital